Digital Transformation and Human Potential in the AI Era

Krastev Viliyan Krastev
https://orcid.org/0000-0001-5456-247X
University of Economics in Varna, Bulgaria

Chandni Rani
https://orcid.org/0009-0009-0806-6147
Chandigarh University, India

Olga Ergunova
https://orcid.org/0009-0006-2267-8121
Peter the Great St. Petersburg Polytechnic University, Russia

Pooja Kansra
https://orcid.org/0000-0003-2229-0662
Lovely Professional University, India

Tanveer Kajla
https://orcid.org/0000-0002-5528-9804
NALSAR University of Law, India

IGI Global
Scientific Publishing
Publishing Tomorrow's Research Today

Vice President of Editorial	Melissa Wagner
Director of Acquisitions	Mikaela Felty
Director of Book Development	Jocelynn Hessler
Production Manager	Mike Brehm
Cover Design	Jose Rosado

Published in the United States of America by
IGI Global Scientific Publishing
701 East Chocolate Avenue
Hershey, PA, 17033, USA
Tel: 717-533-8845 | Fax: 717-533-7115
Website: https://www.igi-global.com E-mail: cust@igi-global.com

Library of Congress Cataloging-in-Publication Data

LCCN: (CIP Data Pending)
ISBN13: 9798337386126
Isbn13Softcover: 9798337386133
EISBN13: 9798337386140
British Cataloguing in Publication Data
A Cataloguing in Publication record for this book is available from the British Library.

Table of Contents

Detailed Table of Contents

that AI has to potential to reduce administrative burdens and promote inclusivity and data-driven decision-making. This chapter emphasizes balancing innovation with ethics and advocates for the responsible use of AI to foster sustainable growth and a healthy workplace.

The role of generative artificial intelligence in the process of training and work of marketers is shown.The purpose of the presented survey was to determine ways to improve the educational process that includes generative artificial intelligence, as well as to form a realistic attitude among students towards tools of this type. The study showed that students are well acquainted with AI and use it extensively. The attitude towards AI is quite realistic: there are no expectations that it will do the work for students. But the aid of AI in learning is highly appreciated. The demand of acquiring knowledge in this area is urgent, mainly through new teaching methods. There are also high expectations regarding personalized learning. The obtained results will help to improve the preparation of students for their future professional activities. The proposed survey methodology can be used for annual monitoring of the situation.

Emotional Intelligence plays an important role in the progressively involved digital workplace where face-to-face interactions are often less prioritized by digital infrastructures like emails, social media networks, and ICT tools. Emotional Intelligent leaders make more empathetic and harmonious decisions, reduce conflicts, and resilience approach towards the virtual environment. The chapter sheds light on Digital Emotional Intelligence (DEQ) in management decision-making in a hybridized workplace. The chapter conducted PRISMA research methodology and Daniel Goleman's EI Model to investigate and synthesize the literature in the management and administration area. The studies on DEQ are very limited, therefore the findings are novel and practical in the present digitalized workplace for decision-

Preface

INTRODUCTION

It is with great enthusiasm that we present this edited volume, *Digital Transformation and Human Potential in the AI Era*, a work born from the recognition that human resources stands at the epicenter of one of the most profound technological evolutions of our time. As we navigate this rapidly changing digital landscape, HR professionals are not merely adapting to new tools— they are redefining their role, competencies, and strategic influence within organizations.

Today's HR leaders face an environment shaped by Artificial Intelligence (AI), Machine Learning (ML), the Internet of Things (IoT), and big data analytics. These technologies are no longer optional enhancements; they are integral to the strategic operations and competitive advantage of modern organizations. At the forefront of this evolution, AI and ML empower HR teams to automate routine tasks, redirecting human effort toward high-impact, value-added initiatives. From deciphering workforce trends to optimizing talent strategies, these technologies enable HR professionals to uncover patterns that were once hidden within vast and complex datasets. Predictive analytics, for example, can help organizations identify high-potential employees early in their careers and design targeted growth pathways that maximize both individual and organizational potential.

As this transformation unfolds, new AI capabilities are expanding HR's possibilities even further. Generative AI offers the ability to produce tailored language, imagery, and code—supporting personalized employee communication, content creation, and learning experiences. Meanwhile, Agentic AI introduces autonomous systems capable of acting on defined objectives, streamlining processes from recruitment to performance management. Together, these advancements signal an era in which AI is not simply supporting HR operations but actively reshaping them.

A recurring theme throughout this book is the imperative for fairness, transparency, and ethical stewardship. Data-driven practices must not only improve accuracy and efficiency but also reinforce equity and trust. As HR analytics grow increasingly sophisticated, leaders must prioritize ethical AI use, safeguard against bias, and ensure responsible data governance. Digital literacy, critical thinking, and technological fluency are now essential competencies—cornerstones that will enable HR professionals to lead with insight, integrity, and confidence.

This volume is guided by two overarching objectives:

1. **To cultivate a future in which humans and technology work in harmony within HR functions.**

This involves establishing ethical guidelines, building digital capabilities, and creating supportive infrastructures that empower HR professionals to leverage AI, ML, and data analytics effectively. Our goal is to equip organizations with forward-thinking strategies that foster innovation, enhance operational efficiency, and support a culture of adaptability and continuous learning.

2. **To highlight the indispensable role of Human-Computer Interaction (HCI) in shaping responsible, human-centered AI adoption in HR.**

By emphasizing "human-in-the-loop" approaches, this book demonstrates how effective HCI design can mitigate algorithmic biases, strengthen decision quality, and preserve the humanity of HR processes. HCI ensures that as technology becomes more pervasive, people remain at the center of work—supported, not overshadowed, by intelligent systems.

This book is written for a diverse and forward-looking audience:

- HR professionals navigating profound technological transformation
- Executives seeking strategic insights into the future of work
- Technology practitioners exploring applied AI solutions
- Academics and students studying HR, business, and emerging technologies
- Anyone curious about AI's expanding role in shaping organizational life

As editors, our hope is that this reference work serves not only as a scholarly contribution but as a practical guide—one that empowers readers to embrace digital transformation while championing human potential. The journey ahead is dynamic and demanding, yet filled with opportunity. By cultivating a digital mindset and upholding ethical, human-centered principles, HR professionals can lead their organizations into a future defined by agility, innovation, and equity.

ORGANIZATION OF THE BOOK

Chapter 1: The Use of Information and Communication Tools of Social Networks in Humanitarian Education

Our opening chapter illuminates how human-computer interaction (HCI) and social media–based information and communication technologies (ICT) are reshaping educational environments in Russia and China, with important implications for future workforce readiness. Here, the authors demonstrate how digital learning ecosystems—rooted in platforms familiar to students—enhance communication, promote interdisciplinary collaboration, and support self-directed learning. The chapter highlights the growing importance of developing digital competencies early, framing education as a foundational element of future HR development. At the same time, it acknowledges challenges related to privacy, digital literacy gaps, and institutional readiness. Ultimately, this chapter shows that integrating HCI into everyday learning tools is not simply a pedagogical innovation but a strategic investment in preparing students for the digital labor market.

Chapter 2: Artificial Intelligence and the Future of HRM—Balancing Innovation and Ethics

Chapter 2 explores the dual promise and peril of AI in HR management. By streamlining recruitment, improving forecasting, and strengthening retention strategies, AI offers extraordinary opportunities for organizational efficiency and agility. Yet the authors also stress that these advantages bring ethical complexities: algorithmic bias, opacity, and risks to data privacy require vigilant oversight. This chapter argues powerfully for a balanced approach—one where innovation is tempered by ethical governance, regulatory safeguards, and human-centered supervision. The authors reinforce that while AI can reduce administrative burden and enhance inclusivity, its responsible adoption demands transparency, accountability, and ongoing human involvement.

Chapter 3: Artificial Intelligence in Professional Marketing Education—A Student Perspective

This chapter shifts the lens to marketing education, revealing how students perceive and engage with generative AI as both a learning partner and a professional tool. Survey findings indicate that students hold realistic expectations about AI's capabilities, valuing it as an aid rather than a substitute for their own work. They express strong interest in developing deeper knowledge and skills related to

AI, particularly through innovative teaching methods and personalized learning pathways. The authors emphasize that integrating generative AI into educational programs equips future marketing professionals with the digital fluency required in a rapidly evolving industry. The chapter concludes with a replicable methodology for ongoing monitoring of student attitudes—an invaluable resource for educators.

Chapter 4: Digital Emotional Intelligence in the Hybrid Workplace

In this chapter, the authors explore how emotional intelligence—long recognized as vital to effective leadership—takes on new significance in digitally mediated work environments. Using PRISMA methodology and Goleman's EI framework, the chapter examines how Digital Emotional Intelligence (DEQ) shapes decision-making in hybrid contexts where interactions increasingly occur through ICT tools. The findings offer timely insights into four key DEQ quadrants that support self-awareness, self-management, social awareness, and relationship management. As organizations continue to adopt hybrid models, this chapter provides a novel, research-driven guide for leaders seeking to navigate the emotional complexities of digital work with resilience, empathy, and clarity.

Chapter 5: Digitalization in University Training Using VR/AR and Its Implications for HR Development

Chapter 5 offers an in-depth look at the transformative power of VR/AR technologies in professional and pedagogical training. Through empirical data from two Kazakh universities, the authors demonstrate how immersive tools dramatically improve engagement, creativity, and skill acquisition. Students report VR/AR as especially effective for mastering complex, practice-oriented tasks, while trained instructors note that these technologies elevate teaching quality and their own professional development. The chapter identifies both benefits and challenges, contributing valuable insight into how VR/AR can shape not only modern higher education but also future HR development by cultivating more capable, digitally fluent professionals.

Chapter 6: Economic Sector Development in the Digital Transformation Era

In this chapter, the authors provide a comprehensive analysis of how digital transformation is reshaping organizational structures across different economic sectors. They highlight the growing reliance on digital tools to improve efficiency, reduce costs, and modernize management practices. A key insight is the shift from traditional, closed business models to modular, platform-based architectures that demand new forms of agility. The chapter also explores how digitalization influences HRM practices in industrial settings, identifying trends and offering recommendations to enhance workforce performance. It serves as an essential resource for HR specialists seeking to optimize personnel management in rapidly evolving economic landscapes.

Chapter 7: Ethics and Bias in AI-Powered HR Systems

Chapter 7 confronts one of the most critical issues facing HR today: the ethical vulnerabilities of AI-driven systems. Through case examples—such as biased recruitment tools and culturally insensitive emotion-recognition technologies—the authors illustrate how algorithmic decisions can perpetuate systemic inequalities. They analyze technical, organizational, and societal sources of bias, providing a multidisciplinary evaluation of risks. Importantly, the chapter offers actionable guidance, including dataset auditing, transparent model design, and collaborative governance frameworks. This chapter serves as both a warning and a roadmap, urging HR leaders to ensure that technological advancement never outpaces ethical responsibility.

Chapter 8: Exploring the Impact of AI on Employee Spirituality

This chapter offers a unique and thought-provoking perspective on the intersection of AI, spirituality, and workplace well-being—particularly within the BFSI sector. Drawing on survey data from 501 employees, the authors reveal a positive relationship between AI integration and employee spirituality, suggesting that technology can support mindfulness rather than undermine it. The research introduces the concept of "technological spirituality," describing how AI-driven tools can foster clarity, intuition, and emotional balance. With both theoretical and practical implications, this chapter expands the conversation beyond efficiency and performance, reminding us that digital transformation must also account for human wholeness.

Chapter 9: Organizational and Methodological Conditions for Personalized Corporate Training Through HCI

In Chapter 9, the authors tackle a pervasive challenge in corporate learning: the fragmentation of e-learning content and the erosion of structured competency development. They propose organizational and methodological frameworks to design personalized, coherent training programs grounded in HCI principles. Drawing from research and applied experience, the chapter presents models and tools for developing training systems that are aligned, scalable, and strategically grounded. It highlights the importance of intentional instructional design to ensure that digital training programs not only look modern but truly build professional capacity.

Chapter 10: Robotic Process Automation in HR Operations

This chapter examines the strategic role of Robotic Process Automation (RPA) in modernizing HR operations. Despite its widespread success in other fields, RPA adoption within HR remains conservative but increasingly promising. The authors detail how RPA can enhance recruitment, onboarding, payroll, data management, and compliance by automating repetitive tasks and enabling data-driven insights. They also identify common adoption challenges, offering practical solutions to guide organizations through implementation. The chapter reinforces the central message of this volume: automation, when thoughtfully integrated, allows HR teams to shift from administrative maintenance to strategic leadership.

Chapter 11: The Transformative Power of AI in Recruitment

Our final chapter focuses on one of the most rapidly evolving HR domains: recruitment. The authors analyze how AI is reshaping every phase of the hiring process—from sourcing and screening to assessment and selection. Drawing on current industry insights, they highlight AI's capacity to improve efficiency, reduce costs, and enhance candidate matching. The chapter also outlines potential risks and areas for improvement, offering strategic recommendations to ensure AI strengthens—rather than disrupts—the recruitment process. By synthesizing emerging trends and practitioner perspectives, this chapter provides a valuable blueprint for designing recruitment systems that are both technologically advanced and human-centered.

Collectively, these chapters underscore the vast potential and deep responsibility that accompany digital transformation in the AI era. Each contribution adds nuance to our understanding of how technology can elevate human potential—provided we design, govern, and implement it with care.

CONCLUSION

As we conclude *Digital Transformation and Human Potential in the AI Era*, we find ourselves reflecting on the extraordinary breadth and depth of insight offered across these chapters. Together, they present a rich mosaic of perspectives that illuminate not only the transformative power of digital technologies but also the profound responsibility we share in shaping their role in human development, organizational life, and society at large.

Across the volume, a consistent message emerges: technology alone does not define the future—people do. Whether through the adoption of AI in recruitment, the integration of VR/AR in professional training, the cultivation of digital emotional intelligence, or the ethical oversight required to mitigate algorithmic bias, the chapters reinforce that the human element remains central. Digital transformation is not a passive process; it is an intentional redesign of how we learn, work, lead, and connect.

The contributions in this book highlight both tremendous opportunity and essential caution. We see how intelligent systems can elevate HR into a more strategic, data-driven force; how immersive learning tools can inspire deeper engagement; how AI-supported mindfulness can foster well-being; and how personalized digital ecosystems can transform corporate training. Yet we also observe clear risks—ethical vulnerabilities, privacy concerns, competency gaps, and structural inequities—that must be addressed with rigor and foresight.

As editors, we are encouraged by the collective call for balance: technological innovation must be guided by ethics, by empathy, and by a steadfast commitment to human potential. The concepts of human-in-the-loop design, digital literacy, transparent governance, and inclusive digital ecosystems appear throughout this volume as indispensable foundations for the future. They remind us that meaningful digital transformation is not simply achieved through the deployment of advanced tools, but through cultivating the capacities, cultures, and values that allow those tools to serve the common good.

We hope this reference work inspires its readers—whether HR professionals, educators, executives, students, or technologists—to engage with digital transformation not as a challenge to endure, but as an opportunity to shape. The future of work is not predetermined; it is being crafted now through the choices we make, the systems we design, and the ethical commitments we uphold. By embracing innovation with intention, humility, and humanity, we can create workplaces and learning environments that are more adaptive, equitable, and deeply aligned with the aspirations of the people they support.

Chapter 1

The Use of Information and Communication Tools of Social Networks in the Framework of the Study of Disciplines of the General Humanitarian Cycle

Anastasya Byshevskaia
https://orcid.org/0000-0003-1122-9794
Smolensk Sport University, Russia

Zhivutskaya Irina
Smolensk State University of Sports, Russia

Xiaoquan Zhang
Shenyang Normal University, China

ABSTRACT

This chapter explores the potential of human-computer interaction (HCI) and the use of information and communication tools (ICT) embedded in social media platforms to empower human resources in the context of higher education in Russia and China. It investigates how digital learning environments, supported by HCI technologies, contribute to the development of students' digital competencies, self-directed learning, and engagement. The findings highlight the effectiveness of social media-driven

DOI: 10.4018/979-8-3373-8612-6.ch001

interaction in enhancing communication between students and educators, promoting interdisciplinary collaboration, and increasing motivation. The chapter also addresses challenges related to privacy, digital literacy, and institutional adaptation. The authors conclude that incorporating HCI through familiar digital tools plays a key role in shaping modern educational practices and preparing students for the demands of the digital labor market.

INTRODUCTION

According to numerous authors, scientific and technological progress, as well as the active immersion of young members of society in the cyber space, demands for the use of information and communication technologies (ICT) in the educational process. Social networking sites expand the possibilities of educational digital technologies: the placement and dissemination of teaching materials and tools; the establishment of social connections between students and teachers; the speed and scale of information transmitted to students; the arrangements of public conversations on educational issues; project work inituation, etc. (Dyachkova & Tomyuk, 2017)(Kergilova & Sazonova, 2017)(Kinyashina, 2021). From the technical, didactic, pedagogical and organizational aspects the use of social networks as an available platform for the interaction of all participants in the learning process is convenient for the higher education system (Koch & Melnik, 2019)(Manyaev & Shipitsin, 2018)(Proskuryakov, 2014).

Based on foreign experience, A.V. Fedeshchenko (2012) cites more than 20 arguments in favor of the use of social networks in the educational process, among which the following are of the greatest interest to our research: the generation of communication skills in a virtual environment and the search for reliable sources of information; the establishment of joint activities between the educators and the classmen, which increases the accessibility of the research process and raised motivation for independent educational patterns and resources; ensuring the continuity of the educational procedure, the possibility of detailed planning of the undergraduates' academic and research work (Fedeshchenko, 2012).

A.M. Bakirova (2017), Podchalimova G.N., Belova S.N. (2018), D.I. Kozlov (2024) note the need for higher school teachers to comply with modern information realities, the need to prepare for the use of social networks in giving and receving knowledge (Sayfutdinova et al., 2017)(Podchalimova & Belova, 2021)(Kozlov, 2024). At the same time, domestic researchers consider that the potential of applying social networking sites in the learning process can be offset by a number of disdadvantages. (Ivanko & Ushenko, 2015)(Gutorova, 2019)(Guzhova, 2020). A wide variety of rows and concerns over these issues are caused by such drawbacks as the high risk of uncontrollable Internet addiction, distraction of students' attention to other content, eruption of “clip-based” thinking, decreased attendance at offline classes at the university, distortion of forms of social interaction between students and teachers, misinterpretation by mentors the meaning of various concepts that truly became a widespread phenomenon of communication in social networks (Resnyanskaya & Kuzmina, 2016)(Selezenev & Skripak, 2013)(Semenovskikh, 2014). Despite the growing scientific interest in the problem under study, it should be noted that modern Russian authors do not take into account the inner motives of the use of information and communication technologies in teaching subjects of various backgrounds. Thematic research works are mostly local and multidirectional in nature. There are different ranges of academic disciplines, the social networks taken and assests for the entire project cycles (Malysheva, 2013)(Shcherbakova & Timashova, 2020).

There is an ultimate necessity to go into analysis in the potential of social networks to enhance the efficiency of the learning process in teaching miscellaneous subjects, both core and non-core. The objective of this work was to identify the preferences of students in regards to information and communication technologies of social networks in the framework of mastering the disciplines of the general humanitarian cycle in higher education (philosophy, sociology, marketing, management, integrated child safety). Methods and organization of research. In order to clarify the results of social research for subsequent implementation, in January-February 2024, a sociological survey (using the written questionnaire method) of students of three Smolensk universities was conducted. The following universities were on focus: Smolensk State University of Sports, Smolensk branch of the International Law Institute, Smolensk Branch of the Financial University under the Government of the Russian Federation.

The outcomes of the preliminary pilot study (N=40) caused the additional list of popular social networks shaping resources in Russia that are associatively perceived and recognized by the majority of respondents as messengers, in particular Telegram, Viber, Whatsapp. The total number of respondents was 165 people (N=165) aged 18 to 23, of whom 79 (47.9%) were males and 86 females (52.1%). The conclusion drawn from the study, Answering the question about which social networks/messengers they are registered in, a big number of the audience indicated “Vkontakte” and “Telegram” – 99.4% and 97.6%, respectively. Whatsapp ranks third in popularity with 81.2%, Viber ranks fourth with 40.6%, and Odnoklassniki (One classmates) ranks fifth with 29.1% (Figure 1).

Figure 1. Preliminary pilot study

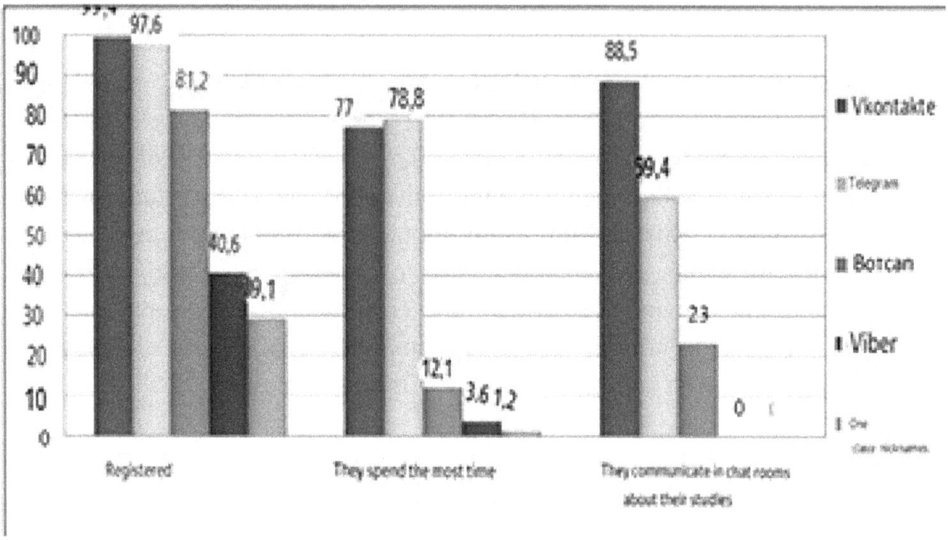

Moreover, the respondents spend most of their time on Telegram (78.8%) and the Vkontakte social network (77%). Whatsapp, Viber, and Odnoklassniki are much less popular at 12.1%, 3.6%, and 1.2%, in turn. The above mentioned data correlate with the answers to the question "In which social networks/messengers have communities been created and in which you communicate with your classmates on issues related to your studies?". Thus, 88.5% chat about their studies on Vkontakte, 59.4% on Telegram, and 23% on WhatsApp. In the Odnoklassniki social network and the Viber messenger, students do not interact with academic issues. Surprisingly, when answering a similar question about direct communication with a teacher, students indicated the following: 90.3% of respondents regularly communicate with a teacher on VKontakte, 37.6% on WhatsApp, 26.7% on Telegram and 4.2% on Viber. Thus, Vkontakte, Telegram, and WhatsApp are the most attractive platforms for communication among both students and teachers. Indisputable evidence of the students' need for information and communication interaction with the teacher on social networks are the answers to the question "Which sources of information did you use most frequently while preparing for classes in the humanities?": 67.9% of respondents voted for the answer "Electronic sources posted by the teacher on social networks (personal page, specially created community etc.).", 43.6% prefer to use electronic sources (thematic websites, electronic libraries) recommended by the teacher, 41.8% – various educational and informational websites (www.studme.org, www.studref.com, www.sdamna5.ru and others similar), 38.2% opted for preparation for classes based on paper sources (textbooks, teaching aids, thematic magazines), 12.1% choose electronic sources hosted in the information and educational environment of the university where they study and special educational programs. platforms (Moodle and similar). It is obvious that most students are attracted to compiling and arranging their work for classes by means of electronic sources and are more willing to apply the devices highly recommended by the teacher. Ultimately, the active use of social networks by higher school teachers to post educational materials will allow students to be directed to high-quality and reliable teaching materials. To the question "Do you use social media to communicate with a teacher about your studies?" 90.3% of respondents answered in the affirmative, 54.5% indicated that "it helps to quickly receive information about any changes in the educational process," 20% "the teacher can explain something if I don't understand." This is made in a lecture or seminar session," 15.8% "it encourages to build an individual trajectory of the educational process." 9.6% of students indicated no need for direct communication with the teacher, while 4.8% each noted the options "it's inconvenient for me" and "I don't need it." Thus, 1/5 of students use social media to receive additional explanations from the teacher, more than half – rather to clarify organizational issues (Figure 2).

Figure 2. Students' preferable sources of information

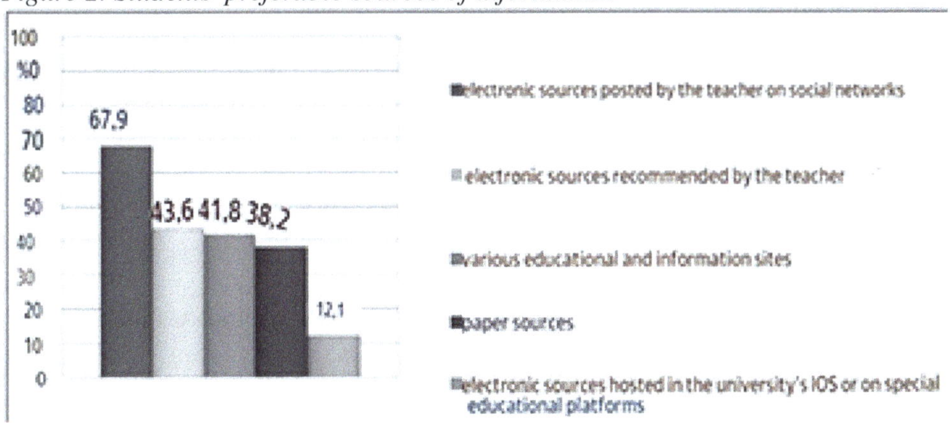

It is believed that students themselves recognize the importance of diversifying the methods of information and communication exchange with their teachers. Specifically, more than three-quarters of students (78.1%) expressed a desire to engage with their teachers on educational matters through social media. Additionally, 44.8% of participants highlighted the necessity of establishing a dedicated chat or channel on platforms like VKontakte or Telegram, where students can quickly access supplementary educational materials. 33.3% indicated their interest in being able to privately message their teachers with questions about the curriculum. The relevance of this demand from contemporary students for broadening the scope of interactive online communication with educators on social media is in part due to the fact that many students are balancing part-time jobs. Recent studies by Russian scholars have shown that a considerable number of full-time students are also employed. This dual commitment often has a detrimental impact on academic performance and future career prospects for young individuals, as it leads to missed classes and difficulty in bridging knowledge gaps later on. According to the survey results, 72.2% of students work on a permanent or temporary basis, combining study with work. Answering the question "Have you ever missed classes because of work," 77.5% of students answered in the affirmative. The results of the answer to the question "Does your work activity affect the successful acquisition of a future profession?" were distributed as follows: 60.5% of respondents believe that work definitely hinders the development of a future profession, 15.5% of students hold the opposite view, since their secondary employment is related to their future profession, 24% of respondents could not give an unambiguous answer.

Figure 3. Distribution of student responses to the question about the impact of work (secondary employment) on the successful acquisition of a future profession

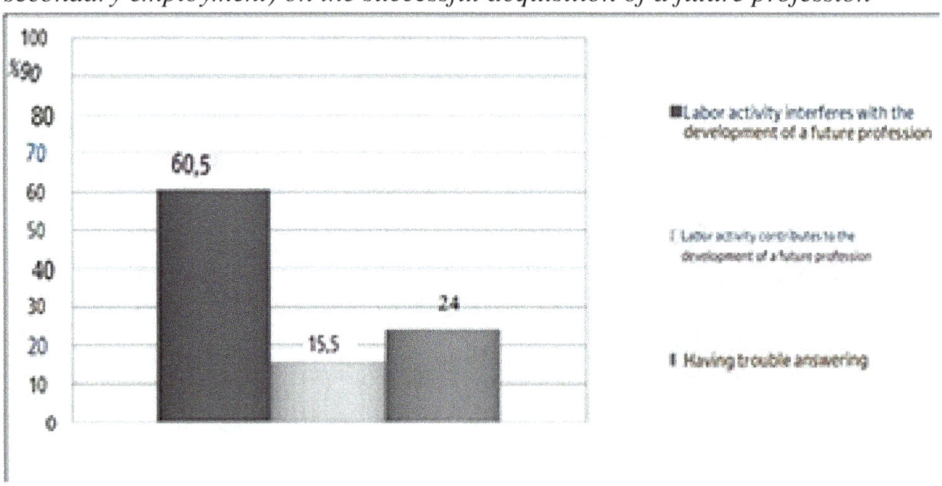

Responding to the question "What steps taken by the teacher could enhance your academic performance?" The majority of employed students expressed the importance of posting lecture material in both written and video forms – 77.5% of respondents, 58.1% of participants wished to have the ability to connect with a teacher for virtual consultations at a designated time, and 56.6% of individuals would appreciate a dedicated chat or discussion on platforms like Vkontakte or Telegram. Thus, most students who miss classes due to their job commitments acknowledge the detrimental impact of working on their ability to master professional knowledge.

By offering a unique opportunity for students to reach out to teachers for resources and additional guidance using social media, a significant number of students would make use of this option.

In recent years, the global pedagogical community has seen an increasingly active discourse on the use of social networks in professional education. Often, teachers and methodologists are skeptical about the possibility of using networks as a pedagogical means of teaching, since traditionally social networks are considered an environment for spending free time and having fun. Based on foreign experience, A. V. Fedeshchenko (2012) gives more than 20 arguments in favor of using social networks in the educational process. 1. Fashion, almost all students are familiar with such a social network as "Facebook" are happy to have the opportunity to use its resources in the learning process. 2. Free access. As a rule, educational institutions are forced to buy special software and maintain servers for storing digital data and organizing communication on the network. Social networks provide this for free. 3. Often, the information systems and educational platforms used by the university require special training, complex access. Therefore, students appear there only when necessary, while they go to social networks several times a day. 4. Social networks have functionality that allows teachers to quickly share relevant information with students. 5. The use of social networks in the learning process allows modern students to master the communication skills and skills for quickly searching for information that are necessary in the 21st century. 6. Social networks do not limit students' opportunities to share their knowledge and skills within the framework of the educational environment of the university. On the contrary, information posted by students on social networks can be accessed in many countries around the world. 7. Collaboration with various web resources becomes more convenient: through social networks, students and teachers can exchange and discuss the content of thematic sites, and demonstrate interesting information finds to each other. 8. Due to the active use of social networks for educational purposes, students no longer perceive them exclusively as a means of entertainment or informal communication. An understanding of the full range of possibilities for using social networks in future professional activities comes. 9. The implementation of the educational process with the support of social networks provides additional opportunities for those students who, due to various circumstances, cannot attend a face-to-face lesson in person. 10. This point logically follows from the previous one: supporting learning with resources and communication capabilities of social networks ensures the continuity of the educational process. In addition, students and teachers get the opportunity to interact at their convenience, and not only during class time. There is an opportunity for more detailed planning of joint work. 11. The use of social networks in the educational process allows to increase the level of communicative competencies not only of students, but also of teachers. 12. Teachers get the opportunity to conduct lectures in an interactive mode. Students, while listening to a lecture, can ask questions and discuss the material in a microblog, without disturbing their classmates and the teacher. 13. Social networks allow you to involve students' parents in the educational process. We note that although it is not customary for universities to involve parents in the educational process, this opportunity will allow for more effective educational control. 14. An important feature of the use of social networks is the availability of special applications for mobile phones. Thus, a student and a teacher can communicate on academic matters from anywhere in the world. 15. Using social networks allows increasing the social responsibility of students due to environmental friendliness: there is no need to print out a large amount of handouts, you can simply attach them to the page as a file. 16. Using social networks during class time increases students' self-discipline: a number of teachers have noticed that young people are less likely to use networks for entertainment or other purposes unrelated to the lesson content. 17. Students who are shy in class feel more comfortable in social networks and are less embarrassed to ask the teacher a question on a topic that interests them. 18. Insufficient equipment in classrooms or technical problems do not always allow the teacher to demonstrate the prepared digital material. They can be demonstrated in a social network in a virtual study group by downloading the necessary files in advance. In this way, students will see the proposed materials immediately during class using their smartphones. 19. A discussion of the material that began in class can be continued in a social network. This opportunity will allow students to spend more time actively learning through discussion. 20. Using social networks reduces the social barrier between teachers and students in the communication sphere. 21. It becomes possible for students and teachers to jointly create educational content. Students are transformed from passive consumers, objects of the educational process, into creative subjects, forming a new Internet reality. 22. Social networks help teachers to better understand and remember students. When a young person creates a profile (page) on a social network, they create their own unique content: they post photos, drawings, describe their personal interests, political and religious views. Teachers are given the opportunity to learn more about the student's personality, their values and interests, and, accordingly, offer them information, topics or tasks that may interest them. 23. Some social networks, such as Facebook, have a large selection of applications that can be used for educational purposes. Without detracting from anything stated above, the following are of greatest interest for this study: developing communication skills in a virtual environment and searching for reliable information; establishing joint activities between a teacher and a student, which leads to increased accessibility of the research process and increased motivation for independent educational activities; ensuring the continuity of the educational process, the possibility of detailed planning of the student's educational and research work.

It should be noted that this article was published by the author in 2012, that is, more than ten years ago, and is in a sense prophetic. Subsequently, social networks took a strong position among the information and communication technologies used in Russia and abroad.

It should be noted that our colleagues from Kazakhstan A.A. Bukaeva and A.T. Magzumova (2015) in their work identified a distinctive feature of learning through social networks. The authors called it "distance-interactive learning" because this feature is expressed in the ability to acquire knowledge through interactivity, that is, interaction with other participants in the educational process "at a distance", that is, at a distance. The choice of social networks as a platform for organizing distance-interactive learning has, according to scientists, a number of advantages. The principles of building many social networks, such as identification, communication, presence on the site, relationships, groups, reputation, exchange, search, integration with other offers are very well suited for creating a study group in the online space of a social network. Placing an educational resource on the basis of social networks automatically establishes direct effective communication between the teacher and the student, between the student and the student. The advantages of using social networks are also as follows: their resources are absolutely free; the convenience of mailing and notification services about information, which makes them convenient in communicating with students; conditions are created for a student who, for some reason, missed a lesson, to observe educational activities and even take direct part in them online.

According to A.A. Bukaeva and A.T. Magzumova (2015), despite the fact that social networks cannot be the only means of online learning, their educational opportunities are clearly underestimated. Interest in social networks is associated with the need for educational institutions to establish direct effective communication with participants in the educational process and consumers of educational services. The online community will serve as an additional "informal bridge" between the teacher, student and employer.

N.V. Kergilova and O.K. Sazonova (2017) were among the first Russian researchers to point out that VKontakte is the most popular social resource among Russian students and can be considered as an educational resource in organizing students' extracurricular activities. The experience of the mentioned researchers in using the information and communication capabilities of the VKontakte social network as a teaching tool in addition to classroom lessons in studying psychological and pedagogical disciplines is interesting. In particular, teachers of the psychological and pedagogical faculty of the Gorno-Altai State University created a group in the VKontakte social network called "Pedagogy and More". In their work "Using Social Networks in the Educational Process of the University (using the VKontakte Group "Pedagogy and More" as an example)," the authors described in great detail their own experience of using the social network in the educational process at the university and, importantly, conducted a sociological survey among students, thereby providing feedback. So, let's turn to the experience of colleagues. The group they created is a social and educational environment that allows a group of people, in this case students and teachers, united by a common interest, to communicate. The experience of using the study group "Pedagogy and More" for educational purposes provided researchers with the opportunity to highlight the following advantages of using social networks in the educational process:

1) since students spend more and more time on social networks, which allows them to communicate successfully in an informal setting, in the same information environment they can gain new knowledge that leads to more effective mastery of the discipline;
2) the student and the teacher, interacting on a social network, behave more freely, which allows the student to ask questions on the discipline without fear of critical assessment from classmates;
3) the student has the opportunity to communicate online not only with the teacher, but also with his classmates, which makes it possible to organize conferences and dialogues, especially before the examination session; 4) the teacher becomes a participant in a social network for the student, that is, interaction at the vertical level is replaced by interaction at the horizontal level, which inspires confidence on the part of the student and improves the process of assimilation of the material;
4) the teacher has the opportunity to quickly inform students about upcoming plans.

The authors of the work paid special attention to the information content of the virtual study group "Pedagogy and More". This resource allows you to centrally post information in the news feed, upload documents, video, audio, photo materials. In order to effectively organize the educational process, the materials are arranged as follows:

1) in the "Documents" section, students get access to work programs, to methodological instructions for organizing independent work, as well as to the topics of essays, reports, and requirements for their implementation;
2) in the main section, the workload and the teacher's academic schedule are presented, as well as current announcements about consultations and retake dates;
3) video materials, where students can watch video lectures or thematic films, as well as reporting video materials;
4) audio files-lectures of leading teachers and psychologists, as well as music that can be used for educational purposes.

One of the mobile and priority opportunities in organizing independent work of students is the ability to send the teacher their work in a personal message, which allows working with the sent documents in the online review mode.

The authors pay special attention to the educational resources of the virtual group "Pedagogy and More"

1. The created group provides an opportunity to solve the curator's educational tasks. This format allows you to receive information necessary for the educational process: announcements about upcoming events, holidays, rehearsals.
2. The news feed can be used for educational purposes. To increase students' motivation during the learning process, you can post short interesting articles about great people and their achievements, bright slides with deep interesting philosophical statements, high-quality information on psychological and pedagogical disciplines.
3. Using the teacher's page for educational purposes. The student audience is always interested in facts from the teacher's life and this interest can be used for educational purposes. When a teacher accepts a student's request to be a "friend", he thereby gets the opportunity to interest him in good quality information of a social, cultural, psychological, pedagogical nature.

Thus, the social network "VKontakte" allows you to use its resources for educational and educational purposes, which allows the teacher to keep up with the times.

Feedback from the authors of the study was carried out by conducting a sociological study (using the survey method) among students. Answering the questionnaire, students expressed their opinions on the necessity and usefulness of the created group, as well as on some shortcomings of the resource. The survey results revealed that respondents have a predominantly positive attitude towards the introduction of social networks into the educational process, but some students expressed concerns that social networks would interfere with the learning process.

The authors once again emphasize that the value of social networks for organizing the educational process has not yet been sufficiently assessed. Many managers, teachers and students are skeptical about the possibility of using virtual space to achieve educational goals, since social networks are perceived as a form of leisure. However, social networks in pedagogical activity make it possible to solve various problems: effectively organize the collective work of a study group, develop educational projects online, as well as carry out international exchanges and plan self-education of students.

In conclusion of their work, N.V. Kergilova and O.K. Sazonova (2017), based on sufficient experience in using a virtual study group on the VKontakte network, essentially agree with A.V. Feshchenko and highlight the positive aspects of using social networks in the educational process. Firstly, the use of social networks allows the teacher to save a lot of time. Secondly, the virtual space of the social network makes it possible to build informal interaction between the teacher and students. Thirdly, the use of the presented material in a group allows all participants to independently or jointly create online educational content: glossaries, articles, discussions, multimedia libraries, which stimulates independent cognitive activity, helps to improve the skills of comprehensive assessment and comparison of the information received. Fourthly, the interaction between the teacher and the student ensures the continuity of the educational process. Fifthly, the virtual space facilitates the uploading of video and audio materials to the study group. Sixthly, it allows students to build an individual educational trajectory. Kinyashina Yu.B. (2021) in her work "Features of the use of social networks in the process of studying at a university" proposes to divide the network educational resources of the university into main (strategic resources presented in the form of an educational portal with all the information about the areas of training, access to library resources, creation of personal accounts, etc.) and auxiliary (additional communication resources between subjects through social networks, e-mail). The researcher emphasizes that since the strategic resources created by the university are mandatory for use, and additional resources are used exclusively on the initiative of the participants in the educational process (teacher, study group, student), then the greatest interest is in assessing the capabilities of auxiliary components, that is, social networks.

A study of student behavior in social networks revealed the following three models of student behavior in the VKontakte social network. The first model of planned behavior (students' presence in certain social network groups with specific goals (completing assignments, exchanging information, communicating with the teacher); identifying themselves with a clearly defined circle of users; following established norms, respectful attitude toward the teacher; limiting the use of social networks for other (e.g., entertainment) purposes; trusting the group leader). The second model of one's own beliefs (students use social networks more as a platform for communication than for educational activities; being in a group and identifying oneself with the group; participating in educational discussions with one's own goals and intentions (passing exams, paying off debts, searching for ready-made educational assignments); having one's own opinions and positions; possible violations of norms and rules of conduct).

Model of problematic behavior (lack of a clear goal; the user visits different pages, channels; making numerous subscriptions; joining different groups without particularly identifying oneself in them; diversity of interests; distraction from educational processes; minimal influence of the opinion leader, etc.).

The author emphasizes that all the above-mentioned models of behavior are typical of student youth, and their integrated nature is observed. At the same time,

Yu.B. Kinyashina notes that the greatest danger for young citizens is the model of problematic behavior, which excludes them from educational activities, disrupts socialization mechanisms, and develops dependence on the virtual environment. In this regard, the teacher needs to manage communication with the study group on social networks, monitor content, maintain connections with "opinion leaders", and direct the discussion to a business (educational) format. Thus, social networks act as the most important auxiliary tool in the educational environment of the university. Being a convenient, modern and technological resource for the implementation of the educational process, they are able to solve many educational tasks of the teacher: from posting, storing and transmitting information to the student audience to organizing discussions, exchanging opinions, and conducting project activities. The main advantage of social networks is the wide coverage of all students, even those who are inclined to ignore the educational process. At the same time, the unpreparedness of the teaching staff to work in the virtual space, the skeptical attitude of teachers to online learning, the lack of requirements for mastering this format of classes, difficulties in the technical organization of this process (access to the Internet, equipment of classrooms) can become deterrents to the widespread use of social networks in the education system.

G.B. Saifutdinova, S.A. Livshits, S.S. Usachev (2017), D.I. Kozlov (2024) notes the need for higher education teachers to comply with modern information realities and the need to prepare for the use of social networks in teaching activities. Let us dwell on the works of these authors in more detail. In particular, G.B. Saifutdinova, S.A. Livshits, S.S. Usachev (2017) consider the issue of the possibilities of using social networks as a means of increasing the effectiveness of the educational process of physical education for students of non-core universities. Scientists note that physical education teachers in non-core higher education institutions regularly face the problem of increasing the effectiveness of the educational process of physical education for students in their discipline. In modern realities, social networks are one of the opportunities for introducing students to physical education and a healthy lifestyle and provide an answer to a number of tasks:

- understanding the social significance of physical education and its role in personal development and preparation for professional activity;
- mastering a system of practical skills and abilities that ensure the preservation and strengthening of health;
- expansion of the circle of those wishing to engage in various sports more intensively and increase their physical activity;
- formation of a motivational and value attitude towards physical education, a healthy lifestyle mindset.

In the course of the study conducted by the authors at the Kazan State Power Engineering University (KSPEU), it was revealed that the following organizational and pedagogical conditions contribute to the increase in the effectiveness of the educational process of physical education among students:

- use of information and communication technologies in the learning process;
- organization of operational control of student knowledge and skills;
- popularization of a healthy lifestyle and sports achievements;
- motivational and value attitude towards physical education classes.

The implementation of the identified organizational and pedagogical conditions is carried out through students' interest in information technologies, search engines and social networks. Despite the fact that KSPEU successfully operates a single electronic educational environment "Electronic University", which provides access to multimedia educational content, the university attaches great importance to working with students in social networks. Thus, to popularize a healthy lifestyle and sports achievements of students and teachers, KSPEU uses information technologies of social networks popular among young people. On the basis of the Department of Physical Education, as part of a thematic circle, teachers created a group in the social network VKontakte (https://vk.com/fizkulturaplanettatarstan) to popularize the achievements of the department in the framework of a healthy lifestyle and physical fitness among students. Almost 100% of students are registered in the social network VKontakte, which frees teachers from explaining technical aspects. In modern conditions, social networks can be used as:

- a program for quick exchange of text messages;
- a bulletin board.

Thanks to social networks, students are given the opportunity to contact their teachers with questions and comments directly during preparation for practical classes. Thus, the psychological barrier is removed; it is much easier to start a meaningful Internet dialogue between a student and a teacher online. In addition, the capabilities of social networks allow, for example, to post educational videos, drawings, photographs, audio recordings and documents. Forums, voting, surveys, comments provide great opportunities for joint and independent work. It should be noted that these advantages of social networks are also mentioned by A. V. Fedeshchenko (2012).

In general, the use of information technologies of social networks in the learning process allows solving problems of developing creative thinking, initiative and independence of the student, provides an opportunity to apply the knowledge gained in the learning process in solving practical problems; to form a motivational and value-based attitude towards physical education, a focus on a healthy lifestyle, physical self-improvement and self-education, and a need for regular physical exercise. At the same time, online communication with students in different systems puts forward increased requirements for the qualifications of the university teaching staff and accounting of the time spent, which should be reflected both in the qualification requirements and in the results of certification and remuneration of the teaching staff. The use of information technologies and social networks in the educational process is an option for the development of pedagogical activity as a system that takes into account new content, form and technologies in education with a focus on independent acquisition of knowledge by students in any branch of science, in any subject, which increases the competitiveness of Russian graduates in the labor market. N.V. Kergilova, O.K. Sazonova (2017) indicate the need for advanced training of teachers in the formation of ICT competencies; studying the pedagogical possibilities of social networks; developing and testing effective methods of their application in the educational space; material and moral encouragement of teachers through holding all kinds of competitions on the use of social networks in education. Touching upon the issue of the need to apply additional efforts to the organization of the educational process in the modern information and communication space, the authors believe that in the very near future this will become an objective reality for most higher education workers in connection with the transition to new federal state educational standards. In the new conditions, teachers will have to learn to work with students more flexibly and interactively. According to D.I. Kozlov (2024), the digital transformation of higher education has made significant changes in the professional activities of higher education teachers. Today, teachers must have a variety of digital tools. An important condition for the productive organization of the modern educational process at a university is the professional mobility of a teacher, one of the characteristics of which is his ability to use social networks in pedagogical activities. The availability of cognitive and educational resources in social networks, technical and multimedia capabilities, as well as the ability to maintain professional and educational connections in the online environment make social networks an important actor in the modern learning process and require higher education teachers to develop a special competence - competence in the use of social networks in the educational process of a university (ISUSEP). In his work, the researcher defines the competence of a teacher in the field of ISUSEP as possession of a set of competencies (information, communicative and multimedia), including knowledge, skills in the field of ISUSEP, as well as experience in using social networks in the educational process of a university. Information competence is determined by the information function of social networks, which ensures the exchange of various information containing elements of both a personal nature and news, educational, and educational nature. It is an integrative quality of personality, which is "the result of reflecting the processes of selection, assimilation, processing, transformation, and generation of information into a special type of subject-specific knowledge that allows developing, accepting, predicting, and implementing optimal solutions in various fields of activity." The communication function of social networks consists of people interacting with each other, establishing various contacts: friendly, business, professional, educational, which is possible if users have communicative competence, which is a set of knowledge of "ways of interacting with people around and at a distance, skills in working in a group, mastering various social roles in a team." Social networks today are not only a platform for communication, but also a full-fledged media resource, as they have a wide range of multimedia capabilities that combine varieties of audio, video, photo and text publications, as well as other forms of presentation. Consequently, multimedia competence, characterized as "the ability to freely use various methods and means of presenting, perceiving and transmitting information using modern multimedia technologies to solve any communication problems", is a mandatory component of competence in the field of ISSOPV. Thus, the structure of a teacher's competence in the field of ISSOPV can be represented by information, communication and multimedia components, including the necessary knowledge, skills and practical experience in the relevant professional activity. According to D.I. Kozlov (2024), it is advisable to develop a teacher's competence in the field of ISSOPV in the context of his professional growth and development within the framework of additional professional education in the training of a higher education teacher and advanced training in additional educational programs of the relevant content. The process of developing competence in the field of ISSOPV should be based on key methodological approaches: systemic, competence-based, andragogical and personally oriented, which will contribute to both improving the professional skills of teachers and their personal growth. Thus, a teacher who has competence in the use of social networks will ensure the implementation of the educational process of the university in the paradigm of personalization. At the same time, a number of modern Russian researchers (A.F. Ivanko, G.V. Ushenko, 2015; N.A. Gutorova, 2019; I.V. Guzhova, 2020) note in their works that the potential for using social networks in the educational process can be negated by a number of negative aspects. It should be noted that similar concerns were expressed by domestic teachers more than 10 years ago. Thus, R.S. Seleznev, E.I. Skripak (2013), T.V. Semenovskikh (2014), M.A. Resnyanskaya, S.V. Kuzmina (2016) expressed the opinion that long-term presence of students in social networks contributes to the formation and further development of Internet addiction, the dispersion of students' attention to extracurricular content, the spread of "clip" thinking and the deterioration of mental skills with complex information, a decrease in attendance of offline classes at the university, a distortion of the forms of social interaction between students and teachers, a transformation of students' worldviews and an increase in the socio-cultural gap between teachers and students, and a misinterpretation by teachers of the meaning of a number of concepts that have entered the practice of communication in social networks. In addition, referring to the study of the negative aspects of the use of social networks in the educational process, A.A. Bukaeva and A.T. Magzumova (2015) notes the following problematic points:

1. lack of convenient tools specifically designed for educational purposes (e.g. keeping an electronic register or journal), as in learning management systems;
2. lack of access to social networks from school and university classrooms;
3. active communication, extensive information flow and abundance of entertainment content along with educational content, which distract from the educational process;
4. high degree of time and labor costs for organizing and supporting the educational process in the context of continuous learning in a social network for the teacher;
5. openness of the educational space to the entire Internet community, which is unacceptable or uncomfortable for the educational process;
6. impossibility of assessing the work of the teacher in social learning for the purpose of paying him. N.V. Kergilova, O.K. Sazonova (2017) identified the following negative aspects of using social networks in the educational process: unwillingness of the teaching staff to use the capabilities of social networks in their professional activities; a large amount of work on organizing and supporting a study group in the context of continuous learning; lack of open access to social networks from university classrooms.

Yu.B. Kinyasheva (2021) pointed out that the positive potential of using social networks during training can be offset by a number of negative aspects manifested in the subsequent behavior of young citizens: the development of Internet addiction, decreased physical activity and deterioration in health, a decrease in literacy standards, distraction from other content, and distortion of forms of real interaction. It is obvious that the use of network resources in the educational process is dictated by modern living conditions, but at the same time it should be dosed, being an auxiliary tool for teachers and students.

Research by N.A. Gutorova (2019) is devoted to the study of the ethical component of communication between teachers and students in social networks. The author notes that the Internet has created a fundamentally new communication environment. In the virtual space, the user has the opportunity to create an alternative version of himself, try on various social roles, and hide from reality. Electronic networks provide opportunities for interpersonal and group communication that is not constrained by any framework: "Openness, mass character, intimacy - all these are not contradictions here, but synonyms that characterize a new quality of human communication. The analysis of works by Russian and foreign authors conducted by the researcher showed that social networks allow for a more attentive attitude to the interests of the student, but at the same time require openness from the teacher, in which many of them see a certain threat to their own status. But the fact is that the format of online communication was formed in interpersonal communication, but began to be used in public professional and business communications. Therefore, in the Internet environment, tendencies towards increased colloquialism and expressivization of communication are manifested. Moreover, we are talking not just about changing communication habits, but about a completely differently constructed system of communication between the student and the teacher. The teacher ceases to be a bearer of sacred knowledge, since the development of the Internet provides enormous opportunities for self-education. Moreover, the recommendations of the Ministry of Education and Science of the Russian Federation for the development of the Code of Professional Ethics of the Pedagogical Community speak of the equality of all participants in the educational process, the teacher recognizes the importance of the student's personality, takes the position of an equal participant in communication. This is quite consistent with the horizontal communication in social networks to which modern young people are accustomed. In order to find out the specifics of communication between teachers and students in social networks, the author conducted a sociological study (using the questionnaire method) of teachers in Moscow and St. Petersburg. In his work, in order to substantiate the features of communication, the author actively uses the concepts of "digital native" and "digital immigrant", following M. Prensky (2001). Representatives of the younger generation, who have used gadgets and Internet communication technologies since childhood, the so-called "natives" are used to always being online and quickly receiving the necessary information. Older people, called "Immigrants", transfer the rules of secular etiquette to virtual communication and are careful in sharing personal information online. "Immigrants" evaluate "natives" by their own standards, first of all, this concerns the attitude to technology. "Immigrants" do not believe that students will be able to study with gadgets, because they themselves studied differently, "natives" do not understand why study differently, if their life primarily requires working with gadgets. Despite the differences in their approaches to online communication, digital natives and immigrants are forced to build effective communication in real life, primarily in the education system. The author draws attention to the fact that in scientific publications of teachers of Russian universities, even in cases where the need to use social networks is recognized, possible risks and negative consequences are emphasized. For the most part, this is due to the aforementioned contradiction between the perception of reality by "digital natives" and "digital immigrants", in this case, students and teachers. V. L. Izmagurova (2017) identifies two lines of behavior for teachers (primarily school teachers) on the Internet: "The first is when the teacher values his inner space, and therefore does not go online, or if he has his own account, but does not add students as "friends". The second line is when the teacher includes his students in the circle of Internet "friends" and contacts them on social networks". The researcher considers the second line of behavior to be a priority - the teacher can become an agent of infosocialization for students: "The teacher's participation in the online life of students requires great responsibility, he is actually deprived of privacy on social networks. This must be understood and accepted. In general, the results of the sociological study by N.A. Gutorova (2019) showed that the use of social networks requires certain self-presentation skills, since almost any user becomes a participant in public communication. The problem of blurring the boundaries of personal space in social networks has become noticeable also because the audience of social networks has matured. Those who used to use accounts for personal interests now use them to solve professional issues and feel especially strongly how their personal space is turning into a work office. Two trends are associated with this: migration to other social networks and the popularization of netiquette.

Thus, survey data show that VKontakte is becoming the main platform for working with young people, accordingly, teachers who created accounts specifically for this purpose practically do not publish personal information in them. Here it is appropriate to refer to the idea of "scalable sociality" that social networks can build, while within the framework of one account it is possible to provide for the possibility of implementing both personal and business communication, just as in one apartment you can find a place to meet with friends and an important meeting.

Fearing excessive openness of social networks, a teacher can artificially limit himself and not use all the possibilities of this technology. According to the survey, we see how few teachers use social networks for project or research activities together with students. "Digital footprints" force the modern user (not only the teacher) to be more attentive to what information he posts in his account, what he comments on, including during private correspondence. The simplest solution to this problem is to minimize your presence in social networks. In addition, "digital natives" feel more confident on this platform than most of their teachers, but at the same time do not have their life experience. Most problems can be solved with the help of clear rules that are mandatory for all participants in communication. Modern teachers, at a minimum, include in these rules an indication of the time when you can "write" to them on social networks and expect to receive a response. It is necessary to pay attention to the use of other people's texts and the distribution of confidential information (for example, the distribution of screenshots of private correspondence, and phrases can be taken out of context). It is even possible to include a separate course in the curriculum dedicated to information ethics, at least until such work is carried out in schools.

The practice of using social networks in the educational process is taking shape before our eyes. We still have a weak idea of how many higher education teachers have an account on social networks and how they use it, especially when it comes to regional universities, which determines the importance of further research in this area.

For representatives of the "digital generation", an account on a social network is both a living room and an office. It is difficult for "digital immigrants" to accept the new rules for organizing working time and space. The older generation, having minimal experience in using social networks, is often inclined to demonize them, and the general situation with the privacy of Internet communication and the pressure of public opinion on teachers who post materials in social networks that allegedly do not correspond to their status, only worsens the situation. Meanwhile, social networks are a platform for communication, which in itself continues to be the same as in reality. Thus, summing up the theoretical review of Russian studies on the presented topic, it became possible to establish that the majority of works are devoted to the features of the use of information and communication technologies of social networks as an additional means of teaching at the university: the possibility of free and prompt placement of educational materials, rapid exchange of information, creation of new forms of communication between teachers and students. Often, researchers focus on the positive and negative aspects of the use of social networks in education, as well as the problem of ethics in interaction in the networks of all participants in the learning process. It is relevant that the authors raise the question of the compliance of the qualifications of a university teacher with the requirements that the digitalization of modern education places on him.

At the same time, little attention is paid to recording the achievements of students (in academic and extracurricular activities), realized through the use of social networks.

Despite the growth of scientific interest in the problem under study over the past 10-15 years, it should be noted that modern domestic authors do not take into account the specifics of the use of information and communication technologies in teaching disciplines of different focus. Thematic research papers are often local and multidirectional. The types of academic disciplines, social networks used and forms of work in them vary. As an example, we can cite the works of N.A. Malysheva (2013), I.V. Shcherbakova, M.V. Timasheva (2020), who study the practice of using information and communication technologies of social networks in the process of teaching students of individual specialties or disciplines, respectively. There is an obvious need to study the potential of social networks to improve the efficiency of the educational process in teaching various subjects, both specialized and non-specialized, in higher education institutions of various focus areas.

ANALYSIS OF THE FINDINGS

The results obtained enable us to infer about the vast potential of utilizing social networking technologies in teaching humanities subjects in higher education. The study identified the prevalent social networks employed by teachers and students for educational purposes, forming the basis of the experiment (Vkontakte and Telegram). The researchers observed that students integrating educational materials from social networks into their learning process tend to show better academic results. In contrast to previous studies, social networks are viewed as an essential component of the learning environment within higher education.

CONCLUSION

- Vkontakte and Telegram are the favored social networks among students for both casual interactions and educational exchanges;
- Students rely heavily on digital resources when preparing for humanities classes, preferring materials shared by teachers or recommended by them;
- There is a clear demand from students for expanded avenues of communication with teachers, particularly through specialized chats and direct interactions on Telegram and Vkontakte;
- Enhancing communication with teachers on social media platforms is crucial, especially considering the prevalence of part-time job commitments among contemporary students.

The exchange of ideas between educators and students in the process of mastering subjects is a dynamic and evolving network of connections. Continuous enhancement and availability of information and communication technologies create possibilities to utilize social media platforms in the academic setting, fostering the growth of innovative teaching methods. The significance of this research lies in the education system's need for digitalization and the emergence of fresh communication techniques in transmitting information between instructors and learners. The study focuses on analyzing contemporary students' inclination towards internet-based communication tools, while evaluating the utilization of social media technologies in teaching liberal arts subjects at the college level. A survey was conducted among students in key institutions of higher learning in Smolensk.

At present, online resources are underappreciated in the academic arena among traditional full-time students. The primary research tool used was a sociological survey (employing a written questionnaire technique). The feedback obtained from students at various universities in the Smolensk area enables the authors to infer the potential of information and communication technologies in higher education. A questionnaire was developed by the authors, covering the main communication features of popular social networks in Russia. Additionally, participants were invited to provide their suggestions and feedback in a dedicated section of the questionnaire. The study yielded a comprehensive statistical database on students' preferences regarding the utilization of social media technologies in the instruction of liberal arts subjects at the college level.

REFERENCES

Dyachkova, M. A., & Tomyuk, O. N. (2017). Social networks as an educational resource. *Pedagogical education in Russia.*, (12), 141–146.

Fedeshchenko, A. V. (2012). Social networks in education: Analysis of experience and prospects of development. *Humanitarian informatics. Tomsk.*, (6), 124–134.

Gutorova N.A. (2019). Features of teacher-student communication in social networks: an ethical aspect // The sign: the problematic field of media education. No.2(32). pp.7-16.

Guzhova I. V. (2020). Problems of formation of digital literacy of youth in social networks // Sign: problematic field of media education . No. 4(38). pp.14-25.

Ivanko, A. F., & Ushenko, G. V. (2015). Educational opportunities of Facebook // Bulletin of MGUP. No.6. Access mode: https://cyberleninka.ru/article/n/obrazovatelnye-vozmozhnosti-facebook (date of application: 07.11.2017)

Kergilova, N. V., & Sazonova, O. K. (2017). The use of social networks in the educational process of a university (on the example of the VKontakte group "Pedagogy and not only"). *Siberian Pedagogical Journal.*, (6), 87–92.

Kinyashina, Yu. B. (2021). Features of the use of social networks in the process of studying at a university. *Izvestiya Tula State University. Humanities*, (2), 126–133.

Koch I. A., Melnik A.V. (2019). Social networks as a means of communication in the educational environment of the university // Society and power. N° 1 (75). C. 31-41

Kozlov, D. I. (2024). Competence of a teacher in the field of using social networks in the educational process of a university / Scientific notes. electronic scientific journal of Kursk State University. N° 1 (69). Access mode: http:// api-mag.kursksu.ru/api/v1/get_pdf/5219 / (date of reference 03/31/2024)

Malysheva, N. A. (2013). The role of social networks in the model of distance learning for students of art specialties // Scientific journal of KubGAU. No.86. Access mode: https://cyberleninka.ru/article/n/rol-sotsialnyh-setey-vmodeli-distantsionnogo-obucheniya-studentov-hudozhestvennyh-spetsialnostey (Date of reference: 03/31/2024)

Manyaev, A. G., & Shipitsin, A. I. (2018). Prospects of using social network technology in university education. *Innovación Educativa (México, D.F.)*, (5), 148–157.

Podchalimova G.N., Belova S.N. Digital transformation of the system of additional professional education at the university // Human capital. 2021. No. S5-3 (149). pp. 78-85.

Proskuryakov, A. S. (2014). Education in the context of globalization. The use of social networks in the educational process // Bulletin of the Voronezh State Technical University. No.3-2. T10. Access mode: https://cyberleninka.ru/article/n/obrazovanie-v-usloviyah-globalizatsii-ispolzovanie-sotsialnyh-setey-v-obrazovatelnom-protsesse (Date of application: 03/31/2024)

Resnyanskaya, M. A., & Kuzmina, S. V. (2016). The influence of social networks on the worldview of students. *Young Scientist.*, *4*(9), 61–63.

Sayfutdinova, G. B., Livshits, S. A., & Usachev, S. S. (2017). Information technologies and social networks as a means of improving the effectiveness of the educational process in universities // Problems of modern pedagogical education. No. 56-8. pp. 199-204.

Selezenev R. S., Skripak E. I. (2013). Social networks as a phenomenon of information society and the specifics of social relations in their environment // Bulletin of KemSU. No. 2 (54). pp. 125-132.

Semenovskikh, T. V. (2014). The phenomenon of "Clip thinking" in the educational university environment // Bulletin of Eurasian science – No. 5 (24). Access mode: https://cyberleninka.ru/article/n/fenomen-klipovogo-myshleniya-v-obrazovatelnoy-vuzovskoy-srede/viewer (Accessed 04/01/2024)

Shcherbakova I. V., Timashova M. V. (2020). Vkontakte social network for teaching vocabulary and grammar of the German language // Baltic Humanitarian Journal. Vol. 9. No. 2(31). pp. 317-321

Chapter 2
Artificial Intelligence and the Future of HRM in the Corporate World: Balancing Innovation and Ethics

Aayisha Ahamed
https://orcid.org/0009-0001-7675-8569
Lovely Professional University, Punjab, India

Tawheed Nabi
Lovely Professional University, Punjab, India

ABSTRACT

The use of AI in HRM is pioneering. It has enhanced organizational efficiency and recruitment processes. This chapter digs into the impacts of AI on HRM, emphasizing its ability to simplify the recruitment process. Utilizing AI for trend forecasting, employee retention strategies, and risk mitigation can enhance productivity and satisfaction. Like other technologies that let computers perform tasks requiring human intellect, the use of AI in HR also has limits. Ethical issues like algorithmic bias, lack of transparency, and data privacy are concerns that require robust governance and regulatory framework. This chapter discusses the risks of using AI, like the increasing existing biases and replacing HR roles with AI, and highlights the necessity for human supervision of ethical AI adoption. Regardless, it's evident that AI has to potential to reduce administrative burdens and promote inclusivity and data-driven decision-making. This chapter emphasizes balancing innovation with ethics and advocates for the responsible use of AI to foster sustainable growth and a healthy workplace.

DOI: 10.4018/979-8-3373-8612-6.ch002

1. THE IMPACT OF AI ON HR DECISION-MAKING

AI streamlines recruitment by automating standard tasks, selecting candidates efficiently, and lowering bias, resulting in more efficient and effective hiring approach (Vishwanath, 2023; Ali & Rafi, 2024; Chandratreya, 2024; Dăniloaia, 2024). AI is an enhancement tool, which enhances competencies of human resources by generating insights based on data to improve productivity, job satisfaction, and innovation. This assists organizations stay ambitious in a swiftly changing business environment (Manisha Anil Vhora et al., 2024; Ramli et al., 2024). AI tools enable advanced performance tracking and management by providing cutting-edge analytics, allowing HR experts to make data-driven decisions and personalize employee engagement approach (Ashrafuzzaman et al., 2024). AI simplifies repetitive HR tasks, letting HR experts to concentrate on strategic decision-making and decreasing the administrative workload (Bhattacharya, 2023b; Vishwanath, 2023). AI- oriented HR analytics, including predictive analytics, data mining, and machine learning, allow organizations to take informed decisions regarding talent supervision, employee performance, and retention approaches. This results in better and increased employee satisfaction, reduced attrition rates, and increased productivity (Manisha Anil Vhora et al., 2024). AI tools improve the effectiveness, customization, and growth potential of HR processes, from recruitment to retention. AI-driven candidate tracking structures and computerized onboarding platforms improve effectiveness and reduce turnover (Chandratreya, 2024; Madanchian, 2024). For instance, ChatGPT can optimize HR processes, boost communication, and assist personalized learning and decision-making, resulting in better performance and engagement (Porkodi & Cedro, 2025).

AI and machine learning help HR to make educated decisions based on reliable data trends, improving the accuracy and efficacy of HR procedures (Fomude et al., 2023a). In addition to improving decision-making efficiency of HR Artificial Intelligence can create ethical issues because of algorithmic biases and lack of transparency (Khair et al., 2020). Incorporation of AI in HR presents ethical problems, such as algorithmic bias, and data privacy which ought to be addressed to make sure that Artificial Intelligence complements human skills instead of replacing them (Vishwanath, 2023; Ali & Rafi, 2024; Dăniloaia, 2024) Applicants see screening of resumes done by AI as less reliable and fair than humans, with outcome positivity and AI expertise mediating roles (Cai et al., 2024).

AI's impact on HR and administration is debatable, but HR experts can shape the future by making sure that ethics and fairness are paramount to AI development (Charlwood & Guenole, 2022a). AI is reshaping business decision-making, offering unparalleled opportunities for innovation and efficiency, while advocating for sustainable practices (Kaggwa et al., 2024).

The incorporation of Artificial Intelligence (AI) into Human Resource Management (HRM) has revolutionized the manner in which organizations handle decision-making. AI technologies, including machine learning and predictive analytics, have allowed HR experts to make more educated, data-driven decisions, improving efficiency and accuracy. Nevertheless, the effectual deployment of AI in HR decision-making is dependent on the progress of AI literacy among HR professionals. AI has extremely altered HR decision-making by offering avant-garde tools for acquiring talent, performance management, and planning the workforce. AI-driven analytics allows HR professionals to examine extensive datasets, identify trends, and make forecasts, resulting in more educated decisions. For example, AI-based hiring tools can screen resumes, match candidates with job requirements, and even conduct primary interviews, simplifying the hiring procedure and enhancing the quality of hires (Olaniyan et al., 2023; Ganatra, 2024; Srivastava, 2024).

Moreover, AI enhances decision-making in performance management by providing continuous, objective feedback and personalized development plans. AI-driven performance evaluation tools facilitate more precise assessments, enabling HR professionals to identify skill gaps and align employee development with organizational goals (Ganatra, 2024) (Gupta, 2024) (Khan et al., 2024). AI also plays a crucial role in workforce planning by predicting future workforce needs, optimizing resource allocation, and enhancing strategic decision-making. By analyzing large datasets, AI can forecast turnover trends and inform succession planning, contributing to organizational productivity and efficiency (Vhora et al., 2024) (Manoharan, 2024).

Although it holds significant transformative possibilities, AI in HR decision-making, certain challenges should be addressed. One of the main challenges is the moral implications of adoption of AI, including algorithmic bias, data privacy, and transparency issues. These challenges can sabotage confidence in AI systems and impede their adoption if not handled effectively (Gupta, 2024; Ganagi & Rotti, 2024; Bar-Gil et al., 2024). An additional obstacle is the requirement for HR professionals to learn the required skills and proficiencies to work with AI technologies. The limited understanding of AI among HR professionals can restrict the effective use of AI tools and obstruct the achievement of their complete potential in HR decision-making. (Kim, 2024; Bouhsaien & Azmani, 2024; Arora et al., 2024). Additionally, the incorporation of AI in HR decision-making needs substantial organizational changes, this includes creating strategic frameworks for the adoption of AI and setting up governance structures to guarantee the ethical use of AI. These changes can be difficult and may face opposition from employees and stakeholders (Gupta, 2024; Ganagi & Rotti, 2024; Bar-Gil et al., 2024).

The future of AI in HR decision-making is optimistic, with substantial possibilities for continued advancement and development. One essential area of emphasis is the creation of more sophisticated AI tools that can tackle the ethical and technical challenges linked to the implementation of AI. These tools should be developed with transparency, fairness, and inclusivity in mind, guaranteeing that they conform to organizational principles and moral guidelines (Gupta, 2024; Ganagi & Rotti, 2024; Bar-Gil et al., 2024).

1.1 Enhance the Processes of Recruitment and Talent Acquisition.

Artificial Intelligence decreases time-to-hire and enhance the quality of hires by optimizing the process of candidate sourcing and screening. Automated resume assessment and precise candidate matching for the job role is a significant progress (Jafri et al., 2024; Prasad, 2024; Sasi, 2024). AI can improve matching candidates with jobs, resulting in longer-term job placements and higher retention rates. Tools like the Resume Analyzer use machine learning algorithms to examine job advertisements and resumes, scoring candidates based on the extent to which they fulfill particular criteria. (Bhalke et al., 2024).

AI tools can be used for predictive analytics to predict hiring requirements, enabling organizations make informed decisions to enhance workforce management strategies (Sasi, 2024). For the recruitment process use of AI can increase employer branding which can result in making the organization look more appealing to potential candidates (Baratelli & Colleoni, 2022). AI optimizes candidate sourcing and screening, decreasing time-to-hire and enhancing the quality of hired candidates via tools like chatbots and applicant tracking approaches. AI enhances resume screening precision and candidate review applicability, allowing recruiters to concentrate on strategic decision-making (Zhang, 2024).

Aside from its advantages, AI can perpetuate biases that already exist if not appropriately managed, requiring robust bias recognition and mitigation tactics. There's no doubt that AI can improve recruitment and talent management by optimizing, automating, and personalizing the hiring strategy, but its impact relies on the quality of data, algorithm, and circumstances, and may raise privacy, safety, accountability, and legal risks (Kiritsi & Adamantidis, 2024). Despite its advantages, AI can increase existing biases if not carefully handled, concerning fairness in candidate selection. (Faqih et al., 2024; Paramita et al., 2024). AI refines recruitment by making hiring procedures more efficient, precise, and inclusive. Nevertheless, organizations must address challenges like bias and privacy matters to leverage AI's potential in talent acquisition altogether. This proportion guarantees reasonable and practical recruitment approaches, ultimately improving organizational performance and employer branding.

Figure 1. Recruitment Process of AI

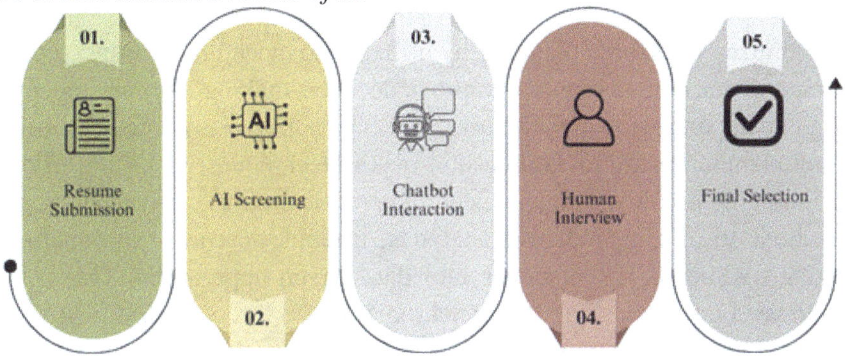

1.2 Improve Employee Retention

AI greatly improves employee retention by leveraging predictive analytics, personalized growth strategies, and enhanced HR strategies. Here's how AI contributes to better employee retention:

AI studies historical data and employee behavior to predict potential risks. This enables organizations to recognize early warning signs and diligently intervene with personalized retention measures. By predicting the gradual reduction of the organization's employees over time, AI helps HR professionals develop targeted retention plans that align with individual employee requirements (Basnet, 2024; Marín Díaz et al., 2023; Paigude et al., 2023). AI-driven tools are capable of personalizing learning experiences, and career development which in turn will improve employee satisfaction and engagement, resulting in positive retention outcome (Kadirov et al., 2024a).

Application of AI in Human Resource Management, for instance natural language processing, and chatbots enable more suitable talent management and employee growth resulting in higher rates of employee retention. Employee engagement and retention are a few among the multiple benefits of successful implementations of AI in HR, emphasizing the AI's potential to transform HR practices (Vaghani, 2024). Assistance of AI in HRM increases productivity by reducing customer sentiments and requests for managerial interventions, thus, improving employee retention (Brynjolfsson et al., 2023). AI-based performance feedback can improve employee productivity, though its disclosure may negatively affect productivity with lengthier tenure in the company mitigating this impact (Tong et al., 2021a).

1.3 Optimize Workforce Planning

AI optimizes workforce planning by utilizing advanced algorithms, predictive analytics, and machine learning to improve decision-making, optimize operations, and align talent strategies with the organization's objectives. AI greatly optimizes workforce planning by improving decision-making techniques, enhancing efficiency, and encouraging employee engagement. The incorporation of AI technology lets organizations to utilize predictive analytics, machine learning, and automation, converting traditional HR practices into data-driven approaches. This shift not only optimizes operations but also synchronizes workforce management with the objectives of the organization.

AI-based HR analytics offer insights into talent management, employee performance, and retention techniques, resulting in informed decision-making (Vhora et al., 2024). Predictive analytics allows predict workforce requirements, allowing proactive adjustments to staffing levels and skill requirements (Rao et al., 2024). AI optimizes workforce planning by improving decision-making, improving efficiency, and fostering strategic HR management. It leverages predictive analytics and machine learning to simplify various HR roles, from recruitment to employee engagement. AI enables forecasting short-term and long-term appointing and recruiting requirements, letting organizations foresee workforce requirements and simplify resource distribution (Ganatra, 2024; Roy, 2021; Saini, 2023).

AI automates routine tasks such as scheduling, managing timesheets, and absence management, letting HR experts concentrate on strategic initiatives (Kumar Tyagi et al., 2023; Popo-Olaniyan et al., 2022; Saini, 2023). AI tools assist in predicting short- and long-term scheduling and recruitment requirements, letting organizations align workforce supply with demand better (Wang, 2024). AI improves recruitment approaches by studying data to recognize ultimate talent, simplify candidate selection, and anticipate candidate success, therefore improving recruitment efficiency and employee productivity (Zhang, 2024a). By automating redundant administrative tasks, AI lets HR professionals to concentrate on strategic initiatives, such as workforce planning and talent administration.

AI improves decision-making in workforce management by providing data-driven understanding which helps organizations to integrate development of employees with goals of the organization to forecast turnover patterns (Rao et al., 2024). AI-based tools simplify hiring processes, personalized learning and development, and improve performance management, resulting in better talent acquisition, and retention (Faqihi & Miah, 2023; Subbaiah & Rajalakshmi, 2024). AI-based sentiment analysis tools observe well-being of employees and their engagement, promoting a positive work atmosphere and decreasing turnover (Popo-Olaniyan et., 2022; Ganatra, 2024).

Incorporating AI in workforce planning needs thorough review of data privacy, possible bias, and ethical implications to create trust and guarantee transparency (Tyagi et al., 2023; Kadirov et al., 2024). Successful deployment of AI relies on getting past pushback from staff, ensuring integration of system, and boosting AI literacy among HR experts (Popo-Olaniyan et al., 2022). AI significantly streamlines workforce planning by improving recruitment, improving employee performance, and facilitating strategic HR management. It automates standard tasks, provides data-driven perspicuity, and helps personalized employee growth, eventually leading to improved organizational efficiency and productivity.

Figure 2. Workforce Planning with AI

Traditional Planning	AI-Driven Planning
Manual forecasting	Automated predictions
Time-intensive analysis	Real-time adjustments
Limited scope	Comprehensive insights

1.4 Boost Performance Management

AI allows real-time feedback and personalized performance-based statistics, shifting away from conventional approaches to better contemporary measures that correspond to career paths of individuals and goals of the organizations. AI-based analytics assist in creating personalised development plans and pre-emptive management plans, enabling unbiased evaluations and improving engagement of employees (Nyathani, 2023; Nayak & Choudhury, 2024; Madhumita et al., 2024).

AI streamlines current processes by improving automation, data flow, and transformation effects, which improves organizational and process-level performance. AI-based solutions in IT operations, such as anomaly detection and predictive maintenance, lead to enhanced performance, reduced downtime, and cost savings (Wamba-Taguimdje et al., 2020; Al-Surmi et al., 2022; Aluwala, 2023). AI enhances decision-making efficiency by providing precise and uniform performance data, which assists in strategic planning and operational progress (Baabdullah, 2024).

AI helps strategic decision-making by incorporating marketing and IT strategies, enhancing operational efficiency and decision precision in complicated problems.

AI-based performance management systems provide more in-depth understandings into employee strengths and weaknesses, helping in strategic talent management and organizational growth (Al-Surmi et al., 2022; Subbaiah & Rajalakshmi, 2024; Madhumita et al., 2024). By providing suitable and constructive feedback, AI systems can increase employee engagement and motivation, resulting in higher productivity and talent retention (Tong et al., 2021).

AI decreases subjectivity and bias in performance assessment, guaranteeing fairer assessments and promoting a more inclusive work atmosphere (Sahay & Kaur, 2021; Subbaiah & Rajalakshmi, 2024; Nyathani, 2023) Ethical and privacy concerns are paramount when incorporating AI into performance management, needing continuous monitoring and robust AI models (Nayak & Choudhury, 2024; Folorunsho et al., 2024). AI is redefining the future outlook of performance management by improving feedback, guiding, and overall talent management approaches. Organizations are encouraged to incorporate AI purposefully to remain determined, improve talent retention, and steer sustainable growth (Nayak & Choudhury, 2024; Subbaiah & Rajalakshmi, 2024; Madhumita et al., 2024).

AI elevates performance management by providing real-time insights., personalized feedback, and enhanced decision-making, resulting in enhanced employee success and organizational growth. However, organizations should address potential challenges, such as employee perceptions and the need for human supervision, to completely realize AI's advantages in performance management. While AI provides significant advantages, it also presents concerns about bias and data privacy, requiring careful implementation and transparency in HR practices (Madanchian, 2024; Basnet, 2024).

Figure 3. AI-based Performance Feedback Loop

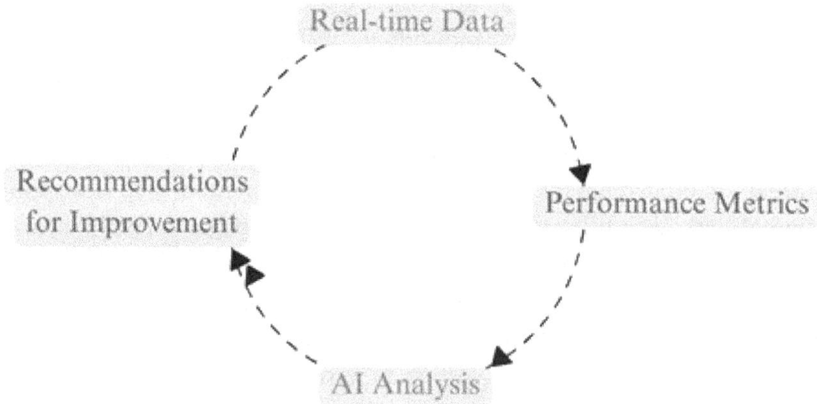

2. ADVANTAGES OF AI IN HR DECISION-MAKING

Incorporating AI into HR decision-making provides a variety of benefits, fundamentally changing conventional HR methods. AI technologies improve efficiency, precision, and strategic decision-making in numerous HR functions, ranging from hiring to maintaining employee loyalty. By utilizing AI-powered analytics, businesses can make strategic decisions that enhance employee satisfaction, lower turnover rates, and increase productivity. Artificial Intelligence (AI) is significantly improving decision-making in Human Resources (HR) by offering insights based on historical data and simplifying various HR tasks.

- AI streamlines the posting of job listings, the assessment of resumes, and the evaluation of candidates, enhancing efficiency and minimizing bias in hiring processes.(Mollay et al., 2024; Srivastava, 2024).
- Systems for tracking applicants that utilize AI technology enhance the selection process, increasing both the efficiency and precision of hiring choices. (Madanchian, 2024).
- Technologies such as deep learning and natural language processing streamline the process of resume evaluation and interview arrangement, improving the experiences of candidates. (Mollay et al., 2024).

AI allows more educated and strategic decision-making by providing predictive analytics, data mining, and machine learning to manage talent, evaluate employee performance, and create retention plans (Ali & Rafi, 2024b; Manisha Anil Vhora et al., 2024; VC, 2024a).

AI simplifies HR operations by automating regular tasks such as hiring, appointing, and performance assessments, decreasing administrative loads, and allowing HR experts to concentrate on strategic functions (Bansal et al., 2022; Bhattacharya, 2023; Vishwanath, 2023) AI provides HR with robust analytical tools that facilitate data-driven decision-making. This has predictive analytics for talent acquisition, workforce planning, and employee engagement, resulting in more informed and strategic HR decisions (Nyathani, 2023; Ali & Rafi, 2024; Popo-Olaniyan et al., 2022; VC, 2024) AI-driven talent analytics optimize talent management by recognizing the most suitable candidates, forecasting employee performance, and customizing development programs to personal needs, thus improving overall organizational performance (Chandratreya, 2024). AI improves the efficiency of HR functions, such as recruitment, onboarding, and performance management, by automating standard tasks and lowering administrative burdens (Stone et al., 2024).

AI has the potential to decrease human biases in HR functions, such as recruitment and performance assessments, by making decisions based on data trends rather than subjective judgment (VC, 2024). AI tools can improve employee participation by providing personalized experiences and understandings of employee satisfaction and productivity, enabling to promotion of a more diligent and motivated workforce (Ashrafuzzaman et al., 2024). AI helps in strategic workforce planning by predicting future workforce requirements and integrating HR strategies with organizational objectives, ensuring that suitable talent is appointed to meet future demands (Popo-Olaniyan et al., 2022; Fomude et al., 2023).

AI in HR decision-making provides substantial benefits, including improved strategic insights, improved efficiency, and competitive advantages. Regardless, organizations should address moral considerations and strategically implement AI to align with their objectives to thoroughly utilize its potential.

2.1 Improved Efficiency

AI tools improve the recruitment process by predicting hiring salaries, optimizing candidate screening, and enhancing onboarding experiences. This leads to reduced costs, time, and effort in recruitment, ultimately increasing HR efficiency (Jiaping, 2022; Alnsour et al., 2024; Jafri et al., 2024). AI automates routine HR duties, for instance, data management, scheduling, and payroll, letting HR concentrate on strategic initiatives. This transition improves operational efficiency by up to 30% and supports more suitable strategic decision-making (Yadav et al., 2023; Sundari et al., 2024). AI allows individualized employee experiences via data analysis, leading to higher engagement, satisfaction, and retention. AI technology also provides real-time feedback and helps employee development (Chinenye Gbemisola Okatta et al., 2024; Manoharan, 2024).

Figure 4. Time saved by AI Automation (Example)

HR Task	Manual Effort (Hours)	AI Effort (Hours)	Time Saved
Resume Screening	20	1	95%
Onboarding	10	2	80%
Attendance Tracking	5	0.5	90%

2.2 Improved Accuracy

Artificial Intelligence (AI) improves precision in HR by improving recruitment, performance management, and decision-making processes using data-driven insights, automation, and avant-garde analytics, along with addressing challenges like data privacy and algorithmic bias. Artificial Intelligence (AI) substantially improves precision in Human Resource (HR) management by improving several functions like recruitment, evaluation of performance, and decision-making.

Machine learning (ML) algorithms, such as decision trees and logistic regression, improve the accuracy of HRM operational processes by providing substantial and ideal assessment approaches (Kumar et al., 2022). AI automates resume screening, conducts big data analysis, and utilizes natural language processing to interact with candidates, boosting the speed and accuracy of candidate screening (Norman & Pahlawati, 2024). AI refines recruitment by making resume screening and candidate conversations automatic. It reduces biases and improves the accuracy of choosing suitable candidates. AI-based systems can manage considerable volumes of data, making the recruitment process more efficient and accurate (Yadav et al., 2023; Kumari, 2024; Manoharan, 2024). AI-based systems offer objective reviews in performance evaluations which lowers subjectivity and increases fairness. These systems utilize data-driven insights and provide real-time feedback, improving the precision and efficiency of performance reviews (Bakar et al., 2024; Sampath et al., 2024). Although AI offers significant advantages for improving precision in human resource management, it is essential to consider the ethical concerns and possible biases associated with these technologies to ensure fairness and transparency in the hiring and assessment processes.

2.3 Improved Employee Experience

Artificial Intelligence in human resource management improves employee experience by improving personalization, automating standard tasks, boosting engagement and retention, and also improving the efficiency of operations and decision-making.

AI applications facilitate hyper-personalized employee experiences by utilizing bots and virtual assistants for systematic, analytical, and communicative tasks. This individualization improves employee dedication and satisfaction (Malik et al., 2022). Artificial intelligence in human resource management can result in a more optimized, measurable, and user-friendly employee interface, improving career progress, and staff service, and equipping organizations for more significant value. The adoption of AI in human resources greatly influences Time-Saving & Cost Reduction, however, automation and real-time experience do not (Nawaz et al., 2024). Platforms powered by AI provide customized training initiatives and ongoing learning opportunities, targeting personal skill deficiencies and aligning with the objectives of the organization. (Ganatra, 2024; Bharadwaj, 2024). AI-driven continuous feedback systems enable employees to monitor their performance and establish attainable goals, leading to improved job satisfaction overall (Ganatra, 2024).

2.4 Cost Savings

Artificial Intelligence in human resource management saves costs mainly by increasing accuracy, enhancing computing power and capacity, and improving personalization, meanwhile, automation and real-time experience do not particularly contribute to cost reduction. AI technologies streamline the process of resume evaluation and preliminary candidate assessments, significantly cutting down on the time and resources invested in hiring. (Kuźniarska & Stańczyk, 2024; Rami, 2024). Chatbots and virtual assistants enable faster interactions with candidates, reducing delays and improving the overall experience of recruitment. (Rami, 2024).

AI-enabled applications automate regular HR tasks such as recruitment, screening, and onboarding, which decreases the time and resources required for these functions. This automation results in substantial cost savings by lowering manual labor and boosting efficiency (Hu, 2023; Khan et al., 2024). AI in human resources management greatly influence Time-Saving & Cost Reduction by factors such as Accuracy, Computing Power and Capacity, and Personalization (Nawaz et al., 2024). Artificial intelligence in human resource management assists companies in saving costs by studying data sets, boosting hiring success, and enhancing the quality of talent (Li, 2018).

3. LIMITATIONS AND ETHICAL CONCERNS

Limitations and ethical concerns of artificial intelligence in human resource management comprise biases and discrimination, privacy incursion, and accountability problems, meanwhile also emphasizing the lack of transparency, impartiality, and reliable management to handle these challenges.

Artificial intelligence in human resource management can improve recruitment efficiency but may result in biased outcomes and systematic drawbacks for marginalized groups (Capasso et al., 2024). Artificial intelligence in human resource management presents challenges such as complexity of phenomena, small data sets, and ethical and legal constraints (Tambe et al., 2019). Difficulties of employing artificial intelligence in human resource management comprise resistance from organization, ethical concerns, technological constraints, and the requirement for new skills (Ghezelseflou, 2023).

AI systems can further increase existent biases, especially gender and racial biases if they are trained on biased data. This can result in unfair recruitment and assessment practices (Valčo, 2023; Du, 2024, Du, 2024; Kumari, 2024). The usage of AI in HRM involves managing considerable amounts of personal data, raising concerns about data privacy and the possibility of mishandling or infringements (Wei & Hong, 2024). The automation of HR jobs through AI can result in job displacement, raising concerns about the future role of human HR experts (Kumar, 2024).

3.1 Data Privacy and Security

AI presents noteworthy security and privacy concerns because of ethical apprehensions associated with this technology, mandating researchers and stakeholders to establish and refine the regulations (Li, 2024). Artificial Intelligence and Machine Learning in human resource management can generate ethical concerns and quandaries, like concerns about the encroachment on personal data and privacy, prejudices, and biased treatment, and probable harm from inaccurate data (Lukaszewski & Stone, 2024).

AI systems in HRM usually process enormous volumes of personal data, raising substantial privacy concerns. Robust data security measures and transparent data handling approaches are vital to mitigate these risks (Sarkar & Arigela, 2024). Guaranteeing adherence to data protection laws, such as the General Data Protection Regulation (GDPR), is paramount. These regulations are prepared to protect individual rights and privacy (Kumar, 2024). The sophistication of AI systems can conceal accountability, making it challenging to determine responsibility for decisions made by AI (Reddy et al., 2024). Over-dependence on AI can undermine human judgment, which is essential for nuanced decision-making in HRM (Valčo, 2023; Wei & Hong, 2024).

To address the concerns of employing artificial intelligence in human resource management, AI ethics is a crucial field that addresses ethical risks and problems in AI systems, addressing privacy, discrimination, unemployment, and security risks whilst improving efficiency and advantages for individuals, organizations, and society (Huang et al., 2023).

Figure 5. AI and Data Privacy Challenges

Challenge	Impact	Solution
Data breaches	Loss of sensitive info	Encryption, access control
Employee consent	Legal and ethical issues	Transparent policies
Compliance with regulations	Financial and reputational	Regular audits

3.2 Bias in Algorithms

Limitations and ethical concerns of artificial intelligence in human resource management, particularly regarding bias in algorithms, include issues of prejudice and systematic disadvantages for marginalized groups, gender and racial biases, privacy and data protection concerns, and the need for transparency and accountability in AI-driven decision-making.

Artificial Intelligence has developed as a substitute for human intelligence. It influences the existence of countless individuals. It imitates humans by solving problems and understanding the tasks. In past couple of years, numerous companies have used several Artificial Intelligence tools like chatbots and face recognition software to meet their recruitment requirements. The companies recruiting need to make the candidates seeking jobs realize that AI-based tools would be free from discrimination and they system would safeguard their privacy (Gupta & Mishra, 2022). According to Aashima Gupta and Mridula Mishra notable unethical issues encountered by the hiring companies are Data privacy and implicit bias.

As per a report published by UNESCO, Women constitute just 22 percent of all AI professionals. Gender biases and stereotyping are perpetuated in AI technologies because of their underrepresentation in the field. Virtual personal assistants such as Siri, and Alexa are “female” by default, which is not an accident. The submissiveness or agreeability they show is a representation of how Artificial Intelligence (AI) might continue to sustain and expand gender bias in our society.

The lack of transparency in AI algorithms makes it challenging to understand and challenge decisions, decreasing accountability and trust. Transparent algorithms are essential for guaranteeing fairness and fostering trust in AI systems. Providing human oversight in AI decision-making processes can help mitigate biases and improve accountability (Du, 2024). Periodically scrutinizing AI systems and including feedback can help adapt and improve algorithms to handle emerging ethical issues (S, 2024).

3.3 Trust and Transparency

AI in HR presents issues about security of jobs, fairness, and privacy, and transparency in AI systems is critical for building trust and optimistic employee perspectives (Sadeghi, 2024). Ethical decision-making by artificial intelligence algorithms can improve clarity and responsibility in human resource management decision-making, resulting in diverse strategy selection (Rodgers et al., 2023).

AI systems in HRM oftentimes lack transparency, making it hard for users to understand how decisions are taken. This ambiguity can result in distrust among employees and stakeholders, as they may feel unsure about the fairness and accuracy of AI-based decisions (, Muskan Kumari, 2024b). Confidence in AI systems is impacted by perceived usefulness, ease of use, and fairness. Ethical and legal issues, such as data privacy and lack of understanding, can decrease trust, making it important for organizations to encourage transparency and increase AI literacy among employees (Du, 2024; Wei & Hong, 2024).

Transparency should be a fundamental value for processing data under the Data Protection Regulations. Transparency should be comprehended relationally in artificial intelligence, with information being a requirement in communication between technology providers and users, and reliability assessments based on contextual aspects (Felzmann et al., 2019).

3.4 Concerns of Job Displacement

While artificial intelligence in human resource management can improve efficiency and decision-making, it presents noteworthy ethical concerns such as job displacement, bias and discrimination, privacy concerns, and the necessity for responsible governance to protect employees' rights and guarantee fairness.

AI systems may improve organizational performance but could result in job displacement for human resources, presenting challenges for management to steer the process of AI adoption (Basu et al., 2023). AI has resulted in job displacement spanning different sectors, raising worries regarding unemployment, skill gaps, and income inequality (Karangutkar, 2023).

AI can automate regular HR tasks, such as recruitment and performance management, which may result in job displacement as AI can substitute role of humans in these areas (Badhurunnisa & Dass, 2023; Shouran & Ali, 2024; Saraswathi et al., 2023; Yorks & Jester, 2024). The introduction of AI mandates redefining job roles and may need training employees to work along with AI systems, potentially replacing those incapable of adapting (Badhurunnisa & Dass, 2023; Saraswathi et al., 2023). Digital skills particularly safeguard against job displacement risk resulting from artificial intelligence, decreasing negative consequences on occupational wage and employment (Chen et al., 2022).

The dawn of artificial intelligence (AI) has brought about a significant period of change across several industries, however, it has also resulted in concerns about job displacement. As AI technologies progress, people are increasingly recognizing that some tasks that are routine and repetitive might be automated., potentially resulting in a change in the job market (Jain, 2023).

4. FUTURE OUTCOMES OF AI IN HR

The future outcomes of AI in HR include improved organizational productivity, optimized operations, improved decision-making, personalized employee experiences, and strategic workforce planning, whilst also showcasing difficulties like ethical concerns, data privacy issues, and possibly job displacement.

AI-assisted HRM can enhance organizational productivity and revolutionize work, workers, and workplaces (Malik et al., 2023). AI in HRM has the prospect of transforming the future of human resource management, but there is a necessity for interdisciplinary collaborations and a unified definition to guarantee its full potential (Pan & Froese, 2023). Artificial Intelligence-based applications in Human Resource Management will influence resource utilization, decision-making, and problem-solving, with additional research required to understand their effect on individual and business outcomes (Budhwar et al., 2022).

AI is transforming hiring process by employing algorithms to interpret data and recognize top talent, streamlines recruitment approaches, and predict candidate success. It also helps in talent management by providing personalized feedback and recommending learning paths (Wuisan et al., 2023; Benabou et al., 2024). AI platforms will analyze comprehensive datasets to anticipate hiring trends, workforce turnover, and skill gaps, advising strategic workforce planning (Popo-Olaniyan et al., 2022; Benabou et al., 2024). The HR discipline has a level of autonomy in shaping the future if it decides to use it; HR professionals ought to acquire the skills to guarantee that ethics and fairness are the focal points of AI development for HR and organizational management. In the use of AI in HR and people management, with HR professionals having the potential to shape the future, both good and bad visions of the future are possible to coexist (Charlwood & Guenole, 2022).

4.1 Advanced Predictive Statistics

Advanced predictive statistics in artificial intelligence (AI) significantly improve the accuracy of talent forecasting in human resource management (HRM) by utilizing sophisticated algorithms and data-driven insights. These technologies allow organizations to make educated decisions about recruitment, employee retention, and performance evaluation, eventually leading to improved management of workforce.

Techniques like Random Forest and deep neural networks (DNN) have demonstrated high accuracy rates (up to 95%) in forecasting recruitment success and employee retention (Yashu et al., 2024; Wahyuning & Sudibyo, 2024). AI models study comprehensive datasets, including candidate attributes and past performance, to recognize high-potential candidates, therefore optimizing the hiring process (Wahyuning & Sudibyo, 2024; Uppal & Awasthi, 2024).

AI-based predictive statistics can foretell employee turnover, letting organizations to execute targeted interventions for at-risk employees, and hence, improving retention and decreasing turnover expenses (Basnet, 2024; Yashu et al., 2024). Advanced predictive statistics in AI improve talent forecasting by incorporating neural networks with Stochastic Gradient Descent and effective feature selection methods such as Logistic Regression, improving prediction precision and efficiency, thereby simplifying candidate evaluations and modernizing recruitment workflows in human resource management (Yassine, & Achchab, 2024).

Figure 6. Predictive Model of AI

4.2 Improved Diversity and Inclusion Measures

The significance of diversity and inclusion (D&I) measures in AI-powered talent forecasting is controlled by several key factors, including representation of data, stakeholder engagement, and operational frameworks. These factors are important for guaranteeing that AI systems encourage fairness and inclusivity in recruitment strategies.

AI systems usually depend on datasets that may not sufficiently represent diverse populations, resulting in biased outcomes. For example, face recognition systems have demonstrated substantial inaccuracies with underrepresented groups, such as dark-skinned women (Brien, 2022). Effective D&I measures should account for several overlapping identities to avoid exclusionary practices in hiring (Kelan, 2023). Engaging various stakeholders in the creation process can improve understanding and application of D&I principles. Workshops have been shown to improve understanding but translating this into practice stays challenging (Bano et al., 2024).

AI can help mitigate unintentional biases in recruitment by impartially selecting candidates and making diverse potential candidate shortlists. Machine learning algorithms can study performance statistics objectively, decreasing subjective biases in assessments (Dwi & Hidayatullah, 2024; Kumari et al., 2024). Conventional performance evaluation systems usually suffer from subjectivity and inefficiency, resulting in skewed results and employee discontent. AI-powered systems manage these limitations by ofering objective reviews based on data-driven insights. For instance, an AI-powered performance rating system established accuracy values ranging from 0.78 to 0.85, greatly outperforming conventional methods (Sampath et al., 2024). This objectivity promotes trust and fairness in the evaluation process, contributing to increased employee loyalty.

Figure 7. AI Recommendations for Improving Workplace Diversity

Metric	Current Status	AI Recommendation
Gender Diversity (Leadership)	20% women	Focus on mentorship
Racial Diversity (Team)	15% minorities	Targeted outreach programs

4.3 Real-Time Decision Support

Employee retention is a crucial challenge for organizations, with increased turnover rates resulting in increased expenses and decreased productivity. AI-powered real-time decision support systems provide a favorable solution by improving HR practices via predictive analytics, personalized techniques, and data-driven insights.

AI systems utilize predictive analytics to recognize employees at risk of exiting, allowing proactive retention plans. For example, deep learning models, such as deep neural networks (DNNs), have shown high precision (92%) in forecasting employee turnover (Yashu et al., 2024). These models examine different HR metrics, including demographics, performance, and engagement levels, to forecast potential attrition.

By recognizing at-risk employees prematurely, HR can implement targeted interventions, such as personalized development plans or enhanced work conditions, to retain invaluable talent. AI enables personalized development plans by examining individual employee data, like performance metrics, engagement levels, and career aspirations. For instance, platforms powered by artificial intelligence can recommend customized training programs, mentorship prospects, and career tracks, improving employee satisfaction and decreasing turnover (Tamizhselvan & Pougajendy, 2024; Vaghani, 2024). Personalization makes employees feel appreciated and invested in, which can remarkably enhance retention rates. Real-time feedback is important for employee development and happiness. AI-powered systems offer prompt insights into employee performance, letting for timely adjustments and modifications. For example, AI-driven performance evaluation systems use natural language processing (NLP) and machine learning to provide objective and constructive feedback, improving the overall assessment process (Sampath et al., 2024). This real-time feedback circle allows employees stay involved and inspired, decreasing the chance of attrition.

AI-driven Management Information Systems (MIS) improve decision-making by providing precise, timely, and objective understandings. This results in more suitable recruitment processes, performance management, and employee participation (Vishwanath, 2023; Fomude et al., 2023; Ashrafuzzaman et al., 2024).

4.4 Improved Employee Well-being

The incorporation of AI in HR procedures can result in higher recruitment efficiency and employee productivity, which is associated with increased job satisfaction and decreased turnover rates. Favourable perceptions of AI in HR are linked to high levels of organizational trust and employee participation (Ganatra & Pandya, 2023; H. Zhang, 2024b).

CONCLUSION

The incorporation of Artificial Intelligence into Human Resource decision-making represents a revolutionary shift in organizational administration. It has profound outcomes for efficiency, and accuracy. With the help of the AI, hiring process, planning workforce, and improving performance management has been simplified allowing HR experts to concentrate on other value-based tasks. Through data-driven understanding, AI enables the recognition of suitable candidates, personalization of employee participation programs, and projection of workforce trends, thus contributing to the overall improvement of the performance of the organization.

The impact of AI on HR decision-making is huge, with AI technologies allowing HR professionals to make more educated, data-driven decisions. Nonetheless, the successful application of AI in HR decision-making relies on enhancing AI literacy among HR professionals. Understanding AI equips HR professionals to manage the intricacies of AI implementation, tackle ethical issues, and enhance the advantages of AI technology in HR decision-making.

As artificial intelligence progresses, creating sophisticated AI tools, strategic plans for adopting AI, and programs to enhance AI literacy will be crucial for unlocking the complete capabilities of AI in human resources decision-making. By tackling the obstacles related to AI implementation and promoting a culture of ongoing learning, organizations can leverage the transformative capabilities of AI to improve HR decision-making and propel organizational success. Even though the potential advantages of AI in HR are significant, its implementation has its own limitations. Ethical issues like, algorithmic bias, lack of transparency, data privacy & security, remain important obstacles that should be addressed in earlier stages. These challenges highlight the importance of creating robust frameworks for bias mitigation, promoting transparency in algorithmic processes, and guaranteeing adherence to data protection regulations. Moreover, the displacement of certain HR roles due to automation requires a redefinition of job roles and highlights the pressing need for reskilling workers to work in collaboration with AI systems. Incorporation of AI into HRM should be done with a commitment to ethical responsibilities and design principles that human-centric. This approach will ensure that AI will enhance, rather than replace human judgment and empathy in decision-making. Human oversight is significant in building trust and ensuring regular audits of AI systems, and transparent communication with stakeholders.

In conclusion, integrating AI in HRM is not only for optimizing operations but also a necessity for organizations to aim to remain competitive in an increasingly data-driven world. However, to fulfil this potential a rational approach is required that combines technological innovation with ethical accountability. By practicing inclusivity and transparency, organizations can utilize AI to enhance organizational performance and the well-being of employees.

REFERENCES

Al-Surmi, A., Bashiri, M., & Koliousis, I. (2022). AI based decision making: Combining strategies to improve operational performance. *International Journal of Production Research, 60*(14), 4464–4486. DOI: 10.1080/00207543.2021.1966540

< Ali, A., & Rafi, N. (2024). Enhancing Human Resource Management Through Advanced Decision-Making Strategies: Harnessing The Power Of Artificial Intelligence For Strategic, Data-Driven, And Judicious Choices. Migration Letters : An International Journal of Migration Studies, 21(S8), 881–889. DOI: 10.59670/ml.v21iS8.9488

Alnsour, A. S., Kanaan, O. A., Salah, M., Alfayyad, L., Hijazi, Y., & Alsharif, D. (2024). The impact of implementing AI in recruitment on human resource management efficiency and organizational development effectiveness. Journal of Infrastructure. *Policy and Development*, *8*(8), 6186. DOI: 10.24294/jipd.v8i8.6186

Aluwala, A. (2023). Optimizing IT Operations with AI-Driven Application Performance Management. *Journal of Artificial Intelligence & Cloud Computing*, *2*(2), 1–6. DOI: 10.47363/JAICC/2023(2)355

Arora, S. S., Chaudhary, P., & Singh, R. K. (2024). Adoption of HR analytics for future-proof decision making: Role of attitude toward artificial intelligence as a moderator. *The International Journal of Organizational Analysis*. Advance online publication. DOI: 10.1108/ijoa-03-2024-4392

Ashrafuzzaman, M., Prince, K. B., & Rahman, A. (2024). INTEGRATING ARTIFICIAL INTELLIGENCE IN HRM: THE ROLE OF MANAGEMENT INFORMATION SYSTEMS IN ENHANCING DECISION-MAKING PROCESSES. *GLOBAL MAINSTREAM JOURNAL*, *1*(4), 1–16. DOI: 10.62304/ijmisds.v1i04.177

Baabdullah, A. M. (2024). The precursors of AI adoption in business: Towards an efficient decision-making and functional performance. *International Journal of Information Management*, *75*, 102745. DOI: 10.1016/j.ijinfomgt.2023.102745

Badhurunnisa, M., & Dass, V. S. (2023). Challenges and opportunities involved in implementing AI in Workplace. International Journal For Multidisciplinary Research, 5(6).

Bakar, A., Albadry, S. A., Jessika, S., & Sunaryo, J. (2024). Analysis of the Use of Artificial Intelligence (AI) in Human Resources Management (HR): Study at PT Semen Baturaja Persero (SMBR). *Enigma in Economics*, *2*(1), 59–62.

Bano, M., Zowghi, D., Mourão, F., Kaur, S., & Zhang, T. (2024). *Diversity and Inclusion in AI for Recruitment: Lessons from Industry Workshop*. /arxiv.2411. 06066DOI: 10.48550

Bansal, S., Agarwal, M., Bansal, D., & Narayanan, S. (2022). *Artificial Intelligence Inroads Into HR*., DOI: 10.4018/978-1-7998-8497-2.ch016

Bar-Gil, O., Ron, T., & Czerniak, O. (2024). AI for the people? Embedding AI ethics in HR and people analytics projects. *Technology in Society*, *77*, 102527. DOI: 10.1016/j.techsoc.2024.102527

Baratelli, G., & Colleoni, E. (2022). Does Artificial Intelligence (AI) Enabled Recruitment Improve Employer Branding? *International Journal of Business and Management*, *17*(2), 45. DOI: 10.5539/ijbm.v17n2p45

Basnet, S. (2024). The Impact of AI-Driven Predictive Analytics on Employee Retention Strategies. *International Journal of Research and Review*, *11*(9), 50–65. DOI: 10.52403/ijrr.20240906

Basu, S., Majumdar, B., Mukherjee, K., Munjal, S., & Palaksha, C. (2023). Artificial Intelligence–HRM Interactions and Outcomes: A Systematic Review and Causal Configurational Explanation. *Human Resource Management Review*, *33*(1), 100893. DOI: 10.1016/j.hrmr.2022.100893

Bhalke, V., Satanure, D., Ghabade, P. S., & Vedalankar, A. (2024).. . *AI-Driven Transformation of HR: Enhancing Recruitment, Training, and Employee Retention, 1–5*. Advance online publication. DOI: 10.1109/asiancon62057.2024.10837981

Bharadwaj, V. (2024). Integrating artificial intelligence in human resource management: A comprehensive overview. *Journal of Management*, *11*(3), 71–78. DOI: 10.34218/jom_11_03_006

Bhattacharya, S. (2023b). The Future of HR: Embracing AI for Smarter and More Human Workplaces. [IJSR]. *International Journal of Scientific Research*, *12*(5), 457–459. DOI: 10.21275/SR23423182128

Bouhsaien, L., & Azmani, A. (2024). The potential of artificial intelligence in human resource management. *Applied Computer Science*, *20*(3), 153–170. DOI: 10.35784/acs-2024-34

Brien, P. (2022). *Diversity and Inclusion in Artificial Intelligence* (pp. 109–134). T.M.C. Asser Press eBooks. DOI: 10.1007/978-94-6265-523-2_6

Brynjolfsson, E., Li, D., & Raymond, L. (2023). Generative AI at Work. DOI: 10.3386/w31161

Cai, F., Zhang, J., & Zhang, L. (2024). The Impact of Artificial Intelligence Replacing Humans in Making Human Resource Management Decisions on Fairness: A Case of Resume Screening. *Sustainability*, *16*(9), 3840. DOI: 10.3390/su16093840

Capasso, M., Arora, P., Sharma, D., & Tacconi, C. (2024). On the Right to Work in the Age of Artificial Intelligence: Ethical Safeguards in Algorithmic Human Resource Management. *Business and Human Rights Journal*, *9*(3), 346–360. DOI: 10.1017/bhj.2024.26

Chandratreya, A. (2024). AI in HR: A Comprehensive Analysis and Framework for Success. INTERANTIONAL JOURNAL OF SCIENTIFIC RESEARCH IN ENGINEERING AND MANAGEMENT, 08(008), 1–11. DOI: 10.55041/IJSREM37020

Charlwood, A., & Guenole, N. (2022). Can HR adapt to the paradoxes of artificial intelligence? *Human Resource Management Journal*, *32*(4), 729–742. DOI: 10.1111/1748-8583.12433

Chen, N., Li, Z., & Tang, B. (2022). Can digital skill protect against job displacement risk caused by artificial intelligence? Empirical evidence from 701 detailed occupations. *PLoS One*, *17*(11), e0277280. DOI: 10.1371/journal.pone.0277280 PMID: 36346798

DĂNILOAIA, D.-F. (2024). EXPLORING THE LANDSCAPE: A LITERATURE REVIEW OF AI'S IMPACT ON HUMAN RESOURCE MANAGEMENT. *European Journal of Public Administration Research*, *3*, 15–22. DOI: 10.47743/ejpar.2024-3-6

Subbaiah, D. S. N., & Rajalakshmi, M. (2024). AI-Powered Strategies for Talent Management Optimization. *Journal of Informatics Education and Research*, *4*(2). Advance online publication. DOI: 10.52783/jier.v4i2.848

Du, J. (2024a). Do Humans Trust AI in HRM? Why Do? Why Not? — Insights from a Decade of Research. *Journal of Research in Social Science and Humanities*, *3*(7), 20–48. DOI: 10.56397/JRSSH.2024.07.04

Du, J. (2024b). Ethical and Legal Challenges of AI in Human Resource Management. *Journal of Computing and Electronic Information Management*, *13*(2), 71–77. DOI: 10.54097/83j64ub9

Du, J. (2024c). Exploring Gender Bias and Algorithm Transparency: Ethical Considerations of AI in HRM. *Journal of Theory and Practice of Management Science*, *4*(03), 36–43. DOI: 10.53469/jtpms.2024.04(03).06

Dwi, M., & Hidayatullah, A. N. A. (2024). Exploring AI's Role in Supporting Diversity and Inclusion Initiatives in Multicultural Marketplaces. *International Journal of Religion*, *5*(10), 5549–5582. DOI: 10.61707/apmwg008

Faqih, M., Sukistini, A. S., Asrianto, A., Siri, A., & Nggandung, Y. (2024). The Impact of AI on Talent Acquisition: Opportunities and Challenges in Modern HR Practices. *Global International Journal of Innovative Research, 2*(11), 2626–2638. DOI: 10.59613/global.v2i11.365

Faqihi, A., & Miah, S. J. (2023). Artificial Intelligence-Driven Talent Management System: Exploring the Risks and Options for Constructing a Theoretical Foundation. *Journal of Risk and Financial Management, 16*(1), 31. DOI: 10.3390/jrfm16010031

Felzmann, H., Villaronga, E. F., Lutz, C., & Tamò-Larrieux, A. (2019). Transparency you can trust: Transparency requirements for artificial intelligence between legal norms and contextual concerns. *Big Data & Society, 6*(1). Advance online publication. DOI: 10.1177/2053951719860542

Samuel Olaoluwa Folorunsho, Olubunmi Adeolu Adenekan, Chinedu Ezeigweneme, Ike Chidiebere Somadina, & Patrick Azuka Okeleke. (2024). Optimizing network performance and quality of service with AI-driven solutions for future telecommunications. International Journal of Frontiers in Engineering and Technology Research, 7(1), 073–092. DOI: 10.53294/ijfetr.2024.7.1.0041

Fomude, A. H., Yang, C., Agordzo, G. K., Serwah, A. V., & Abangbila, L. (2023a). AI Model to Improve HR Decision-Making with Machine Learning Predictions Algorithm. 2023 25th International Conference on Advanced Communication Technology (ICACT), 206–212. DOI: 10.23919/ICACT56868.2023.10079282

Ganagi, M. C., & Rotti, A. A. (2024). A study on Pursuit of Artificial Intelligence in Human Resource Management: A Narrative view. *ITM Web of Conferences, 68*, 01005. DOI: 10.1051/itmconf/20246801005

Ganatra, N. J. (2024). A research paper on how Artificial Intelligence changes the Human Resource Activities inside the organization and provides the significant improvement in workforce working environment for various day to day decisions making along with their efficiency and their productivity. *Journal of Management Research and Analysis, 11*(3), 182–184. DOI: 10.18231/j.jmra.2024.030

Ganatra, N. J. (2024). A research paper on how Artificial Intelligence changes the Human Resource Activities inside the organization and provides the significant improvement in workforce working environment for various day to day decisions making along with their efficiency and their productivity. *Journal of Management Research and Analysis, 11*(3), 182–184. DOI: 10.18231/j.jmra.2024.030

Ganatra, N. J., & Pandya, J. D. (2023). The transformative impact of artificial intelligence on hr practices and employee experience: A review. *Journal of Management Research and Analysis, 10*(2), 106–111. DOI: 10.18231/j.jmra.2023.018

Ghezelseflou, H. (2023). Investigating the Challenges and Opportunities of Using Artificial Intelligence in Human Resource Management. *Journal of Technology in Entrepreneurship and Strategic Management*, *2*(2), 28–36. DOI: 10.61838/kman.jtesm.2.2.4

Gupta, A., & Mishra, M. (2022). Ethical Concerns While Using Artificial Intelligence in Recruitment of Employees. *Business Ethics and Leadership*, *6*(2), 6–11. DOI: 10.21272/bel.6(2).6-11.2022

Gupta, R. (2024). Impact of Artificial Intelligence (AI) on Human Resource Management (HRM). *International Journal For Multidisciplinary Research*, *6*(3). Advance online publication. DOI: 10.36948/ijfmr.2024.v06i03.21444

Hu, Q. (2023). Unilever's Practice on AI-based Recruitment. Highlights in Business. *Economics and Management*, *16*, 256–263. DOI: 10.54097/hbem.v16i.10565

Huang, C., Zhang, Z., Mao, B., & Yao, X. (2023). An Overview of Artificial Intelligence Ethics. *IEEE Transactions on Artificial Intelligence*, *4*(4), 799–819. DOI: 10.1109/TAI.2022.3194503

Jafri, S., Upreti, S., Saiyad, F. B. J., Madhukar, K. S., Chaturvedi, V. M., & Divakaran, P. (2024a). Effectiveness of Artificial Intelligence for Enhancing Decision-Making Process of Recruitment in HRM Process. 2024 IEEE International Conference on Contemporary Computing and Communications (InC4), 1–6. DOI: 10.1109/InC460750.2024.10649327

Jafri, S., Upreti, S., Saiyad, F. B. J., Madhukar, K. S., Chaturvedi, V. M., & Divakaran, P. (2024b). Effectiveness of Artificial Intelligence for Enhancing Decision-Making Process of Recruitment in HRM Process. 2024 IEEE International Conference on Contemporary Computing and Communications (InC4), 1–6. DOI: 10.1109/InC460750.2024.10649327

Jain, A. (2023). Job Displacement Due to Artificial Intelligence and Machine Learning – A Review. *International Journal For Multidisciplinary Research*, *5*(6). Advance online publication. DOI: 10.36948/ijfmr.2023.v05i06.10958

Jiaping, Y. (2022). Enterprise Human Resource Management Model by Artificial Intelligence Digital Technology. *Computational Intelligence and Neuroscience*, *2022*, 1–9. DOI: 10.1155/2022/6186811 PMID: 36479021

Kadirov, A., Shakirova, Y., Ismoilova, G., & Makhmudova, N. (2024a). AI in Human Resource Management: Reimagining Talent Acquisition, Development, and Retention. *2024 International Conference on Knowledge Engineering and Communication Systems (ICKECS)*, 1–8. DOI: 10.1109/ICKECS61492.2024.10617231

Kaggwa, S., Eleogu, T. F., Okonkwo, F., Farayola, O. A., Uwaoma, P. U., & Akinoso, A. (2024). AI in Decision Making: Transforming Business Strategies. *International Journal of Research and Scientific Innovation*, *X*(XII), 423–444. DOI: 10.51244/IJRSI.2023.1012032

Karangutkar, A. A. (2023). The Impact of Artificial Intelligence on Job Displacement and the Future of Work. *International Journal of Advanced Research in Science. Tongxin Jishu, 635–638*. Advance online publication. DOI: 10.48175/IJARSCT-12096

Kelan, E. K. (2023). Algorithmic inclusion: Shaping the predictive algorithms of artificial intelligence in hiring. *Human Resource Management Journal*. Advance online publication. DOI: 10.1111/1748-8583.12511

Khair, M. A., Mahadasa, R., Tuli, F. A., & Ande, J. R. P. K. (2020). Beyond Human Judgment: Exploring the Impact of Artificial Intelligence on HR Decision-Making Efficiency and Fairness. *Global Disclosure of Economics and Business*, *9*(2), 163–176. DOI: 10.18034/gdeb.v9i2.730

Khan, M., Parahyanti, E., & Hussain, S. M. A. M. (2024). The Role Generative AI in Human Resource Management: Enhancing Operational Efficiency, Decision-Making, and Addressing Ethical Challenges. *Asian Journal of Logistics Management*, *3*(2), 104–125. DOI: 10.14710/ajlm.2024.24671

Khan, S., Faisal, S., & Thomas, G. (2024). Exploring the nexus of artificial intelligence in talent acquisition: Unravelling cost-benefit dynamics, seizing opportunities, and mitigating risks. *Problems and Perspectives in Management*, *22*(1), 462–476. DOI: 10.21511/ppm.22(1).2024.37

Kim, S. (2024). Developing AI literacy in HRD: Competencies, approaches, and implications. *Human Resource Development International*. Advance online publication. DOI: 10.1080/13678868.2024.2337962

Kiritsi, A., & Adamantidis, V. (2024). Recruitment and Talent Management in the Modern World Using AI. International Journal of Management. *Knowledge and Learning*, *13*. Advance online publication. DOI: 10.53615/2232-5697.13.151-157

KUMAR, A. (2024). An Analysis of Artificial Intelligence Adoption in the Human Resource Management. INTERANTIONAL JOURNAL OF SCIENTIFIC RESEARCH IN ENGINEERING AND MANAGEMENT, 08(04), 1–5. DOI: 10.55041/IJSREM32681

Kumar, M. R., Sharma, A., Bhargavi, Y. K., & Ramesh, G. (2022). Human Resource Management Using Machine Learning-Based Solutions. 2022 3rd International Conference on Electronics and Sustainable Communication Systems (ICESC), 801–806. DOI: 10.1109/ICESC54411.2022.9885526

Kumar Tyagi, P., Jit Singh, V., Kumar Singh, A., Saxena, A., Tyagi, P., & Mehta, P. (2023). The Impact of Artificial Intelligence-Based Human Resource Management Systems on Organizational Efficiency. 2023 10th IEEE Uttar Pradesh Section International Conference on Electrical, Electronics and Computer Engineering (UPCON), 1727–1731. DOI: 10.1109/UPCON59197.2023.10434792

Kumari, D. A., Karim Shaikh, I. A., Gangadharan, S., Narendra Kiran, P. B., Ramya, S. R., & Nargunde, A. S. (2024). Machine Learning for Diversity and Inclusion: Addressing Biases in HR Practices. 2024 5th International Conference on Recent Trends in Computer Science and Technology (ICRTCST), 182–187. DOI: 10.1109/ICRTCST61793.2024.10578442

Kumari, D. A., Karim Shaikh, I. A., Gangadharan, S., Narendra Kiran, P. B., Ramya, S. R., & Nargunde, A. S. (2024). Machine Learning for Diversity and Inclusion: Addressing Biases in HR Practices. 2024 5th International Conference on Recent Trends in Computer Science and Technology (ICRTCST), 182–187. DOI: 10.1109/ICRTCST61793.2024.10578442

Kumari, M. (2024a). The Effects and Functionality of Artificial Intelligence in Human Resource Management. *INTERANTIONAL JOURNAL OF SCIENTIFIC RESEARCH IN ENGINEERING AND MANAGEMENT*, *08*(04), 1–5. DOI: 10.55041/IJSREM31091

Kuźniarska, A., & Stańczyk, I. (2024). *Artificial Intelligence in HR*. Informa., DOI: 10.4324/9781032678719-6

Li, X. (2018). New thinking of human resource management in the age of artificial intelligence. In 2nd International Proceedings on International Conference on Systems, Computing, and Applications, Francis Academic Press, UK (pp. 133-136).

Li, Y. (2024). Security and Privacy of Artificial Intelligence with Ethical Concerns. *2024 IEEE 9th International Conference on Data Science in Cyberspace (DSC)*, 660–667. DOI: 10.1109/DSC63484.2024.00098

Lukaszewski, K. M., & Stone, D. L. (2024). Will the use of AI in human resources create a digital Frankenstein? *Organizational Dynamics*, *53*(1), 101033. DOI: 10.1016/j.orgdyn.2024.101033

Madanchian, M. (2024). From Recruitment to Retention: AI Tools for Human Resource Decision-Making. *Applied Sciences (Basel, Switzerland), 14*(24), 11750. DOI: 10.3390/app142411750

Madhumita, G., & Dolly Diana, P. PC, N., Narendra Kiran, P. B., Aggarwal, S., & Satish Nargunde, A. (2024). AI-powered Performance Management: Driving Employee Success and Organizational Growth. 2024 5th International Conference on Recent Trends in Computer Science and Technology (ICRTCST), 204–209. DOI: 10.1109/ICRTCST61793.2024.10578371

Malik, A., Budhwar, P., & Kazmi, B. A. (2023). Artificial intelligence (AI)-assisted HRM: Towards an extended strategic framework. *Human Resource Management Review, 33*(1), 100940. DOI: 10.1016/j.hrmr.2022.100940

Malik, A., Budhwar, P., Patel, C., & Srikanth, N. R. (2022). May the bots be with you! Delivering HR cost-effectiveness and individualised employee experiences in an MNE. *International Journal of Human Resource Management, 33*(6), 1148–1178. DOI: 10.1080/09585192.2020.1859582

Manoharan, P. (2024). A Review on AI Driven HR Systems: Revolutionizing HR Systems and Talent Management. *Scholars Journal of Engineering and Technology, 12*(06), 179–184. DOI: 10.36347/sjet.2024.v12i06.001

Marín Díaz, G., Galán Hernández, J. J., & Galdón Salvador, J. L. (2023). Analyzing Employee Attrition Using Explainable AI for Strategic HR Decision-Making. *Mathematics, 11*(22), 4677. DOI: 10.3390/math11224677

Mollay, M. H., Sharma, D. S., Kale, A. P., Anawade, P., & Gahane, S. (2024). *Smart Hiring: Leveraging AI for Effective Employee Selection*. 1–6. DOI: 10.1109/idicaiei61867.2024.10842754

Nawaz, N., Arunachalam, H., Pathi, B. K., & Gajenderan, V. (2024). The adoption of artificial intelligence in human resources management practices. *International Journal of Information Management Data Insights, 4*(1), 100208. DOI: 10.1016/j.jjimei.2023.100208

Nayak, A., Dr, S. S., & Choudhury, S. N. B. (2024). The Future of Performance Management: Leveraging Ai for Better Feedback and Coaching. *Journal of Informatics Education and Research, 4*(2). Advance online publication. DOI: 10.52783/jier.v4i2.649

Norman, E., & Pahlawati, E. (2024). Peran Artificial Intelligence dalam Rekrutmen dan Seleksi: Meningkatkan Efisiensi dan Akurasi dalam MSDM. *Sci-Tech Journal, 3*(1), 45–59. DOI: 10.56709/stj.v3i1.320

Nyathani, R. (2023). AI in Performance Management: Redefining Performance Appraisals in the Digital Age. *Journal of Artificial Intelligence & Cloud Computing, 1–5*. Advance online publication. DOI: 10.47363/JAICC/2023(2)134

Okatta, C. G., Ajayi, F. A., & Olawale, O. (2024). NAVIGATING THE FUTURE: INTEGRATING AI AND MACHINE LEARNING IN HR PRACTICES FOR A DIGITAL WORKFORCE. *Computer Science & IT Research Journal*, *5*(4), 1008–1030. DOI: 10.51594/csitrj.v5i4.1085

Paigude, S., Pangarkar, S. C., Hundekari, S., Mali, M., Wanjale, K., & Dongre, Y. (2023). Potential of Artificial Intelligence in Boosting Employee Retention in the Human Resource Industry. International Journal on Recent and Innovation Trends in Computing and Communication, 11(3s), 01–10. DOI: 10.17762/ijritcc.v11i3s.6149

Pan, Y., & Froese, F. J. (2023). An interdisciplinary review of AI and HRM: Challenges and future directions. *Human Resource Management Review*, *33*(1), 100924. DOI: 10.1016/j.hrmr.2022.100924

Paramita, D., Okwir, S., & Nuur, C. (2024). Artificial intelligence in talent acquisition: Exploring organisational and operational dimensions. *The International Journal of Organizational Analysis*, *32*(11), 108–131. DOI: 10.1108/IJOA-09-2023-3992

Popo-Olaniyan, O., James, O. O., Udeh, C. A., Daraojimba, R. E., & Ogedengbe, D. E. (2022). FUTURE-PROOFING HUMAN RESOURCES IN THE U.S. WITH AI: A REVIEW OF TRENDS AND IMPLICATIONS. *International Journal of Management & Entrepreneurship Research*, *4*(12), 641–658. DOI: 10.51594/ijmer.v4i12.676

Porkodi, S., & Cedro, T. L. (2025). The Ethical Role of Generative Artificial Intelligence in Modern HR Decision-Making: A Systematic Literature Review. *European Journal of Business and Management Research*, *10*(1), 44–55. DOI: 10.24018/ejbmr.2025.10.1.2535

Prasad, Prof. Dr. S. (2024). AI-Powered Talent Acquisition: Enhancing Recruitment Processes in the Digital Age. INTERANTIONAL JOURNAL OF SCIENTIFIC RESEARCH IN ENGINEERING AND MANAGEMENT, 08(06), 1–5. DOI: 10.55041/IJSREM35619

Prithu Sarkar, R. B. N. K., & Sreenivasulu Arigela, P. S. A. K. G. (2024). Ethical Implications of AI Adoption in HRM: Balancing Automation with Human Values. *Journal of Informatics Education and Research*, *4*(3). Advance online publication. DOI: 10.52783/jier.v4i3.1337

Rami, K. (2024). AI in Human Resource Marketing and Its Influence on Recruitment Efficiency. *Journal of Global Economy. Business and Finance*, *6*(12), 7–10. DOI: 10.53469/jgebf.2024.06(12).02

Ramli, R., Wida'atullah, M. R., & Rahayu, Y. S., Rahmat, & Ramly, A. T. (2024). Leadership and Decision-Making to Strengthen HR Competency in AI Emergence. Diversity. *Jurnal Ilmiah Pascasarjana*, *4*(2), 88–103. DOI: 10.32832/djip-uika.v14i2.17024

Reddy, K. S., Kethan, M., Mahabub Basha, S., Singh, A., Kumar, P., & Ashalatha, D. (2024). Ethical and Legal Implications of AI on Business and Employment: Privacy, Bias, and Accountability. *2024 International Conference on Knowledge Engineering and Communication Systems (ICKECS)*, 1–6. DOI: 10.1109/ICKECS61492.2024.10616875

Rodgers, W., Murray, J. M., Stefanidis, A., Degbey, W. Y., & Tarba, S. Y. (2023). An artificial intelligence algorithmic approach to ethical decision-making in human resource management processes. *Human Resource Management Review*, *33*(1), 100925. DOI: 10.1016/j.hrmr.2022.100925

Roy, M. (2021). AI-Powered Workforce Management and Its Future in India. DOI: 10.5772/intechopen.97817

S, S. (2024). Exploring an AI-Based Algorithmic Framework for Ethical Decision-Making in Human Resource Management Procedures. Shanlax International Journal of Management, 11(S1-Mar), 228–234. DOI: 10.34293/management.v11iS1-Mar.8110

Sadeghi, S. (2024). Employee Well-being in the Age of AI: Perceptions, Concerns, Behaviors, and Outcomes. ArXiv, abs/2412.04796. /arXiv.2412.04796.DOI: 10.48550

Sahay, U., & Kaur, G. (2021). Leveraging AI to Drive Organizational Performance through Effective Performance. 2021 Fifth International Conference on I-SMAC (IoT in Social, Mobile, Analytics and Cloud) (I-SMAC), 584–588. DOI: 10.1109/I-SMAC52330.2021.9640761

Saini, A. (2023). AI-Intelligent Automation in Workforce Management: Enhancing the Hourly Work Experience. Journal of Artificial Intelligence & Cloud Computing, 1–13. DOI: 10.47363/JAICC/2023(2)E127

Sampath, K., Devi, K., Ambuli, T. V., & Venkatesan, S. (2024). AI-Powered Employee Performance Evaluation Systems in HR Management. 2024 7th International Conference on Circuit Power and Computing Technologies (ICCPCT), 703–708. DOI: 10.1109/ICCPCT61902.2024.10673159

Sampath, K., Devi, K., Ambuli, T. V., & Venkatesan, S. (2024). *AI-Powered Employee Performance Evaluation Systems in HR Management*. 703–708. DOI: 10.1109/iccpct61902.2024.10673159

Saraswathi, T., Karthikeyan, M., Balakrishnan, C., Nithya, T., Maheswari, B., & Subramanian, R. S. (2023). Artificial intelligence in human resource management: Advancements, implications and future prospects. *International Journal on Recent and Innovation Trends in Computing and Communication*, *11*(11), 266–281.

Sasi, K. P. (2024). Impact of AI in Recruitment and Talent Acquisition. *Human Resource and Leadership Journal*, *9*(3), 78–83. DOI: 10.47941/hrlj.2117

Shouran, Z., & Ali, D. A. (2024). The Implementation of Artificial Intelligence in Human Resources Management. *Journal of International Conference Proceedings*, *7*(1), 244–258. DOI: 10.32535/jicp.v7i1.2993

Srivastava, S. R. (2024). Transforming Talent Acquisition: How AI is shaping modern HRM. *International Journal of Science and Research Archive*, *13*(2), 1236–1244. DOI: 10.30574/ijsra.2024.13.2.2252

Stone, D. L., Lukaszewski, K. M., & Johnson, R. D. (2024). Will artificial intelligence radically change human resource management processes? *Organizational Dynamics*, *53*(1), 101034. DOI: 10.1016/j.orgdyn.2024.101034

Sundari, S., Silalahi, V. A. J. M., Wardani, F. P., Siahaan, R. S., Sacha, S., Krismayanti, Y., & Anjarsari, N. (2024). Artificial Intelligence (AI) and Automation in Human Resources : Shifting the Focus from Routine Tasks to Strategic Initiatives for Improved Employee Engagement. *East Asian Journal of Multidisciplinary Research*, *3*(10), 4983–4996. DOI: 10.55927/eajmr.v3i10.11758

Tambe, P., Cappelli, P., & Yakubovich, V. (2019). Artificial Intelligence in Human Resources Management: Challenges and a Path Forward. *California Management Review*, *61*(4), 15–42. DOI: 10.1177/0008125619867910

Tamizhselvan, V., & Pougajendy, S. (2024). From Data to Insights: Using AI Tool to Improve Employee Involvement and Employee Tenure-Rane Madras. *International Journal For Multidisciplinary Research*, *6*(6). Advance online publication. DOI: 10.36948/ijfmr.2024.v06i06.33512

Tong, S., Jia, N., Luo, X., & Fang, Z. (2021a). The Janus face of artificial intelligence feedback: Deployment versus disclosure effects on employee performance. *Strategic Management Journal*, *42*(9), 1600–1631. DOI: 10.1002/smj.3322

Uppal, A., & Awasthi, Y. (2024). Machine learningbased approaches for enhancing human resource management using automated employee performance prediction systems. *The International Journal of Organizational Analysis*. Advance online publication. DOI: 10.1108/ijoa-07-2024-4643

Vaghani, D. (2024). *Enhancing Employee Engagement and Retention through AI-Powered Human Resource Software Solutions*. The International Journal of Science & Technoledge., DOI: 10.24940/theijst/2024/v12/i5/ST2405-003

Vaghani, D. (2024). *Enhancing Employee Engagement and Retention through AI-Powered Human Resource Software Solutions*. DOI: 10.24940/theijst/2024/v12/i5/st2405-003

Valčo, M. (2023). ETHICAL IMPLICATIONS OF ARTIFICIAL INTELLIGENCE IN HUMAN RESOURCE MANAGEMENT FOR SUSTAINABLE DEVELOPMENT. *The International Conference on Human Resources for Sustainable Development*, 147–160. DOI: 10.51316/icpt.hust.2023.34

VC, K. (2024a). The Role of Artificial Intelligence (AI) and Machine Learning (ML) in HR Decision Making Processes. Shanlax International Journal of Management, 11(S1-Mar), 98–107. DOI: 10.34293/management.v11iS1-Mar.8064

Vishwanath, S. V. (2023). The Future of Work: Implications of Artificial Intelligence on Hr Practices. Tuijin Jishu/Journal of Propulsion Technology, 44(3), 1711–1724. DOI: 10.52783/tjjpt.v44.i3.562

Vhora, M. A., Bhandwalkar, V., & Rege, P. M. (2024). AI-driven HR analytics: Enhancing decision-making in workforce planning. *The Scientific Temper*, *15*(04), 3299–3308. DOI: 10.58414/SCIENTIFICTEMPER.2024.15.4.39

Wahyuning, S., & Sudibyo, S. K. (2024). Leveraging Machine Learning for Talent Acquisition: Predicting High-Performance Candidates in Human Resource Management. *Journal of Management and Informatics*, *3*(1), 87–104. DOI: 10.51903/jmi.v3i1.44

Wahyuning, S., & Sudibyo, S. K. (2024). Leveraging Machine Learning for Talent Acquisition: Predicting High-Performance Candidates in Human Resource Management. *Journal of Management and Informatics*, *3*(1), 87–104. DOI: 10.51903/jmi.v3i1.44

Wamba-Taguimdje, S.-L., Fosso Wamba, S., Kala Kamdjoug, J. R., & Tchatchouang Wanko, C. E. (2020). Influence of artificial intelligence (AI) on firm performance: The business value of AI-based transformation projects. *Business Process Management Journal*, *26*(7), 1893–1924. DOI: 10.1108/BPMJ-10-2019-0411

Wang, A. (2024). Advancing Organizational Effectiveness Through Strategic Workforce Planning and Technology Integration. Advances in Economics. *Management and Political Sciences*, *121*(1), 107–112. DOI: 10.54254/2754-1169/121/20242362

Wuisan, D. S. S., Sunardjo, R. A., Aini, Q., Yusuf, N. A., & Rahardja, U. (2023). Integrating Artificial Intelligence in Human Resource Management: A SmartPLS Approach for Entrepreneurial Success. [ATT]. *Aptisi Transactions on Technopreneurship*, *5*(3), 334–345. DOI: 10.34306/att.v5i3.355

Yadav, M., Kakkar, M., & Kaushik, P. (2023). Harnessing Artificial Intelligence to Empower HR Processes and Drive Enhanced Efficiency in the Workplace to Boost Productivity. *International Journal on Recent and Innovation Trends in Computing and Communication*, *11*(8s), 381–390. DOI: 10.17762/ijritcc.v11i8s.7218

Yashu, Y., Sharma, R., Jain, A., & Manwal, M. (2024). *Enhancing Human Resource Management through Deep Learning: A Predictive Analytics Approach to Employee Retention Success*. 1–4. DOI: 10.1109/iciteics61368.2024.10625175

Yassine, T. K., & Achchab, S. (2024). Predictive Hiring and AI: Elevating Recruitment with Optimized Neural Networks and Gradient Descent. *International Journal of Intelligent Information Systems*, *13*(6), 117–127. DOI: 10.11648/j.ijiis.20241306.11

Yorks, L., & Jester, M. Y. (2024). Applying generative AI ethically in HRD practice. *Human Resource Development International*, *27*(3), 410–427. DOI: 10.1080/13678868.2024.2337963

Zhang, E. Y. A. (2024). *Digitalizations Enhancement in HR Practices: The Impact of Incorporating AI in the Process of Recruitment and Selection. Advances in Economics, Management and Political Sciences, 120(1).* None-None., DOI: 10.54254/2754-1169/120/20242377

Zhang, H. (2024). Exploring the Impact of AI on Human Resource Management: A Case Study of Organizational Adaptation and Employee Dynamics. *IEEE Transactions on Engineering Management*, *71*, 14991–15004. DOI: 10.1109/TEM.2024.3457520

Chapter 3
Artificial Intelligence in the Professional Activity and Education of Marketing Specialists: A Survey of Students' Opinions

Nikolai Pavlov
https://orcid.org/0000-0002-7068-1695
Peter the Great St. Petersburg Polytechnic University, Russia

Luis Cesar Molina Almanza
https://orcid.org/0000-0003-1327-4468
Simon Bolivar Public Institute of Higher Education, Peru

ABSTRACT

The role of generative artificial intelligence in the process of training and work of marketers is shown.The purpose of the presented survey was to determine ways to improve the educational process that includes generative artificial intelligence, as well as to form a realistic attitude among students towards tools of this type. The study showed that students are well acquainted with AI and use it extensively. The attitude towards AI is quite realistic: there are no expectations that it will do the work for students. But the aid of AI in learning is highly appreciated. The demand of acquiring knowledge in this area is urgent, mainly through new teaching methods. There are also high expectations regarding personalized learning. The obtained results will help to improve the preparation of students for their future professional activities. The proposed survey methodology can be used for annual monitoring of the situation.

DOI: 10.4018/979-8-3373-8612-6.ch003

INTRODUCTION

Ideas for using artificial intelligence have been around in science fiction for a long time. But now it is becoming reality.

The set and names of branches of artificial intelligence models vary. Below is a typical list from (White, 2024). Each of these models has made a significant contribution to the development of information technology, each has its own area of application where it is effective.

- Expert systems, which fixed the knowledge of human experts in the form of a set of rules.
- Fuzzy logic, allowing more flexible logical reasoning.
- Machine learning, which made a computer able to improve its functioning.
- Deep learning, in which computers self-learn.
- Natural language processing.
- Computer vision, which allows a computer to recognize objects in the real world.
- Robotics is a complex field that studies the development and design of automated technical systems.

Also, it is necessary to mention other sections.

- Genetic algorithms and Evolutionary computation (Rhinehart, 2018),
- Swarm intelligence (Xue & Shen, 2020).

However, none of these lists is a strict classification. For example, modern generative models are a mixture of Natural language processing and machine or deep learning.

This indicates a high complexity of this field. In view of the noted very wide variety of AI technologies, as well as the breakthrough in the field of generative AI that has occurred in recent years, it seems relevant to concentrate on generative models.

The applications of generative AI in various fields are also very different. Both its applications and teaching methods based on generative AI vary depending on the disciplines (Lahby, 2024a), so in this chapter the emphasis will be on marketing applications and teaching the students of the marketing orientation.

Chapter Focus

The main purpose of this chapter is to figure out the dynamic range of problems related with generative AI that future marketing specialists will face. As the problem is wide and many authors already studied it, the structure of this chapter is as follows.

Part 1 briefly reveals the present rapidly changing situation of generative AI in one of its most important spheres – marketing, and the importance of the ability to deal with it. For this, future marketing specialists should be properly educated.

Part 2 is devoted to the generative AI applications in education both from the point of view of students and teachers. These points of view are interrelated: monitoring students' attitude and usage of generative AI helps to organize curriculum properly, also with the help of Generative AI instrumentation.

Part 3 contains a research of marketing students' opinions about AI in Peter the First St. Petersburg Polytechnic University. The obtained results reveals the present situation and can serve as the useful instrument for improving university education via monitoring the situation.

1. GENERATIVE AI IN MARKETING

1.1. Generative AI in brief

Traditional AI systems are used to make forecasts based on existing data. Recommendations may concern purchases on the marketplace as well as determining which of the company's customers are most likely to buy this or that product.

Generative AI models, according to (Feuerriegel et al., 2023), are capable of creating new content based on templates and structures that they extract from existing data.

Thus, here we see modeling of human creativity.

Generative AI is built on neural networks. Systems based on elements similar to human brain neurons were described long time ago (McCulloch & Pitts, 1943). The main property of such models was their learning ability. For a long time, such systems were quite simple, they could be implemented even with the help of improvised means (Borzykh, 2001).

Neural network models have been included in the arsenal of researchers for a number of years, for example, in the SPSS and Statistica packages (Ashabokov et al, 2025). Actually, neural networks were just another, not the simplest and not the most accurate, tool for data analysis.

There were also attempts to use such models for image recognition and natural language. For this, some algorithms were introduced, for example, image convolution.

Generative AI tools have been constantly evolving since their launch in 2018 (Ali, 2023). These models use both new algorithms and a huge network size, and have proven to be capable of making a breakthrough in the field of AI.

The author of (Malyshev, 2024), as many other authors, distinguishes the following types of generative AI:

- general, capable of performing many different tasks;
- limited, specializing in a specific task;
- superintelligence, which is a project of the future, capable of surpassing humans or even all humanity.

Stanislaw Lem in his book "Summa Technologiae" (Lem, 1978) pointed out the emergence of this type of intelligence in the future. He drew an analogy between an intelligence amplifier and a physical strength amplifier. Both, he believed, are necessary for the progress of humanity.

Generative neural networks are classified by their functionality (Malyshev, 2024). Here are some examples.

- Text generation – CharacterAI, BingAI.
- Image creation – Dall-E, Kandinsky, Shedevroom.
- Video editing – Runway - Gen-2, Nvidia Eye Contact.
- Sound processing – Adobe Enhance, Voice.AI.
- Productivity enhancement – DeepL, Any Summary, Grammarly.
- Entertainment – RoomGPT, Outfits AI.
- Universal use – ChatGPT, YandexGPT, GigaChat.

Not only their potential is now obvious, but also their impact on the labor market (Eloundou et al., 2023). But the limitations and dangers of these instruments are still far from being revealed.

There is also intense competitive struggle between developers. In early 2025, a publicly available Chinese chatbot with AI, DeepSeek, appeared, with functions similar to ChatGPT and YandexGPT. Although its work is still somewhat unstable (Vologzshanin, 2025; Rechetnikova, 2025), and some topics are subject to censorship (Lu, 2025), it can be assumed that it will create serious competition for leading artificial intelligence manufacturers. Another breakthrough could be the use of ChatGPT 5 (D'Cruze, 2025).

The functionality of existing generative artificial intelligence is improving almost every day. The quality of generated images is improving, the context of previous requests is remembered, and work with large texts is allowed.

All this suggests that the situation with artificial intelligence is extremely dynamic:

- the set of tools is expanding;
- their functionality is improving;
- the results are becoming more useful for practical work.

Therefore, future specialists should be prepared for the challenges of the coming years while still at university. They must be able to assess the capabilities of the latest generative artificial intelligence systems and use them effectively both in their learning and in their professional activities. To achieve this, it is necessary to improve the training of students in the field of generative artificial intelligence.

1.2. The Present State of Generative AI Development

According to Gartner Hype Cycle Research Methodology (Chandrasekaran, 2024), emerging technologies related to generative artificial intelligence can reach the Plateau of Productivity in 2...5 years, that is, just when today's students will start working.

- The hype regarding Generative AI itself has already begun to subside.
- AI-augmented Software Engineering is at the peak of the hype wave.
- Prompt Engineering is approaching the peak of hype, which has become, to some extent, a way of adapting to the specifics of modern generative AI.
- AI Trust, Risk and Security Management is on its way to the peak of hype. This is a framework ensuring the responsible and secure usage of AI. It is aimed to manage risks, support compliance and increase trust in AI systems.
- A little further from the peak of hype is AI Supercomputing. It deals with the large computational resources for training advanced AI models, which are critical for achieving breakthroughs in increasing the capabilities of AI.
- Finally, at the initial stage of the path to hype is Disinformation Security. It is a number of technologies that can address disinformation to help enterprises protect their brand and their online presence. Technologies include deep fake detection, impersonation prevention and reputation protection.

1.3. Opportunities and Risks of Generative AI

This topic has already been widely covered in literature, but for the sake of completeness, it is necessary to briefly outline the positive and negative aspects of generative AI.

Positive features (Quillian, 2025) are as follows.

- An extensive knowledge base with quick and easy access to it, which is much better than traditional information search engines.
- Understanding user prompts, including long, incoherent and containing typos. Naturally, better results are obtained in response to correctly composed prompts.
- Ability to understand and remember context. One can conduct a dialogue based on previous prompts and responses of generative AI system.
- Ability to generate ideas and solve problems, adapting to the roles given by prompts.
- Communication in many languages. It is officially stated that ChatGPT supports 58 languages, although in reality this number can be doubled (Howarth, 2024).
- Availability. There is the possibility of free access, although often – not to full functionality.

However, generative artificial intelligence has also certain disadvantages (Quillian, 2025).

- Hallucinations. A plausible list of references may contain non-existent sources. Another example: a list of attractions in St. Petersburg, made by generative AI, has absolutely nothing to do with reality. The results produced by AI must be thoroughly verified!
- Generative AI is not a calculator, but a predictor or advisor. If mathematical calculations are required, it can recommend a method, but the calculations will have to be done by a person.
- Generative AIs have problems with humor and logic. The author of (Quillian, 2025) believes that both AI humor and AI logic are not based on human living experience, but only on training data. However, it is possible that something useful can be extracted from more of less large series of generated responses.
- Confidentiality. Your prompts are remembered to improve future work and to better understand natural language. You should not enter personal data or financial documents.
- Ethics of plagiarism. Publishing unedited AI-generated texts may be considered plagiarism, and sometimes it leads to the spread of false information due to possible hallucinations. It is also possible that the response of AI will be too similar to existing materials from real authors. Although there are no clear laws regarding these problems yet, fragments of text generated by AI should be pointed out and their content should be carefully checked.
- Bias. It should be remembered that responses of AI are based on the data on which it was trained. This is related with the country in which the AI de-

velopment took place, culture, certain points of view of its developers. The possibility of such distortions should be closely monitored.

We must also not forget about the threats posed by generative AI (Mylrea, 2025; Kumar, 2024).

- Deliberate disinformation.
- Deepfakes.
- Content of appeals containing threats and violence.
- Cybersecurity threats.

The idea of the strategic danger of using AI in medical analysis has spread in the medical world. If this function is completely transferred to AI, which will even do it faster and better than a person, human qualifications may be lost, and it will become much more difficult to cope with new medical challenges. Another possibly dangerous thing is changing human employees by robots and AI assistants.

This is another reason why not only in medicine, but also in other areas of AI application, it should remain just an assistant, but not replace a person (Bergalieva & Keulimzhaeva, 2024; Petrov, 2023).

All this indicates the need of the serious studying of various aspects related with generative AI. The author of (Chichulin, 2023) lists the competencies required for an operator working with AI. These are:

- development of generative AI systems from refining the problem to integrating it into the activities of an industry organization;
- management and maintenance of such systems;
- data analysis and problem solving with the help of such systems;
- ensuring the development of AI systems using the latest achievements in this area.

These are not just the activities of IT specialists. Success can be reached only with close interaction with those, who use the results obtained by generative AI systems. Here we speak about marketing specialists.

1.4. Applications of Generative AI in Marketing

According to (Zhu, 2024; Singla et al., 2024), in 2024 organizations began to use generative AI widely. It is expected to have a great effect. Many business functions are implemented with its help. But it is better to apply these technologies where they bring value. The most popular applications are (in per cent of respondents):

- just in marketing – 34% (content support, personalized marketing, lead identification and prioritization in sales);
- in product development – 23% (design, literature review, preliminary simulation and testing; actually, this is also marketing),
- in service operations – 13% (the answer is ambiguous).
- in IT – 17% (including Help desk chatbot, Help desk AI Assistant).

Other, less common applications included:

- human resource management,
- risk management,
- developing a corporate strategy,
- finance management,
- supply chain and inventory management.

And a very modest role generative AI has in manufacturing.

Possible results of applying generative AI in marketing (Kukitz, P, 2024) are as follows.

- Reduction of expenses of creative advertising campaigns and unique features of the image of a company.
- Generation of text, images, video and audio content.
- Improvement of products and services.
- Improvement of interaction with consumers, improvement of user experience (Davide, Sciannamè and Ceconello, 2024).

This is due to new functions of generative artificial intelligence (Patrecia, 2025).

- Automated content creation. This is most useful for repetitive tasks. It saves time and resources.
- Augmented reality: interactive demonstrations of the product, virtual try-ons or immersive experiences. In the future there are perspectives in a wider sphere: Extended Reality which is the combination of augmented, virtual and mixed realities.
- Accurate segmentation of the audience by behavior and preferences.

New opportunities for marketing communications supported by generative AI are also described in (Büyüksomer & Tekeoğlu, 2024).

It is clear that marketing applications of generative AI

- are widely used;
- perform specific functions.

Advantages of using generative AI in marketing (Kukitz, 2024) are:

- ease of access, convenient interface between the user and the platform);
- relatively low cost: there are free solutions on the market;
- fast connection, practically unrelated with traditional barriers of digitalization: in some cases – just a simple authorization is necessary to start working;
- scalability and easy improvement for specific tasks due to API connection, which reflects the openness of AI to improvements.

But at the same time, there are risks in using generative AI in marketing (Kukitz, 2024):

- the possibility of critical errors in AI recommended decisions;
- ethical issues, which have already received much attention (Heyder, Passlack and Posegga, 2023); they include privacy violation, plagiarism, manipulation.
- hallucinations; in this case false advertising, strange drawings, non-existent landmarks (Duke & Giudici, 2025) – plausible, but incorrect results that undermine user trust (Yaprak, 2024). Of course, the identified errors are eliminated one by one. But there is no guarantee that others will not appear.

The presence of both pros and cons of using generative AI is also described in (Israfilzade, 2025).

This duality is also considered in detail in (Rosenberg, L, 2023). Interactive generative media are considered in this work as "personalized, adaptive and interactive content that is deployed in real time for maximum involvement and optimization of influence on individually targeted users". However, almost the same functions are considered in (Rosenberg, 2023) as sources of great danger. There is a danger of starting an intense struggle for the buyer, offering content, color scheme, fonts and other elements of advertising messages depending on gender, age, lifestyle of the person to whom the advertising is directed. At the same time, in the process of self-learning based on the results of the implemented impacts, they will become more and more aggressive and actually turn into manipulation. The same applies to dialogue with customers, which will also increase the possibilities of manipulating them.

Thus, AI will be able to create personalized, interactive and adaptive media, that is a powerful, but dangerous tool for influencing users.

The need for a balanced approach to this tool in marketing is indicated in (European Commission, 2024). A new direction has also emerged (Duke & Giudici, 2025). It is called "Responsible AI" or "Ethical AI".

A systematic review of literature sources on enhancing marketing communications with generative AI is given in (Büyüksomer & Tekeoğlu, 2024).

The authors are confident that the potential of generative AI has not yet been fully revealed.

Based on all of the above, there is an urgent need to master the proper use of generative AI in marketing.

1.5. Regulations on Using Generative AI

The EU supports the development of AI (European Commission, 2024). AI Innovation Package, the launch of AI Factories and the Coordinated Plan on AI can be mentioned. Together, these measures are supposed to guarantee safety, fundamental rights and human-centric AI, and stimulate investments and innovations in AI across the EU.

However, this package also includes Regulation, declaring systematized rules on AI (European Commission, 2024). Here are its main points.

- High-risk systems include scoring and manipulation systems. A fine is imposed for using such systems. In particular, it restricts:
  - facial recognition using cameras in public spaces;
  - scoring to assess the likelihood of loan default based on behavior on social networks;
  - creation of databases for facial recognition of data from the Internet;
  - an AI-powered interface that affects the subconscious.
- Limited-risk systems that require user awareness.
- Minimal-risk systems: video games, spam filters.

In the United States (Lafferly, 2025) the regulations are being developed, but different states plan to introduce regulations in 2026. They include marking AI generated content, privacy protection, risk management, prevent discrimination in employment decisions, prohibiting deep fakes, digital replications, manipulation.

The situation in this area is also changing rapidly. For example, shortly after the appearance of the Chinese DeepSeek system, restrictions were introduced on its use (Lu, 2025). They include (Luo & Dan, 2025) labelling of AI generated content.

The detailed regulations worldwide is described in (Sherman, 2024).

The situation in this area is also changing rapidly. This is another argument in favor of the need to study generative AI and its applications.

2. AI IN EDUCATION

2.1. AI as an Assistant for Students

Generative AI has great prospects in the field of higher education development.

The boom in the use of neural network chatbots, based on a large language model, by students, primarily Russian ones, began with the publication that a diploma thesis was written in 23 hours using a chatbot and successfully defended (Abramov, 2023; Zhadan, 2023). As a result, the student received a document on education, but the problem of attitude to such a practice arose (Vorobjev, 2023; Keffer, 2023).

This precedent inspired students. Among them, many followers appeared who hoped that AI would do all the work for them. Basically, such attempts were not successful. Recommendations for writing diploma theses using neural networks also appeared. Source (Neural networks for writing a thesis, 2024) offers several neural networks for this, describes the complexities of the process, including their additional training. In (Greceva, 2024), the need for caution in using chatbots at work is indicated. It becomes clear that the need to create a detailed task and further train the chatbot to solve it requires special competencies and does not greatly simplify the process of writing a thesis. Rather, it can make it even more complicated.

Counteraction to the practice of generating thesis using chatbots has also begun. Standards for the percentage of generated text were introduced, anti-plagiarism systems began to recognize generated texts. However, it is not possible to find legislative acts prohibiting the use of AI in education.

As a counteraction to the recognition of generated texts, recommendations appeared on how to make the generated text undetectable (Mustakrimov, 2023). A 2024 study performed by the National Research University Higher School of Economics (HSE University, 2024) is devoted to the issues of combating generated texts.

However, it soon became obvious that it is impossible to prohibit the use of AI by students (Mikhailov, 2023). It is only necessary to direct this process properly, since it has great potential (Ningsih & Lahby, 2024). In recent years, a number of works have appeared that provide recommendations for changing the educational process, for example, (Garkusha & Gorodove, 2023; Lahby, 2024a).

The main possibilities of AI in education are as follows (Amar & Benchouk, 2024).

- Virtual Mentor.
- Voice Assistant.
- Smart Content Maker.
- Presentation Translator.
- Global Courses Support.
- Automatic Assessment.

- Personalized Learning.

Although the idea of individual selection of a number of subjects by students is not new (Othman, 2023), generative AI has introduced new features to the individualization of learning (Yuyun & Suherdi, 2023; Randieri, 2024). But AI analysis of students' successes and failures aimed on the selection of individual tasks is understood to be a very complex thing (Mikhalev, 2020), and obviously a matter of the future.

But it is wrong to believe that generative AI, after overcoming its shortcomings, will be undoubtedly useful in all possible educational tasks. For example, on one hand, personalized learning is certainly a step forward compared to the "1 teacher – many students" system. But on the other hand, the perception of new information is many times better when interacting with a real person, not a robot.

So the generative AI, as in other cases, is thought of as an auxiliary tool, just an assistant in the foreseeable future (Trapeznikov & Zinovieva, 2024).

2.2. Generative AI as a Teachers' Assistant

Universities' attitudes towards generative AI in education vary widely (Alexandrova, 2024): from prohibiting its use by students to encouraging its use.

World trends in education related with generative AI are listed in (Koroleva et al., 2025). These are thefollowing.

- Immersive approach to learning.
- Learning through dialogue with AI.
- Explanation of ethical issues in using AI.
- Smart textbooks (personalized content and recommendations).
- Assessment using augmented reality.

The authors of (Lahby et al., 2024) examines various learning systems based on AI. Among them, the PolyGloT framework stands out. It is a new framework for teachers and students, designed to create, curate and participate in personalized learning paths of digital education. This open, adaptable and universal framework facilitates the design and consumption of adaptive learning. It involves various educational goals, covering interactive activities and complex assessment tasks.

However, its implementation in a university is a complex task that requires a major restructuring of the existing educational process. In addition, it requires training not only students, but also teachers.

In general, as of early 2025, publications consider prospects rather than real experiences.

Therefore, the practice of individual use of AI by teachers and students is more common.

2.3. Studies on Generative AI in Education

As shown above, the process of implementing generative AI into the process of higher education is far from being complete. Therefore, it is necessary to monitor the attitude of students and teachers towards it. This will help to decide what is more important: to conduct training that will form an informed attitude towards AI, or to improve certain functions of the generative AI itself and methods of its use.

The topics of research have varied from using the results of AI as one's own text and monitoring this (Davalos & Yin, 2024) to assessing the benefits of generative AI for students and teachers.

For example, a student noted (Khadzakos, 2024) that generative AI can be:

- a teacher answering questions, giving a summary of lectures and seminars;
- a text editor, highlighting the essence of the material, setting its style.
- a programmer, creating things according to technical requirements, generating software, correcting errors in programs.
- a foreign-language interlocutor.

In 2023 and 2024, a number of large-scale studies were also conducted in different countries. (Deschenes & McMahon, 2024) – 360 undergraduate and graduate students at Harvard University, (Chan & Hu, 2023) – 399 students in Hong Kong, (Mamikonyan, 2023) – 1272 students in cities with a population of over one million in the Russian Federation, (Buyakova et al., 2024) – 1597 students and 250 teachers at Tomsk State University, (Aleshkovsky et al., 2025) – 52919 students at Russian universities. A number of publications are summarized in (Vetrova, 2024).

This gave an initial general picture of the use of generative AI by students and, to some extent – by teachers.

Generative AI is already used quite widely and for a variety of tasks. Most students have a positive attitude towards it. High accuracy of assistance to students is noted, half of the teachers use generative AI to develop educational materials. The emergence of learning management systems based on generative AI is expected, which will reduce the number of failures in learning.

But the situation is changing quite quickly, so the results of such studies quickly become outdated. The authors (Amar & Benchouk, 2024) note both the fundamental similarity of skills required for effective teaching of subjects based on generative AI, and the difference in methods depending on the disciplines: engineering, marketing, art. And the situation with the use of generative AI varies in different universities.

Therefore, it is necessary to conduct research within individual universities and specialties. And among them, it is advisable to study such a popular direction of student training as marketing.

3. MONITORING THE STUDENT'S OPINIONS AND EXPERIENCES

3.1. Research Problem

Within the framework of this approach, the proposed chapter describes a study of the opinions of students – future marketers of the Institute of Industrial Management, Economics and Trade of Peter the Great St. Petersburg Polytechnic University on the use of generative AI in their educational process and future work.

Research objectives were to determine,

- to what extent the students are familiar with generative AI and in what ways they have used it;
- what do they think about the benefits and potential of AI in education and professional activities;
- how and to what extent is AI used in their learning process;
- how do they evaluate the potential of AI concerning the improvement of the education process.

3.2. Methodology

The study was conducted in the form of an electronic questionnaire among undergraduate and graduate students. The questions suggested a choice of fixed options, but had an additional item "Other". Among the answers to some questions, this item was left blank, which indicates a successful choice of options by developers of the questionnaire.

To avoid careless answers, the survey did not contain mandatory questions. For more frank answers, it was anonymous. Each student was sent a link to an electronic questionnaire.

A total of 91 responses were collected from marketing students (73 from the undergraduate program and 18 from the graduate program). This amounted to about 40% coverage. The percentage of responses allows to estimate the level of interest in the proposed topic among respondents. Obviously, it is not very high.

The collected data were grouped by the level of education.

The study is exploratory in nature, allowing to identify the main trends at a qualitative rather than quantitative level.

The authors tried to make the questionnaire not very long, to make the answers more thoughtful and not careless. The questionnaire is divided into the following sections.

The first part is the respondents' experience of using generative AI, their opinions on using this tool in their studies and future work, their wishes for mastering it.

The second part is devoted to students' opinions about the work of teachers using generative AI.

The third part concerns opinions on generative AI in marketing in the present and future.

The final, fourth part contains questions about the student himself: level of study: undergraduate or graduate level; year of study; plans for work in the field of marketing.

As to terminology, the author used a bit simplified terms that are widely spread among students.

3.3. Research Results

Question 1. What are the benefits of using neural network based chatbots in education, in your opinion (multiple variant answer)? The results are shown on Figure 1.

Here and below UG means undergraduate level, G – graduate.

Figure 1. Percentage of Answers About Benefits of Using Chatbots

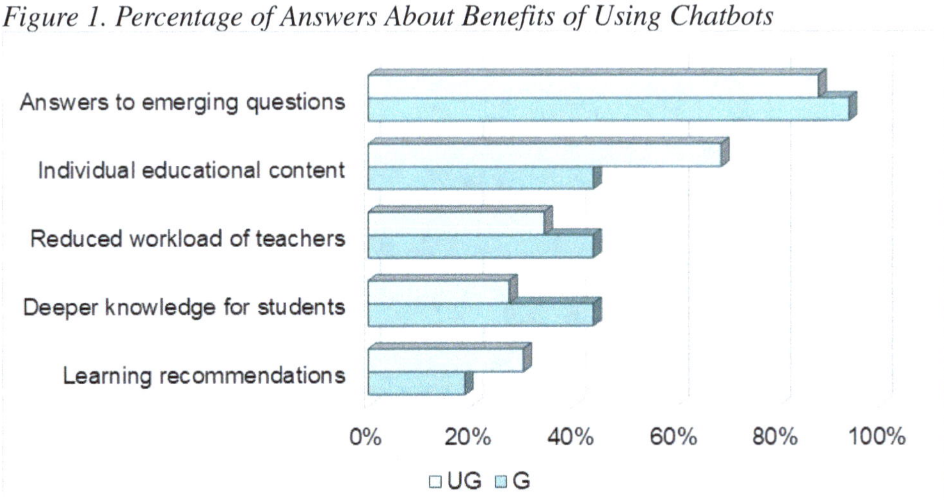

It is clear that the most popular answer is getting information, which is quite realistic.

Among undergraduates, there are high expectations for individualized learning content. They are also waiting for recommendations on how to improve the learning process more than graduates, although this is an unpopular answer.

It is nice to see that making teachers' work easier is in third place.

Hopes for gaining deeper knowledge, which is higher among graduates, are still quite modest.

Recommendations are:

- to teach how to ask questions, addressing AI correctly, to get relevant answers, to convince students not to trust AI-generated answers completely;
- to consider implementing a personalized learning management system, for example, PolyGloT (Lahby, 2024b);
- to develop methods aimed not at getting ready-made answers to homework or an exam question, but at gaining knowledge.

Similar recommendations on this issue are also available, for example, in (Wazan et al., 2023) and other works.

Almost all points, except the first, can be solved by implementing an automated learning system based on generative AI. But this is obviously a matter of the future.

Question 2. Then it is necessary to ask about the attitude to this. What is your attitude towards the use of neural networks in the educational process? Answers are shown on Figure 2.

Figure 2. Distribution of Answers About Attitude Towards Neural Networks in Educational Process

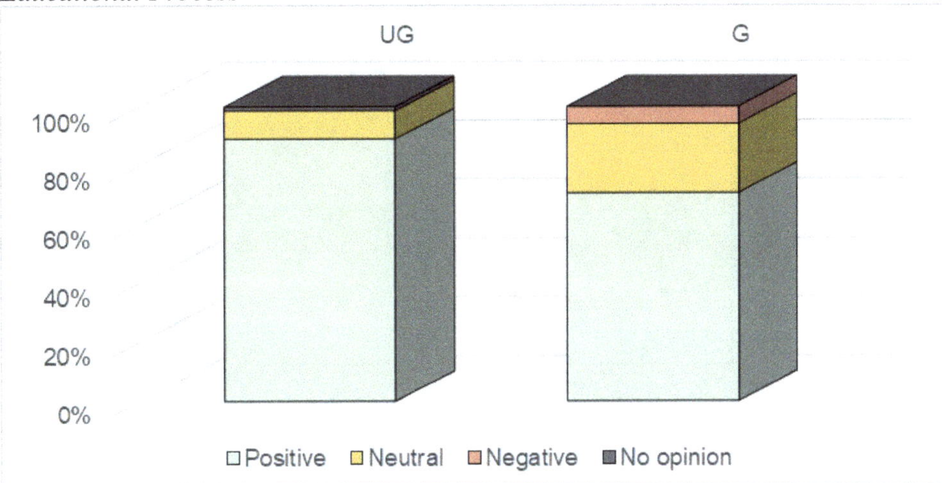

General optimism is visible, although for graduates everybody of which already have had a certain experience, it is somewhat reduced, being replaced by a neutral and even negative attitude.

Recommendations are: to teach the correct usage of generative AI from the beginning of training, explain its capabilities and, just from the beginning, to teach how to evaluate various generative AI tools to choose the most suitable one.

Question 3. To what extent do you think you can trust the information from chatbots? See Figure 3 for the results.

Figure 3. Percentage of Different Attitude to the Results Generated by AI

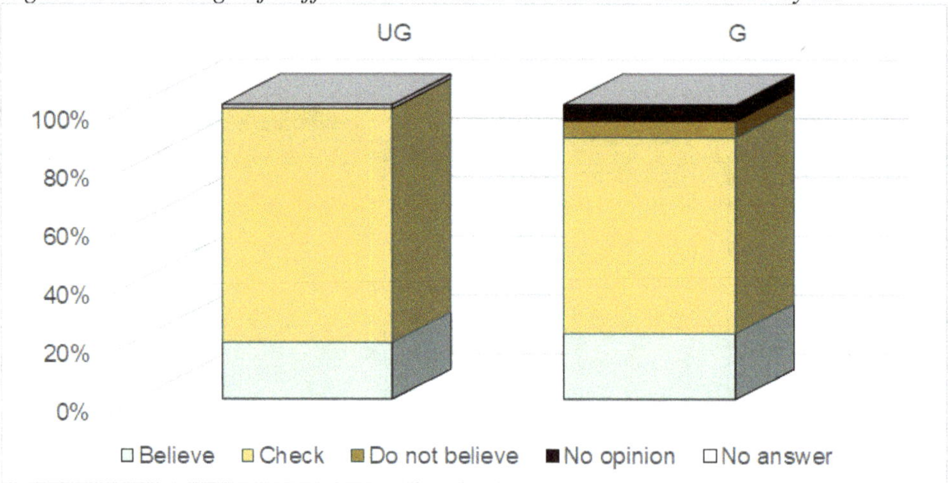

It is clear that the attitude is quite realistic: relatively few respondents trust it without hesitation. Interestingly, the level of trust among the graduate students is somewhat higher. But the overwhelming majority is ready to use the answers of generative AI only after verification. Some of the undergraduates did not give an answer, but some graduates do not trust the materials provided by AI, apparently based on their experience, including the defense of their Bachelor's thesis. A certain number of graduates doubt to give the definite answer or just do not have a definite opinion.

The recommendations are the same: to teach the correct usage of generative AI.

Question 4. How do you check the materials provided by the chatbots? It is related with the previous one. The answers of those who indicated that they check the materials provided by AI were considered. From Figure 4 the following can be seen.

Figure 4. Percentage of Respondents, Using Different Ways to Check AI-Generated Results

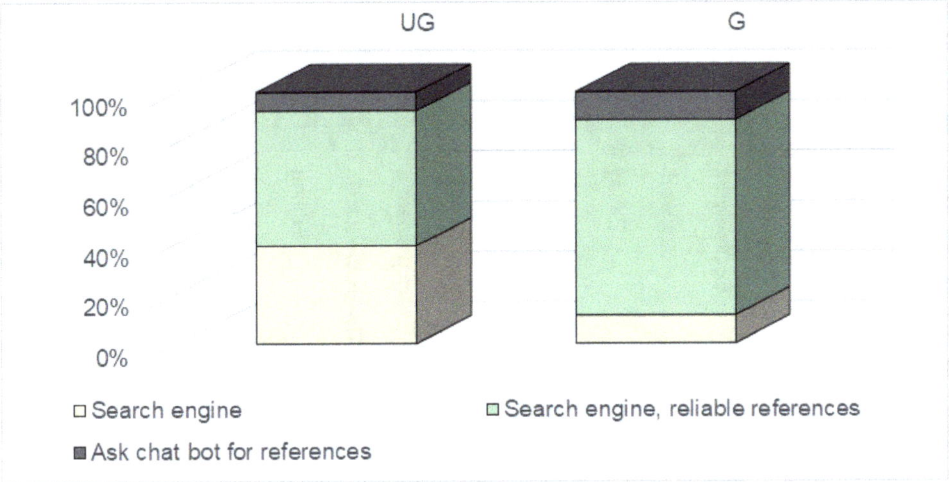

It is clear that graduate students are more careful in choosing data sources and more often than undergraduates, make the chatbot provide links to the materials provided.

Unfortunately, not all chatbots provide reference links at all, and often these are links to Wikipedia or other not very reliable sources. So, in fact, such links also need to be checked.

Recommendations: emphasize the importance of carefully checking the information provided by the generative AI.

Question 5. What tasks can neural network technologies help with in the learning process and which ones have you ready used? See Figure 5 for results.

Figure 5. Opinions about Neural Network Technologies

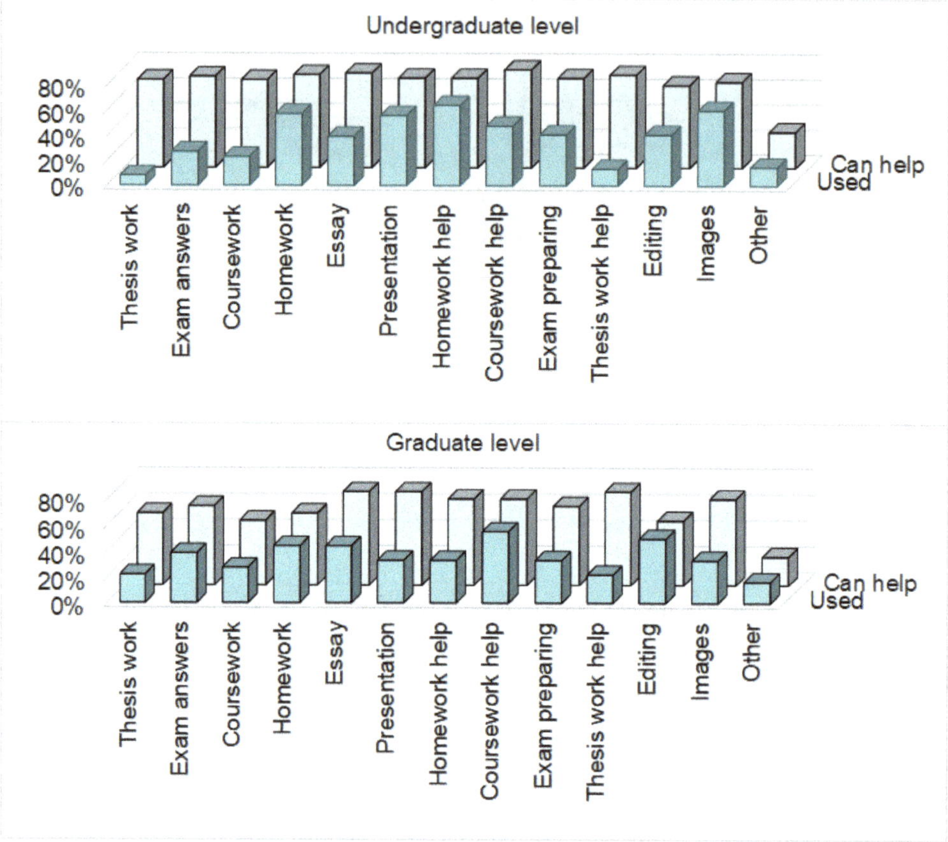

The horizontal axis shows the answers from "criminal" to "welcomed" in the opinion of the authors (they are broken down in the questionnaire).

- Writing a graduation thesis.
- Answering exam questions and/or tests.
- Writing a term paper.
- Doing homework.
- Preparing an essay.
- Preparing reports and presentations.
- Finding answers to homework questions.
- Finding materials for a term paper.
- Finding materials to prepare for exams and/or tests.
- Finding materials for a graduation thesis.
- Editing materials.

- Working with images.
- Other.

Undergraduate students are more optimistic, including on “criminal” points, but used the capabilities of generative AI less. Apparently, graduates have already encountered disappointment in the ability of generative AI to do all the work for them.

As for help at work, graduates are more disappointed. Interestingly, graduates use text editing capabilities more often, although they are more pessimistic about this capability than undergraduates.

Recommendations are:

- to explain the advantages, risks, and difficulties of using generative AI for various tasks, starting with routine ones, such as editing texts and preparing presentations, and then moving on to more complex ones that require creative approach: generating images, literature reviews, and forming detailed texts from abstracts. In this case, it is necessary to emphasize only the auxiliary role of generative AI and the need for serious personal participation in the listed actions.
- to provide an opportunity to gain experience in practical classes.

Question 6. What is your attitude to the various functions of chatbots? Answers: 5 – very positive, 4 – rather positive, 3 – neutral, 2 – rather negative, 1 – very negative. On Figure 6 “undesirable” functions are closer to the viewer.

Figure 6. Attitude to Neural Network Functions

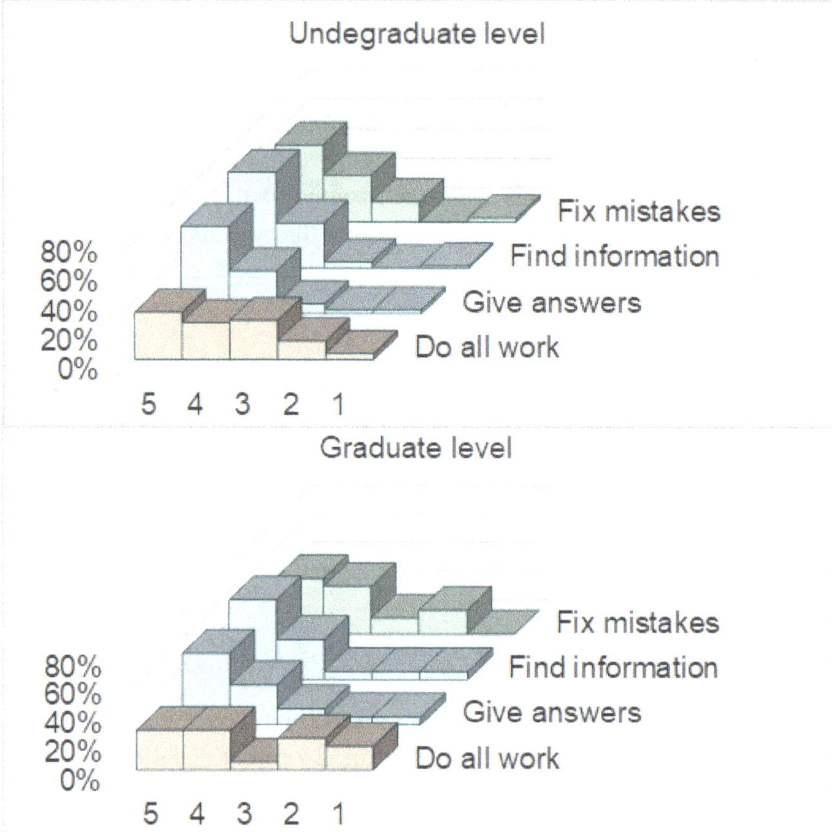

It is clear that although graduate students are not so optimistic on all questions as undergraduates, especially on the first function, many of them still hope that generative AI will do all the work for them.

Items 2 and 3 are similar, but item 3 implies a less specific search, in fact, similar to a request to an information retrieval system. It should be noted that these systems already use built-in AI tools.

Interestingly, graduates have little faith that AI will help them correct errors in prepared materials.

Recommendations are:

- to explain that generative AI will not be able to do all the work for the student. One way to explain this, according to the authors' experience, can be to give an assignment to review a book created by a generative AI, for example, “More Clever with AI: How to Use ChatGPT to Achieve Success and Build

Wealth". In this book, the features of the generated texts are obvious: vagueness, lack of meaning, excessive verbosity, lack of logic.

- to teach how to compose prompts correctly. This is critically important at the current level of development of generative AI. A large number of books are devoted to this problem, for example, (Bozkurt, 2024);
- to explain that error correction is at least a joint matter of generative AI and the user.

Question 7. What neural networks did you use? The answers are shown on Figure 7.

Figure 7. Neural Network Based Instruments Used

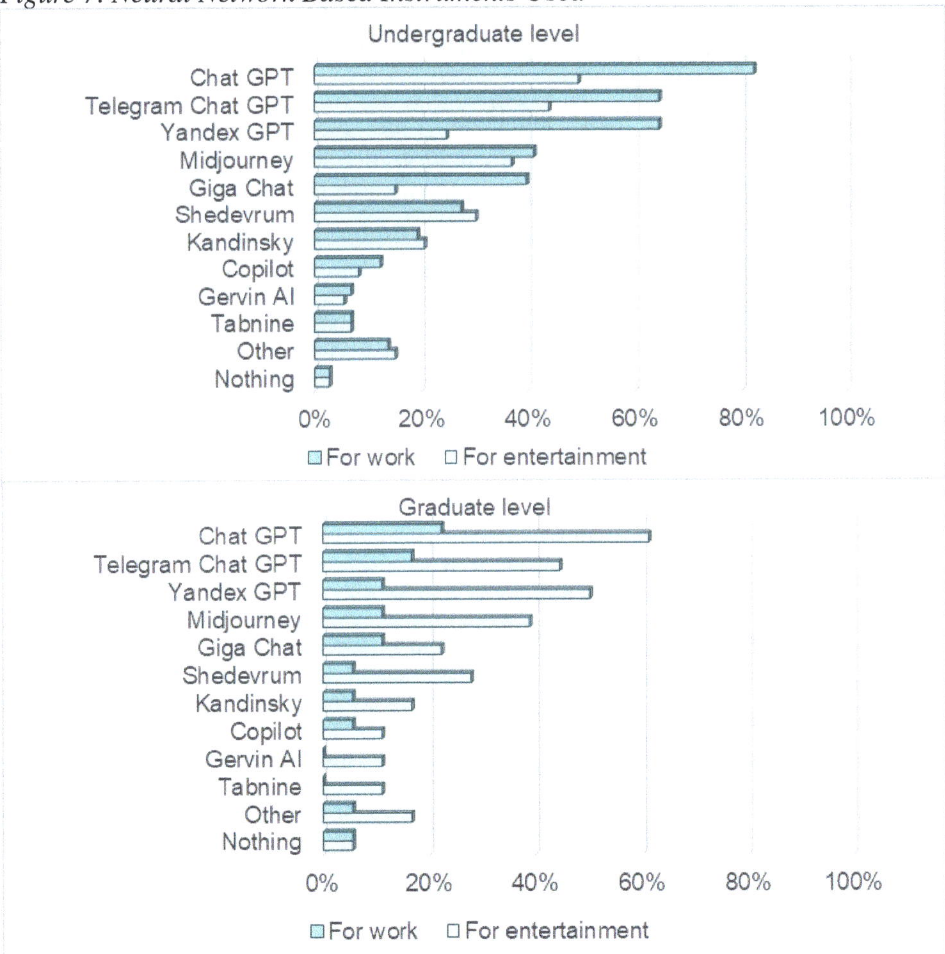

It is interesting that graduates use generative AI much more often for entertainment than for study. Most likely, this is explained by the fact that in previous years there was no training in the useful use of generative AI. Here you can clearly see the difference between students of different years of admission, which indicates a high dynamism of the situation and the need for annual monitoring of the dynamic changes.

The rating of the tools used is almost the same for both groups. Among the popular ones are both domestic and foreign generative AI systems. The most famous and the first widely advertised tool, ChatGPT, retains its leadership. Other foreign tools include Copilot for general use and Tabnine for assistance in programming.

As for the purpose of generative AI tools, it is mainly general. Midjourney is quite popular. It is a tool for working with images, and for educational purposes.

Among Russian-language generative AI systems, Yandex GPT and Giga Chat from Sber turned out to be popular.

Yandex GPT (Sorokin, 2024), launched in 2023, is designed to generate text, images, conduct dialogues, provide information, assist in learning and creativity, and solve business problems. It can understand many languages. It is integrated into the Yandex search queries, the Alice voice assistant, and various products, such as smart speakers. The limitations include: dependence on training data, possible inaccuracy and neutrality of responses.

Gigachat from Sberbank (Perov, 2024) is a multimodal neural network consisting of the following components: ruGPT-3 for writing texts, the FRED-T5 language model, ruCLIP for working with images and texts, and Kandinsky for creating images and videos. The only language is Russian. Its features are: creating text, writing program code, generating images, creating presentation plans, writing poetry, writing essays, etc.

Some respondents also checked the Other item. This indicates the need for further in-depth research.

Recommendations. The authors believe that it is better to use generative AI instruments in the native language. Two stages of translation can introduce additional distortions into the query result.

In addition, the English-language AI is trained (mostly?) on English-language sources. This most likely causes trouble in language analysis tasks as well as book and paper references for writing graduate work.

The students should also be oriented to search for newly emerging generative AI tools. For the questionnaires similar to the one described in this chapter, in the future it is reasonable to ask for the names of the generative AI instruments used.

It is important for teachers to be ready for changes in the landscape of generative AI toolkit and prepare students for this.

Question 8. Is it necessary to train the use of neural networks for education and work of a marketer? Here the shift has already been made to the direction of training students. To make the question more concrete, the future specialty of education is mentioned.

Of course, graduates have a clearer idea of the prospects for their future work. The obtained results are presented on Figure 8.

Figure 8. Levels of Necessity of Neural Networks for Marketers

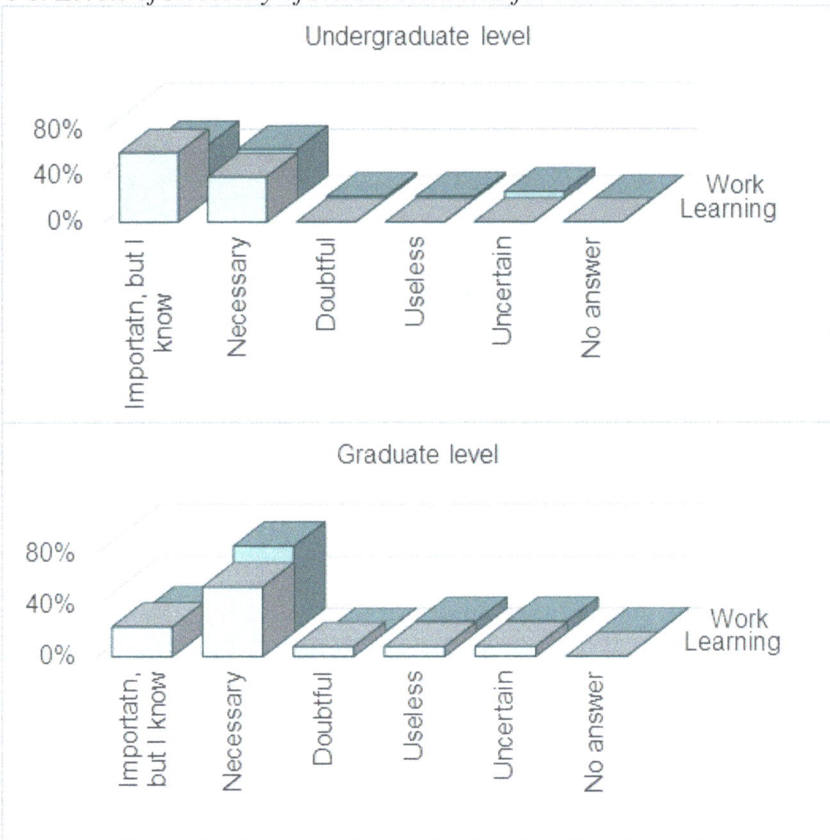

It is interesting that many undergraduates are confident in their knowledge, while most graduates believe that training is necessary, especially for the future work. Obviously, this is due to their experience in the process of education. Besides that, some graduates already have experience of practical work in organizations. That can be the reason why they attach greater importance to the need for knowledge and skills in the field of generative AI for their future career.

Several graduate students also have some doubts about the need for training in the use of generative AI, while undergraduates do not.

Recommendations. From the very beginning of training, it is important to familiarize students with the advantages and limitations of using generative AI in marketing, starting with its help in solving marketing tasks. This will help to acquire an adequate opinion about generative AI.

Question 9. Do you think that the use of neural networks in education can improve the learning outcomes? See Figure 9 for results.

Figure 9. The Role of Neural Networks in Improving Learning Outcomes

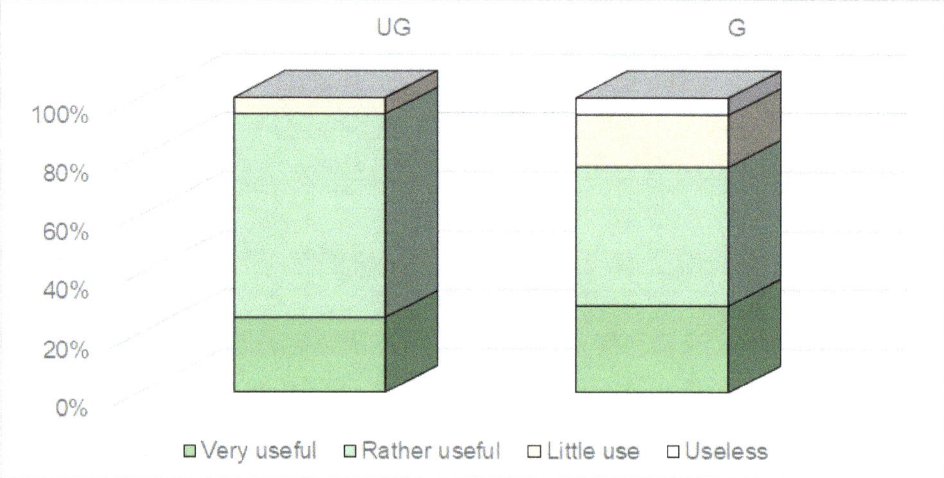

Opinions of graduates: on one hand, most of them think that including neural networks into their educational process is useful, but at the same time, the share of those who think it is of little use or completely useless is also increasing.

Obviously, the opinion of all respondents is not very optimistic. Perhaps this is due to a negative experience of using generative AI tools due to not proper dealing with them. It is also possible that there was an unsuccessful experience of trying to pass assignments completely prepared by generative AI, or a negative attitude of teachers to the usage of such tools.

Recommendations. It is important to teach students how to correctly compose prompts, starting with solving the simplest problems of the initial period of study. Then they will see the capabilities of generative AI and will evaluate them higher, though more realistically. One way or another, they will have to work under the conditions of widespread generative AI tools in all areas of activity.

Question 10. What do you think is the future of neural networks in education? (Figure 10).

Figure 10. Opinions about the Future of Neural Networks in Education

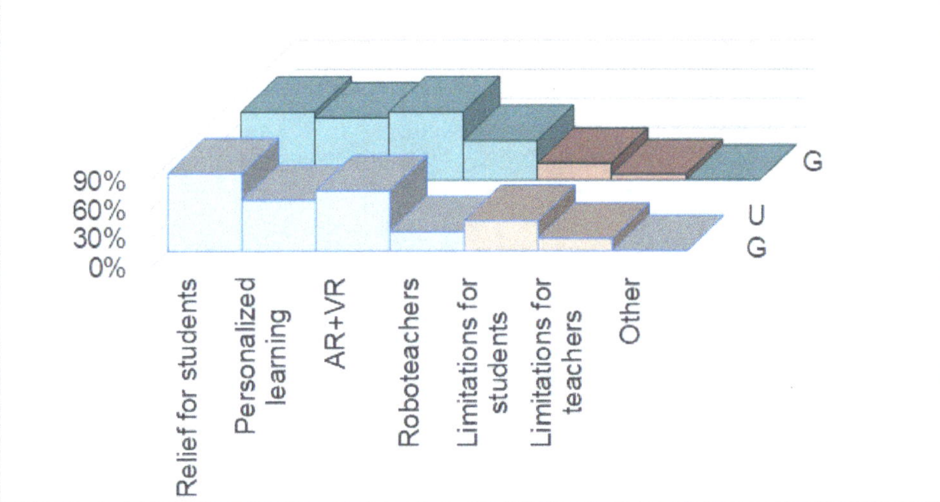

The desire to make one's life easier turned out to be the strongest among students. Great hopes are also related with personalized learning. However, this is most likely only a general idea. AR and VR look attractive as well. Graduate students are more positive than undergraduates in their attitude towards robotic teachers. As for the negative aspects – restrictions of the usage of generative AI by teachers and students – there are some concerns here too.

However, these restrictions are necessary, even at the legislative level, as was already mentioned above in this chapter.

Recommendations. The role of introduction of generative AI in increasing creativity and promoting teamwork is widely discussed in literature. However, it appeared that many students simply want to make their lives easier by using generative AI. It is necessary to show that generative AI can really help, but primarily in solving routine tasks. The learning process should be changed from an emphasis on manual search and literature review to solving truly creative problems, but containing a component of routine work, in which generative AI can help.

It is also necessary to explain the ethical and legislative features of the usage of generative AI; to create a proper attitudes towards the use of AI at the university. This will be very useful in future professional activities.

Question 11. In what form would you like to master the use of artificial intelligence in marketing? Results – on Figure 11.

Figure 11. Preferable Ways to Learn Generative AI

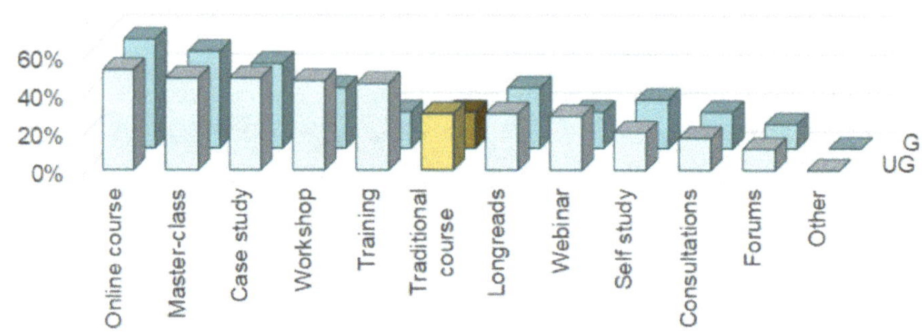

First of all, the relative unpopularity of the traditional academic course – lectures, practical exercises, the exam – is striking, especially among graduate students. The popularity of online courses can be explained by the fact that they have become widely spread during Covid 19 pandemic, and in addition, this way of learning does not require much time to visit university. In addition, the practice of putting lectures into a handwritten abstract word by word has now been a thing of the past. There are printed materials, presentations, numerous sites with educational contents for students, finally, you can ask AI a question. The popularity of viewing records of practical classes in TEAMS while preparing home works is also noted. Nowadays, students appreciate the possibility of repeated viewing of complex moments. This is an individual pace of mastering the educational material.

Finally, traditional lectures are difficult for the Generation Z students to comprehend. They are hardly perceived by the Generation Z, inclined to clip thinking (Tyugashev, 2025).

The remaining preferred forms of training have a pronounced practical orientation.

Self studies, although indicated by some respondents, are not very popular.

It should also be noted that in this question it appeared to be possible to list all the methods of mastering the material, no "Other" answers were noted.

Recommendations:

- The identified unpopularity of traditional academic courses requires their restructuring.
- The main attention should be paid to practical tasks, to solving real problems. Training courses should focus on the phenomena occurring in the environment. A fruitful subject is to find new trends and explore them using generative AI.

Question 12. How do some of your teachers feel about the fact that students use neural networks? It is a multiple response answer. See figure 12 for the collected results.

Figure 12. Teachers' Attitude to Neural Networks Usage by Students

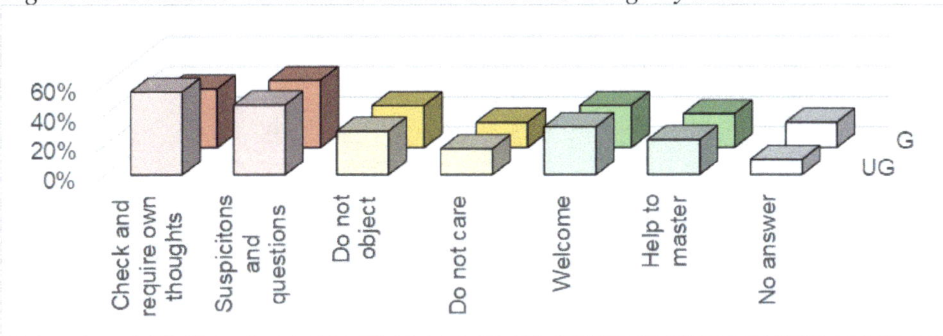

On the horizontal axis, the answers are located from "strictly prohibitive" to "helpful".

It can be seen that most teachers feel negative about the usage of AI. The indifferent options are not very popular. Quite many teachers welcome the usage of generative AI. Unfortunately, so far only a few teachers help students to master it.

Recommendations:

- On the one hand, the commonness of generated texts requires more attentive reading and thorough analysis of students work from teachers, so that the text does not have characteristic drawbacks of generated texts that were discussed above.
- On the other hand, this question revealed that teachers should pay more attention to help students in mastering generative AI or at least clearly determine their position. Currently, one cannot remain indifferent to this issue.

Question 13. Does some of your teachers use AI for educational purposes (multiple response answer)? Findings can de seen on figure 13.

Figure 13. Opinion of Students about Teachers' Usage of AI

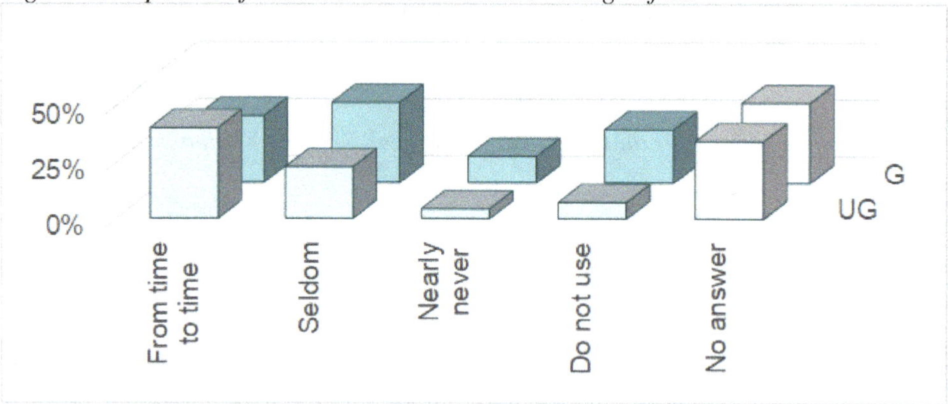

Here a large percentage of the absence of answers should be noted. Perhaps this was because students do not pay much attention for this thing. Maybe it does not catch the eye.

It is also interesting that many undergraduate students believe that most teachers use generative AI. This may be because undergraduate courses are more general, fundamental, and for them more AI based elements are already implemented.

As for the graduate students, their opinions were divided. It can also be due to the specifics of disciplines, many of which are new, introduced for the first time due to the dynamism of marketing (Kotler, Kartajaya and Setiawan, 2023).

Question 14. How would you react if the teachers used AI technology to evaluate your knowledge and work? Answers are on figure 14. Answers in the questionnaire were somewhat longer and more clarified:

- Positively, this would be an objective assessment.
- Neutral, I don't care.
- Negatively, I do not want AI to give me an assessment.
- I find it difficult to answer.

Figure 14. Attitude Towards Checking Students' Knowledge by AI.

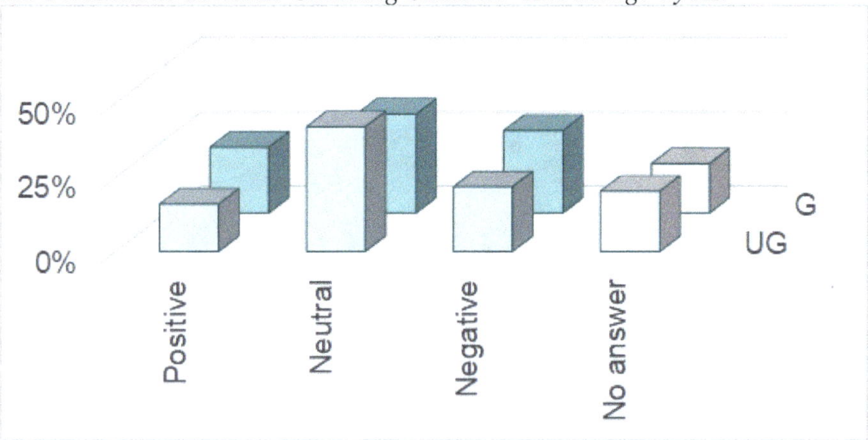

The number of "No answer" and "Negative" opinions is quite noticeable. The most popular answer is "Neutral".

Those who support AI checking rely on the absence of subjectivity in the given grades. Not so seldom students disagree with the evaluation of their work.

Recommendations. The opinion of the authors is that students should be informed about the procedure for assessing their knowledge, emphasizing that generative AI plays just an auxiliary role. Then, obviously, the attitude towards automated assessment will improve.

The next section of the questionnaire was dedicated to more professional aspects of the application of generative AI.

Question 15. Do you agree that AI will change the approach to marketing in the future? The answers were given on a scale: "Completely agree", "Rather agree", "Rather disagree", "Completely disagree" with the option of "No opinion". The results are on figure 15.

Figure 15. Agreement to the Future Changes in Marketing Caused by AI

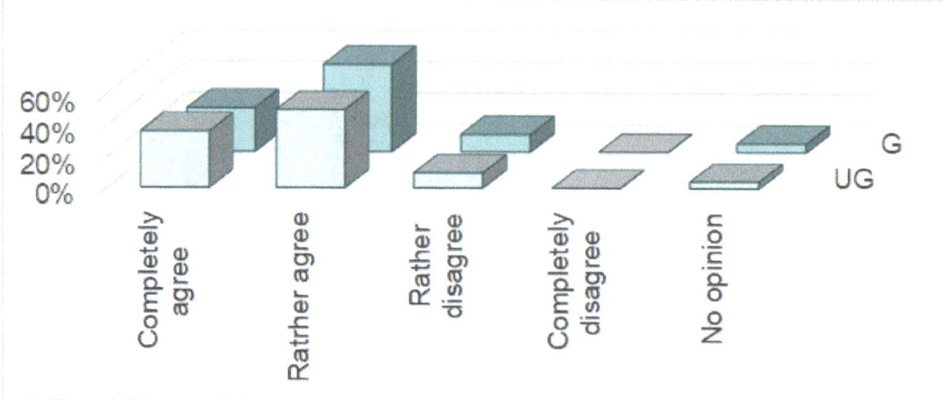

The most popular answer is "Rather agree". Perhaps the effect of avoiding extreme statements worked here. Some respondents do not have an opinion. There are no people who completely disagree that changes will occur.

In general, the answers correspond to expectations that are expressed in numerous sources.

Recommendations. Students are ready to accept the upcoming changes, it is necessary to prepare them for these changes in a proper way.

Question 16. (It was the most difficult). In your opinion, what is the impact of AI on marketing activities? It was necessary to evaluate various aspects of marketing activities:

- High accuracy of targeting for advertising.
- Improved multimodality of content (text + image + video)
- Improved customer experience in using chatbots and voice communication with them.
- Personalized offers based on buyer behavior.
- Modernization of research and decision making.
- Quick response to trends and changes in customer's preferences.
- Predictive analytics.
- Competitor analysis.
- Optimization of promotion campaigns.
- Automation of labor-intensive and repetitive tasks.
- Successful launch of new products.
- Optimization of the pricing process.
- Reduction of marketing costs.
- Other impacts.

Assessments were given on a scale: 5 – very strong, 4 – rather strong, 3 – of medium strength, 2 – rather weak, 1 – very weak. See figure 16 for the obtained results.

Figure 16. Opinions About the Impact of AI on Different Elements of Marketing

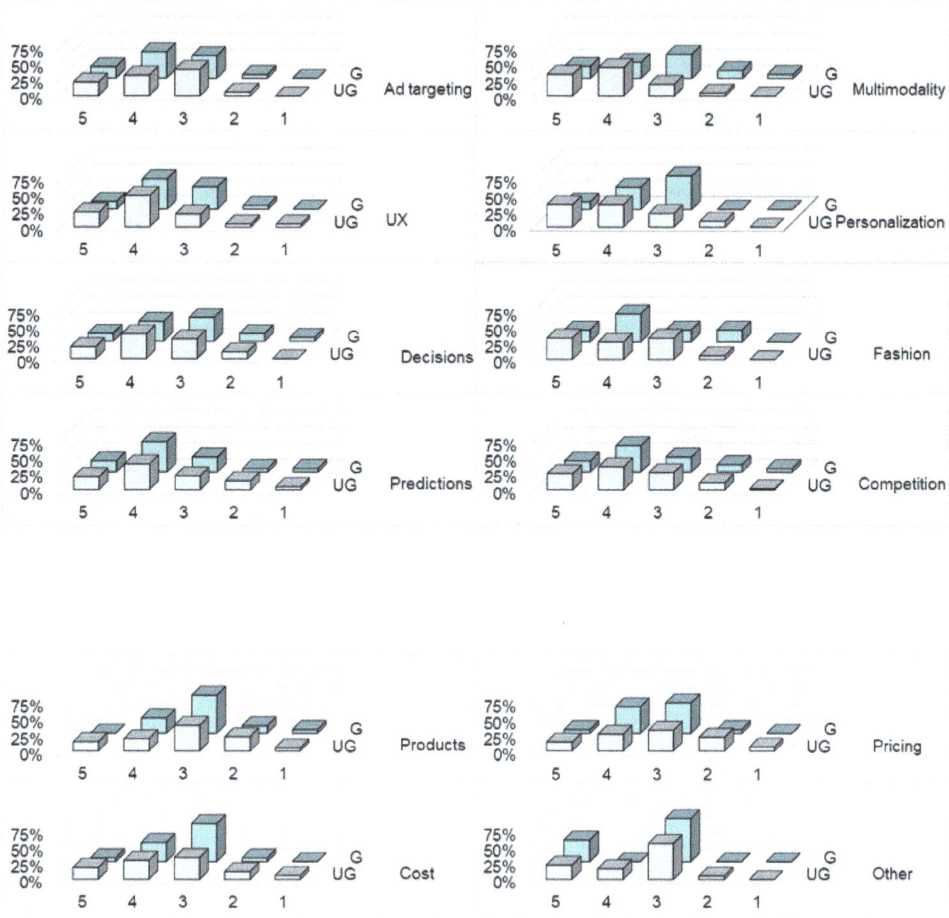

Here, too, in most cases the answer was 4. The exception was assessments of a strong impact on "Personalized offers based on customer behavior", "Following fashion" and "Automation of routine work" for undergraduate students. Graduates are more reserved.

There is also a significant predominance of grades 3 for "Successful products" – for the undergraduates and, especially, for the graduates; "Cost reduction" – for graduate students; "Other types of activity" – for both undergraduate and and graduate students. But this is most likely explained by the typical assessment of an unknown phenomenon.

Recommendations. The use of generative AI in marketing is just beginning, these are only the first steps. In literature, even in recent years, mostly recommendations are given, not description of real implementations. At the same time, negative experience of using generative AI in marketing is accumulating (Pavlidis, 2025).

Therefore, the main thing is to teach students to independently find new tools, evaluate them, be realistic about the results they produce, and, as usual, consider them only as assistants whose activities require careful monitoring.

Another recommendation is to develop the creative potential of students. They will have to find and use new areas of application of generative AI in marketing.

The last section allowed us to obtain information about the respondents themselves.

- The number of bachelors and masters (the data is given above);
- Their plans regarding their future profession are shown in the figure 17.

Figure 17. Career Plans

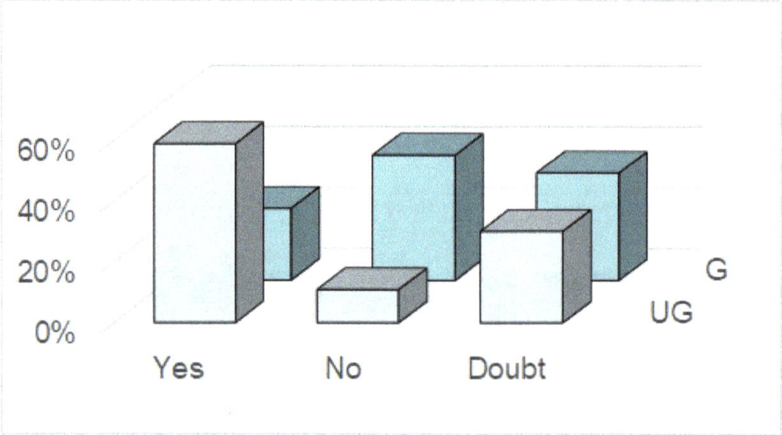

The result is rather strange at first glance.

The first possible reason is that the number of respondents is small, which could have introduced an error.

The second, more important, is that undergraduate students obviously initially came to the marketing specialization, while undergraduates of various specializations, including technical ones, receive a master's qualification in marketing. Marketing is a very broad field, useful for specialists in many professions. So the results of graduates indicate the popularity of marketing direction among future specialists in different fields.

Recommendations. It is necessary to think over the content of the course taking into account the different specifics of bachelor's education of future masters. This is a very difficult task.

CONCLUSION

The incomplete coverage of the target audience may have introduced some inaccuracies, but a detailed analysis of each question revealed a number of interesting facts.

Overall, the students are well acquainted with generative AI and use it extensively. The attitude towards AI is quite realistic: there are few expectations that AI will do the work for students. But the aid of AI in learning is highly appreciated.

An understanding of the great role of generative AI in the future has been revealed, both in the educational process and in professional activities. The demand for acquiring knowledge in this area is urgent, mainly through new teaching methods. There are also high expectations regarding personalized learning.

From the teaching side, it is necessary to reveal the possibilities and limitations of generative AI, and also to teach students to navigate successfully in a very dynamic field from which great results are expected, not all of which are clearly visible at the present time. It is important for improving the learning process today, but it is still more important for their future professional activities.

Although the implementation of a personalized learning management system is a complex task that requires fundamental, but not yet fully understood changes in the learning process, teachers can already improve the process of mastering generative AI by students. Having mastered the capabilities of generative AI, they will be able to prepare teaching materials more effectively.

Both students and teachers have to keep up with the rapid progress of generative AI.

The proposed questionnaire can serve as a basis for systematically collecting data on student opinions. It is important to have a feedback about their opinion. It may be correct or not. Knowing it, it is possible to direct their learning process. But it will be only possible if teachers can clearly see the perspectives of generative artificial intelligence.

Prospects

In the future, it would be advisable to ensure that respondents are interested in a high level of responses so that the results can be broken down by year of study.

This will also help to correctly orient students from the beginning of their studies and give them the knowledge that they need most.

It should be noted that the difference in responses is influenced not only by the number of years spent at the university, but also by the difference in previous digital experience. This can be seen in the results of (Aleshkovsky et al., 2024): the higher the year, the less is experience in using generative AI. On the other hand, in (Buyakova et al., 2024) it is noted that junior students are more optimistic about the prospects for the implementation and use of generative AI in higher education.

Therefore, it is advisable to conduct such studies regularly in order to track the dynamics of changes in attitudes among students of the same class.

In addition, the questionnaire should probably include a number of open-ended questions that will help to identify emerging opinions not covered by the developers of the questionnaire.

In the future, it is planned to create a similar questionnaire for teachers. It will help to monitor the generative AI assisted educational process thoroughly.

REFERENCES

Abramov, A. (2023). A Neural Network Wrote a Thesis for a Russian Student in One Evening. Teachers are Shocked – How to Check Knowledge now? https://www.msk.kp.ru/daily/27460/4714947/

Aleshkovsky, I. A., Gasparishvili, A. T., Narbut, N. P., Kruhmaleva, O. V., & Savina, N. E. (2025). Russian Students on the Possibilities and Limitations of Using Artificial Intelligence in Education. *Bulletin of Peoples' Friendship University of Russia. Series. Sociology*, *24*(2), 335–353. DOI: 10.22363/2313-2272-2024-24-2-335-353

Alexandrova, E. (2024). Artificial Intelligence in Education: Good or Bad? *The World of Robotics*. https://roboticsworld.ru/it-ai/iskusstvennyy-intellekt-v-uchebe-blago-ili-zlo/

Ali, F. (2023). GPT-1 to GPT-4: Each of OpenAI's GPT Models Explained and Compared. *MUO*. https://www.makeuseof.com/gpt-models-explained-and-compared/

Amar, S., & Benchouk, K. (2024). The Role of Generative AI in Higher Education: Fostering Teamwork and Interaction as a Virtual Teaching Assistance. In Lahby, M., Maleh, Y., Bucchiarone, A., & Schaeffer, S. E. (Eds.), *General Aspects of Applying Generative AI in Higher Education*. Springer., DOI: 10.1007/978-3-031-65691-0_3

Ashabokov, B. A., Tashilova, A. A., Kesheva, L. A., Teunova, N. V. (2025). Implementation of a neural network model in the Statistica 12 for mudflow frequency forecasting. *Nauka Innovatsii Tekhnologii*. doi: .DOI: 10.37493/2308-4758.2025.1.2

Bergalieva, A. N., & Keulimzhaeva, A. Zh. (2024) The Influence of Artificial Intelligence on Disease Diagnosis. *Science Bulletin* 12 (81), Vol. 1, 1586–1593. https://www.vestnik-nauki.com/article/19367

Borzykh A.K. (2001). Universal Self-Learning System from Matchboxes. *Computer Tools in Education*, 90–94.

Bozkurt, A. (2024). Tell me Your Prompts and I will Make Them True: The Alchemy of Prompt Engineering and Generative AI. *Open Praxis*, *16*(2), 111–118. DOI: 10.55982/openpraxis.16.2.661

Buyakova, K. I., Dmitriev, Y. A., Ivanova, A. S., Feshchenko, A. V., & Yakovleva, K. I. (2024). The Attitude of Students and Teachers Towards the Use of Tools with Generative Artificial Intelligence in the University. *Education in Science*, *26*(7). Advance online publication. https://cyberleninka.ru/article/n/otnoshenie-studentov-i-prepodavateley-k-ispolzovaniyu-instrumentov-s-generativnym-iskusstvennym-intellektom-v-vuze. DOI: 10.17853/1994-5639-2024-7-160-193

Büyüksomer, A. E., & Tekeoğlu, A. N. T. (2024). Enhancing Marketing Communications with Generative AI: A Systematic Literature Review. *Journal of Industrial Policy and Technology Management*. https://www.jipat.org/index.php/jipat/article/view/188

Chan, C. K. Y., & Hu, W. (2023). Students' Voices on Generative AI: Perceptions, Benefits, and Challenges in Higher Education. *International Journal of Educational Technology in Higher Education*, *20*(1). Advance online publication. DOI: 10.1186/s41239-023-00411-8

Chandrasekaran, A. (2024). Gartner Hype CycleTM for Emerging Technologies. Gartner. https://www.gartner.com/en/articles/hype-cycle-for-emerging-technologies

Chichulin, A. (2023). *AI operator*. Guide for the Artificial Intelligence Operator. Publishing Solutions.

D'Cruze, D. (2025). GPT-5 Launch Plan Revealed: All ChatGPT Users to get Free Access, but Plus, Pro Users to get More. *Business Today*. https://www.businesstoday.in/technology/news/story/gpt-5-launch-plan-revealed-all-chatgpt-users-to-get-free-access-but-plus-pro-users-to-get-more-464449-2025-02-13

Davalos, J., & Yin, L. (2024). Do AI Detectors Work? Students Face False Cheating Accusations. Bloomberg.com. https://www.bloomberg.com/news/features/2024-10-18/do-ai-detectors-work-students-face-false-cheating-accusations

Davide, S., Sciannamè, M., & Ceconello, M. (2024). *User Experience + Artificial Intelligence*. Springer Nature., DOI: 10.1007/978-3-031-77521-5

Deschenes, A., & McMahon, M. (2024). A Survey on Student Use of Generative AI Chatbots for Academic Research. *Evidence Based Library and Information Practice*, *19*(2), 2–22. DOI: 10.18438/eblip30512

Duke, T., & Giudici, P. (2025). *Responsible AI in Practice: A Practical Guide to Safe and Human AI. Apress eBooks*. Apress., DOI: 10.1007/979-8-8688-1166-1

Eloundou, T., Manning, S., Mishkin, P., & Rock, D. (2023). GPTs are GPTs: An Early Look at the Labor Market Impact Potential of Large Language Models. *arXiv* (Cornell University). doi: /arxiv.2303.10130.DOI: 10.48550

European Commission. (2024). Regulatory Framework on AI *Shaping Europe's digital future*. European Commission. https://digital-strategy.ec.europa.eu/en/policies/regulatory-framework-ai

Feuerriegel, S., Hartmann, J., Janiesch, C., & Zschech, P. (2023). Generative AI. *Business & Information Systems Engineering*, *66*(1), 111–126. DOI: 10.1007/s12599-023-00834-7

Garkusha, N., & Gorodove, Ju. (2023). Pedagogical Opportunities of ChatGPT for Developing Cognitive Activity of Students. *Vocational Education and Labour Market*, *1*(52), 6–23. DOI: 10.52944/port.2023.52.1.001

Greceva, I. (2024). How to Write a Diploma or Term Paper Using a Neural Network. *Softline.ru*. https://softline.ru/about/blog/kak-napisat-diplom-ili-kursovuyu-s-pomoshyu-nejroseti

Heyder, T., Passlack, N., & Posegga, O. (2023): Ethical Management of Human-AI Interaction : Theory Development Review, in: *The Journal of Strategic Information Systems : Incorporating International Information Systems*, Amsterdam: Elsevier, Jg. 32, Nr. 3, S. 101772, 1–50, doi: DOI: 10.1016/j.jsis.2023.101772

Howarth, J. (2024). Languages Supported by ChatGPT. Exploding Topics. https://explodingtopics.com/blog/chatgpt-supported-languages

Israfilzade, K. (2025). Benefits and Risks of Generative AI in content marketing. *Adauniversity*. https://www.academia.edu/123673514/Benefits_and_Risks_of_Generative_AI_in_Content_Marketing. doi: DOI: 10.5281/ZENODO.13731679

Keffer, L. (2023). Minister of Education and Science Falkov Urged not to Punish a Graduate who Wrote his Thesis Using ChatGPT. *Kommersant*. https://www.kommersant.ru/doc/5812075

Khadzakos, N. (2024). 21st Century Student: How to Use AI in the Learning Process? *Habr*. https://habr.com/ru/articles/820375/

Koroleva, D., Pivovarova, X., Zagranichmy, A., Kolabinova, A., Andreeva, A., Podlipskaya, Y., Arzumanyan, M., & Ronanchenko, A. (2025). *Global Education Trends in the Russian Context* – 2025. Ioe.hse.ru. https://ioe.hse.ru/edu_global_trends/2025/

Kotler, P., Kartajaya, H., & Setiawan, I. (2023). *Marketing 6.0*. Wiley.

Kukitz, P. (2024). Challenges and Prospects of Implementing Generative Artificial Intelligence Tools in Business Marketing Activities. *Economic Development Research Journal*. 22–30.

Kumar, S. (2024). Risks from Generative AI. https://ssrn.com/abstract=4858973 or http://dx.doi.org/DOI: 10.2139/ssrn.4858973

Lafferly, J. (2025). Generative AI Regulations – What Your Business Needs To Know for 2025. https://www.salesforce.com/blog/generative-ai-regulations/

Lahby, M. (Ed.). (2024a). Empowering Digital Education with ChatGPT. *CRC Press is*. doi: DOI: 10.1201/9781032716350

Lahby, M. (Ed.). (2024b). *General Aspects of Applying Generative AI in Higher Education*. Springer Nature., DOI: 10.1007/978-3-031-65691-0

Lahby, M., Maleh, Y., Bucchiarone, A., & Satu, E. S. (Eds.). (2024). *General Aspects of Applying Generative AI in Higher Education*. Springer., https://www.alibris.com/search/ebooks/isbn/9783031656903

Lem, S. (1978). *Summa Technologiae*. Insel Verlag.

Lu, D. (2025). We Tried out DeepSeek. It Worked Well, Until we Asked it about Tiananmen Square and Taiwan. *The Guardian*; The Guardian. https://www.theguardian.com/technology/2025/jan/28/we-tried-out-deepseek-it-works-well-until-we-asked-it-about-tiananmen-square-and-taiwan

Luo, Y., & Dan, X. (2025). China Releases New Labeling Requirements for AI-Generated Content. *Lexology*. https://www.lexology.com/library/detail.aspx?g=1e66cce9-1936-4e63-96f0-5fdf378a8a04

Malyshev, I. O. (2024). Overview of Modern Generative Neural Networks: Domestic and Foreign Practice. *International Journal of Humanities and Natural Sciences, 1-2*(88), 168–171. https://cyberleninka.ru/article/n/obzor-sovremennyh-generativnyh-neyrosetey-otechestvennaya-i-zarubezhnaya-praktika. DOI: 10.24412/2500-1000-2024-1-2-168-171

Mamikonyan, O. (2023). Half of Russian Students Use Neural Networks in Their Studies. *Forbes.ru*. https://www.forbes.ru/forbeslife/495175-polovina-rossijskih-studentov-ispol-zuut-nejroseti-v-ucebe

McCulloch, W. S., & Pitts, W. (1943). A Logical Calculus of the Ideas Immanent in Nervous Activity. *The Bulletin of Mathematical Biophysics, 5*(4), 115–133. DOI: 10.1007/bf02478259

Mikhailov, E. (2023). Students Cheat From ChatGPT. Is Education Under Threat? (It's Not That Simple). *Afisha Daily*. https://daily.afisha.ru/culture/25132-studenty-spisyvayut-u-chatgpt-obrazovanie-pod-ugrozoy-vse-ne-tak-prosto/

Mikhalev, M. (2020). Individualization is Useless if the University Thinks in the Old Way. *RBC Trends*. https://trends.rbc.ru/trends/education/cmrm/5fe06c989a794774a4861cd3?from=copy

Mustakrimov, V. (2023). GPT for Students. Publishing Solutions. https://mybook.ru/author/vyacheslav-mustakimov-2/gpt-studentam-580promptov-sposobnyh-reshit-lyubuyu/

Mylrea, M. (2025). The Generative AI Weapon of Mass Destruction: Evolving Disinformation Threats, Vulnerabilities, and Mitigation Frameworks. *Interdependent Human-Machine Teams*, 315–347). Academic Press. doi: .DOI: 10.1016/B978-0-443-29246-0.00007-9

Neural Networks for Writing a Thesis (2024). giga.chat. https://giga.chat/help/articles/ai-for-diploma.

Ningsih, W., & Lahby, M. (2024). The Potential of GPT in Education. *Chapman and Hall/CRC eBooks*, 247–263. doi: .DOI: 10.1201/9781032716350-17

Othman, M. H. (2023). Students' Perceptions and Understanding of Elective Courses and Their Effects on Academic Performance. [MJSSH]. *Malaysian Journal of Social Sciences and Humanities*, *8*(3), e002171. DOI: 10.47405/mjssh.v8i3.2171

Patrecia, M. (2025). The Future of Marketing: AI Transformations by 2025. *ContentGrip*. https://www.contentgrip.com/future-ai-marketing/ or DOI: 10.61796/ijaifd.v1i4.185

Pavlidis, E. (2025). The Good, the Bad, and the Ugly: Generative AI in Marketing in 2025. *SIXGUN*. https://sixgun.com.au/insights/the-good-the-bad-and-the-ugly-generative-ai-in-marketing-in-2025/

Perov, R. (2024). How to Use the GigaChat Neural Network in 2025. *Hi-Tech Mail*. https://hi-tech.mail.ru/review/109793-kak-polzovatsya-nejrosetyu-gigachat/#anchor17157754334643962

Petrov, D. (2023). How Artificial Intelligence is Changing the Future of Medicine. *Forbes.ru*. https://www.forbes.ru/mneniya/488597-kak-iskusstvennyj-intellekt-menaet-budusee-mediciny?utm_source=yandex.ru&utm_medium=organic&utm_campaign=yandex.ru&utm_referrer=yandex.ru

Quillian, C. (2025). *AI for Life*. Adams Media.

Randieri, C. (2024). Council Post: Personalized Learning And AI: Revolutionizing Education. *Forbes*, *12*(Aug). https://www.forbes.com/councils/forbestechcouncil/2024/07/22/personalized-learning-and-ai-revolutionizing-education/

Rechetnikova, M. (2025). What is the DeepSeek Neural Network: a Chatbot with an Internet Search Option. *RBC TrendS*. https://trends.rbc.ru/trends/industry/67920b739a794768fab8fe92

Rhinehart, R. R. (2018). Genetic Algorithms and Evolutionary Computation. *ASME Press eBooks*, 243–252. doi: .DOI: 10.1115/1.861opt_ch14

Rosenberg, L. (2023). Generative AI as a Dangerous New Form of Media. *Proceedings*, 165–170. doi: .DOI: 10.54808/imsci2023.01.165

Sherman, N. (2024). AI Regulations Around the World. Mind Foundry. Acceptable at: https://www.mindfoundry.ai/blog/ai-regulations-around-the-world

Singla, A., Sukharevsky, A., Yee, L., & Chui, M. (2024). The State of AI in early 2024: Gen AI Adoption Spikes and Starts to Generate Value. *McKinsey & Company*. https://www.mckinsey.com/capabilities/quantumblack/our-insights/the-state-of-ai/

Sorokin, V. (2024). How to Use YandexGPT in 2025. *Hi-Tech Mail*. https://hi-tech.mail.ru/review/109799-kak-polzovatsya-yandexgpt/#anchor171575595670418014

Trapeznikov, V., & Zinovieva, E. (2024). Neural Networks and Generative AI in Higher Education: International Experience and Russian Practice. *Russian International Affairs Council*. https://russiancouncil.ru/analytics-and-comments/analytics/neyroseti-generativnyy-ii-v-vysshem-obrazovanii-mezhdunarodnyy-opyt-i-rossiyskaya-praktika/

Tyugashev, E. (2025). Clip thinking – a modern form of zero-dimensional thinking. *BULLETIN of Samara State Technical University. Series. Philosophy (London, England)*, *7*(1), 91–102. https://journals.eco-vector.com/2658-7750/article/view/692897/208432

University, H. S. E. (2024). Survey on the Use of Artificial Intelligence by University Students. *Ict.moscow*. https://ict.moscow/projects/ai/research/opros-o-primenenii-iskusstvennogo-intellekta-uchashchimisia-vuzov/.

Vetrova, E. (2024). AI in Education: Statistics, Implementation, Advantages, Problems. *VirtRe*. https://virtre.ru/articles/artificial-intelligence/ii-v-obrazovanii-statistika-vnedrenie-preimushhestva-problemy

Vologzshanin, G. (2025). What Can the Chinese Neural Network DeepSeek Do on Android and How is it Better than ChatGPT – AndroidInsider.ru. *Androidinsider.ru*. https://androidinsider.ru/obzory-prilozhenij/chto-umeet-kitajskaya-nejroset-deepseek-na-android-i-chem-ona-luchshe-chatgpt.html

Vorobjev, D. (2023). 'They'll Find a Loophole': Analyst on Banning a Chatbot for Writing Diplomas. *National News Service – NSN*. https://nsn.fm/nauka-i-tehnologii/naidut-lazeiku-analitik-ne-verit-v-zapret-chat-bota-po-napisaniu-diplomov

Wazan, A. S., Taj, I., Shoufan, A., Laborde, R., & Venant, R. (2023). How to Design and Deliver Courses for Higher Education in the AI Era: Insights from Exam Data Analysis. *arXiv (Cornell University)*. doi: /arxiv.2308.02441.DOI: 10.48550

White, J. (2024). People Want to Know: Which are the Top Seven Branches of Artificial Intelligence? *Tech Rays*. https://techrays.net/top-seven-branches-of-artificial-intelligence/

Xue, J., & Shen, B. (2020). A Novel Swarm Intelligence Optimization Approach: Sparrow Search Algorithm. *Systems Science & Control Engineering*, *8*(1), 22–34. DOI: 10.1080/21642583.2019.1708830

Yaprak, B. (2024). Generative Artificial Intelligence in Marketing: The Invisible Danger of AI Hallucinations. *Economica Işletme Ve Yonetim Dergisi*, *8*(2), 133–158. DOI: 10.7596/jebm.1588897

Yuyun, I., & Suherdi, D. (2023). Components and Strategies for Personalized Learning in Higher Education. *Systematic Reviews*. Advance online publication. DOI: 10.2991/978-2-38476-054-1_23

Zhadan, A. (2023). I Defended my Thesis, which I Wrote Using ChatGPT. https://journal.tinkoff.ru/neuro-diploma/

Zhu, Z. (2024). What Businesses Can Learn from McKinsey's 2024 Global Survey on AI Adoption. Mitchell E. Daniels, Jr. School of Business. https://business.purdue.edu/daniels-insights/posts/2024/global-survey-on-ai-adoption.php

Chapter 4
Digital Emotional Intelligence in Hybridized Workplace: Does it Fortitude Decision-Making

Sukhmeet Kaur
https://orcid.org/0000-0002-3363-6844
INTI International University, Malaysia

Babita Yadav
Doctor Harisingh Gour Central University, Sagar, India

Saloni Devi
University of Jammu, India

ABSTRACT

Emotional Intelligence plays an important role in the progressively involved digital workplace where face-to-face interactions are often less prioritized by digital infrastructures like emails, social media networks, and ICT tools. Emotional Intelligent leaders make more empathetic and harmonious decisions, reduce conflicts, and resilience approach towards the virtual environment. The chapter sheds light on Digital Emotional Intelligence (DEQ) in management decision-making in a hybridized workplace. The chapter conducted PRISMA research methodology and Daniel Goleman's EI Model to investigate and synthesize the literature in the management and administration area. The studies on DEQ are very limited, therefore the findings are novel and practical in the present digitalized workplace for decision-makers. The chapter concluded four DIEI quadrants corresponding to four digital skills, and competencies for self-awareness, social awareness, self-management, and relationship management which fortitude decision-making

DOI: 10.4018/979-8-3373-8612-6.ch004

1. INTRODUCTION

Conventionally, it could be argued that the employees should be qualified and their job skills must be matched with their job characteristics. It has been important for organizations to understand, evaluate, and utilize their emotions and those of others. Communication skills, mutual trust, resilience of emotions, empathetic thinking, and self-perception have pushed organizations to reach desired performance. In the age of digital communication, digital competencies, the ability to use techno-devices, to learn new digital skills, digital awareness, and openness to acquire digital skills, are another step forward to meet competition. The way of doing work has been extremely transformed, post the COVID-19 pandemic. It is right to say that managing emotions, technical knowledge, the Internet of Things, and emotional intelligence are as important as digital intelligence.

Today, we experience emotions that flash daily and need to recognize them and manage the rate of innovation, creativity, and information flow. Dynamics of emotions are the most important investment in creating a strong sense of convenience and commitment. The chapter outlines the understanding of how digital technologies and human emotions interplay with each other and permeate every aspect of decision-making. We must be vigilant not to lose our train of thought and emotions in the cloud of the Internet of Things, Machine Learning, Metacognition, Metaverse, and Artificial Intelligence. Emotions are complex, and like the weather of the day. The state of feelings changes multiple times on a particular day. A classical theory of emotions proposed six basic states of emotions: happiness, sadness, fear, anger, surprise, and disgust (Ekman, 1992). In the real world, these emotions are coached by our body language, tone, and facial expressions that help in expressing, communicating, and surviving. With the advent of the digital world, these emotions are less visible behind the curtain of digital interfaces. However, human emotions are the same, but now we primarily connect through digital technologies. The synchronicity of body language, actions, and facial expressions is beaten by emojis and digital emotions (Kramer et al., 2014). (Cherbonnier & Michinov, 2021) massive experiment (N = 689,003) showed that emotions can spread throughout social networking sites. The study suggests that expressing emotions on social networking sites is contagious even without any presence of non-verbal clues and in-person interaction. Digital emotions can be experienced in one's physique with the interface of the digital environment around us, for instance, smartphones, smartwatches, online streaming sites, social texting sites, electronic gadgets, etc., through which we express, communicate, and act. Emoji is a new non-verbal online language and is 80% more effective in communicating thoughts and emotions on digital platforms (George et al., 2023).

With the excessive practice of using digital tools and social networking sites, users are increasingly tangled with multimedia interactions, i.e., audio, texts, visuals, illustrations, animations, and virtual realities. This makes people deal with a bulk of emotional cues in the digital context (Steinert & Dennis, 2022). In academic literature, digital circumstantial and emotional intelligence are being pointed out in terms of digital well-being. (Bhattacharya et al., 2023), emotion contagion (Goldenberg & Gross, 2020; Kramer et al., 2014), digital emotion regulation (Wadley, Smith, et al., 2020) and digital emotional intelligence(Audrin & Audrin, 2023).

1.1 Emotional Intelligence

Emotional Intelligence (EI) has a significant role in our essential and professional lives. EI has gained momentous interest in academic and organizational studies. EI has shown its impact on navigating burnout (Szczygiel & Mikolajczak, 2018), better work attitude (Miao et al., 2017), and better task performance(Salovey & Mayer, 1989). EI is described as "the ability to monitor one's own and others' feelings and emotions, to discriminate among them, and to use this information to guide one's thinking and actions"(Salovey & Mayer, 1990; p.189).

1.2 Digital Emotional Intelligence (DEQ)

The concept of digital emotional intelligence (DEQ) has already been used in many business industries (Kaur & Sharma, 2021). AI has tremendously impacted retail (Eubanks, 2022) However, the understanding of EI in the digital context we live in today and communicate in has changed. In the field of management administration, (Kaur & Sharma, 2021) emphasized that AI has the power to expand human intelligence and empower smart decision-making. Artificial Intelligence can be used to observe and analyze employees' emotions and moods before and after making decisions. AI can detect stress-related behavior, tone, and attitude toward the decision-making process.

Recently, (Audrin & Audrin, 2023) introduced a concept of "digital emotional intelligence," emphasizing it as "EI in a digital world (p.3). Authors labeled 'digital ability emotional intelligence' (dAEI) progress from 'digital competencies'(DC) and 'trait emotional intelligence' (TEI) to evaluate digital emotional intelligence. (Völker & Mannheim, 2021) advocate that the more people are emotionally intelligent, the more responsive they are toward emotional information. A notable study (Pitts et al., 2012) investigated that emotional intelligence positively predicted team viability when virtual teams communicate online. (Warrier et al., 2024) showed that the effectiveness of communication can positively increase the effectiveness of decision-making.

Taken together, this strong literature highlights the role of online behavior or digital emotional intelligence in digital interaction and collaboration, which can lead to accessing our emotion recognition and management, and higher performance, better decision-making, conflict management, and emotion management.

The chapter aims to understand the importance of digital emotional intelligence in making management decisions.

(1) RQ1 What is the development of Digital Emotional Intelligence (DEQ) in the management and administration field?
(2) RQ2 What is the role of Digital Emotional Intelligence (DEQ) in strengthening decision-making in a hybrid workplace?
(3) RQ3 How can digital interactions and Goleman's Emotional Intelligence Model (EI) be applied in a hybrid workplace?

2. RESEARCH METHODOLOGY

2.1 Research Approach

The study used qualitative and exploratory methods to explore the development of DEQ in a management administration setting. It is a conceptual study based on a systematic literature review to gain deeper insights into the concept of DEQ and its role in decision-making in digital interaction. A systematic literature review (SLR) identifies transparent and quality review processes that enable researchers to integrate past databases and existing knowledge (Sambunjak et al., 2021).

2.2 Materials and Methods

To inquire about the concept of digital emotional intelligence in the modern management world, a systematic literature review was carried out with the purposively knowing the characteristics of emotional intelligence and digital interaction within the management disciplinary area. We aimed to review the current literature related to digital emotional intelligence in the management discipline. We followed the guidelines (Page et al., 2021), PRISMA 2020 flowchart in Figure 1 for the final development of the concept.

2.3 Search Location Strategy

The collection of related studies was done through the research database 'Google Scholar, Web of Science,' and 'EBSCO' portals with relevant management and administrative chapters from 2019 to 2024. The following search terms were used in combination: ("Emotional Intelligence" OR "Digital Intelligence" OR "Virtual

Intelligence" OR "Digital Emotional Intelligence") AND ("Business" OR "Management" OR "Administration").

2.4 Inclusion and Exclusion Criteria

To explore the scope, the author established four inclusion criteria. First, the articles had to be interrelated to emotional intelligence and digital interactions or interventions together. Second, the article had to be a full-text article written in English. Third, the article originally focused on management or business-related outcomes or applications. The last criterion was five from (2019-2024). Meanwhile, the exclusion criteria contain (1) articles that are not focused on emotional intelligence or digital interactions together; (2) articles from non-management disciplines; (3) articles written in non-English; and (4) articles that only focus on emotional intelligence but not digital interactions or context. To delimit the search, the rejected documents include misprints, pre-print publications, and false positives, i.e., do not address the defined research question criteria.

Figure 1. SLR for the Development of DEQ

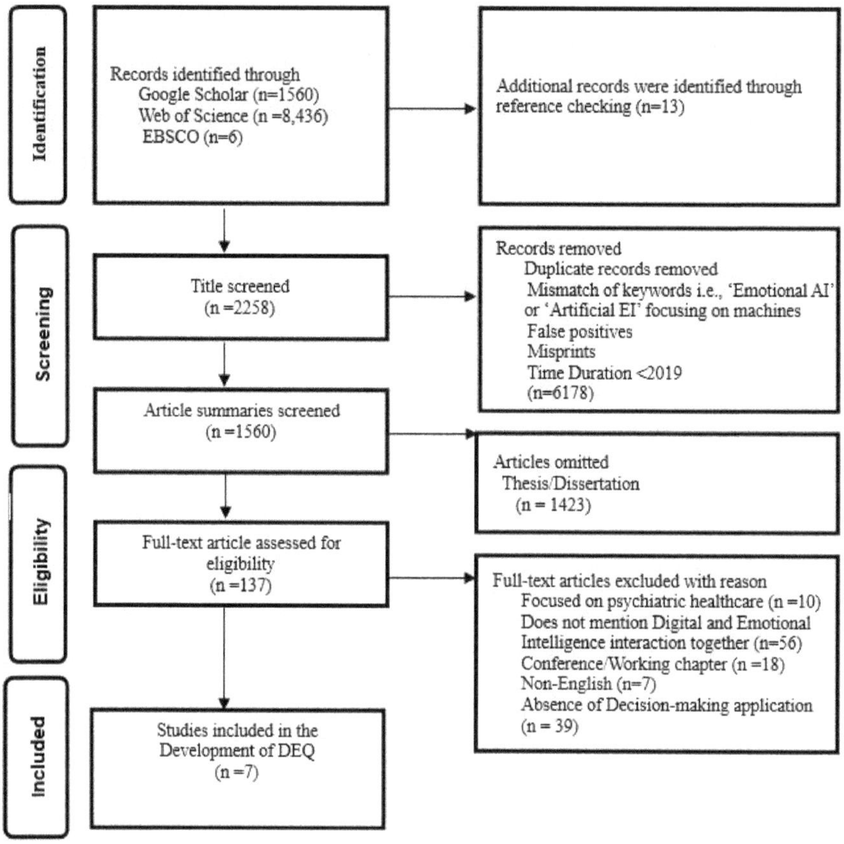

Source: Flowchart of SLR (PRISMA Method)

3. FINDINGS AND DISCUSSION

3.1 DEQ-Management and Administration Field

Emotion Intelligence is explained as "the subset of social intelligence that involves the ability to monitor one's own and others' feelings and emotions, to discriminate among them, and to use this information to guide one's thinking and actions" (Salovey & Mayer, 1990; p.189). Research on emotions has enormously increased in the fields of engineering, technology, medical science, computer science, and psychology. It is very common to be influenced by emotions in our daily routine and at the workplace. The real conversations are entirely different from online chats and interactions. Unprofessional feedback, comments, or updates on digital platforms may play with our emotions and lead to wrong decisions. Therefore, the development of digital emotional intelligence (DEQ) in the management field is imperative to understand. The findings (Table 1) of the SLR support that the development of DEQ is very limited and emerging in the management and administration field.

Table 1. SLR of DEQ Development

Source	DEQ Development
(Audrin & Audrin, 2023)	Developed a "Digital Emotional Intelligence" conceptual model with two key linkages: 'Trait Emotional Intelligence' - 'Digital Competence' and 'Digital Competence'- 'Ability Emotional Intelligence.' DEQ positively supports tasks on remote hybrid teams, virtual teams, organizational performance, and digital learning setups
(Kumar & Martin, 2023)	'Artificial Emotional Intelligence' was used to detect the changes in emotions, body language, and gestures in human-machine interaction-based technology.
(Leeuw & Joseph, 2023)	DEQ can assist individuals in agile workplace environments, such as dealing with ambiguity, uncertainty, misunderstanding, digital distractions, and prioritizing tasks. DEQ enables more informed decisions by considering the viewpoints and emotions of others.
(Santana & Díaz-Fernández, 2023)	DEQ offers the essential digital competencies to navigate organizational challenges to adapt HRM with AI DEQ is an emerging theme for performing technological tasks where decision-making is required.
(Yeke, 2023)	'Digital Intelligence 'and 'Emotional Intelligence' are inseparable in business-making tasks and decisions. A strong connection between a 'Digital Mindset,' 'Digital Efficiency,' and 'Emotional Intelligence' can enable one to understand the warmth, concerns, and emotions of business administration tasks.
(Audrin & Audrin, 2024)	DEQ can support in assessment of the performance of EI adapted to digital contexts The mingling of digital dimensions in EI can be assessed with media richness and media synchronicity theories.
(Vicci, 2024)	'AI Emotional Intelligence' allows ethical-moral-based judgment and decisions. Digital emotional experience creates empathy and connectedness with technology-related tasks like education, health, and the management industry.

Source: Author

The task-technology fit (TTF) theory stems from information systems research (Vanduhe et al., 2020). The concept of task-technology fit was established by focusing on the fit between the individual, the task, and the technology. The theory of TTF states that the higher the fit between digital systems (software, hardware, and data), the individual abilities (experience, training, motivation) will contribute a better performance; therefore, tasks associated with technology will be accomplished with accuracy (D. L. Goodhue, 1998). In the practical world, most knowledge workers depend on digital data and platforms for sharing, collaborating, and allocating job duties. To cope with digital stress and improve cognition and emotional response, individuals make efforts to find potential options to regulate it (D. L. Goodhue, 1998; Lazarus & Folkman, 1984; Tarafdar et al., 2007; Vendramin et al., 2021). In the digital context, TTF represents the fit between the explicit digital task knowledge (sharing files, type of data, presentation, communication) and responsiveness towards technology or digital interactions (present state of consciousness, i.e., knowing what, how, and which technology) that contribute to better decision-making outcomes. This alignment involves digital emotional intelligence, reducing the technostress factor, and increasing decision-making quality and accuracy. Research indicates that TTF theory accentuates the alignment of the critical role of digital response with emotion-cognition response in facilitating decision-making tasks. Theory has been implemented in many other areas of research: virtual teams (Zigurs & Khazanchi, 2008), team performance (Fuller & Dennis, 2009), and managerial decision-making (D. Goodhue et al., 2000). Digital emotional intelligence individuals are more sensitive in interpersonal digital networks. The intelligent use of emotions during digital conversation provides possible accuracy of decisions. Emotion recognition and regulation make people more confident and creative. Nonetheless (Nasef Zaki et al., 2018) argued that emotional intelligence is an additional factor in making decisions valuable, where experience and time also play a substantial role. The digital space is jam-packed with a lot of information, relevant or irrelevant, organized or unorganized, organic or inorganic, and accurate or inaccurate. It is not necessary to consider all digital cues, data, and algorithms in decision-making. Numerous studies found that digital-based texts or communication are perceived as less predictable for emotional and social tasks than non-social-emotional tasks due to their less information or dubious communication cues (Rice, 1992; Rice et al., 1989). However, the relationship between the individual and performance "fits" when the medium or information is rich (Rice, 1992). The media richness theory (MRT) concept was introduced by (Daft & Lengel, 1983), which encapsulates coping strategies with communication challenges such as unclear and confusing messages or conflicting interpretations of messages. MRT ranks the "media richness" based on the competence to process it. For instance, face-to-face is the richest medium with instant feedback, multiple cues, natural language, and personalized (Daft & Lengel, 1986). User experience "media leanness" with restricted feedback and cues like impersonal documents, databases, rules, and regulations (Daft & Lengel, 1986). Therefore, the hierarchy of media richness is elucidated by (1) handling multiple information cues at the same time, (2) rapid feedback, (3) language variety, and (4)

Person focus (Bodensteiner, 1970; Daft & Lengel, 1983; Lengel & Daft, 1988). To highlight the research objective, Table 2 merges the above two theories.

Table 2. Theoretical Development of DEQ

TRADITIONAL MEDIA (MEDIA RICHNESS & TASK-TECHNOLOGY FIT THEORY)		
Information Medium	**Information Richness**	**Task Fit**
Face-to-Face	Highest	The alignment or fit of technical assistance or technology tools intensifies in executing tasks or sets of tasks with increased technological functionalities and performance.
Telephone	High	
Written & Personal (Letters & Memos)	Moderate	
Written & Formal (Bulletin Documents)	Low	
Numeric Formal (Computer Output)	Lowest	
DIGITAL MEDIA		
Websites, Blogs, Video Clips, Digital Records	Lowest	The alignment or fit of technical assistance or technology tools intensifies in executing tasks or sets of tasks with increased technological functionalities and performance.
Audio Notes, Audio Calls, Instant Messages	Low	
Social media	Moderate	
Video Conferencing, Live Chat, Chatbots	High	
Virtual Worlds (AI, VR, AV, Metaverse)	Highest	

Source: Adopted Model (Daft & Lengel, 1983; p.8 & D. L. Goodhue & Thompson, 1995)

3.2 DEQ in Decision-making-Managerial Implications

Emotional Intelligence allows us to be 'emotionally awake' to our own and those of others. We can make balanced decisions based on digital information and acquaintances. The succeeding section will explore how digital emotional intelligence intertwines with decision-making. Supervision of digital protocols, technology acceptance, trust, and virtual team motivation is significant for the effectiveness of online virtual members. (Rezgui, 2007). High emotional intelligence can affect the strengths of rational decision-making on virtual communication platforms. (Warrier et al., 2024).

(Ahmad et al., 2023) examined that excessive use of artificial intelligence in our daily lives leads to the loss of human decision-making power. The study shows that

27.7% of the loss of decision-making is due to dependency on artificial intelligence. The computerized work and boundless applications result in dependency, laziness, and limits in decision-making. This time-saving digital assistance essentially disables the human emotional cognition process by lowering cognitive capabilities (Jarrahi, 2018); increasing technostress (Tarafdar et al., 2007); lessening intuitive and creative problem-solving in decision-making (Ghosh et al., 2019). The study argues that intuition affects decision-making, which is an intrapersonal aspect of emotional intelligence (Dane & Pratt, 2007).

COVID-19 initiated sudden and unintended virtual teams with no previously cited directions and operating guidelines to recognize emotions and communicate accordingly. Joining online sessions and virtual conferences was more limited to attending than being emotionally present. The transition from interacting at a regular workplace to home or virtual workspaces leads to more seamless familiarity with technology and more seamless avoidance of unwanted anxiety. However, the failure to adapt led to technostress, i.e., the inability to use and learn digital technologies (Kaur et al., 2024; Tarafdar et al., 2007). Emotional intelligence competencies will assist in coping with digital adversities (Warrier et al., 2024). The role of emotion in decision-making is important. The quality of decision-making can be improved with highly thoughtful emotions (Perkins, 2023; Spicer & Sadler-Smith, 2005). Therefore, emotional intelligence helps in the decision-making process by considering all relevant information online (Alzoubi & Aziz, 2021; O, 2004).

3.3 Digital Interactions with Goleman's EI Model

The future of digital emotional intelligence (DEQ) proves industries using emotion analytics in decision-making, using an emotion chip, and emotion recognition. Companies are using empathy and emotional understanding to modify their entire workplace with an emotive business. Digital Interaction refers to the communication and exchange of information or experience that occurs through digital platforms like emails, video conferencing, virtual events, online chats, social media platforms, webinars, text messaging, online classes, etc. Therefore, (Figure 2.) connecting digital interactions with Goleman's emotional intelligence model would guide us in assessing individual DEQ. For the third research question, we refer to the use of Daniel Goleman's model (2002) with four domains.

Digital Interactions with Self-Awareness

It is the first and most significant quadrant of EI. Self-awareness is a basic ability to understand how we feel and recognize how it can impact others in social relationships and digital interactions.

Digital Interactions with Self-Management

Self-management is the second quadrant of EI. It is the ability to regulate one's emotions, feelings, and thoughts in a sense of self-connectedness to others.

Digital Interactions with Social Awareness

Social Awareness is the third quadrant of EI. It is sensing what others are thinking and feeling, and reading the situation using empathetic and organizational capacity.

Digital Interactions with Relationship Management

It is the last quadrant of EI that pulls together all three quadrants to create relationship management on digital interactions. This quadrant also refers to "friendliness with a purpose" to influence others' reactions to make a good decision, manage conflicts, and work with teams.

Figure 2. Digital Interactions-Goleman's EI Model (DIEI)

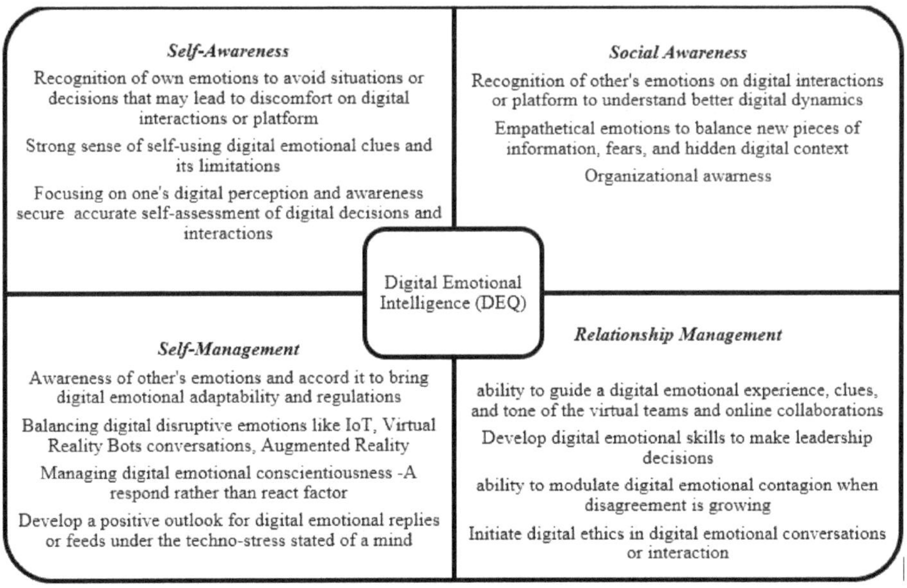

Source: Author's Work

4. CONCLUSION AND LIMITATIONS

Digital emotional intelligence (DEQ) is an emerging interest in management and organizational studies. The ability to digitally sense the emotional response of others and self to use effective information or data to make decisions and act accordingly. DEQ allows us to apply real-time digital data from smart technologies and environments to build intelligent connections and smart decisions. However, the studies on DEQ also vary with the context of the studying environment for instance, the literature based on "digital Emotion Regulation (ER)" as a "process in which people evaluate their emotions about their current goals and decide whether to modify them and, if so, select which regulation strategy to use" (Wadley et al., 2020). Some researchers identified ER as a motive for using digital tools. For example, using digital music platforms to cope with stress and problems (Wadley, Krause, et al., 2020). Balancing terms like Digital Well-being ((Cao & Li, 2023) and Digital Literacy (Estrada et al., 2022) also studied the behavioral and emotional responses in digital settings. In the business world (Yeke, 2023) specified that digital intelligence and emotional intelligence cannot be disconnected from each other and should be harmonized with each other. Authors would like to quote a line from Roger Ebert (1992): "*Your intellect may be confused, but your emotions will never lie to you.*"

The study is limited to the explorative-descriptive research method. Future research can embed hypothesis testing to reveal strong empirical results, which is not the aim of this study. It is anticipated that the discussion presented above will be developed with extended models given intelligence disciplines such as social sciences, psychology, marketing, technology, and human behavior. Further studies can also investigate other management applications such as leadership style, personality type, coping, decision fatigue, analysis, or choice paralysis.

REFERENCES

Ahmad, S. F., Han, H., Alam, M. M., Rehmat, M. K., Irshad, M., Arraño-Muñoz, M., & Ariza-Montes, A. (2023). Impact of artificial intelligence on human loss in decision making, laziness and safety in education. *Humanities & Social Sciences Communications*, *10*(1), 1–14. DOI: 10.1057/s41599-023-01787-8 PMID: 37325188

Alzoubi, H. M., & Aziz, R. (2021). Does emotional intelligence contribute to quality of strategic decisions? The mediating role of open innovation. *Journal of Open Innovation*, *7*(130). Advance online publication. DOI: 10.3390/joitmc7020130

Audrin, C., & Audrin, B. (2023). More than just emotional intelligence online: Introducing "digital emotional intelligence.". *Frontiers in Psychology*, *14*(1). Advance online publication. DOI: 10.3389/fpsyg.2023.1154355 PMID: 37205063

Audrin, C., & Audrin, B. (2024). Emotional intelligence in digital interactions – A call for renewed assessments. *Personality and Individual Differences*, *223*, 112613. https://doi.org/https://doi.org/10.1016/j.paid.2024.112613

Bhattacharya, S., Bhattacharya, S., Vallabh, V., Marzo, R. R., Juyal, R., & Gokdemir, O. (2023). Digital Well-being Through the Use of Technology-A Perspective. *International Journal of MCH and AIDS*, *12*(1), e588. DOI: 10.21106/ijma.588 PMID: 36683649

Bodensteiner, W. D. (1970). *Information channel utilization under varying research and development project conditions: an aspect of inter-organizational communication channel usage.*

Cao, S., & Li, H. (2023). A Scoping Review of Digital Well-Being in Early Childhood: Definitions, Measurements, Contributors, and Interventions. *International Journal of Environmental Research and Public Health*, *20*(4), 1–20. DOI: 10.3390/ijerph20043510 PMID: 36834204

Cherbonnier, A., & Michinov, N. (2021). The recognition of emotions beyond facial expressions: Comparing emoticons specifically designed to convey basic emotions with other modes of expression. *Computers in Human Behavior*, *118*. Advance online publication. DOI: 10.1016/j.chb.2021.106689

Daft, R., & Lengel, R. (1983). Information Richness. A New Approach to Managerial Behavior and Organization Design. *Research in Organizational Behavior*, *6*, 73.

Daft, R., & Lengel, R. (1986). Organizational Information Requirements, Media Richness and Structural Design. *Management Science*, *32*, 554–571. DOI: 10.1287/mnsc.32.5.554

Dane, E., & Pratt, M. G. (2007). Exploring Intuition and its Role in Managerial Decision Making. *Academy of Management Review*, *32*(1), 33–54. DOI: 10.5465/amr.2007.23463682

Ekman, P. (1992). An argument for basic emotions. *Cognition and Emotion*, *6*(3–4), 169–200. DOI: 10.1080/02699939208411068

Estrada, F. J. R., George-Reyes, C. E., & Glasserman-Morales, L. D. (2022). Security as an emerging dimension of Digital Literacy for education: A systematic literature review. *Journal of E-Learning and Knowledge Society*, *18*(2), 22–33. DOI: 10.20368/1971-8829/1135440

Eubanks, B. (2022). *Artificial Intelligence for HR: Use AI to Support and Develop a Successful Workforce* (2nd, illustr ed.). Kogan Page. https://books.google.nl/books?id=NGBuzgEACAAJ

Fuller, R. M., & Dennis, A. R. (2009). Does fit matter? The impact of task-technology fit and appropriation on team performance in repeated tasks. *Information Systems Research*, *20*(1), 2–17. DOI: 10.1287/isre.1070.0167

George, A. S., George, A., & Baskar, D. (2023). Emoji Unite: Examining the Rise of Emoji as an International Language Bridging Cultural and Generational Divides. *Partners Universal International Innovation Journal*, *01*(4), 183–204. DOI: 10.5281/zenodo.8280356

Ghosh, B., Wilson, J. H., Burden, A., & Daugherty, P. H. (2019). *Taking a Systems Approach to Adopting AI*. Harvard Business Review. https://hbr.org/2019/05/taking-a-systems-approach-to-adopting-ai

Goldenberg, A., & Gross, J. J. (2020). Digital Emotion Contagion. *Trends in Cognitive Sciences*, *24*(4), 316–328. https://doi.org/https://doi.org/10.1016/j.tics.2020.01.009 PMID: 32160568

Goodhue, D., Klein, B., & March, S. (2000). User evaluation of IS as surrogates for objective performance. *Information & Management*, *38*(2), 87–101. DOI: 10.1016/S0378-7206(00)00057-4

Goodhue, D. L. (1998). Development and Measurement Validity of a Task-Technology Fit Instrument for User Evaluations of Information System. *Decision Sciences*, *29*(1), 105–138. https://doi.org/https://doi.org/10.1111/j.1540-5915.1998.tb01346.x

Goodhue, D. L., & Thompson, R. L. (1995). Task-Technology Fit and Individual Performance. *Management Information Systems Quarterly*, *19*(2), 213–236. DOI: 10.2307/249689

Jarrahi, M. H. (2018). Artificial intelligence and the future of work: Human-AI symbiosis in organizational decision making. *Business Horizons*, *61*(4), 577–586. https://doi.org/https://doi.org/10.1016/j.bushor.2018.03.007

Kaur, S., Katoch, G., & Zahidi, F. (2024). A Bibliometric Review on Technostress : Performance and Scientific Approach. *Prestige International Journal of Management & IT- Sanchayan, 13*(1), 21–40.

Kaur, S., & Sharma, R. (2021). Emotion AI: Integrating Emotional Intelligence with Artificial Intelligence in the Digital Workplace. In P. K. Singh, Z. Polkowski, S. Tanwar, S. K. Pandey, G. Matei, & D. Pirvu (Eds.), *Innovations in Information and Communication Technologies (IICT-2020)* (pp. 337–343). Springer International Publishing. https://doi.org/https://doi.org/10.1007/978-3-030-66218-9_39

Kramer, A. D. I., Guillory, J. E., & Hancock, J. T. (2014). Experimental evidence of massive-scale emotional contagion through social networks. *Proceedings of the National Academy of Sciences of the United States of America*, *111*(24), 8788–8790. DOI: 10.1073/pnas.1320040111 PMID: 24889601

Kumar, H., & Martin, A. (2023). Artificial Emotional Intelligence: Conventional and deep learning approach. *Expert Systems with Applications*, *212*, 118651. https://doi.org/https://doi.org/10.1016/j.eswa.2022.118651

Lazarus, R. S., & Folkman, S. (1984). *Stress, Appraisal, and Coping*. Springer Publishing Company. https://books.google.nl/books?id=i-ySQQuUpr8C

Leeuw, R. T., & Joseph, N. (2023). Reciprocal Influence between Digital Emotional Intelligence and Agile Mindset in an Agile Environment. *Administrative Sciences*, *13*(11). Advance online publication. DOI: 10.3390/admsci13110228

Lengel, R. H., & Daft, R. L. (1988). The Selection of Communication Media as an Executive Skill. *The Academy of Management Perspectives*, *2*(3), 225–232. DOI: 10.5465/ame.1988.4277259

Miao, C., Humphrey, R., & Qian, S. (2017). A meta-analysis of emotional intelligence and work attitudes. *Journal of Occupational and Organizational Psychology*, *90*(2), 177–202. DOI: 10.1111/joop.12167

Nasef Zaki, H., Saeed Ahmed Abd-Elrhaman, E., & Ghoneimy Hasanin Ghoneimy, A. (2018). The Effect of Emotional Intelligence Program on Decision Making Style. *American Journal of Nursing Research*, *6*(6), 524–532. DOI: 10.12691/ajnr-6-6-21

O, Y.-L. (2004). Intelligent Information Systems for Decision Support. *International Conference on Artificial Intelligence, IC-AI, 1*, 326–332.

Page, M. J., McKenzie, J. E., Bossuyt, P. M., Boutron, I., Hoffmann, T. C., Mulrow, C. D., Shamseer, L., Tetzlaff, J. M., Akl, E. A., Brennan, S. E., Chou, R., Glanville, J., Grimshaw, J. M., Hróbjartsson, A., Lalu, M. M., Li, T., Loder, E. W., Mayo-Wilson, E., McDonald, S., & Moher, D. (2021). The PRISMA 2020 statement: An updated guideline for reporting systematic reviews. *BMJ (Clinical Research Ed.)*, *372*. Advance online publication. DOI: 10.1136/bmj.n71 PMID: 33782057

Perkins, M. (2023). Academic Integrity considerations of AI Large Language Models in the post-pandemic era: ChatGPT and beyond. *Journal of University Teaching & Learning Practice*, *20*(2). Advance online publication. DOI: 10.53761/1.20.02.07

Pitts, V. E., Wright, N. A., & Harkabus, L. C. (2012). Communication in Virtual Teams : The Role of Emotional Intelligence. *Journal of Organizational Psychology*, *12*(3/4), 21–34. DOI: 10.1016/j.chb.2012.06.001%5Cnhttp://

Rezgui, Y. (2007). Exploring virtual team-working effectiveness in the construction sector. *Interacting with Computers*, *19*(1), 96–112. https://doi.org/https://doi.org/10.1016/j.intcom.2006.07.002

Rice, R. E. (1992). Task Analyzability, Use of New Media, and Effectiveness: A Multi-Site Exploration of Media Richness. *Organization Science*, *3*(4), 475–500. DOI: 10.1287/orsc.3.4.475

Rice, R. E., Hughes, D., & Love, G. (1989). Usage and Outcomes of Electronic Messaging at an R&D Organization: Situational Constraints, Job Level, and Media Awareness Organization: Situational Constraints, Job Level, and Media Awareness. *Office Technology and People*, *5*(2), 141–161. DOI: 10.1108/EUM0000000003532

Salovey, P., & Mayer, J. D. (1989). Emotional intelligence. *Imagination, Cognition and Personality*, *9*(3), 185–211. DOI: 10.2190/DUGG-P24E-52WK-6CDG

Sambunjak, D., Cumpston, M., & Watts, C. (2021). *Module 1: Introduction to conducting systematic reviews. In: Cochrane Interactive Learning: Conducting an intervention review. Cochrane*. Cochrane. https://training.cochrane.org/interactivelearning/module-1-introduction-conducting-systematic-reviews

Santana, M., & Díaz-Fernández, M. (2023). Competencies for the artificial intelligence age: visualisation of the state of the art and future perspectives. In *Review of Managerial Science* (Vol. 17, Issue 6). Springer Berlin Heidelberg. https://doi.org/DOI: 10.1007/s11846-022-00613-w

Spicer, D. P., & Sadler-Smith, E. (2005). An examination of the general decision making style questionnaire in two UK samples. *Journal of Managerial Psychology*, *20*(2), 137–149. DOI: 10.1108/02683940510579777

Steinert, S., & Dennis, M. J. (2022). Emotions and Digital Well-Being: On Social Media's Emotional Affordances. *Philosophy & Technology*, *35*(2), 36. DOI: 10.1007/s13347-022-00530-6 PMID: 35450167

Szczygiel, D. D., & Mikolajczak, M. (2018). Emotional intelligence buffers the effects of negative emotions on job burnout in nursing. *Frontiers in Psychology*, *9*. Advance online publication. DOI: 10.3389/fpsyg.2018.02649 PMID: 30627113

Tarafdar, M., Tu, Q., Ragu-Nathan, B. S., & Ragu-Nathan, T. S. (2007). The impact of technostress on role stress and productivity. *Journal of Management Information Systems*, *24*(1), 301–328. DOI: 10.2753/MIS0742-1222240109

Vanduhe, V., Cemal Nat, M., & Al-Delawi, H. (2020). Continuance Intentions to Use Gamification for Training in Higher Education: Integrating the Technology Acceptance Model (TAM), Social Motivation, and Task Technology Fit (TTF). *IEEE Access : Practical Innovations, Open Solutions*, *20*, 1. DOI: 10.1109/ACCESS.2020.2966179

Vendramin, N., Nardelli, G., & Ipsen, C. (2021). Task-Technology Fit Theory: An Approach For Mitigating Technostress. In *A Handbook of Theories on Designing Alignment Between People and the Office Environment* (pp. 39–53). Routledge/Taylor & Francis Group. https://doi.org/DOI: 10.1201/9781003128830-4

Vicci, D. H. (2024). Emotional Intelligence in Artificial Intelligence: A Review and Evaluation Study. SSRN *Electronic Journal*. https://doi.org/DOI: 10.2139/ssrn.4818285

Völker, J., & Mannheim, C. (2021). Tuned in on senders' self-revelation: Emojis and emotional intelligence influence interpretation of WhatsApp messages. *Computers in Human Behavior Reports*, *3*, 100062. https://doi.org/https://doi.org/10.1016/j.chbr.2021.100062

Wadley, G., Krause, A., Liang, J., Wang, Z., & Leong, T. W. (2020). Use of music streaming platforms for emotion regulation by international students. *Proceedings of the 31st Australian Conference on Human-Computer-Interaction*, 337–341. https://doi.org/DOI: 10.1145/3369457.3369490

Wadley, G., Smith, W., Koval, P., & Gross, J. J. (2020). Digital Emotion Regulation. *Current Directions in Psychological Science*, *29*(4), 412–418. DOI: 10.1177/0963721420920592

Warrier, U., Shankar, A., & Belal, H. M. (2024). Examining the role of emotional intelligence as a moderator for virtual communication and decision making effectiveness during the COVID-19 crisis: Revisiting task technology fit theory. *Annals of Operations Research*, *335*(3), 1519–1535. DOI: 10.1007/s10479-021-04216-8 PMID: 34539017

Yeke, S. (2023). Digital intelligence as a partner of emotional intelligence in business administration. *Asia Pacific Management Review*, *28*(4), 390–400. DOI: 10.1016/j.apmrv.2023.01.001

Zigurs, I., & Khazanchi, D. (2008). From Profiles to Patterns: A New View of Task-Technology Fit. *IS Management*, *25*(1), 8–13. DOI: 10.1080/10580530701777107

Chapter 5

Digitalization in Professional Training in Universities UsingVR/AR and HR Development

Bibigul Vasic
https://orcid.org/0000-0002-8723-1703
Faculty of Applied Sciences in Niš, Serbia

Rysty Kerimbayeva
https://orcid.org/0000-0003-0430-1831
Taraz University Named After M.Kh. Dulaty, Kazakhstan

Gulnar Sibagatova
https://orcid.org/0009-0006-9191-9857
K. Zhubanov Aktobe Regional Univesity, Kazakhstan

Yulia Kuznetsova
https://orcid.org/0009-0000-1556-0156
Aktobe Regional University Named After K. Zhubanov, Kazakhstan

ABSTRACT

This work is devoted to the study of the potential of using VR/AR technologies in the training of professional and pedagogical specialists and their impact on the development of HR in higher education. Consideration of these aspects will help to identify the main advantages of digital tools for the educational ecosystem, identify challenges and propose approaches to their effective integration. In a study conducted among 224 students of Taraz University named after M.H. Dulati and Aktobe Regional University named after K. Zhubanov, the use of VR/AR showed

DOI: 10.4018/979-8-3373-8612-6.ch005

a noticeable improvement in students' engagement in the educational process, increasing their creativity and motivation. Students rated these technologies as an effective tool for mastering complex practical skills and improving understanding of educational material. Teachers who have been trained to work with VR/AR have also confirmed an increase in their qualifications and an improvement in the quality of the educational process.

INTRODUCTION

The modern world is undergoing a rapid digital transformation that affects all areas of life, including education. In a dynamically changing labor market, the higher education system faces the need not only to train professionals with relevant competencies, but also to ensure the development of personnel capable of working effectively in the digital economy. One of the key directions of this transformation is the use of virtual and augmented reality (VR/AR) technologies, which open up new horizons in training and staff development.

The use of VR/AR technologies makes it possible to model professional processes, improve students' practical training and increase their involvement in the educational process. This trend is especially significant for the training of professionals in pedagogical specialties, where real-world practice often requires significant resources and difficult conditions. In addition, the integration of VR/AR contributes to the development of innovative approaches to talent management, which plays a key role in increasing the competitiveness of universities.

The relevance of our chosen topic is emphasized not only from an educational point of view, but also from an economic and socio-cultural one. Professions in the fields of art, design, engineering, medicine and other creative fields require high qualifications and an innovative approach. VR and AR can help shape future generations of professionals with the necessary skills and abilities for a successful career. This paper is devoted to the study of the potential of using VR/AR technologies in the training of professional and pedagogical specialists and their impact on the development of HR in higher education. Consideration of these aspects will make it possible to identify the main advantages of digital tools for the educational ecosystem, identify challenges and propose approaches to their effective integration.

Description of Materials and Methods

The study of the use of virtual and augmented reality in teaching professional and creative specialties includes a variety of research methods. The analysis of the methodological base in this area allowed us to identify several methods that were subsequently applied in pedagogical research:

1. A literary review of the available scientific articles, studies and publications related to the use of VR and AR in education. This helps to understand the status of the field, identify shortcomings, and identify unresolved issues.
2. A survey with teachers, students, and other participants in the educational process to collect data on their experiences using VR and AR.
3. Monitoring the progress of classes using VR and AR in order to study the interaction of students and teachers with these technologies. Long-term observation and analysis of long-term effects allows us to identify how deeply the use of VR and AR technologies affects the professional development of students and graduates of creative specialties.
4. Ethical analysis of the use of VR and AR in education, including data privacy, security and socio-cultural issues.

RESULTS

1. Virtual Reality: Evolution and Modern Technologies for Creating Artificial Worlds

Virtual reality is an artificial world created using technological means. A person perceives it through sight, hearing, touch and other senses. Although elements of the VR industry have existed for several centuries, it has been formed relatively recently in its modern technological and complex form.

Device prototypes and the first mentions of virtual reality (VR) and augmented reality (AR) technologies date back to the middle of the 20th century. However, the modern terminology and understanding of these concepts were formed in the early 1990s. Jaron Lanier first used the term «virtual reality» (Lanier, 2018), and the term "augmented reality" was mentioned in the work of authors Caudell Thomas et al., 1992).

Due to the rapid development of technologies in the field of VR and AR, terminology in this field is constantly evolving. Nevertheless, the concept of the real-virtual continuum, proposed in the work of Milgram, Paul, and colleagues (Skarbez R, et al., 2021), remains relevant and is of fundamental importance for understanding the spectrum between reality and virtuality (Cipresso et al., 2018). Figure 1 shows an illustration demonstrating this concept (**Figure 1**).

Figure 1. The real-virtual continuum

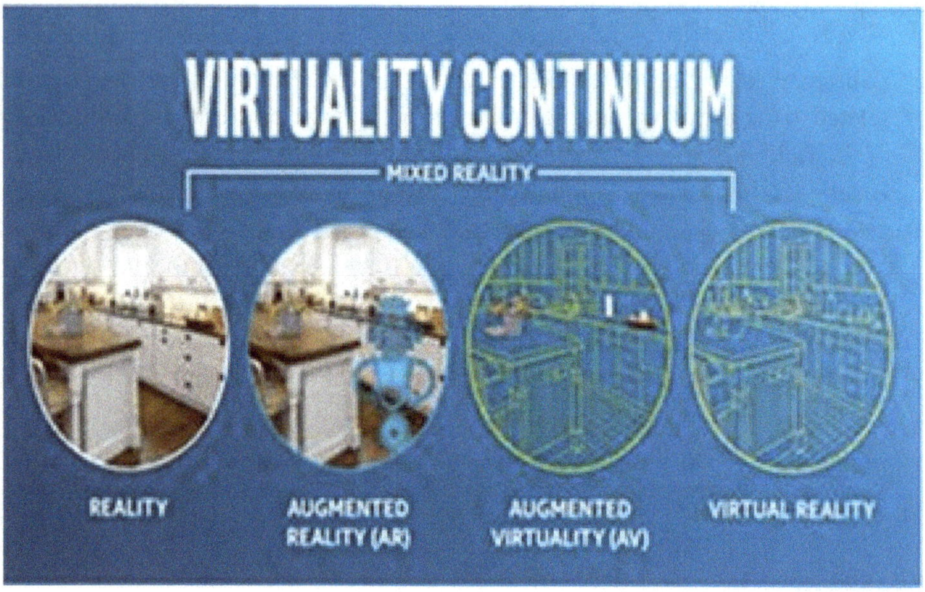

Sensorama became one of the first devices capable of immersing the user in virtual reality. This device, created by Morton Heilig in 1957, largely anticipated modern VR technologies. By design, it was a stationary installation with a screen for watching videos, providing complete immersion in what was happening. A special landing module with vibration was built into the device, transmitting the movements occurring on the screen. Sensorama was also equipped with stereo sound, a wind and odor generator, creating a presence effect. In fact, it can be considered one of the first examples of a 3D cinema, despite the fact that the quality of the content left much to be desired.

Shortly before **Sensorama** appeared, **Philco** engineers Brian and Komo presented an invention that became a significant step in the development of virtual reality technologies. They have developed the first modern helmet with a display (**HMD**), called **Headsight.** The device used video screens that displayed the movements of each eye, and the camera allowed you to change the angle of inclination depending on the user's head turns. This invention has largely anticipated modern VR headsets.

In 1968, the Sword of Damocles system became widely known due to developments carried out at the Lincoln Laboratory at the Massachusetts Institute of Technology. A unique feature of this device, created by the efforts of engineers, was not only the display of stereoscopic images and tracking user movements in space, but also the ability to overlay machine graphics on real objects. In fact, this gadget became the first helmet related to interactive virtual reality systems.

In 1980, an innovative gadget appeared — Eye Tap glasses, developed by Canadian scientist Steve Mann, who is considered a pioneer in the field of wearable electronics. Being a talented engineer, he has made a significant contribution to the development of digital technologies. Back in school, Mann created the first portable computer designed to work with video equipment. The device was powered by a MOS Technology 6502 processor and housed in a metal frame placed in a backpack.

In 1990, the first Virtuality system was introduced. The author of the first VR gaming system was Jonathan Valdern, who demonstrated it at the Computer Graphics exhibition. One of the two versions presented looked like a helmet with two LCD displays providing a resolution of 276x372 pixels for each eye.

The second version of the system was a full-fledged arcade machine. In this variation, the player controlled a virtual racing car using the steering wheel, which created an exciting presence effect. Despite its impressive appearance and popularity, Virtuality's commercial success turned out to be modest — just over 50,000 copies were sold on the market during its entire existence.

In 1992, the first prototype of a room was presented, in which the walls were used as screens for displaying stereoscopic images. Students of the University of Illinois developed this system. To fully immerse themselves in the virtual environment, users wore special glasses with built-in stereoscopes. The system also used a controller that allowed interaction with virtual reality objects. In addition, the technology made it possible to track the position of the user's head and hands, enhancing the effect of presence.

Today, only a small number of companies use CAVE systems. Their main applications include design, training, and ergonomics testing. Compared to VR headsets, such rooms provide a better immersion in virtual reality and are considered professional solutions in this field ((Isabelle Pivotto, et al., 2024).

The main advantages of CAVE over virtual reality (HMD) helmets are high visualization quality, wide viewing angle, minimal delay in image transmission, and the ability to see your own body. The latter factor reduces the likelihood of loss of coordination and motion sickness, which makes the system more comfortable for the user.

In 1993, SEGA introduced its VR headset concept at CES (Consumer Electronics Show). The prototype device featured built-in stereo speakers, two LCD displays, and a planned cost of $200.

The development required significant financial investments, but it never went on sale. SEGA representatives claimed that the headset provided an incredibly realistic image. However, the project was closed because the company expressed concerns that due to the high degree of realism, users may have problems perceiving the world around them.

In 1999, VirtusSphere appeared, an innovative development that was a spherical structure designed for games using digital reality glasses. The sphere with a diameter of 3 meters was mounted on a platform with wheels, which allowed it to rotate freely, providing the user with complete freedom of movement inside.

The project impressed investors due to its high level of immersion in the virtual environment. However, like many other similar developments, VirtuSphere was unable to receive sufficient funding. To avoid financial collapse, the creators sold the remaining copies to museums and military organizations on time.

2012 was a landmark year for virtual reality thanks to Oculus VR. This period coincided with the heyday of crowd funding platforms, which played a key role in popularizing VR technologies. The enthusiast Palmer Lucky, whose vision of the development of virtual reality helped to avoid the oblivion of this technology became particularly famous. He became the author of one of the most successful fundraising campaigns: at his suggestion, about 10 thousand people supported the project, investing about 2.5 million dollars in the development of branded VR helmets.

After completing work on the Oculus Rift DK1 project, the company began developing the next generation of VR glasses. The new version received an improved screen with high image quality, as well as a more ergonomic design. The impressive results have attracted the attention of both developers and investors, which has significantly increased interest in the headset.

In 2015, Facebook acquired the company founded by Palmer Lucky for $2 billion. This deal provided Oculus with a stable future and provided financial freedom for further development of the hardware and software complex. The purchase of Oculus was a confirmation of the promise of virtual reality technologies.

By the end of 2023, several factors can be identified that contribute to the spread of VR technologies in education:

1. Reducing the cost of equipment. Modern VR systems, suitable for both professional and home use, have become more affordable due to recent price reductions.
2. The rapid increase in the number of VR applications. Currently, there are thousands of programs that support virtual reality technologies, and their number continues to grow rapidly.
3. Increased investment in VR. Annual investments in the field of virtual reality exceed 2.5 billion dollars. Since 2012, the volume of investments has been constantly increasing, and this growth is not expected to slow down in the near future.
4. Expanding the number of major VR manufacturers in Europe. There are more than 300 companies developing VR solutions on the market. Corporations such as Oculus, HTC, and Sony Technologies are leading players, and the use of virtual reality has become standard practice.

5. The spread of VR in various industries. Virtual reality technologies are actively used not only in the gaming industry, but also in mechanical engineering, oil and gas, energy, metallurgy and telecommunications.

Virtual reality has the potential to radically change the approach to learning, making it more exciting and immersive. The use of VR in educational processes covers several key areas:

1. Practical training. Virtual reality allows students to gain experiences that are not available with traditional methods. Using VR headsets, students can interact with various objects and simulations, which facilitates learning through practice.
2. Improved visualization. Thanks to VR technologies, complex concepts become more understandable, as they are presented in the form of interactive 3D models. For example, using augmented reality applications, students can study the internal structure of the human body or recreate historical events in virtual space.
3. Effective assimilation of the material. Virtual reality promotes better memorization of knowledge and skills compared to traditional learning methods due to its interactivity and engagement.
4. Distance learning. VR technologies allow students to learn even from a distance, ensuring that students participate in virtual classrooms and joint educational events, regardless of their physical location.

Virtual reality can significantly improve the quality of education, making learning more interactive and immersive (Fedchenko A.D., 2020). With the help of VR, students can gain practical experience, visually explore complex topics and improve their knowledge and skills, including distance learning.

VR has also played an important role in solving the urgent problem of 2021, the COVID-19 pandemic. This year, a series of two free educational simulations dedicated to the coronavirus was released. According to the developers, the project was created with the participation of doctors who worked with infected patients in Washington and California. These simulations help to master the basics of using personal protective equipment, diagnosing the disease, as well as inpatient treatment methods (www.patentlyapple.com, 2021).

In the industry, VR is actively used to train new employees using specialized virtual simulators. They teach the rules of working with dangerous or expensive equipment, reducing risks to workers' lives, preventing possible breakdowns and minimizing harmful effects on the environment.

Neuroscientists from Neuro-Insight, a company specializing in the study of the human subconscious mind in a business context, conducted a study aimed at measuring the brain's response to augmented reality. About 150 people participated in the experiment, who were asked to complete tasks on translating foreign phrases. One group used the Google Word Lens AR application, while the other worked with traditional Google Translate, which does not support augmented reality. The results showed that the level of engagement among users of AR technologies was almost twice (1.9 times) higher than those who performed the task without them. This suggests that augmented reality contributes to more efficient and productive work compared to traditional methods.

Based on these data, the development of AR applications for managers could significantly facilitate their daily activities. For example, such technologies could display their positions above employees, remind them of tasks and show a timer until they are completed, mark shelves with documents and provide brief annotations when hovering over them. These functions would make it possible to speed up work processes and improve management efficiency. However, the constant use of such solutions can reduce the level of independence of employees, since their skills will develop only with AR tools, limiting opportunities without them.

In modern conditions, for successful development, companies need to undergo a digital transformation, which implies not just the introduction of new technologies, but also a profound change in business processes.

2. Transformation of VR Technology Into HR Strategy

A particularly significant aspect of this transformation is the modernization of the HR strategy. With the development of artificial intelligence in industry, the requirements for personnel, their qualifications and competencies are constantly changing. One of the key areas of HR policy is the training and development of employees, because they are the main resource that ensures the competitiveness of the company.

VR technologies, which are already actively used in the field of vocational training, play a leading role in this process. Traditional methods of personnel training are gradually losing relevance, especially against the background of the introduction of artificial intelligence in industrial enterprises. As an innovative approach, it is worth using virtual reality to train production staff. This will allow not only developing practical skills in a safe environment, but also to create various scenarios of production processes, minimize the risks of injury and prepare employees for possible emergency situations.

Earlier, the results of the author's research on the use of VR technologies in various fields, including HR and employee training at industrial enterprises of the energy complex using a teacher simulator, were published. As part of the study, the development of the "Teacher Simulator" simulator was presented, which acts as a virtual reality tool designed to improve the effectiveness of personnel training in the energy industry.

The Vireim corporate VR platform has been recognized for its effectiveness in staff training. The system allows you to practice certain skills through interaction with virtual equipment, which helps to reduce the number of production errors when performing technological processes.

The analysis of existing experience in the field of VR training, as well as the practice of using VR technologies in large enterprises, allowed the authors to identify the key prerequisites for the introduction of VR training in companies in the industrial sector. These aspects were reflected in the SWOT analysis (Table 1).

Table 1. SWOT analysis of prerequisites for the introduction of VR training for professional development

Strengths: **- Significant financial resources of higher education institutions allow us to invest in the purchase of VR equipment and the introduction of VR technologies.** **-Traditional teaching methods do not allow us to fully simulate real educational and industrial conditions, especially to recreate emergency and emergency situations.**	**Weaknesses:** **- In the HR services of professional enterprises, there are no specialized departments responsible for staff development and training.** **- The interaction between the HR department and the production departments is not properly established.**
Opportunities: - Implementation of artificial intelligence technologies in educational and production processes. - The functioning of training centers based on industrial enterprises. - Sufficient financial resources to organize their own VR classes on the territory of enterprises.	Threats: - Low efficiency of VR-learning application. - Insufficient preparation of managers for the integration of VR technologies into training. - Difficulties in mastering VR technologies by older workers.

Earlier, the need and importance of transforming the HR strategy in the framework of training specialists, in parallel with the introduction of innovative solutions into production processes, was noted. In the course of the study, the authors found that the advantages of VR training correspond to the strategic goals of the HR service, which is presented in Table 2.

Table 2. Implementation of VR training in professional training and HR service

<table>
<tr><th colspan="3">VR Training Stages</th></tr>
<tr><td rowspan="6">1. The stage of preliminary adaptation of the innovative technology of personnel training in the HR service.</td><td>Evaluation and study of personnel management processes</td><td>-Identification of difficulties in personnel management;
-Defining goals and objectives for improvement</td></tr>
<tr><td colspan="2">Determining the need to introduce advanced personnel training technologies in the HR department</td></tr>
<tr><td colspan="2">Determining the optimal innovative technology for personnel training (VR training, gamification, and others).</td></tr>
<tr><td colspan="2">Analysis of management and employee perceptions regarding the introduction of new personnel training technology</td></tr>
<tr><td colspan="2">Identification of potential risks in the implementation of advanced personnel training technology.</td></tr>
<tr style="display:none"></tr>
<tr><td rowspan="5">Development of a plan for integrating VR training into the HR HR management system</td><td colspan="2">Creating a team of specialists</td></tr>
<tr><td colspan="2">Assessment of the existing technical infrastructure</td></tr>
<tr><td colspan="2">Setting criteria and requirements for the implementation of VR training</td></tr>
<tr><td colspan="2">Creating a technical specification for the implementation of VR training</td></tr>
<tr><td colspan="2">Development of risk mitigation measures during technology implementation</td></tr>
<tr><td rowspan="6">Implementation of the VR training implementation process in the HR department</td><td rowspan="2">Creation and development of VR training</td><td>methodology VR equipment</td></tr>
<tr><td>Creation and development of programs for VR-learning</td></tr>
<tr><td colspan="2">Conducting VR learning testing by developing an experimental version.</td></tr>
<tr><td colspan="2">Launching and integrating VR learning into the workflow</td></tr>
<tr><td colspan="2">Implementation of VR training in the current HR management system</td></tr>
<tr><td colspan="2">Assessment of potential risks and development of mitigation measures</td></tr>
<tr><td rowspan="3">Analysis of the effectiveness of the implementation of VR training in the HR personnel management system</td><td colspan="2">Analysis of the effectiveness of VR-learning in the HR system.</td></tr>
<tr><td colspan="2">Analysis of the implementation of VR training in the current personnel training system</td></tr>
<tr><td colspan="2">Analysis of the implementation of VR training in the current personnel training system</td></tr>
</table>

In addition, VR training expands the possibilities of individual and group training, providing a personalized approach to employee development. Technology helps not only to develop technical skills, but also contributes to the improvement of soft competencies such as conflict management, public speaking and stress tolerance (A.E. Bajurov, 2019). The inclusion of VR methods in the HR strategy allows not only to form highly qualified teams, but also to strengthen the innovative image of the company, which increases its competitiveness in the labor market (Table 3).

Table 3. Relationship of the key advantages of VR training with the long-term goals of the HR strategy

Strategic objectives in HR strategy Advantages of using VR technologies in training	**Strategic objectives in HR strategy Advantages of using VR technologies in training**
Improving the process of integrating university graduates as new employees into the workforce	Adaptive training of university graduates (new employees) in practical skills, including personalized programs depending on the level of training, as well as injury prevention among inexperienced employees.
Creating a comfortable and safe working environment.	Ensuring a safe learning environment for staff, especially during the adaptation period, which helps to increase their safety level.
Application of modern methods of training and professional development of employees.	VR learning is an innovative technology that modernizes and enriches the learning process.
Forming a team capable of quickly adapting to work with advanced equipment and new technologies in production processes.	VR training will ensure the rapid development of programs for mastering new equipment or innovative technologies introduced into production, allowing personnel to learn without restrictions on the number of attempts.
Formation of a team of highly qualified specialists.	VR training promotes the development of both technical skills (necessary for specific tasks) and flexible competencies, including public speaking and conflict management skills.
Organization of events aimed at improving the emotional atmosphere and relationships in the team	Within the framework of VR training, programs are available that help strengthen the emotional state of employees, such as, for example, meditation practices during a break. This is especially important for reducing stress and tension among workers involved in harsh production conditions.

Table 3 shows the relationship between the key advantages of VR training and the long-term strategic goals of the HR department, emphasizing that virtual reality is becoming an effective tool for training and adapting personnel. The use of VR technologies allows us to create personalized training programs adapted to the level of training of employees, which is especially important when integrating new specialists into the team. In addition, VR contributes to the creation of safe working conditions, providing simulation of potentially dangerous situations without endangering the life and health of personnel. This not only minimizes the risk of injury, but also increases the overall level of professional training of employees (Rêgo et al., 2024).

3. Augmented Reality: Concept, Technology and Its Impact on Modern Society

The research also highlights that augmented reality should be considered as a concept, not just as a technology. This is because some of its functions may be specific to other digital systems or technologies, not just AR applications. With the development of technology over time, it becomes possible to more clearly understand the full potential of both augmented and virtual reality, which leads to the emergence of different definitions of these technologies, including from different scientific and practical points of view (Sanjeev N.,2019).

The implementation of augmented reality assumes that a real-time computer adds digital elements with virtual objects to the image of the real environment on the screen of various devices, such as a tablet, smartphone or a special headset. This technology does not replace the real environment with an artificial one, but only enriches it with additional effects that cannot be conveyed using traditional means such as presentations, books or videos. Augmented reality allows you to create visual effects that are impossible to observe in real life, such as a deer walking on a keyboard or hares running across a room.

Augmented reality is based on hardware and AR applications, which are developed using special software. Other programs that support various augmented reality effects can also be used to create a full-fledged AR application. The hardware includes devices through which virtual images are displayed. Smartphones and tablets are the most popular and affordable devices for working with augmented reality. In addition, various headsets such as augmented reality glasses are also used to demonstrate AR. These devices can be diverse: for example, Smart glasses look like ordinary glasses and belong to augmented reality devices, while AR Box or ClassVR headsets resemble helmets that are worn on the head (**Figure 2**).

Figure 2. Augmented Reality hardware

In order for augmented reality to function on these devices, they must be equipped with sensors and processors that can meet the high demands required to work with AR. The main hardware components of augmented reality devices are:

- Processor, which is a key element for data processing. It is responsible for the speed of the device and its ability to handle tasks that require high computing power, in addition to performing standard functions such as smartphone operation.
- A graphics processor (GPU) that processes visual information, such as displaying an image on a device screen. Augmented reality requires powerful graphics processors to make it easy to create and overlay digital content.
- Sensors that allow the device to receive information about the external environment and understand its surroundings. The following sensors are important for augmented reality: depth sensors to measure distance and depth, a gyroscope to determine the angle and position of the device, proximity sensors to estimate the distance to objects, an accelerometer to detect changes in speed, movement and rotation of the device, as well as a light sensor to measure brightness and light intensity.

The second key element of the augmented reality system is software, where the process of creating an AR experience begins. It is conventionally divided into two categories: platforms for the development of augmented reality, which include external libraries with various effects, 3D objects, images and other elements, and augmented reality applications created on these platforms. The operation of augmented reality software (or platform) is based on three basic principles that make it possible to realize the effect of augmented reality:

- Understanding the environment, which gives the device the ability to detect key points and flat surfaces, creating a map of its surroundings. This allows you to accurately place virtual objects on these surfaces.
- Motion tracking, which allows the device to determine its location in relation to the environment. This allows virtual objects to be precisely positioned at the desired points on the screen.
- Illumination assessment, which helps the device to take into account the current illumination conditions in the surrounding space. This allows virtual objects to be placed in conditions similar to real lighting, increasing the realism of the image.

It is important to emphasize that the augmented reality effect arises due to the close relationship between hardware and software. If they are not compatible or the necessary components are missing, for example, if the hardware is not equipped with sensors for measuring light intensity, then the software's capabilities for assessing illumination will be useless, and vice versa. Now, there are several platforms on the market for developing augmented reality applications. One of the most popular is:

- Unity 3D with AR Foundation (https://unity.com/unity/features/arfoundation) is a multifunctional environment based on Unity 3D, which is recognized as a universal platform for creating cross-platform AR and VR applications. The environment, designed specifically for augmented reality development, allows you to create applications and run them on various mobile AR devices and headsets. It implements all the basic functions to support platforms such as iOS (ARKit), Android (ARCore), Hololens (Microsoft mixed reality), Magic Leap (Spatial OS) and Web (browsers). Unity's unique features are also available, including photorealistic rendering, physics, device-specific optimization, and many other features.;
- ARCore (https://developers.google.com/ar?hl=en) is a platform from Google for creating augmented reality applications. In the AR application market, ARCore is considered a complete software development kit (SDK) and one of the reliable tools for creating AR applications on the Android platform. ARCore also supports SDKs of other popular development environments such as Android NDK, Unity 3D with AR Foundation, iOS, Unreal and Web. These SDKs provide their own (native) An API for implementing basic AR functions such as motion tracking, environmental awareness, and light estimation.
- Vuforia (https://developer.vuforia.com/) has established itself as a powerful tool in the augmented reality industry, offering a wide range of functions. It includes image recognition technologies, object tracking, and cloud-based recognition services. Vuforia uses real-time computer vision technology to work with two-dimensional and three-dimensional objects. When viewed through the camera of a smartphone or tablet, it allows developers to create and interact with virtual objects, placing them relative to real-world objects in such a way as to create the impression that the virtual object is part of a real environment. Vuforia supports various platforms, from mobile devices to augmented reality glasses. Its versatility makes it a popular choice for developers seeking to create AR applications in various fields, including education.;
- ARKit (https://developer.apple.com/augmented-reality/arkit/) is an augmented reality platform that takes full advantage of the Apple ecosystem. ARKit integrates seamlessly with iOS development, especially with tools like Reality Kit, Reality Composer Pro, and Reality Composer for iOS, and

Reality Converter, which greatly simplify the process of creating AR apps for iOS. This set of tools allows you to take into account lighting conditions and recognize the dimensions of the surrounding space, which ensures the most accurate integration of virtual objects into the real world. One of the advantages of ARKit is its compatibility with most modern iOS devices, which opens up many opportunities for interacting with the environment, learning and working, making ARKit one of the most flexible and scalable platforms for augmented reality.

In addition to the aforementioned platforms, there are many other tools for creating augmented reality, each with its own advantages and disadvantages, corresponding to different user needs. These augmented reality development platforms provide developers and users with several key capabilities:

- Gesture recognition, which allows users to interact with the environment through hand and body movements. This feature can be used to control games, navigate the interface, or manipulate virtual objects.
- Object recognition, which allows the software to identify and track familiar objects in augmented reality scenes. This feature opens up opportunities for creating interactive applications in which users can interact with physical objects through their device's camera.
- Creation of 3D models that can be created from scratch or based on templates and accurately displayed in the context of augmented reality. These models can be used for educational purposes, modeling, or in game applications.
- Augmented reality platforms also support image detection and tracking, which allows the software to identify images at a certain distance and monitor them as they move in AR space. This feature is often used to add interactive elements and additional information to processes or phenomena.

The artificial intelligence in the application determines the location of an object using key points and planes into which the space captured by the camera is divided. This process is based on GPS, gyroscope, compass, and other sensors that track the user's position. Various augmented reality libraries perform such tasks. The ability to recognize images, such as 2D labels, and overlay additional content on them is one of the responsibilities of these libraries. In addition, libraries should include functions that support the operation of the device, which extends the functionality of augmented reality applications.

4. Digital Transformation in Education: the Introduction of VR/AR and the Development of HR in Universities

The mixed (hybrid) reality model, also known as the virtual continuum (Fig. 2), was first described in 1994. This concept defines a system in which elements of the real and virtual worlds exist simultaneously and can interact in real time. There are two intermediate links within this continuum: augmented reality (AR) and augmented virtuality (AV). Augmented reality is closer to the physical world by adding digital objects to it, whereas augmented virtuality is an expanded virtual environment that includes elements of the real world.

Polevoda and others identified the key components of this model:

1. Full reality is the physical world around us that exists without digital additions.
2. Virtual reality is a completely artificial digital environment created using modern computer technology.
3. Augmented reality is a physical world enriched with virtual objects and additional sensory data.
4. Augmented virtuality is a virtual space in which elements of the real world are integrated.

Augmented reality developed in parallel with virtual reality until 1990, when scientist T. Codell first coined the term "augmented reality". In 1992, L. Rosenberg created one of the first operational AR systems for the US Air Force. The exoskeleton he developed allowed the military to control equipment remotely from a remote control center (**Figure 3**). In 1994, J. Martin presented the first AR production in the theater, dancing in Cyberspace, where acrobats performed movements in an augmented virtual environment.

Figure 3. L. Rosenberg's exoskeleton

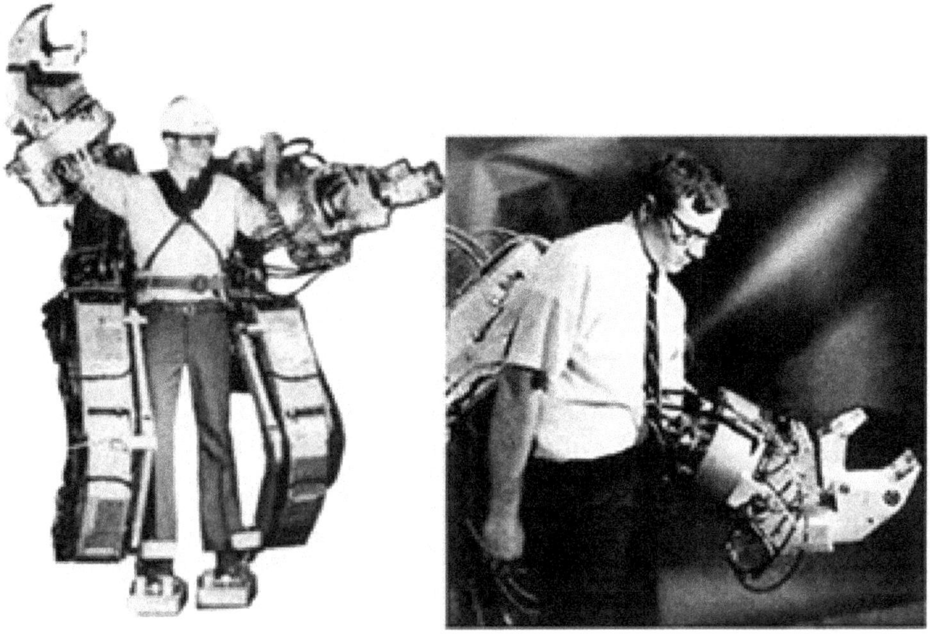

In the educational process of the university, the effectiveness of mastering the material is largely determined by the degree of student involvement. Studies have repeatedly confirmed that information is remembered better if it is repeated many times and affects several senses at once. According to the "Learning Pyramid" developed by American scientists R. Karnikau and F. 4), the best results in memorization are achieved with the practical development of skills and knowledge, since this method has the highest efficiency (**Figure 4**).

Figure 4. The learning pyramid

Visual materials contribute to the student's concentration. The representation of complex processes in the form of simple components, graphs or diagrams makes their perception more accessible. Group discussion allows you to look at the problem from different perspectives, and active participation helps you better remember key details through repeated repetition of information (Klimovich, 2019).

Any created virtual object or process can be used an unlimited number of times without significant expenditure of time and resources. Although the production and use of such materials may be subject to licensing restrictions, there is always the possibility of developing and publishing content under a free license. A virtual model or simulator does not replace real experience, but allows you to prepare for a practical situation in as much detail as possible. In recent years, VR and AR technologies have become in demand in higher education, actively being introduced into the educational process in both foreign and domestic universities.

In 2017, a study based on an analysis of scientific literature on the use of VR/ AR technologies in choreography showed that the most advanced AR technology at that time was Microsoft's Kinect AR sensor-based computer vision system. This technology opens up new perspectives for studying dance movements and improving choreography-teaching methods. The authors suggest that an improved version of Microsoft's Kinect V2 may even be used as a virtual dance teacher of the future.

Another study examined the possibilities of augmented reality in the process of teaching geography at the faculty of a Turkish university. The authors noted that

AR technologies help students better master complex and abstract disciplines. The results of the study showed that the use of AR contributes to improving academic performance, reducing cognitive load and is generally a useful tool in teaching geography, especially in the field of geomorphology. At the same time, the students demonstrated a positive attitude towards the use of this technology in the educational process.

The Russian Federation has also accumulated significant experience in using VR/AR technologies in the educational process. Lomonosov Moscow State University (MSU) and its partners are implementing a full cycle of development of virtual, mixed and augmented reality technologies. The work is carried out from the stage of creating mathematical models and studying physiological aspects to the development of hardware and software.

One of the university's key projects is a simulator of work on the ISS, which includes modeling the surface of the Moon and Mars. This is a mixed reality stand designed to simulate space missions and practice extravehicular and planetary activities. The university has already established an inter-faculty competence center for machine learning and virtual reality, and is implementing a number of projects to introduce VR/AR into school and higher education. Because of this work, a new faculty of space research was opened, which launched a master's program on the technological foundations of virtual and mixed reality.

Since 2013, Ufa State Aviation Technical University has been operating a three-dimensional visualization laboratory, which is a virtual reality room. It is equipped with a full set of VR equipment and peripherals, which allows you to track the gaze and movements of users, as well as interact with virtual objects. This makes it possible to conduct complex virtual experiments in the laboratory, work out technological operations with prototypes of systems and mechanisms, as well as train specialists for hazardous and remote industries. The laboratory is also used to improve the skills of modeling specialists, as it allows analyzing objects and processes in a virtual environment.

For example, the Department of Mechanical Engineering Technology uses a virtual reality room for practical industrial design classes. Students are provided with a virtual workshop site where they place equipment in accordance with safety regulations. Each change made is evaluated separately, and a unified enterprise model is created through the joint efforts of the participants. The laboratory also allows specialists from different fields to work in a shared virtual space.

Additionally, in April 2021, the Russian Science Foundation completed a project of virtual tours of Russia's leading scientific laboratories, including university research centers. Work on the 360° Science project began in 2017 and is a series of spherical panoramic images of laboratories of Russian universities and scientific institutes.

These virtual tours allow users to navigate through rooms, explore equipment, and receive detailed information through text, audio, and video inserts.

A similar experience of introducing virtual and augmented reality technologies is observed in the Republic of Belarus. One example is the Educational Center for Life Safety of the Ministry of Emergency Situations, on the official website of which you can take a virtual tour, being acquainted with the training grounds of the center. An important feature of the institution is its well-developed material base, which provides training in protection skills and emergency response. The center has more than 30 interactive platforms covering the topics of transport, fire, environmental and industrial safety, civil defense, criminal safety, health and meteorological risks, as well as nuclear and radiation safety.

The learning process is based on the principles of a game methodology, where students immerse themselves in a realistically simulated emergency. This approach increases emotional perception, contributing to the deep assimilation of knowledge. Interactive simulators and simulators based on VR, AR, Internet of Things and computer vision technologies are actively used in the educational process. Similar centers operate in China and South Korea, but there are no analogues in the CIS countries yet. The effectiveness of such initiatives is confirmed by statistics: in Belarus, over the past five years, the number of deaths in emergencies has decreased by 1.2 times, while the death rate among children has decreased by six times.

Currently, the Republic of Kazakhstan is implementing the Industry 4.0 project, which also involves the introduction of VR/AR into the professional and industrial environment. Thus, the Ministry is implementing a project to create seven model digital factories (JSC "AK Altynalmas", JSC "Eurasian Foods", JSC "Kentau Transformer Plant", JSC "Khimpharm", LLP "Karlskrona", LLP "Baltextil", LLP "Almaty Fan Plant") in order to demonstrate digital technologies and effects from digitalization, popularization of Industry 4.0 and the development of government support measures.

One example of a pilot project in the field of VR education in Kazakhstan is the introduction of virtual laboratories in secondary schools for teaching physics, chemistry and biology. These virtual labs allow students to conduct experiments in a safe and controlled environment, increasing their interest in natural science subjects and improving their understanding of complex concepts.

In the field of AR, one of the notable projects has been the use of augmented reality to study the history and culture of Kazakhstan. With AR applications, students can visualize historical events, architectural monuments, and important cultural sites directly in the classroom, making history lessons more interesting and memorable.

An analysis of existing VR and AR technologies and tools used in higher education in teaching creative students demonstrates the growth and diversity of innovations in this field. Let us mention some of the key technologies and tools: Virtual Reality (VR):

HTC View and Oculus Rift: These high-quality VR headsets provide the user with a wide field of view and a high degree of immersion. They are used in educational programs to teach design, architecture, and art.

PlayStation VR: This is a more accessible VR platform used in some educational programs to teach game design and virtual art.

- Google Cardboard and Google Daydream: These affordable solutions can be used with smartphones. They allow a wide range of users to get acquainted with VR technology.

Virtual Reality Software: There are many virtual reality programs and applications designed specifically for learning, such as Tile Brush (for creating 3D paintings and models) and Gravity Sketch (for 3D modeling).

Augmented Reality (AR):

- Hardcore and Market: These platforms are developed by Google and Apple respectively and allow developers to create AR applications for mobile devices. They are used to create interactive learning applications.
- Halolens: These augmented reality headsets developed by Microsoft allow users to interact with virtual object designs in the real world. They are used in education to create educational applications and simulations.

Zip Works and Vuforia: These are tools for creating your own AR applications and content used for educational purposes.

- AR software: There are applications such as SketchAR (which helps artists draw in the real world using AR) and Augment (which allows you to create visualizations of 3D models) that can be used in teaching creative professions (http://scirraconstruct.ru, 2025). Cloud and online resources:
- Unity and Unreal Engine:

These popular game engines are used to create VR and AR applications and simulations.

- SketchUp and Blender: These programs are widely used in the architectural and design fields and can be integrated with VR and AR to visualize projects.

The analysis of the mentioned technologies and tools allows educational institutions and professionals in creative specialties to choose the most appropriate resources for the development of training programs and enriching the learning experience of students (Rêgo et al., 2024).

When working with students of creative specialties, it is important to implement practical programs that help them design on a computer and then implement them in the real world. For example, Aktobe Regional University named after K.Zhubanov uses the SketchUp program, which teaches students how to create and edit a model in three-dimensional graphics. SketchUp is intuitive and very easy to use, as it is designed for none-professionals, and allows you to achieve the desired result relatively quickly and simply using tools familiar from childhood - "ruler", "pencil", "protractor", "eraser" in three planes.

As practice shows, the use of virtual reality (VR) and augmented reality (AR) in the educational process requires the development of specific pedagogical techniques and strategies that can maximize the potential of these technologies in education.

The analysis of pedagogical literature allowed us to highlight the advantages of using virtual and augmented reality in education:

- Increase students' motivation and interest.
- Improve practical skills.
- Reduced training and equipment costs.
- Opportunities for collaboration and feedback.

The experimental and practical part of our research was conducted on the basis of the Department of "Social Psychology" M.H.Dulati Taraz University departments consisting of 104 students of the educational programs "6B03111 - Psychology in the social sphere" and "7M03111 - Psychology in the social sphere and professional activity" and the Department of "Artistic Labor and Design" of Aktobe Regional University named after K.Zhubanov. Students of the specialties 6B01405 - "Visual art, artistic labor, graphics and design", 6B02102 - "Design" in the number of 120 people took part in the sociological survey. A total of 224 students participated in the study.

Thus, when conducting a survey among students to identify the use of virtual and augmented reality techniques, the following results were obtained. To the question "Have you used VR or AR for educational purposes?" about 74% answered "Yes", 26% - "No". When explaining which specific VR or AR technology they had experience with, more than 60% indicated mobile applications, 40% - VR headsets. To the question "Do you rate how the use of VR or AR has affected your learning (positively, negatively, and neutrally)?" - positive – 77%, neutral -23%, negative - 0%. To the question "What did you like most about using VR or AR in your studies?"

To the question "Are there any problems or difficulties that you have encountered when using VR or AR for educational purposes?" the students identified the following problems:

- Technical difficulties: problems with the installation and configuration of VR/AR equipment, as well as possible failures or incompatibilities with devices;
- Disorientation: In a virtual environment, students can sometimes feel disoriented or confused, especially if they are new to using VR;
- Physical fatigue: Prolonged use of VR headsets can cause physical fatigue, discomfort, or dizziness;
- Lack of content: lack of educational applications and content for specific educational purposes in the field of VR and AR;
- Availability of equipment: Not all students may have access to the necessary equipment, which may create inequalities in the learning environment;
- Equipment costs: VR headsets and AR devices can be expensive, which may limit accessibility for students with limited financial resources;
- Social isolation: Using VR can sometimes lead to a feeling of isolation from the real world and social contacts;
- Learning difficulties: Some students may have difficulty learning new skills related to the use of VR and AR in their studies.

The results of the survey among the teachers of the department (17 people) Based on the experience of using VR and AR, we have shown the following results. To the question "Do you use virtual reality (VR) or augmented reality (AR) in your training courses?" - 64% of teachers answered "Yes", 36% answered "No". Among the advantages, they highlighted immersion in a virtual environment that simulates real scenarios or phenomena, visualization of abstract and complex concepts, interaction in virtual environments, personalized learning materials and assignments, the opportunity to develop analysis and decision-making skills, interactive and exciting learning materials. To the question "Are there any challenges or difficulties that you have encountered when integrating VR and AR into the educational process, and how do you solve them?" the following results were obtained (Table 4).

Table 4. Challenges and difficulties in integrating VR and AR into the educational process

Difficulties	Challenges
1. Technical difficulties:	
The need to set up and maintain VR and AR equipment can be difficult for teachers and students. Technical failures can lead to interruptions in the learning process.	Provide sufficient training and support for working with technological equipment. This may include conducting training seminars and providing technical support in case of problems.
2. Availability of equipment:	
Not all students may have access to the necessary VR and AR equipment, which may lead to learning disparities.	Consider providing access to the equipment in educational institutions or libraries. It is also possible to develop alternative learning materials for students who do not have access to equipment.
3. Lack of content:	
A lack of educational apps and content for VR and AR can limit learning opportunities.	Encourage teachers and students to create content. Collaborating with developers to create educational apps can also be beneficial.
4. Time and financial costs:	
The integration of VR and AR may require additional time and financial resources for the preparation of educational materials and teacher training.	Conduct pilot projects and performance assessments to ensure that investments are worthwhile. Provide teachers with support and the opportunity to develop their skills.
5. Integration into the curriculum:	
Integrating new technologies may require changing curricula and courses, which can be a complex process.	Work with the administration of the educational institution to make changes to the curricula and study plans to take into account VR and AR as integral components of learning.

Monitoring the course of classes that use virtual reality (VR) and augmented reality (AR) in order to study the interaction of students and teachers with these technologies requires a systematic and methodical approach. The observation was based on the following scheme:

1. Planning and preparation, defining the purpose of research, aspects of interaction between students and teachers: student engagement, reaction to learning materials and technologies, etc.
2. The choice of observation methodology: direct on-site observation or video recording followed by analysis.
3. Preparation of the necessary surveillance equipment, including cameras, microphones, notebooks and pencils for writing.
4. Conducting observation: choosing a place of observation, recording the course of the lesson, including the actions of students and teachers, their reactions, questions, comments, video recording.

5. Data analysis: transcription and categorization of material according to specific topics or criteria (for example, student activity, types of questions and answers, etc.). Identification of successful strategies for using VR and AR and detection of problematic situations.
6. Creating a report and presenting the results: a structured report that includes a description of the monitoring process, identified trends, and recommendations for improving interaction.

One of the significant aspects of the digital transformation of education using virtual and augmented reality (VR/AR) technologies is digital inequality, which manifests itself in the unequal accessibility of these technologies to students from different social groups. Despite the potential of VR/AR to significantly improve the quality and effectiveness of learning, the absence of a detailed analysis of equipment and content accessibility may exacerbate socio-economic disparities among learners.

Special attention should be paid to ethical risks associated with the implementation of VR/AR. Among the main risks are dependence on the virtual environment and data privacy concerns. Extended exposure to the virtual environment may lead to dependency issues, negatively impacting students' social interactions and psychological well-being. Additionally, the protection of personal data and student privacy is critical, as the use of VR/AR involves the collection and processing of large amounts of personal information, requiring robust data protection mechanisms and strict adherence to ethical standards.

To mitigate these risks, regular monitoring of VR/AR technology accessibility is necessary, alongside ensuring equitable conditions for all students to use these technologies. It is also essential to develop and implement ethical standards aimed at protecting students' mental health and data privacy.

One of the significant aspects of the digital transformation of education through virtual and augmented reality (VR/AR) technologies is digital inequality, reflected in the unequal accessibility of these technologies to students from various social groups. Despite the potential of VR/AR to significantly enhance the quality and effectiveness of education, the lack of a detailed analysis regarding the accessibility of equipment and content may exacerbate socio-economic disparities among learners.

A comparative analysis of the effectiveness of VR/AR technologies versus traditional educational methods demonstrates significant advantages for the former. According to research, students who utilized VR showed a 75% better retention of material compared to those employing traditional methods. Student engagement when using AR technologies increased by approximately 50%, and accuracy in practical tasks improved by 30-40%, thanks to clearer material presentation and the possibility of repeated practice in a safe virtual environment.

Modern trends in EdTech are actively developing towards microlearning, especially through the application of AR technologies. Microlearning involves delivering concise and focused educational units that students can quickly learn and immediately apply in practice. For instance, AR applications are already extensively used for brief training in technical skills, languages, and practical operations, providing interactive and visually engaging instructions directly within real-world contexts.

The conclusions obtained from observations of the course of classes using virtual reality (VR) and augmented reality (AR) have become valuable data for analyzing the effectiveness and success of integrating these technologies into the educational process (**Figure 5**).

Figure 5. The results of observations of the course of classes that use virtual reality (VR) and augmented reality (AR)

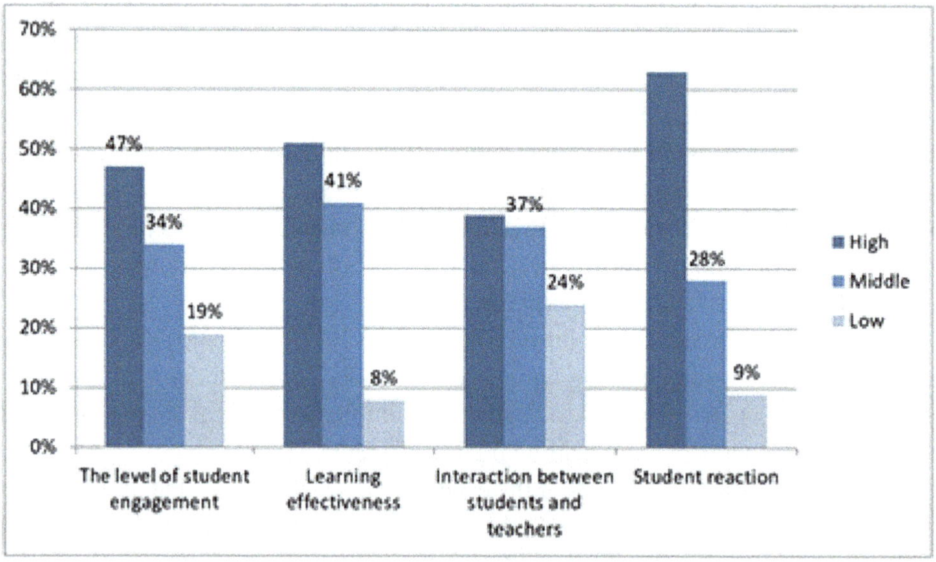

Based on the observations, recommendations were developed on the use of VR and AR in education, which include mandatory training of teachers and students for maximum efficiency, the creation of high-quality educational content and ensuring the availability of technological equipment. In addition, it is important to integrate these technologies into curricula and regularly evaluate their effectiveness, as well as take into account the diversity of student needs and maintain cooperation with the industry to access new developments.

The results of the study confirm the hypothesis that the integration of VR/AR technologies into the educational process has a positive effect on the development of professional skills of students of creative specialties and contributes to the improvement of teachers' qualifications, which, in turn, affects the development of HR in the higher education system.

Various methods were used to conduct the study, including literature review, questionnaires, observation, and long-term analysis of the impact of VR/AR technologies on the learning process.

The literary review method was the first stage of the research and allowed us to identify existing scientific papers and publications related to the use of VR/AR in educational practice. He helped us to assess the status of the use of these technologies in education, to identify the main problems and challenges faced by educational institutions in their implementation. This method also allowed us to identify key areas for the practical application of VR/AR, as well as to understand in more detail the issues related to the development of HR in higher education. The literature review showed that despite the progress in the use of these technologies, there is a need for further development of methodological approaches and wider implementation of innovative practices in the educational process.

The survey of students and teachers, which was attended by 224 people, provided valuable data on the perception of VR/AR technologies in education. Students and teachers answered questions about their experience using these technologies, their impact on the educational process, as well as the level of teachers' training to work with VR/AR. The questionnaires included questions concerning not only technological aspects, but also pedagogical, psychological and ethical features of the introduction of these technologies. The survey results showed that the majority of participants positively assess the use of VR/AR in education, especially in the context of practical disciplines such as design and visual arts. Students noted that such technologies make it possible to more effectively assimilate educational material, develop creativity and increase motivation to learn.

The observation method, which was conducted in real-world educational settings at the departments of Taraz University and Aktobe University, allowed us to better understand how students and teachers interact with VR/AR during the educational process. We observed the classes in which these technologies were used, analyzed how they affect students' engagement and their ability to work with visual and creative tasks. Long-term observation has shown that the use of VR/AR significantly improves the understanding of complex concepts, develops creativity and helps students to better assimilate material in the field of design and visual arts. The observations also revealed certain challenges related to technical support and the need for additional training for teachers. A long-term analysis has shown that positive changes in learning become more pronounced over time, and students and teachers begin to actively use new technologies to solve professional problems.

CONCLUSION

The results of the study confirm the importance of integrating VR/AR technologies into the educational process, especially for the preparation of students of creative specialties such as design and psychology. In a study conducted among 224 students of M.H. Dulati Taraz University and K.Zhubanov Aktobe Regional University, the use of VR/AR showed a marked improvement in student engagement in the educational process, increasing their creativity and motivation. The students appreciated these technologies as an effective tool for mastering complex practical skills and improving the understanding of educational material. Teachers who have learned how to work with VR/AR have also confirmed the improvement of their skills and the improvement of the quality of the educational process. These results are consistent with the findings of other researchers who emphasize the positive impact of VR/AR on the educational environment, especially in the context of creative and practice-oriented disciplines. Many works focus on the fact that virtual and augmented reality technologies allow creating interactive and personalized learning environments, which improves learning outcomes and promotes deeper development of professional skills.

However, despite the positive results, the study also revealed some challenges related to technical aspects and the training of teaching staff. Despite the positive assessment of VR/AR technologies, many teachers expressed the need for additional training and support to use these tools more effectively. This opens up prospects for further research in the field of teacher training and HR development in higher education, where an important aspect will be the creation of specialized courses and trainings for teachers on the use of new technologies. It is also worth continuing to study the long-term impact of VR/AR on the professional development of students and graduates, which will allow for a more accurate assessment of the impact of these technologies on their career growth and demand in the labor market. In general, these studies confirm that the use of VR/AR has great potential to improve the quality of education and training of highly qualified specialists, and requires further innovative approaches in teaching and managing educational processes.

Thus, virtual reality (VR) and augmented reality (AR) are powerful tools that can change the educational landscape, making the learning process more interactive and efficient. Observations and research confirm their potential to improve student engagement, enhance learning effectiveness, and create more accessible educational environments. However, for the successful integration of VR and AR into education, it is necessary to pay attention to technical, content and educational aspects, as well as provide training and support for teachers and students. Further research and collaboration between educational institutions and industry will help maximize the potential of these technologies, creating an enriched educational environment for future generations of students.

REFERENCES

Apple has won a major patent relating to real-time Acoustical Ray Tracing that takes Spatial Audio to new dimensions for VR Environments. (2021) https://www.patentlyapple.com

. Bajurov A.E. (2019) Virtual reality in education. Current issues in aviation and astronautics. M.,T. 3, 633-635.

Caudell Thomas, P., & David, W. Mizell. (1992) Augmented reality: An application of heads-up display technology to manual manufacturing processes. Proceedings of the Twenty-Fifth Hawaii International Conference on. 2. IEEE.

Cipresso, P., Giglioli, I., Raya, M. A., & Riva, G. (2018). The Past, Present, and Future of Virtual and Augmented Reality Research: A Network and Cluster Analysis of the Literature. *Frontiers in Psychology*, *9*, 2086. DOI: 10.3389/fpsyg.2018.02086 PMID: 30459681

. Fedchenko A.D. (2020) Virtual Reality in Modern Technologies of Professional Education. Bulletin of the Master's Degree. M., 1(100), 47-48.

Lanier, J. (2018). Virtual Reality: The Promise of the Future. *Interactive Learning International*, *8*(4), 275–279.

. Klimovich R.R. (2019) Implementation of Virtual Reality Technology in Education. Scythian. Student Science Issues, N°8 (36), 30-100.

Pivotto, I., Matias, V., & William de Paula, F. (2024). CAVE automatic virtual environment technology to enhance social participation of autistic people: A classification and literature review. *Research in Autism Spectrum Disorders*, *117*, 1–21.

Rêgo, B. S., Lourenço, D., Moreira, F., & Pereira, C. S. (2024). Digital transformation, skills and education: A systematic literature review. *Industry and Higher Education*, *38*(4), 336–349.

Sanjeev, N. (2019). Augmented Reality and Virtual Reality in Education. Myth or Reality. *International Journal of Emerging Technologies in Learning*, *14*(3), 203–228. DOI: 10.3991/IJET.V14I03.9289

Skarbez, R., Smith, M., & Whitton, M. C. (2021). Revisiting Milgram and Kishino's Reality-Virtuality Continuum. *Frontiers in Virtual Reality*. Advance online publication. DOI: 10.3389/frvir.2021.647997

SketchUp. (2025) URL: http://scirraconstruct.ru/news/vse-o-vozmozhnostyax-programmy-sketchup/

Chapter 6
Economic Sector Development Specifics in the Era of Digital Transformation

Roman V. Okorokov
https://orcid.org/0000-0002-3403-6373
Peter the Great St.Petersburg Polytechnic University, Russia

Anna A. Timofeeva
http://orcid.org/0000-0001-7031-9971
Peter the Great St.Petersburg Polytechnic University, Russia

Ismael M. Diomande
http://orcid.org/0009-0005-6767-4012
Peter the Great St.Petersburg Polytechnic University, Russia

Khudhur Khudhur
Peter the Great St.Petersburg Polytechnic University, Russia

Luc Tri Tuyen
Institute of Information Technology, Hanoi, Vietnam

ABSTRACT

The study provides analysis of development of digital transformation of leading companies taking into account specifics in new economic conditions. It is shown that in order to improve organization management, use of digital technologies is becoming a key factor to increase efficiency and reduce costs while scale of implementation of digital projects varies across economy sectors due to industry specifics

DOI: 10.4018/979-8-3373-8612-6.ch006

and heterogeneity of new technologies spread. It is noted that main feature of digital transformation is need to change company business models affecting internal and external environment associated with gradual transition from closed core processes to modular architecture platform models. The study highlights that digitalization processes affect traditional approaches to HRM in industrial companies. Current HRM development trends are identified taking into account digital technologies influence. A number of recommendations to improve employee efficiency are proposed. The research results can be used by HR specialists to optimize approaches to personnel management in digital era.

INTRODUCTION

The current stage of human community development is characterized by the intensive formation of the digital economy. Digital transformation is extremely relevant for any company or organization, as the world is becoming more and more digital, and the effective use of technology is a prerequisite for competitiveness. Digital transformation makes it possible to reduce the time spent on the production of goods or services, improve product quality, optimize business processes and improve communication between employees and customers. In addition, digital technologies provide valuable information about customer behavior, which allows to adapt business strategies, improve marketing and fine-tune products and services to meet customer needs (Okorokov & Timofeeva, 2023).

Given the emerging new opportunities for innovative development, government and corporate programs and projects have been consistently implemented in recent years in Russia and other countries to build a digital economy for the systematic implementation of digital technologies in many areas: industry, finance, public administration, healthcare, education, social activities, etc. For global context, initiatives such as China's "Made in China 2025" and the EU's "Digital Europe" strategy illustrate how regions adapt to digital challenges. These programs emphasize sustainability and ethical governance, offering benchmarks for analyzing Russia's approach (L. Yu, 2019).

DIGITAL TRANSFORMATION OF LEADING COMPANIES

Leading companies, primarily in the energy, financial and telecommunications sectors are examples of successful implementation of digital transformation projects in the Russian economy.

First of all, we would like to note the results of the activities of Russian companies in the energy sector, in particular, the Gazprom Neft PJSC digital transformation program, which includes several areas (Sulejmanov, 2024):

- digital production and operations (optimization of production processes, digitization of supply chains and logistics operations);
- digital products and services (development of digital products and services for customers, for example, intelligent fuel quality control technologies);
- digital solutions for customers (innovative solutions, for example, contactless payment for fuel using a mobile application);
- digital technologies and innovations (active use of technologies such as the industrial Internet of Things, blockchain and artificial intelligence (AI) to improve business processes and develop new products and services, create digital counterparts of drilling rigs, wells, etc.);
- competencies and culture (investing in digital skills and employee education, creating an innovative culture for the introduction of digital technologies and effective innovative solutions).

The Company has developed a technology strategy as part of the implementation of Gazprom Neft's Innovative Development Program for the coming years with a total expected impact of more than 100 billion rubles in cost savings and the involvement of more than 100 million tons of reserves.

Digitalization in the financial sector is also one of the most relevant area, it allows to improve the quality of services provided and ensure a high degree of security (Tsindeliani et al., 2022). The main examples of digitalization in the financial sector include:

- online banking (banks open accounts for customers, conduct transactions and financial consultations through online platforms, simplifying access to financial services);
- digital wallets (allow customers to store money, make payments and transfers as well as receive discounts from using banking services);
- fintech companies (the fintech companies sector covers various areas of finance, from lending and investing to financial management);

- big data and analytics (big data analysis helps companies study trends and customer behavior, assess risks and make good decisions);
- blockchain and cryptocurrencies (provide new opportunities in the field of finance, including fast and secure transactions and new forms of investment).

The main trend of digitalization in the financial sector is associated with the transition to remote customer service, manifested in the ever-increasing number of online banking customers. The three leaders in the digitalization of banking business are led by Sberbank of Russia PJSC, Tinkoff Bank JSC and Alfa-Bank JSC, while Sberbank is the leader, having formed its own digital ecosystem uniting more than 30 companies with a variety of services.

The digital ecosystem of Sberbank PJSC includes the following products and services (Maiorov, 2022):

- Sber online mobile application (conducting banking operations, paying bills and receiving cashback through the mobile application);
- SberHealth medical platform (allows clients to receive medical consultations, make appointments, and purchase medical services online);
- Sber retailtainment-platforms (combine fitness centers, cafes and other entertainment as well as banking services and products);
- SberInvestor (a platform for new and experienced investors to access exchange-traded instruments and trade on international markets);
- Sber technological hub (research in the field of data, artificial intelligence and other technologies);
- SberUnity platform (support for startups and new business projects, assistance to entrepreneurs in obtaining financing, advice from experienced businessmen), and others.

Globally, India's fintech firms, such as Paytm, excel in financial inclusion via mobile platforms, contrasting with Russian banks' ecosystem-centric models. This raises questions about balancing innovation with accessibility, particularly in underserved regions (Singh, 2020).

The leader of digital transformation in the telecommunications industry is Rostelecom PJSC, which implements the following projects: the portal for state and municipal services, the identification and authentication system, the system of interdepartmental electronic interaction and the universal biometric system for all organizations.

Digital transformation affects the development of the telecommunications industry in the following areas:

- increasing network speed and stability (introducing the latest technologies, such as 5G, to ensure high connection speed and stability for users);
- implementation of cloud and virtualized technologies (cloud computing, network functions virtualization and software-defined networking allow flexible management of networks and resources, provide services, improving quality and productivity);
- increased operational efficiency (the introduction of digital solutions and automation of business processes allows telecom operators to improve their operations and increase efficiency);
- creation of new services and products (the emergence of new digital solutions, for example, smart home, smart city, wearable devices, etc., which allow customers to improve their lifestyle and increase their comfort level).

According to experts, the introduction of AI technologies will bring 46.5 trillion rubles to Russia by 2035, while the main economic effect will be achieved in the industry. New technologies will also be most in demand in finance, logistics and healthcare, but their implementation will be determined by the companies' ability to increase annual investments in the field of AI by 12 times.

The scale of implementation of digital transformation projects varies across sectors of the Russian economy due to industry specifics, heterogeneity in the spread of new digital technologies, etc. However, the following common features can be noted that are changing traditional approaches to service provision due to the active digitalization of industries (Nikonova & Ivasenko, 2023):

- changing customer behavior and expectations (speed, convenience and the ability to receive a service remotely have become basic needs);
- formation of digital ecosystems by industrial and financial organizations;
- customer-oriented service provision, development of mechanisms for wide data exchange, including through the use of open software interfaces;
- active penetration of information technologies into the financial market, including interaction between market participants, government agencies and regulators;
- growing importance of the operational and cybersecurity risks.

Modern companies, both public and private, are forced to constantly adapt to the new conditions of the digital environment, resort to the use of relevant methods of improving efficiency, which includes, among others, improving personnel management, developing medium- and long-term human resource management strategies to achieve the target of increasing competitiveness.

With the introduction of new digital technologies permeating all areas of organizations, the human resource management is also undergoing significant changes. Digitalization processes have significant development potential, radically changing the life of every employee and the business environment of companies. For example, tracking the actions and activities of the staff using mobile devices allows to get up-to-date information about each employee, and the introduction of modern motivation tools allows to individually configure employees to achieve higher performance indicators.

MATERIALS AND METHODS

The purpose of this study is to systematize the processes, factors, business models and results of the digital transformation of organizations based on a generalization of the practices of leading companies in a number of industries and sectors of the economy, highlighting the processes of digitalization of human resource management aimed at improving staff performance.

To achieve this objective, it is necessary to solve the following tasks:

- systematize the factors, business models and results of the digital transformation of leading organizations in a number of economic sectors;
- show that the processes of digitalization of industrial systems management imply the improvement of not only technological, but also human potential throughout the entire production chain;
- clarify the classification of psychological methods for eliminating the influence of the human factor in the management of industrial facilities in order to increase the potential of future human-computer systems;
- identify current trends in the development of human resource management, taking into account the impact of new digital technologies;
- propose a number of recommendations aimed at improving the efficiency of employees in organizations.

The research methodology is based on the systematic approach and includes general scientific and special research methods such as analysis, synthesis, classification, inductive generalization, concretization and systematization.

RESULTS AND DISCUSSION

The implementation of digital transformation models is carried out through the introduction of digital technologies in various functional areas of organizations. The scientific literature notes the lack of unity in approaches to the processes of digital transformation, which necessitates the systematization of the applied models. Based on a detailed analysis of the activities of a number of leading industry companies, the study (Cenzharik et al., 2020) suggests several characteristic models of the digital transformation.

Model #1 (General Electric Co as an example) assumes the end-to-end penetration of digital ideology into a functioning business. The introduction of digital tools takes place at the level of the main business processes, which affects both the corporate strategy and the business model. This model is characterized by the presence of many risks due to the high requirements for internal readiness on the part of both staff and top management.

Model #2 (Gazprom Neft PJSC, Sberbank PJSC as an example) implies the creation of a portfolio of digital projects without affecting the main business processes of the company, while projects can be either embedded in the main business processes or isolated into the separate business units. This model assumes a phased implementation of technologies and allows to accurately assess the effects due to the focus on a specific business process.

Model #3 (Yandex.Taxi, TripAdvisor as an example) implies creating a business entirely in a digital environment. Such companies best meet the trends of digital transformation by creating value based on the platform-based business models.

The gradual transition from closed at the level of the main business processes of an individual company to platform models with modular architecture is a key feature of the digital restructuring (as illustrated in Table 1) which presents the main characteristics of the models considered using a balanced scorecard in which the digital technologies are separated into an independent subsystem.

Modern companies operating on the principle of a platform business model (Airbnb, Amazon, TripAdvisor, etc.) are changing the traditional relationship between consumers and sellers, becoming major players in the market in a short time, and scaling rapidly through the creation of a digital structure and the use of innovative online technologies.

The digital transformation of the energy industry, outlined in the "Energy Strategy of Russia until 2035" as one of the most important tasks in its implementation, implies a qualitative increase in the level of public administration, coordination and monitoring processes, the introduction of industry platform solutions and digitalization of the interaction with all subjects.

Table 1. Digital transformation models within the framework of the company's balanced scorecard

Company's BSC	Model #1	Model #2	Model #3
Finance (shareholders' interests)	The company's budget	Project budget	The company's budget
Training and development (staff)	Full-time staff with a high degree of involvement in digitalization processes	Digital competencies are designed for a specific project	Full-time staff with digital competencies
Internal processes	All processes within the core business	Digitalization processes are separated into a separate project	All processes within the framework of the main (digital) activity
Customers	All groups of the company's clients	A separate segment of current customers or potential new customers	All groups of the company's clients
Digital technologies	Integrated into the main processes	Integrated into a digital project without affecting the main processes	Integrated into the main (digital) processes

Compiled from (Cenzharik et al., 2020)

Digital transformation is carried out, among other things, by including the platform solutions and digital technologies directly into the production processes of industrial enterprises. The platform solution is an automated information system with Internet access that allows users to solve their technological and functional tasks, reducing transaction costs and increasing labor productivity. Currently, a large number of the automated information systems of various architectural solutions with many classes are used. The classification of the most popular information systems includes the following types: control systems; information management systems; access control systems; monitoring and resource management systems; production management systems (Aminov & Lyandau, 2023).

The production management system is the only element in this classification that directly contributes to the creation of added value of the final product, respectively, influencing the process of digital transformation, increasing labor productivity and reducing costs. Therefore, the use of production management systems ensures the most efficient and balanced use of all system resources and the accurate implementation of the set plan.

An example of a digital solution that is part of the information infrastructure is the digital twins, which are actively being implemented today in the process of energy extraction, processing and transportation. Digital twins are mathematical models created to visualize technological and physical installations, containing information about engineering systems, automation tools, their service life and maintenance periods, and a description of physics-chemical processes. As a result, digital twins make it possible to combine existing infrastructure into the one interconnected system and synchronize the work of all its parts. The basis for digital twins is the information system designed to optimize production processes and create additional sources of statistical data.

The main functional purpose of information systems is a set of operations: data collection, storage and processing; presentation of data in a convenient form, depending on the purpose; formation of the data interconnection structure. The main components of information systems include a database, software modules responsible for data processing and a user interface for working with information systems.

Gazprom Neft PJSC, which is actively implementing multifunctional information systems in the production processes, can be mentioned as an illustration of the digitalization of the oil and gas sector. Thus, the work of the Production Control Center is based on complex machine learning algorithms that accumulate data from a large number of metrological devices covering the entire technological network of Gazprom Neft PJSC, which will optimize 80% of operations. The data of more than 30 thousand accounting sensors is collected in a single digital model for monitoring and adjusting the operation of devices, developing troubleshooting measures. The Production Control Center operates on the principles of Industrial Internet of Things technology, combining information transmitted from all sensors with systems, data monitoring algorithms, big data and applications (Aminov & Lyandau, 2023). Comparative analysis reveals that companies like Shell Energy (Europe) and Sinopec (China) deploy similar digital twin technologies but prioritize carbon footprint reduction. For instance, Shell integrates AI to align extraction processes with EU environmental standards, underscoring the role of sustainability in digital strategies (Onukwulu et al., 2025).

HUMAN FACTOR IN INDUSTRIAL FACILITIES

In general, the operation of the fuel and energy complex today largely depends on the human factor, that is, the inherent ability of the operator, who controls numerous parameters of the production facilities, to accurately manage the technological complex to ensure its trouble-free operation without significant negative economic and social consequences (Okorokov & Timofeeva, 2022).

According to experts, almost 45% of accidents at the energy facilities, 60% of the plane crashes, 80% of the marine accidents and 90% of the car accidents are caused by personnel, and on average, a human operator, even in optimal working conditions, can make one or two mistakes for every 100 current operations. Such human errors committed by the operators are not accidental, as thousands of parameters are under their control when managing production facilities. For example, the operator of a large thermal power plant controls about 1,500 parameters of a steam generator, turbine and electric generator, up to 70 regulators, over 300 remote objects, up to 100 technological tasks and 300 alarm boards (Okorokov et al., 2024).

Let us note the most significant factors affecting the professional activity of a human operator (Biswas & Dutta, 2021):

- discrepancy between his psychophysiological capabilities and the requirements of the organization of technological processes;
- variety of the arising situations, their logical complexity as well as the variability of tools for solving tasks;
- monotony of the operator activity;
- requirement of the constant readiness and high responsibility for the results obtained.

The analysis of operator activity and error conditions reveals the characteristic features of the work of a human operator, clarifying the specifics of the difficulties of mastering both the elements and the entire structure of the managed system, which includes a set of professional knowledge, the education of personal qualities, skills and abilities necessary for the operator (Table 2).

There are two main ways to eliminate the errors of operators when managing complex industrial facilities. The first area focuses directly on the employee and his actions, the second – on the technical means and objects of the operator's influence, which are subject to automation and further implementation as control systems.

Table 2. Top-10 most significant factors affecting the operator

1	work experience
2	intelligence (creativity)
3	age
4	qualification
5	discipline
6	absent-mindedness
7	nervousness
8	attitude to danger
9	resoluteness
10	ability to manage stress

Compiled from (Okorokov & Timofeeva, 2022)

The methodological basis of the improvement strategy covers the possibilities of using the positive aspects of the human operator and at the same time the advantages of technical systems, which leads to the formation of an integrated human-machine control system.

FEATURES OF HUMAN-MACHINE INTERACTION

The characteristic features of a person that make it possible to effectively integrate the personnel into a human-machine control system are the ability of a human to adapt to the variability of the external environment, to be selective in building a logical decision chain. Intuition is also an important property, which allows, along with formalized methods, to predict the further development of events and make choices in difficult situations in the presence of contradictory initial data. The combination of such qualities and characteristics determines the success of a person performing basic functions when working as an operator: making difficult decisions, replacing technical control systems in case of their failures and ensuring the operability of controlled equipment. The advantages of technical control systems over humans are their high speed of operations, high accuracy and the ability to work in the difficult conditions of technological processes.

The main task of improving the operation of human-machine systems is a balanced combination of the best characteristics of personnel and technical control systems, which is based on the principles of synthesis maximizing the reliability of the operator in given specific conditions. The essence of this principle is to compensate for the negative characteristics of a person, which are replaced by the positive properties of control machines as well as in the exhaustive application of the characteristic advantages of personnel, which is ensured by a relevant system of technical means. The purpose of this strategy for improving the human-computer system implies the supremacy of man over machine. Control machines are assigned the role of a subordinate element, regardless of their level of perfection.

The basis for the synthesis of human advantages and technical systems is the creation of adaptive automated systems in which this synthesis is carried out based on the coordination of the main parameters of technical systems and management characteristics of the operators as well as the identification of the information environment that ensures the coordination of information flows circulating between technical and biological elements of the human-computer systems (Prostejovsky et al., 2019).

The introduction of such control systems, which ensure a rational combination of the positive qualities of a human operator and technical means based on automated control systems for technological processes creates a working environment in which the likelihood of errors by personnel is significantly reduced.

It is not possible to completely eliminate the impact of personnel errors because the introduction of automated control systems turns the operator into a passive element. The lack of the active control and monotony in work reduce the sharpness of reaction, worsen operational thinking, lead to the loss of vigilance. Replacing a physical object with an information model with mnemonics or pictographs alienates the operator from real behavior, while the ultimate purpose of controlling the object is replaced by a game (to create the required location of certain icons on the display) which reduces the importance of the objectives and responsibility for the actions performed.

Various methods and mechanisms are used to increase the operator efficiency. Since the main emotional and volitional quality of a human operator is readiness for emergency actions, he must be able to mobilize himself in the case of accidents. It is necessary to use appropriate professional selection mechanisms for operators as well as to organize their continuous and periodic training in real conditions. For this purpose, industrial companies periodically conduct operator retraining as well as trainings at work sites (Alyushin et al., 2020).

The modern personnel training system is implemented, firstly, on the basis of studying the principles of equipment operation, operating rules and safety techniques using specially designed virtual complexes, and, secondly, personnel are trained in the skills of maintaining normal and emergency modes on simulators of the operator's workplace and technological processes.

Professional psychological selection also allows increase the effectiveness of operators as a set of measures aimed at ensuring that only people who can master the profession and functional responsibilities in a timely manner get into positions. This is effective both for hiring and for transfers; it is also mandatory if the employee has committed violations during the operation of the equipment. It is important to check whether applicants for vacant positions have the necessary qualities to eliminate dysfunctional behavior (incompetence, inconsistency of the position, resulting errors in work, causing damage).

Training centers for personnel of the Russian energy companies implement professional development and professional retraining programs for the enterprise specialists using modern innovative technologies. Operators and engineering staff are trained to accurately respond to the most complex changes in the actual operation of energy facilities, not only in theory, but also “play out” normal and emergency situations in training. This practice of continuous training on simulators supports the working tone of operators and reduces the influence of the human factor.

PSYCHOLOGICAL METHODS OF OPERATOR ERRORS ELIMINATION

The development of high-precision psychophysiological methods of monitoring the work of various functional systems of the body and an increase in the number of monitored functions still does not completely solve the problem of eliminating the influence of the operator errors and does not provide definitive results on monitoring the condition of the human operator, moreover, it can significantly complicate his activities due to the use of a large number of sensors and applied control tests.

One of the most promising directions in solving this problem is the development of a theory of the individual norm in assessing the human condition, according to which the current state of the operator should be determined not by the generally accepted average statistical criteria, but by establishing the degree of remoteness from them of the individual norm.

According to modern concepts, the priorities formed by the staff play the main role in the formation of the ability to competently assess the situation at all stages of the equipment maintenance. For the competent assessment of a problematic situation and awareness of the connections between events, it is necessary to take into account the information abilities of the human brain, which are also far from unlimited.

Various methods are offered to assess priorities, for example, the hierarchy analysis method. The maintenance personnel of the equipment of a particular industrial facility makes up the list of critical elements that primarily determine the safety of this equipment, while they do this using their experience, knowledge and intuition, that is, they set the priorities of these elements themselves. Their opinions are used as answers to the set of questions, each of which is logically related to the main functional task (for example, maintaining a technological process, optimizing or improving the service of an industrial system). Further, they are transformed into the quantitative indicators of consistency and confidence, and if these values fall within a certain range, it is assumed that this human operator is competent and ready to manage and maintain the equipment in question. Next, the prioritized critical elements are compared with the similar characteristics presented in the official guidance documents. If the maximum errors between these values are not greater than the permissible value, depending only on the number of identified critical elements, then it can be argued that the results of the safety analysis are verified, and the operator is aware of the quality of the elements and is ready to manage the process of improving the quality of service, that is, the model representations of the safety analysis coincide with the understanding of the safety problem by personnel. According to this model, the manageable size of the allocated critical elements in any system can vary within 5-10 events.

Such monitoring of the human operator's mentality, using the algorithm described above, is essential in improving the efficiency of maintenance of any technological systems, and, consequently, in ensuring their reliability and safety. It is only necessary to understand the limits of the possible application of this criterion as well as the fact that when developing modern equipment maintenance technologies, it is necessary to use the systematic approach and probabilistic methods. We must also not forget about the real possibilities, it is necessary to constantly analyze the inconsistencies between the real results and model proposals that have accumulated in recent years in the industry, and constantly look for new solutions. It is required to introduce the modern methods for assessing and ensuring the reliability of technical systems. A promising approach is to evaluate using mathematical analysis based on the probability theory, including probabilistic security analysis, which includes the following:

- emergency event analysis and event tree development;
- analysis of the serviced system and development of failures tree;
- creating a database;
- assessment of the reliability of the system, taking into account failures for common reasons;
- development of the integrated risk model for industrial equipment elements;
- analysis of the errors in personnel actions.

It should be noted that the implementation of these measures to reduce operator errors cannot guarantee the absolute reliability of the "human" link of modern human-computer systems. A person is always a person: even any healthy operator with the necessary professional skills and competencies may experience adverse mental conditions leading to a violation of the quality of his work. The scale of these states has a fairly wide range: from a state of heightened arousal (euphoria) to extreme fatigue. Therefore, methods of managing the human operator's condition have appeared that are associated with the activation of natural psychological processes, including the methods of psychological influence (functional music, stimulation of biologically active points) and the social methods aimed at correcting work and rest regimes, improving sanitary and hygienic conditions (El Bouti & Allouch, 2020).

Due to the widespread introduction of digital technologies and the digitalization of technological processes, the new methods began to be added in addition to the psychological methods (Fig. 1), based on the concept of transferring decision-making functions from humans to control systems and AI techniques, which is a logical complement to the above-mentioned concept of machine adaptation to humans, and its implementation can significantly improve the quality of management of modern industrial systems (Kuznetsova & Konovalov, 2020). Thus, for energy companies, the use of AI systems will optimize the production process in accordance with the technological features of the equipment, implement resource and energy-saving policies on a large scale, find optimal operating modes of the equipment, reduce current costs of the economic and financial resources and promptly solve problems in the event of an emergency (Khrennikov & Lyubarsky, 2022)(Borowski, 2022).

Figure 1. Classification of the psychological methods of the operator errors elimination in industrial systems

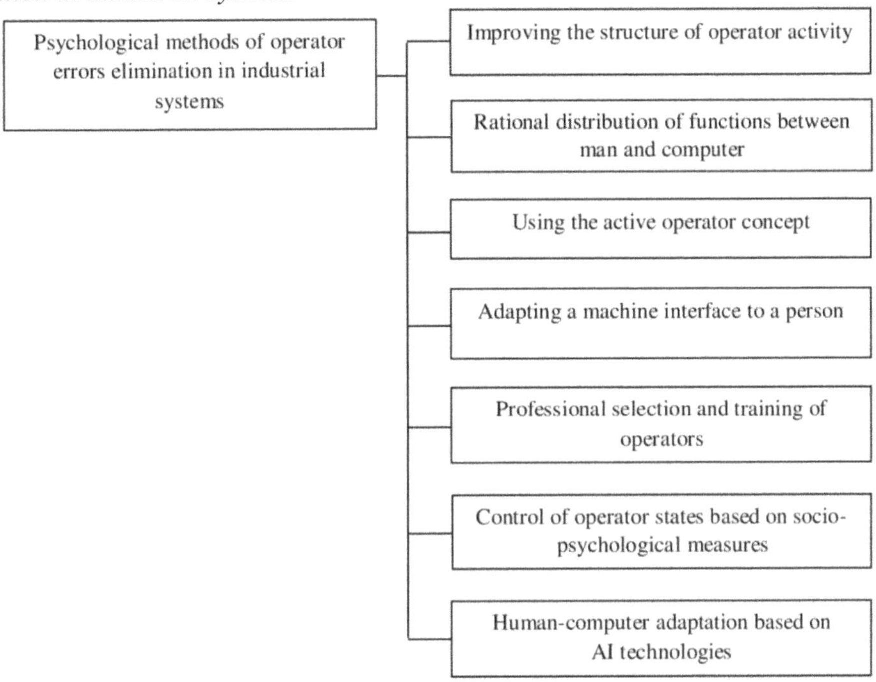

At the same time, it should be emphasized the need for early legislative adoption of the ethical standards regarding the development of AI technologies, regulating their use in the information technology and social sphere, in order to curb the possible abuse by intruders and to prevent the illegal and inhumane applications of AI against society when committing cybercrimes (Pyankova et al., 2024) (Omotunde & Ahmed, 2023).

The EU's AI Act enforces strict ethical guidelines (e.g., algorithmic transparency), whereas Russia's regulatory frameworks remain nascent. This gap heightens risks of misuse, particularly in data privacy and accountability.

Further, in order to achieve the purpose of the study, it seems advisable to divide trends in the field of personnel management into traditional and digital, emphasizing the changes associated with the introduction of AI systems. Traditional trends in the personnel management include general directions of the natural development of society related to the transformation and revision of patterns of behavior in teams, values of corporate culture of organizations, etc.

DIGITAL TRENDS IN HRM

Traditional trends in the human resource management (HRM) include the changes taking place today in organizations, for example, the desire of generation Z (people born in the late 1990s and actively using digital gadgets) to work in a mixed manner, implementing elements of the hybrid or remote work (Bresler et al., 2020).

Based on the analysis of current digital trends and the introduction of innovations in the field of personnel management, presented by the authors of the study (Ng et al., 2021) (Cherep et al., 2022), let us identify the following areas of AI systems use:

1. Generative AI (systems capable of generating text, images and voice can help both in the process of working in an organization and in hiring staff). This type of AI system has many potential applications.
2. Data Factories (representatives of B2B solutions that help route large amounts of data and optimize information storage).
3. Cloud Solutions (cloud services hosted outside the company's infrastructure).
4. Component Software (a set of modules that allow software to be upgraded without the intervention of programmers).
5. Hyper-Automation (full automation of the business processes, capable of increasing productivity and efficiency).
6. AI Software (developing software products capable of monitoring and evaluating employee actions and responding promptly to changes).

AI technologies, like other information and communication technologies, have a significant impact on the field of personnel management and approaches to HRM. In many developed countries, a number of AI systems have already been introduced into the activities of companies at various levels (Johnson et al., 2022). In Russia, such solutions are gradually being applied in many organizations, primarily energy, financial and telecommunications, but the management of domestic companies should take into account both the positive and negative experiences of foreign colleagues.

Currently, one of the significant trends in the HRM is the implementation of predictive models (as a direction for the development of AI-based software). Predictive models allow evaluate the behavior of company personnel and how they will perform in a particular team job, anticipating the condition of employees in advance. For many people, this may seem off-putting and a deterrent, because a person tends to transfer some of the responsibility in the decision-making process of AI-based software. However, in many cases it turns out to be useful, as this approach will allow identify a motivated and stress-resistant employee in advance, which can affect the overall productivity and efficiency of the company due to the delegation of more important work tasks to such an employee.

The authors' analysis of the literary sources made it possible to identify the characteristic features of modern trends in the field of HRM taking into account the impact of new digital technologies as illustrated in Table 3.

Table 3. Current trends in HRM and their main characteristics

Characteristics	Elements of digitalization	Description
Generation Z strives for hybrid work	Employee monitoring software related to ERP systems	Generation Z prefers to work in a mixed format. Companies are implementing corporate management systems to monitor employees
The increasing importance of soft skills	Using AI and machine learning (ML) for recruitment	Flexible skills help with work and affect its effectiveness. Teamwork is highly appreciated by employers. Companies use AI and ML in their work with staff
Focus on work-life balance and employee well-being	Using mobile applications for personnel management and communication with employees	Companies pay attention to the well-being of their employees, trying to create a comfortable environment. Managers use mobile apps to monitor employees on the go
Strengthening the role of HR analytics in decision-making	Automation of routine tasks in HR processes	Analytics has become an integral part of HRM. Routine HR processes are automated using specialized software
Increasing importance of corporate culture and values of the organization	Using social media to recruit staff and increase employee loyalty	Corporate culture plays a big role and is a current trend these days. Social networks are used to select staff and find the best specialists
Increased flexibility in work schedules and working conditions	Using cloud technologies for storing and processing personal data of employees	A new generation of employees prefers flexible work schedules, and companies are trying to provide them with this opportunity. Organizations use cloud solutions in their work
Increasing importance of diversification and inclusivity in recruitment	VR and AR technologies in staff training	Virtual (VR) and augmented (AR) reality technologies help train staff in complex technological processes. Many innovative companies pay special attention to inclusivity when selecting positions
Sustainable Development	AI-driven carbon footprint tracking	Companies adopt systems to monitor environmental impacts, e.g., logistics firms using digital platforms to track CO_2 emissions

Compiled from (Laas, 2023) (Ranjan & Foropon, 2021)

Working remotely from home or elsewhere has a number of advantages, including saving resources, reducing absences due to illness, a more comfortable environment and complete freedom of movement, which generally has a positive effect on the employee motivation. The use of digital communication gadgets, the balance of work and social life can strengthen as a whole the corporate culture and the emotional state of the employee.

At the same time, there are also a number of difficulties of the remote work that HR managers of organizations strive to overcome:

- reducing the degree of the staff involvement in the corporate environment (employees are only busy with work, which reduces their interest in activities and further development);
- problems with communication between employees, for example, a long wait for a colleague to answer an urgent question;
- reducing the opportunities for non-material staff motivation;
- dependence on a stable Internet connection, which endangers not only communication within the company, but also outside it.

The study (Osorio & Madero, 2024) revealed the following main features of the remote form of work:

1. This type of employment is best suited for knowledge workers with a high level of care and perseverance, often with higher education.
2. There are certain limitations of this remote work format: geographical and industry-specific.
3. Learning processes within the framework of remote work proceed differently than in the offline format, which requires significant efforts to adapt such a work schedule.

Special attention should be paid to the industry-specific features of remote work. There are a number of specialties in which this type of employment is unacceptable, such as medical experiments and research; physical labor requiring special equipment and facilities; heavy industry and some types of services. In such cases, the direct presence of a specialist at the workplace is extremely necessary.

Despite the limitations faced by employees in the above-mentioned fields of activity, there are also those in which remote work makes it possible to optimize the production processes and ensure the effective fulfillment of tasks. A significant proportion of remote employees are associated with sectors of the economy, the nature of their activities does not depend on the specific location and is mostly based on intellectual work and work with digital technologies. So, in the first half of 2024, information technology, finance and marketing were named the most popular areas for remote work.

The new Generation Z employees create new requirements for the workflow style, which, in turn, will require the development of new digital solutions for effective personnel management. In order to strengthen social ties within the team, it can be recommended to introduce additional activities into the workdays of employees, such as practicing cyber sport together; conducting online briefings in a non-standard dress code; brainstorming sessions, etc.

Mobile solutions for monitoring employees "on the go" allow to evaluate the effectiveness of their work and optimize the activities of different departments and the company as a whole. In addition, digital tools for staff development and training, including those based on AI, help significantly save time and improve the quality of work.

Recently, the remote work format has been gaining more and more popularity and provides a number of organizations with higher financial performance than the usual full-time schedule. Employees in such companies are more engaged in fulfilling their official duties, without being distracted by personal conversations with colleagues inherent in office employment.

Based on the results of summarizing a number of sources, the following main areas of increasing staff motivation in remote work are identified (Dudnikov et al., 2024):

1. Conducting personal online meetings with employees to discuss the specifics of their activities. Employees need to receive feedback on the work done and discuss development paths within the company with the head.
2. Conducting informal weekly online team meetings. Within the framework of remote work, the company and its employees are often depersonalized, which leads to a lack of communication and a violation of socialization. During such meetings, the degree of staff involvement in the company's activities increases as well as the level of communication and trust between colleagues.
3. Connect to work meetings with the webcameras on. Visual contact allows employees to feel involved in common activities and monitor the emotions of colleagues. When the webcameras are turned off, the effect of an empty room is created, employees complain that they cannot properly evaluate their work and the degree of interest of the audience.
4. Organization of face-to-face events. This measure allows get to know your colleagues personally and form an idea of your team. In face-to-face meetings, the process of adapting new staff is faster.
5. Providing opportunities for the continuous professional development. It is important for intellectual workers to constantly develop in their profession and relevant digital technologies. Modern companies create knowledge bases where they upload the courses necessary for starting work and professional development as well as pay for third-party information resources.
6. Organization of the online community. The so-called "Club of interests" allows find like-minded people and see colleagues not only as employees of the company with their job responsibilities, but also as individuals.
7. The use of the Objectives and Key Results format by the organization's management when setting objectives. An employee engaged in the remote work will perform a set of tasks according to a schedule convenient for him.

8. Financial rewards of employees based on the results of closed projects or at the end of the financial year.
9. The introduction of elements of the bonus system (voluntary health insurance policies, travel compensation, etc.) helps to see the company as a caring employer and increases staff loyalty.

The study (Starodubceva, 2021) presents the existing barriers to the introduction of the remote work format in organizations and measures to eliminate them, in particular, an increase in the likelihood of uncoordinated work of different departments was noted, which, in turn, can be solved by introducing a set of motivational measures. The adaptation of a company's correct motivation policy can have a significant impact on the employee management processes and increase the effectiveness of remote work. The formation of trusting, but at the same time controlled relationships between managers and remote employees will contribute to professional development and increase the overall level of satisfaction with the quality of work and life of employees. Online meetings of employees through video conferencing systems, organization of their interaction in popular social networks and widespread introduction of the elements of material and non-material incentives can contribute to achieving the company's business objectives.

In contrast to Russia, remote work in India and Brazil faces infrastructural barriers (e.g., rural Internet access), emphasizing the need to tailor digital strategies to local conditions (Cavalcante et al., 2021).

Despite the fact that the processes of digitalization and the introduction of digital tools in the field of HRM provide many advantages, it should be noted that it is necessary further develop the processes for humanizing personnel management methods. Currently, the value of communication skills and the importance of employee qualities such as empathy and creative thinking are only increasing; HR managers must take all these elements into account when making personnel decisions and evaluating the work of company staff.

Thus, it can be argued that the future of HRM lies in a harmonious combination of traditional management methods and new digital technologies designed to improve the quality of work and life of employees as well as the efficiency of corporate processes.

There are differences in approaches to HRM in Russia and a number of other countries, in which the key component is the role of a manager in the form of a staff assistant. At foreign enterprises, human resources are usually viewed from a personality-oriented perspective, which means that the HR specialist is viewed more as an employee's "advocate" than as an agent of the organization. This personality-oriented approach to personnel management is facing increasing pressure from the traditional productivity- and performance-oriented management practices prevailing in large multinational corporations (Karakulin, 2019).

A number of Russian companies are now beginning to apply a comprehensive system of motivation and rewards, including a combination of material and non-material incentives. At the same time, many organizations do not implement the format of non-material incentives, everything is stimulated only by the allocation of bonuses in monetary form.

In modern organizations, a systematic approach in the field of personnel management should be applied. It is extremely important to pay attention to new trends and the introduction of modern management tools, to monitor the changes taking place in society. An immense role in modern companies is played by the personal qualities of HR managers and their attitude to the work they do as well as their flexible skills.

The impact of digital transformation cannot be offset, as its processes take place independently of the functioning of companies and the activities of managers. History has seen examples of companies resisting progress and change, and for many of them the resistance ended in bankruptcy or the sale of the business.

SECTORAL DIGITAL TRENDS

The modern implementation of digitalization of the agricultural sector is based on the basic innovations such as nano-, bio-, information and communication digital technologies. First of all, building a system of business processes in the agro-industrial complex in the context of digital transformation involves electronic document management and automated processing of big data flows in order to significantly improve the efficiency of operations.

For example, an approach based on the use of the Internet of Things (IoT) as a tool for the digital transformation of agricultural production makes it possible to automate the full cycle of agrotechnical work related to crop production and animal husbandry. At the same time, hardware elements play an important role here: peripheral equipment (sensors), communication channels (wired and wireless), and web platforms for creating industry-specific applications. The introduction of such digital technologies creates the prerequisites for a gradual reduction in direct human involvement in the agricultural production processes.

A number of software products that provide services for processing agrotechnological data collected using specialized sensors can be cited as examples of successful implementation of digital transformation projects in the agricultural sector. Thus, Rigtech and kSense IoT platforms make it possible to automate the control of agricultural machinery, storage and processing of agricultural products, monitoring of land and livestock management processes. The Smart4agro product provides a cloud-based Geographic Information Systems (GIS) service for management decision-making, monitoring and forecasting farmland conditions (Efremov & Kovalev, 2023).

The digital transformation of logistics systems began to take place at the active pace after 2020 due to the coronavirus pandemic, as it was necessary to develop new approaches to working with customers, simplify contactless payment processes and methods of delivering products. For large logistics companies, it was necessary to build a digital foundation as soon as possible and implement the information infrastructure to ensure the continuity of business. First of all, logistics companies developed digital services for working with customers: processing requests and complaints, purchasing and paying for services online, which simplified interaction with customers and reduced the complexity of processing requests (Okorokov et al., 2021).

For example, the Russian Railways JSC implemented the Freight Transportation system, which organizes e-commerce in the company's services, and the Intertran digital project to monitor cargo movement from abroad to Russia, taking into account multimodal transportation. The company's "Digital Transformation Strategy" reflects the need to implement eight digital platforms in all business directions, including, in particular, multimodal passenger and cargo transportation, the work of a linear infrastructure operator, transportation process management and maintenance of the transport logistics hubs.

It is planned to use robotic devices with AI and driverless technologies to significantly improve the service logistics and digitalize the customer service. For example, Russian Railways JSC is introducing digital twins as the most important digitalization tool for virtual forecasting of the company's real business processes. The Autoagent digital twin optimizes the processing of transportation documents for empty and loaded wagons, and the Electronic Pretensionist digital twin makes claims for the delivery/dispatch of products, improving the quality of cargo transportation. The Transportation Process Management digital platform carries out the planning of freight transportation by rail, creates the addressable plan for bringing trains to port stations, dispatches processes, generates daily train schedules and effective management of traction resources. To organize the transportation process, this digital platform with AI support processes information on cargo transportation schedules, repair plans and regulatory data, compares it with actual data and makes optimal decisions (Nazarova & Treiman, 2023).

In Europe, companies like DHL leverage AI for "green logistics", optimizing routes to reduce CO_2 emissions. Such cases highlight how digitization can align with environmental goals – a dimension requiring deeper exploration in Russia (Bobylev et al., 2018) (Dzwigol et al., 2024).

The digital transformation of educational services is a complex multidimensional phenomenon that includes both a multitude of problematic factors and a set of ways to resolve them productively. The study (Boguslavsky & Neborsky, 2023) identified a number of key socio-technological risks of the digital transformation of educational services, presented in Table 4, which are relevant for other sectors of the economy.

Table 4. Key risks of the digital transformation of educational services

	Types of risks	Brief description of the risks and resolution methods
1	The risk of replacing humans with AI	The prospect of replacing teachers with robots and chatbots. Minimizing this risk: lifelong education to build individual trajectories and adapt to new conditions; adaptation programs and counseling by psychologists
2	The risk of loss of identity by a person	Loss of semantic orientations, values of education, decrease in demand for knowledge and scientific research. The educational sphere should provide tools for searching for meanings, maintaining social connections and expanding the boundaries of one's mentality
3	Risks of social distancing, alienation	The risks of human immersion in the world of algorithms and robots that replace live communication, business and everyday communication. Minimizing risks through interpersonal training, increasing motivation and developing emotional intelligence
4	Risks of loss of privacy	Invasion of privacy, violation of personal boundaries by destructive influence on the will. Resolution through the improvement of human relationships with digital technologies at a level that does not replace skills or personal characteristics
5	The risk of increase in mental disorders	The gap between the speed of digital technology development and the adaptation of the human mentality to new conditions. Minimization through mandatory digital hygiene training at all age stages
6	The risk of rising inequality	The division of society into separate strata in terms of accessibility and quality of education. Resolution through the restructuring of professional education; setting up courses for specific skills and individual routes, in search of one's own identity

Compiled from (Boguslavsky & Neborsky, 2023)

The digital transformation of educational services in Russia presupposes the achievement of the following objectives:

- reducing inequality in access to new technologies through the development of a digital educational environment;
- eliminating digital inequality by updating the content, forms and methods of educational work, introducing digital teaching materials into practice and moving towards a personalized educational process.

Three types of work are provided for the implementation of the first objective:

1. Upgrading of the digital infrastructure of education: connecting all educational institutions to the Internet, developing the digital infrastructure of educational institutions and the digital system of the educational process.
2. Revision of the procedure and structure of certification, assessment and monitoring: creation and commissioning of new digital control and measuring materials, tools for all types of assessment activities, creation of a system that integrates

the collection, storage and exchange of information about the successes and confirmed results of participants in the educational process.

3. Creating universal access to constantly updated and expanding digital educational and methodological resources, tools and services.

To achieve the second objective, work is aimed at shaping the digital transition, improving the quality of education, rebuilding educational institutions and moving to a personalized model of the educational process as follows:

- creation of a domestic network of the innovative digital education platforms, transfer of the practical part of this work to educational institutions;
- designing and developing a regulatory framework for the digital transformation of education;
- introduction of a system for monitoring and supporting the dissemination of educational processes of digital transformation of educational institutions.

Thus, these works aimed at bridging the digital divide are closely related, while the work of the first group is supportive. The full implementation of the results obtained here is impossible without improving the regulatory framework for the digital transformation of education, which is part of the work of the second group (Avdyushkin, 2023).

In the context of progressive formation of the digital economy, the existing methods of teaching students at universities require changes. Currently, there is the active discussion in Russia about the need to switch to new educational standards of higher education, which form a set of the relevant competencies for each area of the future professional activity for students during their studies at the university. The training of students according to existing standards is focused more on the training of imitation specialists who know a little about everything, rather than on the training of creative innovators who know everything in a particular field of activity (Okorokov & Timofeeva, 2020).

The creation and operation of new digital industries will require high-tech specialists, whose training differs significantly from the traditional form existing in technical universities aimed at developing an extensive set of competencies, which, with limited training time, does not allow for the formation of in-depth knowledge in the field of future activities. We need a different system for training specialists to work together in high-tech teams to manage the production processes of the digital economy. Such future specialists should have the wide range of professional competencies as a set of knowledge, skills and experience as well as the key competencies that are essential for the effective functioning of each component system.

The digital transformation has led to a change in our daily experiences and learning methods. As a result of the increased needs and expectations of students in the high-tech teaching methods, the modular learning has become one of the most popular educational methods these days.

In modular learning, subjects are studied in short block modules, each focusing on a specific topic, allowing students to select the courses they are interested in and assemble them in the required sequence to complete the program. This learning model is more flexible and customizable, allows students to build their own educational trajectory, and gives students the opportunity to have access to learning wherever it is convenient, for example, in an online format.

In order to meet the requirements of digital transformation, modular learning must have two key characteristics:

- interactivity (students should be able to actively participate in learning, for example, by communicating with other students, working in a group on projects, using new technologies);
- adaptability (modular learning should provide a personalized approach, depending on the requirements of each student). This can be achieved by providing students with personalized learning programs customized to their interests as well as providing practical examples for independent work.

The implementation of the modular learning model will increase the competitiveness of Russian universities in the educational services market in the era of digital transformation. This significantly corresponds to current trends in the training of specialists at the world's leading universities, where priority attention is given to the development of education as the basis for the formation of human intellectual potential (Pismensky & Safonova, 2022).

CONCLUSION

Based on the results of the study, it can be concluded that digital transformation provides the significant advantages to modern organizations in the new socio-economic conditions, including increased productivity by reducing operating costs, optimizing business processes, monitoring and managing risks and improving communications between employees and customers. In addition, digital technologies provide the valuable information about customer behavior, which allows companies to adapt business strategies and improve marketing, contributing to the creation of better products and services. At the same time, the scale of implementation of digital transformation projects varies by economic sector due to the presence of industry specifics and the heterogeneity of the spread of new technologies.

Digital transformation is a global phenomenon, yet its implementation reflects regional priorities: China focuses on technological sovereignty, the EU on ethics and sustainability, and Russia on integrating digital solutions into traditional industries. Strengthening resilience requires addressing not only technological gaps but also environmental impacts, such as data center energy consumption and e-waste.

As a result of the work carried out, it was shown that the simultaneous processes of digital transformation and traditional transformations in economic systems have a significant impact on the activities of organizations and their performance indicators. It was noted that in order to increase competitiveness, modern companies should pay constant attention to analyzing markets, the external and internal environment, monitor changes taking place in society, and assess the risks of introducing new digital technologies. A prerequisite for the implementation of this approach is the comprehensive business transformation, in which the introduction of digital technologies is accompanied by the improvement of both organizational management structures and human resources, including the development of new competencies and the growth of production management culture.

Human resource management remains one of the most important components of the management activities of any organization that requires close attention and control. Personal development of employees, the system of motivation and bonuses, consideration of the wishes of employees of different generations, the introduction of elements of hybrid or remote work, the use of innovative digital systems including those based on AI – all this has a positive impact on the development of companies and improving the efficiency of their activities.

REFERENCES

Alyushin, M. V., Kolobashkina, L. V., Golov, P. V., & Nikishov, K. S. (2020). Adaptive Behavioral Model of the Electricity Object Management Operator for Intelligent Current Personnel Condition Monitoring Systems. *Advanced Technologies in Robotics and Intelligent Systems.*, (502). Advance online publication. DOI: 10.1007/978-3-030-33491-8_38

Aminov, K. A., & Lyandau, Yu. V. (2023). Digital transformation of the oil and gas complex as a way to increase the efficiency of production processes in the fuel and energy sector [in Russ.]. *Innovation and investment.*, (1), 258–261.

Avdyushkin, V. V. (2023). Digital technologies in education // Pedagogy: current issues of theory and practice. Collection of articles of the III International Scientific and Practical Conference. Penza: Science and Education. pp. 20-22. (in Russ.)

Biswas, A., & Dutta, P. K. (2021). *Novel Approach of Automation to Risk Management: The Reduction in Human Errors*. EAI/Springer Innovations in Communication and Computing., DOI: 10.1007/978-3-030-49795-8_65

Bobylev, S. N.. (2018). Indicators for digitalization of sustainable development goals in PEEX program. *Geography, Environment, Sustainability*, *11*(1), 145–156. DOI: 10.24057/2071-9388-2018-11-1-145-156

Boguslavsky, M. V., & Neborsky, E. V. (2023). Methodological approaches to digital transformation of education: risks and solutions // Conceptual framework of pedagogy and education: A collective monograph. Blagoveshchensk: BSPU Publishing. pp. 54-64. (in Russ.)

Borowski, P. F. (2022). *Digital Transformation and Prosumers Activities in the Energy Sector. Intelligent Systems in Digital Transformation*. Springer International Publishing., DOI: 10.1007/978-3-031-16598-6_6

Bresler, M., Galiullina, S., & Gerasimova, D. (2020). Transformation of the values of Generation Z-Residents of the digital society of sustainable development. In *E3S Web of Conferences* (Vol. 208, p. 09043). EDP Sciences.

Cavalcante, A. M.. (2021). 5G for remote areas: Challenges, opportunities and business modeling for Brazil. *IEEE Access : Practical Innovations, Open Solutions*, *9*, 10829–10843. DOI: 10.1109/ACCESS.2021.3050742

Cenzharik, M. K., Krylova, Yu. V., & Steshenko, V. I. (2020). Digital transformation of companies: Strategic analysis, influencing factors and models [in Russ.]. *Bulletin of St. Petersburg University. Economy.*, *36*, 390–420. DOI: 10.21638/spbu05.2020.303

Cherep, A., Voronkova, V., & Androsova, O. (2022). Transformational changes in organizational management and human resources in the digital age. Baltic journal of economic studies, 8(3), 210-219.

. Dudnikov, T.E., Okorokov, R.V., Timofeeva, A.A., Filyanina, E.A. (2024). Formation of proposals for improving the principles of personnel management in the context of remote work // Natural Sciences and Humanities Research. No. 4(54). pp. 448-451. (in Russ.)

Dzwigol, H.. (2024). Digitalization and energy in attaining sustainable development: Impact on energy consumption, energy structure, and energy intensity. *Energies*, *17*(5). Advance online publication. DOI: 10.3390/en17051213

Efremov, A. A., & Kovalev, I. L. (2023). Overview of trends in the digital transformation of agricultural production [in Russ.]. *Agricultural Economics*, (1), 50–57. DOI: 10.29235/1818-9806-2023-1-50-57

El Bouti, M. Y., & Allouch, M. (2020). Analysis of human factors for enhancing safety and security management system in fossil and renewable power plants. *International Journal of Safety and Security Engineering*, *10*(4), 491–500.

Johnson, P. C., Laurell, C., Ots, M., & Sandström, C. (2022). Digital innovation and the effects of artificial intelligence on firms' research and development – Automation or augmentation, exploration or exploitation? *Technological Forecasting and Social Change*, *179*. Advance online publication. DOI: 10.1016/j.techfore.2022.121636

Karakulin, A. Yu. (2019). Foreign experience in the use and development of human resources // Bulletin of the Altai Academy of Economics and Law. No. 12-3. pp. 176-182. (in Russ.)

Khrennikov, A. Yu., & Lyubarsky, Yu. Ya. (2022). Principles of building artificial intelligence systems and their application in the electric power industry [in Russ.]. *Power Engineering*, (3), 22–30.

Kuznetsova, N., & Konovalov, Y. (2020). Enhancing the Safety of Energy Systems Functioning at Their Digitalization // E3S Web of Conferences. Vol. 209. https://doi.org/DOI: 10.1051/e3sconf/ 202020906017

. N.I. Laas. (2023). Prospects for the development of remote employment and career building features in the context of the development of the remote work market // Human resources and Intellectual Resources Management in Russia. No. 2(65). pp. 37-42. (in Russ.)

Maiorov, S. A. (2022). Development of the ecosystem of SberBank PJSC [in Russ.]. *Integral International Journal of Applied Sciences and Technologies.*, (1), 111–117. DOI: 10.55186/02357801-2022-7-1-3

Nazarova, A. N., & Treiman, M. G. (2023). Digital transformation of logistics activities in the implementation of freight transportation by rail // Current issues of modern scientific research. International scientific and practical conference. pp. 13-15. (in Russ.)

Nikonova, Ya. I., & Ivasenko, A. G. (2023). Digital transformation of the financial sector of the Russian economy // International Scientific Research Journal. No. 1(127). pp. 1-8. https://doi.org/ (in Russ.)DOI: 10.23670/IRJ.2023.127.82

Okorokov, R., Timofeeva, A., Filyanina, E., & Benchabane, M. L. (2021). Institutional approach to classification of sustainable digital technologies in service logistics. In *E3S Web of Conferences* (Vol. 258, p. 02018). EDP Sciences.

Okorokov, R. V., & Timofeeva, A. A. (2020). Formation of key competencies of specialists in the era of digitalization // Russia, Europe, Asia: digitalization of the global space. Collection of scientific papers of the III International Scientific and Practical Forum. Nevinnomyssk: SEQUOIA LLC. pp. 522-525. (in Russ.)

Okorokov, R. V., & Timofeeva, A. A. (2022). Improving human potential in the management of electric power systems in the context of digitalization // The role of innovation in the transformation and sustainable development of modern science: A collective monograph. Vol. 66. Ufa: Aeterna LLC. pp. 45-61. (in Russ.)

Okorokov, R. V., & Timofeeva, A. A. (2023). Industry specifics of digital transformation models // Global challenges of digital transformation of markets: A collective monograph. St. Petersburg: POLYTECH PRESS. pp. 681-703. (in Russ.)

Okorokov, R. V., Timofeeva, A. A., & Sapanova, R. (2024). *The role of the human factor in electric power systems in the context of digitalization // Navigating Digital Transformation: Original Research Across Smart Cities, Sustainable Development and Beyond.* Nova Science Publishers., DOI: 10.52305/YMXR0010

Omotunde, H., & Ahmed, M. (2023). *A Comprehensive Review of Security Measures in Database Systems: Assessing Authentication, Access Control, and Beyond.* Mesopotamian Journal of Cyber Security., DOI: 10.58496/mjcsc/ 2023/016

Onukwulu, E. C.. (2025). Integrating sustainability into procurement and supply chain processes in the energy sector. *Gulf Journal of Advance Business Research.*, *3*(1), 76–104. DOI: 10.51594/gjabr.v3i1.68

Osorio, M. L., & Madero, S. (2024). Explaining Gen Z's desire for hybrid work in corporate, family, and entrepreneurial settings. *Business Horizons*, •••. Advance online publication. DOI: 10.1016/j.bushor.2024.02.008

. Pismensky, G.I., & Safonova, S.V. (2022). Leading Russian and foreign universities in the context of digital transformation of education // Human capital. No. 12-2(168). pp. 37-47. (in Russ.)

Prostejovsky, A. M., Brosinsky, C., Heussen, K., Westermann, D., Kreusel, J., & Marinelli, M. (2019). The future role of human operators in highly automated electric power systems. *Electric Power Systems Research*, *175*, 105883.

Pyankova, S. G., Ergunova, O. T., & Dudnikov, T. E. (2024). Trends in the development of the theory of noonomics: Artificial intelligence as a tool for the transition to a new industrial society [in Russ.]. *Ufa Humanitarian Scientific Forum.*, (2), 156–174. DOI: 10.47309/2713-2358-2024-2-156-174

Ranjan, J., & Foropon, C. (2021). Big Data Analytics in Building the Competitive Intelligence of Organizations. *International Journal of Information Management*, •••. Advance online publication. DOI: 10.1016/j.ijinfomgt.2020.102231

Singh, T. (2020). Fintech adoption: A critical appraisal of the strategies of Paytm in India. *IUP Journal of Management Research.*, *19*(4), 7–17.

Starodubceva, A. S. (2021). Employee motivation for remote work // Digital economy: problems and prospects of development. Collection of scientific articles of the 3rd Interregional Scientific and Practical Conference. Kursk: South-Western State University. pp. 395-398. (in Russ.)

Sulejmanov, A. V. (2024). Digital transformation of the Russian oil and gas industry: Status, prospects, systemic problems and ways to solve them [in Russ.]. *The scientific aspect.*, *27*(7), 3340–3345.

Tsindeliani, I. A., Proshunin, M. M., Sadovskaya, T. D., Popkova, Z. G., Davydova, M. A., & Babayan, O. A. (2022). Digital transformation of the banking system in the context of sustainable development. *Journal of Money Laundering Control*, *25*(1), 165–180.

Yu, L. (2019). *"Made in China 2025" China's development strategy through technological innovation*. Universidade de Lisboa.

Chapter 7
Ethics and Bias in AI-Powered HR Systems

Pradnya Bhatkulkar
https://orcid.org/0009-0007-0781-8621
Manipal Global NXT, India

ABSTRACT

This chapter examines the transformative role of AI in HR, highlighting its dual ability to boost operational efficiency while inadvertently reinforcing systemic biases. It analyzes the integration of AI in resume screening, employee monitoring, and workforce analytics, demonstrating how algorithmic decisions are influenced by historical data and design flaws. Examples such as biased recruitment tools and culturally insensitive emotion-recognition software underscore the ethical risks of opaque "black box" systems. Explores technical vulnerabilities, oversight deficiencies, and broader societal inequities, offering a multidisciplinary perspective on bias in AI-driven HR systems. It also provides strategic recommendations for enhancing transparency and ethical AI design through rigorous dataset auditing, bias-mitigation techniques, and collaborative governance frameworks. Ultimately, it serves as a roadmap for HR professionals, technologists, and organizational leaders striving to harness AI responsibly while ensuring that HR advancements align with principles of fairness, inclusion

INTRODUCTION

The integration of Artificial Intelligence (AI) into Human Resources (HR) has ushered in a transformative era, redefining traditional practices across talent acquisition, employee engagement, performance management, and workforce analytics. Organizations now leverage AI-driven tools to automate resume screening, predict

DOI: 10.4018/979-8-3373-8612-6.ch007

employee attrition, personalize learning programs, and optimize recruitment pipelines. These innovations promise efficiency, scalability, and data-driven insights, enabling HR teams to make faster, more informed decisions. Yet, as AI becomes deeply embedded in HR processes, its ethical implications and potential to perpetuate systemic biases have sparked urgent debates. The very algorithms designed to streamline fairness and objectivity risk amplifying historical inequities, undermining the principles of diversity and inclusion they were meant to advance.

Technically, bias can enter when data are unbalanced, labels reflect prejudice, or models rely on traits linked to protected groups (for example, ZIP codes as proxies for race). Common fairness measures include:

- **Demographic parity**: equal selection rates for each group
- **Equalized odds**: equal error rates for each group

To address bias, teams can re-weight data, apply de-biasing algorithms, or adjust outcomes after modeling.

Regulators are also responding. Europe's AI Act classifies certain HR uses as "high risk," requiring transparency and bias audits. In the U.S., the EEOC and state laws demand that AI hiring tools comply with civil-rights protections and inform applicants when AI is used.

Employees report frustration when AI decisions lack explanation—many want clear reasons if a tool affects their promotion, pay, or dismissal. To build trust, organizations should:

- Audit AI systems regularly for fairness
- Provide simple, clear explanations to employees
- Involve diverse staff in AI design and review

By combining technical safeguards, ethical review, and open communication, HR teams can harness AI's benefits while promoting equity and trust in the workplace.

One prominent example is the deployment of AI in resume-screening processes. AI tools trained on historical hiring data risk inheriting existing prejudices, often favoring candidates from certain demographics or educational backgrounds. A notable case is Amazon's AI recruitment tool, which notoriously penalized resumes containing the term "women's" or referencing all-women's colleges. (Marlowe, 2021) It underscores how unchecked algorithms can inadvertently institutionalize discrimination. Similarly, emotion-recognition software employed in employee monitoring can misinterpret facial expressions due to cultural variances, thereby disadvantaging individuals from underrepresented groups. Such biases compromise the integrity and undermining trust and exposing organizations to legal, reputational, and financial risks. The increasing scrutiny from regulatory bodies, such as the European Union's General Data Protection Regulation (GDPR) and the U.S. Equal Employment Opportunity Commission (EEOC), amplifies the need for accountability and ethical vigilance.

Compounding these concerns is the "black box" nature of many AI algorithms. These systems often function with limited transparency, rendering it challenging to audit decision-making processes or elucidate outcomes to stakeholders. HR leaders, in turn, face the dilemma of balancing efficiency gains with the imperative of ensuring fairness and transparency. The absence of clear accountability frameworks exacerbates this challenge, heightening the risk of ethical lapses and potential public backlash.

By critically analyzing these facets, the chapter aims to provide a nuanced understanding of the ethical landscape surrounding AI in HR. It also offers strategic recommendations for organizations to mitigate bias, enhance transparency, and foster equitable outcomes, thereby ensuring that AI technologies contribute positively to the evolving domain of human resource management.

MISSION OF THE CHAPTER

The mission of this chapter is threefold:

1. **To raise awareness about the ethical implications of AI in HR:**

The ethical implications of AI in HR are profound, as algorithms can inadvertently perpetuate historical biases. A seminal example is Amazon's recruitment tool, which discriminated against female candidates due to training on male-dominated resumes (Marlowe, 2021). This underscores how AI systems can institutionalize inequality. Similarly it is demonstrated racial and gender biases in facial recognition technologies, raising concerns about their use in video interviews (De Villiers, 2022). (Tilmes, 2022)highlighted that biased training data in healthcare algorithms led to discriminatory outcomes, a risk paralleled in HR systems. Ethical AI must address these issues through a lens of fairness and justice, as argued and who emphasize embedding equity into system design. (Friedman & Nissenbaum, 1996)

2. **To identify key challenges and risks associated with bias in AI-powered HR systems**:

Artificial Intelligence (AI) has revolutionized human resource management by introducing efficiency and data-driven insights into various HR functions, including recruitment, performance evaluation, and promotion decisions. However, the integration of AI in HR systems has also introduced significant ethical concerns, particularly regarding bias. This section identifies the critical challenges and risks associated with bias in AI-powered HR systems.

3. **Biased Training Data**

AI systems are susceptible to inheriting historical biases embedded within their training datasets. (Ferrara, 2024). If marginalized groups are underrepresented or misrepresented in these datasets, the AI models trained on such data can perpetuate and even amplify existing inequalities. For instance, if historical hiring data reflect discriminatory practices, the AI system may learn to replicate these biases, leading to the exclusion of certain demographic groups from hiring or promotional opportunities.

4. **Opacity of Algorithms**

The "black box" nature of many artificial intelligence (AI) algorithms presents a significant ethical challenge in the realm of human resources (HR). These algorithms often operate in ways that are not easily understandable or accessible to human observers, including those who deploy and utilize them in HR decision-making processes. This opacity undermines procedural fairness, a core principle that ensures decisions are made through a transparent and justifiable process. (Yanamala, 2023). The lack of transparency in AI systems hinders individuals' ability to understand, question, or contest decisions that affect them. For example, when AI tools are used for candidate screening or performance evaluation without clear rationale, users cannot discern the basis of outcomes, limiting their ability to identify or challenge potential biases. This opacity reduces trust in the system's fairness and impedes the detection and correction of discriminatory practices. The problem is exacerbated when proprietary algorithms restrict access to decision-making processes, further undermining accountability.

5. **Impact on Employment Outcomes**

The implications of biased AI systems on employment outcomes are profound. Biased algorithms can establish systemic barriers in hiring and promotion, systematically disadvantaging certain groups. By demonstrating how AI-driven resume screening tools often disadvantage candidates with non-white names, inadvertently reinforcing racial disparities in employment opportunities. Such biases not only hinder diversity but also compromise the meritocratic principles that HR systems aim to uphold.

6. **Feedback Loops**

When biased recommendations are perpetuated over time, they can reinforce existing patterns of workplace homogeneity. For example, if an AI system consistently favors candidates from a particular demographic, this can lead to reduced diversity within the organization. Over time, the homogeneity in hiring and promotion decisions can create a self-reinforcing cycle, further entrenching bias and limiting organizational inclusivity.

7. **To provide a framework for ethical AI implementation in HR**:

To develop a comprehensive framework for the ethical implementation of AI in HR systems. It aims to promote fairness, transparency, and accountability while actively identifying and mitigating biases that may arise in AI-driven HR processes such as recruitment, performance evaluation, and talent management. The chapter seeks to guide HR professionals and organizations in adopting responsible AI practices that uphold ethical standards, protect employee rights, and foster trust in AI-powered decision-making.

UNDERSTANDING BIAS IN AI-POWERED HR SYSTEMS

Artificial Intelligence (AI) systems in Human Resource (HR) management are increasingly used to streamline recruitment, performance evaluation, and employee engagement. While they enhance efficiency, these systems risk perpetuating biases embedded in their data, design, and deployment. Addressing these biases is essential for ethical and equitable HR practices. Below is a structured analysis of the sources, consequences, and mitigation strategies for bias in AI-powered HR systems:

Sources of Bias

A. Data-Driven Bias

Data-driven bias is a critical concern in the deployment of AI systems within human resource management, as these systems are often trained on historical datasets that encapsulate entrenched discriminatory practices and systemic inequities. One major source of this bias arises from the replication of historical discrimination. For instance, if historical hiring data reveals an underrepresentation of women in leadership roles, AI models may inadvertently learn to deprioritize female candidates in future recruitment processes (Rietdijk, 2024). A notable example is Amazon's recruiting tool, which, due to its training on predominantly male resumes, systematically penalized resumes containing gender-specific terms such as "women's," thereby perpetuating gender biases (Chang, 2023).

A key ethical challenge in deploying AI-powered HR systems is data-driven bias, often stemming from unrepresentative training datasets. Underrepresentation of groups such as non-binary individuals and ethnic minorities can skew outcomes in favor of dominant groups, reinforcing existing disparities in hiring and HR practices. This undermines efforts toward organizational diversity and inclusion. The issue is further compounded by the phenomenon of proxy variables. Even when sensitive attributes, such as race or gender, are deliberately excluded from training datasets to prevent discrimination, AI systems can inadvertently reconstruct these patterns of bias (Scatiggio, 2020)This occurs through the use of proxy variables indirect indicators that correlate with sensitive attributes. For example, zip codes may serve as a proxy for socio-economic status, while educational background can reflect social privilege. Although these variables may not be explicitly discriminatory, their correlations with sensitive attributes enable AI models to infer patterns that align with systemic biases. As (Scatiggio, 2020) highlight, the presence of such proxies undermines efforts to sanitize data and eliminate bias, ultimately allowing discriminatory patterns to persist within AI-driven decision-making processes.

Addressing data-driven bias in AI-driven HR systems requires a comprehensive approach. Organizations must diversify datasets to ensure representation of all demographic groups and conduct fairness audits to detect and mitigate bias, using techniques such as adversarial debiasing and fairness-aware machine learning. These practices promote ethical and inclusive HR outcomes. Additionally, measurement bias—where constructs like "leadership potential" reflect culturally biased interpretations—can disadvantage marginalized groups. Bias in AI systems often stems from historical discrimination, unrepresentative data, proxy variables, and subjective constructs. Tackling these issues demands critical evaluation of data practices and algorithm design to counteract systemic inequities.

B. Design-Induced Bias

In the realm of AI-powered Human Resource (HR) systems, design-induced bias refers to biases that originate from the choices and assumptions made during the algorithmic development process. Such biases can have profound implications for fairness, equity, and inclusivity within organizational practices. This section critically examines three primary sources of design-induced bias: proxy selection, optimization goals, and feedback loops.

Proxy Selection: One significant source of bias arises from the selection of input variables that inadvertently serve as proxies for protected characteristics such as race, gender, or age. For instance, utilizing geographical data such as zip codes in predictive models can inadvertently encode racial or socio-economic information, leading to biased outcomes. This occurs because certain zip codes may be demographically homogenous due to historical and systemic segregation patterns. Consequently, decisions based on such proxies can perpetuate existing inequalities and reinforce discriminatory practices within hiring, promotions, or other HR functions. Therefore, it is essential for AI system designers to conduct thorough audits of input variables to ensure that they do not inadvertently reflect or exacerbate societal biases.

Optimization Goals: Another critical consideration is the optimization goals set during algorithmic development. AI systems are often designed to maximize specific outcomes, such as employee retention or productivity. However, prioritizing short-term metrics without considering the broader context can lead to discriminatory effects. For example, optimizing for employee retention may disadvantage groups that have historically experienced higher attrition rates due to systemic workplace inequities (Schwartz et al., 2022). If the system interprets historical attrition data without accounting for these contextual factors, it may undervalue or overlook candidates from marginalized groups. Therefore, setting optimization goals must involve a comprehensive understanding of historical biases and a commitment to promoting equitable outcomes.

Feedback Loops: Feedback loops represent a critical challenge in mitigating bias within AI-powered HR systems, as they can perpetuate historical inequities embedded within organizational data. These loops occur when machine learning models are trained on historical HR decisions, data that may inherently reflect prior discriminatory practices. For instance, if an algorithm is developed using records of past promotion patterns that systematically favored men over women, it is likely to internalize and replicate this bias. Consequently, the system may continue to endorse gender bias, reinforcing and amplifying discriminatory practices over time. (Madhumita, G., Diana, P. D., Neena, P. C., Kiran, P. N., Aggarwal, S., & Nargunde, A. S., 2024)

Feedback loops in AI systems arise primarily from two factors: the use of biased historical data and the reinforcement of these biases as outcomes are fed back into training. This cycle is especially problematic in HR, where AI-driven decisions impact diversity and inclusion. Addressing such loops requires ongoing monitoring, use of representative data, and integration of fairness checks. Techniques like algorithmic auditing, bias correction, and fairness-aware machine learning can support more equitable outcomes. Ultimately, fostering fairness in AI-powered HR systems demands both technical interventions and sustained ethical oversight.

C. Deployment Context Bias

Deployment context bias emerges as a critical concern when integrating AI-powered human resource systems into diverse operational environments. This form of bias is not solely rooted in the algorithmic design or data input but is often a byproduct of the real-world dynamics between technology, human decision-making, and existing organizational and social structures.

Human Overrides and Subjective Decision-Making: One notable facet of deployment context bias is the role of human overrides. Even when AI systems are engineered to provide objective, data-driven recommendations, HR professionals can and often do override these suggestions based on ingrained heuristics, personal experiences, or unconscious cognitive biases. Such overrides may result in the systematic exclusion of candidates from non-traditional backgrounds, thereby perpetuating subjective preferences that the technology was intended to mitigate. This interplay between algorithmic output and human judgment highlights the complexity of achieving true objectivity; human decision-makers are influenced by factors such as familiarity, cultural norms, and even implicit stereotypes. The challenge is exacerbated when organizational cultures implicitly endorse such biases, ultimately undermining the fairness and efficacy of the recruitment process. (Barrett, 2024)

Mismatched Contexts and Domain Adaptation: Another dimension of deployment context bias pertains to mismatched contexts, often arising when AI models are deployed in environments that differ significantly from those represented in their training data. For example, a model trained predominantly on data from traditional corporate employees may struggle to accurately assess the competencies of gig workers or freelancers, whose work patterns, professional skills, and engagement levels diverge from the norm. This discrepancy, known in machine learning as a domain shift or dataset shift, can lead to misinterpretations and skewed assessments. The validity of the AI's outputs is compromised when the underlying assumptions embedded within the training data no longer align with the target environment, resulting in recommendations that may favor certain groups over others inadvertently. (Zhang, 2024)

Structural Inequities and Technological Access: Structural inequities further compound deployment context bias by influencing both the input data and the operational conditions of AI systems. Inequalities in access to essential technological resources such as high-speed internet, quality video interview tools, or even ergonomic work environments can disadvantage candidates from underprivileged backgrounds. When AI systems rely on data collected in contexts where such disparities are prevalent, they may inadvertently mirror and reinforce these societal inequities. The systemic nature of these inequities means that the technology does not operate in a vacuum; rather, it reflects and perpetuates the broader infrastructural disparities that exist within society. This structural bias not only affects candidate evaluation but also has long-term implications for workforce diversity and social mobility. (Kyriakidou, 2025)

Consequences of Bias

AI-powered HR tools, while promising objectivity, often perpetuate or amplify biases embedded in historical data or flawed model design. Such biases may contravene anti-discrimination legislation, exposing organizastions to litigation, financial penalties, and regulatory sanctions. For instance, in the United States, the *Equal Employment Opportunity Act* (EEOA) prohibits discrimination based on protected characteristics such as race, gender, age, and disability. AI systems that disproportionately filter out candidates from marginalized groups, whether through biased resume screening algorithms or predictive analytics favoring specific demographics, risk violating these statutes. (Athanasiou, 2023).A landmark example includes Amazon's discontinued AI recruitment tool, which systematically downgraded female applicants due to historical hiring data skewed toward male candidates.

Similarly, the European Union's General Data Protection Regulation (GDPR) imposes stringent requirements for transparency and accountability in automated decision-making. Article 22 of the GDPR explicitly grants individuals the right to contest decisions made solely by algorithms, mandating human oversight and explainability (GDPR, 2016). HR systems that lack auditable decision trails or fail to disclose bias mitigation strategies may face fines of up to 4% of global revenue under GDPR non-compliance provisions. (Wolff, J., & Atallah, N., 2021)Regulatory bodies, such as France's CNIL, have already begun scrutinizing algorithmic hiring tools for discriminatory outcomes, signaling a growing emphasis on legal accountability (Lacmanovic, S., & Skare, M., 2025).

Beyond fines, organizations risk entering costly consent decrees requiring third-party audits, algorithmic retraining, and compensatory measures for affected individuals. In 2023, the U.S. Department of Justice emphasized that AI systems used in employment decisions must comply with the *Americans with Disabilities Act* (ADA) particularly in accommodating candidates requiring adjustments during AI-driven assessments (Goren, 2024). Legal frameworks globally are evolving to address algorithmic discrimination, with jurisdictions like New York City implementing Local Law 144 (2023), mandating bias audits of automated employment tools prior to deployment.

The legal ramifications of biased AI in HR underscore the urgent need for proactive governance. Organizations must adopt rigorous bias-testing protocols, ensure algorithmic transparency, and integrate human oversight to comply with anti-discrimination laws and data protection regulations. Failure to address these risks not only jeopardizes legal standing but also erodes stakeholder trust, highlighting the imperative for interdisciplinary collaboration between legal experts, data scientists, and HR professionals. As regulatory scrutiny intensifies, the alignment of AI systems with ethical and legal standards will remain pivotal to sustainable HR innovation.

Ethical Failures: Unfair treatment in AI-driven HR systems undermines corporate values and contradicts commitments to diversity, equity, and inclusion (DEI). Ethical AI mandates the prevention of algorithmic discrimination to promote fairness and social responsibility. When AI systems fail to uphold these ethical principles, employee trust deteriorates, leading to dissatisfaction, disengagement, and potential attrition. Organizations committed to corporate social responsibility (CSR) must integrate ethical considerations into AI governance to ensure equitable outcomes for all candidates and employees. (Shneiderman, 2020)

Reputational Harm: The exposure of biased AI-driven hiring or evaluation systems can severely damage an organization's reputation. High-profile cases, such as Amazon's AI-based recruitment tool, which was found to discriminate against women, highlight the risks associated with biased machine learning models. (Kodiyan, 2019). Public backlash, negative media coverage, and consumer distrust can have long-term consequences, affecting brand integrity and employer attractiveness. Organizations that fail to proactively address bias risk losing stakeholder confidence and competitive positioning in the talent market.

Reinforced Inequities: AI-driven HR systems, if improperly designed or monitored, can entrench existing workplace disparities. Biased training data and flawed algorithms can perpetuate systemic discrimination, further marginalizing underrepresented groups. This limits workplace diversity and reduces the potential for innovation, as diverse teams are empirically linked to enhanced problem-solving and creativity. Failing to mitigate bias in AI can reinforce structural inequities, leading to homogenous workforces and stifling inclusive growth.

MITIGATION STRATEGIES

To mitigate biases in AI-powered HR systems, organizations must adopt a comprehensive and multi-faceted approach, integrating technical, organizational, and contextual strategies.

A. Technical Solutions

Audit Training Data: The foundation of AI fairness begins with high-quality, representative training data. Conducting systematic audits helps identify and correct historical biases, underrepresentation, and proxy variables that may inadvertently influence hiring decisions. Ensuring data diversity and applying techniques such as resampling, synthetic data generation, and adversarial testing can enhance fairness in AI models. (Mehrabi, N., Morstatter, F., Saxena, N., Lerman, K., & Galstyan, A., 2021)

Fairness-Aware Algorithms: Developing and implementing fairness-aware algorithms is essential for reducing bias. Techniques such as adversarial debiasing, reweighting, and fairness constraints ensure that AI models prioritize equity. By incorporating bias detection and mitigation frameworks into machine learning pipelines, organizations can proactively address algorithmic discrimination and improve fairness in automated decision-making.

Transparency Tools: Enhancing explainability in AI-driven HR systems is critical for accountability and trust. Explainability frameworks, such as Local Interpretable Model-Agnostic Explanations (LIME) and SHapley Additive exPlanations (SHAP), provide insights into how AI models make decisions. By deploying these tools, HR professionals can scrutinize AI outputs, ensuring alignment with ethical standards and regulatory requirements.

B. Organizational Practices

Diverse Development Teams: Incorporating a broad range of perspectives in AI system design helps identify and mitigate blind spots. Multidisciplinary teams, including ethicists, HR professionals, and individuals from underrepresented backgrounds, can ensure that AI models reflect diverse needs and considerations. Inclusive development teams are instrumental in embedding fairness principles into AI-driven HR processes.

Continuous Monitoring: Bias in AI is not static; it evolves over time as workplace dynamics shift. Establishing ongoing monitoring mechanisms, such as periodic audits and fairness assessments, allows organizations to detect and address bias proactively. Recalibrating AI models based on real-world data ensures sustained fairness and alignment with organizational diversity goals.

Stakeholder Collaboration: Engaging employees, candidates, regulators, and external auditors in AI governance fosters transparency and ethical alignment. Collaborative oversight mechanisms, such as AI ethics committees and external audits, help organizations uphold fairness standards and maintain credibility in AI-driven HR practices.

C. Contextual Adaptation

Environment-Specific Testing: AI models should be validated within specific organizational contexts to ensure reliability. HR applications differ across sectors and employment types (e.g., gig workers vs. corporate employees), necessitating tailored fairness assessments. Rigorous pre-deployment testing and real-world validation enhance model effectiveness and mitigate unintended consequences.

Bias Training for HR: HR professionals must be equipped with the knowledge to recognize and mitigate biases in AI-human collaboration. Providing training on algorithmic bias, fairness principles, and ethical AI use strengthens human oversight and promotes responsible AI adoption. Educating HR teams enhances their ability to challenge and refine AI-generated recommendations effectively.

Infrastructure Equity: Ensuring equitable access to technology is fundamental to reducing bias in AI-driven HR processes. For instance, organizations must consider candidates from diverse socio-economic backgrounds who may lack access to advanced digital tools. (Vivek, 2023). Providing alternative assessment methods, such as phone-based or in-person interviews, enhances inclusivity and prevents digital divide biases.

Addressing bias in AI-powered HR systems requires an integrated approach that combines technical advancements, organizational responsibility, and contextual sensitivity. By implementing robust mitigation strategies, organizations can build fair, ethical, and legally compliant AI-driven HR processes that enhance workplace diversity, equity, and inclusion.

Bias in AI-powered HR systems is a multifaceted challenge rooted in flawed data, design choices, and deployment environments. Left unchecked, it risks perpetuating discrimination and undermining organizational goals. Mitigation requires a combination of technical rigor (e.g., fairness-aware algorithms), organizational accountability (e.g., diverse teams), and contextual awareness (e.g., infrastructure equity). By proactively addressing these issues, organizations can leverage AI's potential while fostering inclusive, equitable workplaces.

TYPES OF BIAS IN AI-POWERED HR SYSTEMS

AI-powered HR systems hold significant promise for streamlining recruitment, talent management, and workforce planning. However, these systems are not immune to bias, often perpetuating or even exacerbating existing inequalities. Bias in AI-driven HR applications can manifest at multiple levels, including data, algorithms, and human decision-making. This chapter examines the primary types of bias in AI-powered HR systems and their implications for ethical decision-making in the workplace.

1. Data Bias

Data bias occurs when the datasets used to train AI models reflect historical disparities, are unrepresentative, or contain flawed measurements. Such biases can skew outcomes, reinforcing existing inequities in HR practices.

Historical Bias

Historical bias arises when training data encapsulates societal inequities, leading AI systems to replicate and perpetuate these patterns. For instance, if an AI model is trained on past hiring data from a company with a history of gender-based pay disparities, it may learn to favor male candidates over female candidates for higher-paying positions. Such biases result from entrenched structural inequalities rather than explicit discriminatory intent.

Representation Bias

Representation bias occurs when certain groups are underrepresented in training data, leading to skewed model performance across demographics (Shahbazi, N., Lin, Y., Asudeh, A., & Jagadish, H. V., 2023) For example, if an AI-driven recruitment system is trained primarily on resumes from candidates in Western countries, it may struggle to accurately assess applicants from diverse cultural and linguistic backgrounds. This can lead to systemic exclusion of underrepresented groups, perpetuating workplace homogeneity.

Measurement Bias

Measurement bias stems from flawed metrics used in model training and evaluation. For example, if an AI system assesses candidates based on "cultural fit" scores derived from current employees, it may inadvertently favor dominant groups while disadvantaging diverse talent. This occurs because the training data reinforces existing workforce composition rather than objectively evaluating candidates' qualifications and potential contributions.

2. Algorithmic Bias

Algorithmic bias emerges from the mathematical and computational processes underlying AI models. It can occur due to flawed optimization objectives, the selection of inappropriate features, or feedback loops that reinforce existing disparities.

Model Bias

Model bias arises when algorithms prioritize spurious correlations rather than meaningful predictors of job performance. For instance, if an AI recruitment model associates leadership potential with masculine-coded language, it may disproportionately recommend male candidates for managerial positions while overlooking equally qualified female candidates.

Optimization Bias

Optimization bias occurs when AI systems prioritize performance metrics such as accuracy without considering fairness constraints. Many AI models optimize for predictive accuracy, which may lead to discriminatory outcomes. For example, an AI system designed to predict employee attrition may disproportionately flag women as higher risks for turnover due to historical patterns of career breaks related to caregiving responsibilities.

Feedback Loop Bias

Feedback loop bias emerges when AI systems reinforce existing disparities through self-reinforcing mechanisms. (Irshad, 2024) highlight how AI-driven performance evaluation systems may favor employees from historically privileged groups if past promotion data is biased. This leads to a cycle where biased decisions inform future predictions, compounding workplace inequalities.

How Algorithms Amplify Bias

Decision trees and ensemble methods

- Trees split on features that maximize information gain. If a proxy feature (e.g. alma mater) correlates with a protected attribute, splits will reinforce that association. Ensembles (random forests, gradient boosting) aggregate many such splits, compounding bias.

Neural networks

- Deep models capture complex, high-dimensional patterns, including unwanted proxies. Without explicit de-biasing layers or regularization, networks can internalize and amplify subtle biases present in training data.

Clustering and embedding

- Unsupervised methods group similar data points. If embeddings encode societal stereotypes (e.g. word embeddings that link "programmer" with men), clustering will segregate candidates by those stereotypes, affecting downstream tasks like recommendation or screening.

Table 1.

Metric	Definition	Interpretation
Demographic parity	The probability of a positive decision is the same for all groups.	Ensures each group is selected at equal rates, regardless of true qualification differences.
Equalized odds	Both true-positive rates and false-positive rates are equal across groups.	Balances types of errors for each group, so no group bears disproportionately high misclassification.
Predictive parity	The precision of positive predictions is equal across groups.	Guarantees that when the model predicts "positive," it is equally reliable for all groups.
Counterfactual fairness	An individual's predicted outcome would remain unchanged if their protected attribute were altered:	Ensures decisions do not causally depend on protected attributes, requiring a causal model.

In order to reduce unfair outcomes, practitioners apply mitigation methods at different stages of the AI lifecycle, selecting each method to support a particular fairness goal.

Pre-processing (for demographic parity)

Before training, the data can be re-balanced so that under-represented groups carry more weight. Techniques such as re-sampling (duplicating examples from minority groups) or re-weighing (assigning higher importance to those examples) help ensure that each group appears at similar rates. This supports equal selection rates across protected groups, as required by demographic parity.

In-processing (for equalized odds)

During model training, fairness constraints can be built into the algorithm's objective function. By penalizing differences in true-positive and false-positive rates between groups, the model learns to equalize its error rates. This approach directly targets the balance of predictive performance across all subgroups, satisfying the equalized odds criterion.

Post-processing (for predictive parity)

After a model has been trained, decision thresholds can be adjusted separately for each group to equalize positive predictive value. In practice, this means calibrating the score cut-offs so that, when the model predicts a positive outcome (for example, "recommend for hire"), it is equally reliable for every group.

By choosing the right intervention at each stage data re-sampling for demographic parity, constrained optimization for balanced error rates, and threshold adjustment for predictive reliability organizations can systematically align their AI systems with their fairness objectives.

3. Human Bias in Programming

Despite efforts to build objective AI systems, human biases inevitably influence their design and implementation. Developers' implicit assumptions, cultural backgrounds, and cognitive biases shape algorithmic decisions in ways that may inadvertently disadvantage certain groups. One well-documented example is facial recognition technology, which has been shown to perform less accurately for individuals with darker skin tones due to the predominance of lighter-skinned male subjects in training datasets (Hardesty, 2018). Similarly, HR systems that filter resumes based on name-matching algorithms may disadvantage candidates with non-Western names if the training data fails to account for regional naming conventions (Sonderling, K. E., Kelley, B. J., & Casimir, L., 2022)

Addressing Bias in AI-Powered HR Systems

Bias in AI-powered HR systems is not merely a technical issue but a reflection of systemic inequities embedded within organizations and society. Addressing these biases requires a multidisciplinary approach that includes technical interventions, ethical oversight, and regulatory frameworks.

Key strategies for mitigating bias include:

- **Transparent Auditing:** Regularly auditing AI models to identify and correct biases in data and decision-making processes.
- **Diverse Training Data:** Ensuring that training datasets include balanced representations of different demographic groups to enhance fairness.
- **Fairness Constraints in Optimization:** Incorporating fairness metrics into AI optimization processes to minimize discriminatory outcomes.
- **Multidisciplinary Collaboration:** Engaging ethicists, HR professionals, and policymakers in the development and deployment of AI-driven HR solutions.

By critically examining data sources, algorithmic design, and deployment practices, organizations can mitigate bias in AI-powered HR systems and foster more equitable workplaces. Ethical AI development must prioritize transparency, accountability, and inclusivity to ensure that HR technologies serve diverse workforces effectively and fairly (Rodgers, W., Murray, J. M., Stefanidis, A., Degbey, W. Y., & Tarba, S. Y., 2023)

4. Framework for Ethical AI Implementation in HR

The rapid integration of artificial intelligence (AI) into human resources (HR) processes necessitates a robust ethical framework to mitigate bias and ensure fairness, transparency, and accountability. The deployment of AI-powered HR systems should adhere to best practices that promote ethical considerations, reinforcing trust among stakeholders and ensuring compliance with legal and regulatory standards.

Bias in AI-driven HR systems often stems from historical data that reflect existing societal inequities. To mitigate such biases, organizations must adopt a comprehensive strategy that includes rigorous auditing of training data, the application of fairness-aware algorithms, and the implementation of diverse and inclusive datasets. These strategies ensure that AI systems do not perpetuate or exacerbate existing biases in hiring, performance evaluations, and career progression decisions.

Audit Training Data

The foundation of AI fairness begins with high-quality, representative training data. Conducting systematic audits helps identify and correct historical biases, underrepresentation, and proxy variables that may inadvertently influence hiring decisions. Strategies for improving data quality include:

- Ensuring Data Diversity: Incorporating data from a wide range of demographic groups to prevent underrepresentation and biased decision-making. This involves collecting data that accurately reflect different genders, ethnicities, socio-economic backgrounds, and other relevant factors.
- Resampling and Data Augmentation: Employing techniques such as oversampling underrepresented groups or generating synthetic data to balance datasets. Synthetic data can be particularly useful in addressing gaps where real-world data are scarce.
- Adversarial Testing: Simulating scenarios where bias might emerge and evaluating AI performance against fairness criteria. By stress-testing models with adversarial examples, organizations can identify potential vulnerabilities and rectify them before deployment.

- Bias Audits and Data Provenance Tracking: Establishing a structured approach to trace data sources and assess their credibility, ensuring that biased datasets are either corrected or excluded from training.

Fairness-Aware Algorithms

Developing and implementing fairness-aware algorithms is essential for reducing bias. Several techniques can be applied to ensure equity in AI decision-making:

- Adversarial Debiasing: Using adversarial learning techniques to train models that minimize biased predictions while maintaining accuracy. This involves incorporating adversarial networks that actively counteract discrimination in decision-making.
- Reweighting and Fairness Constraints: Adjusting algorithmic weightings to counteract inherent biases in datasets. This includes techniques like equalized odds and demographic parity, which ensure that AI models do not favour one demographic group over another.
- Bias Detection Frameworks: Embedding fairness metrics within machine learning pipelines to proactively identify and mitigate potential discrimination. Tools such as IBM AI Fairness 360 and Google's What-If Tool allow organizations to measure and adjust bias levels in their models.
- Continuous Learning and Model Updates: Implementing ongoing monitoring and retraining of AI models using updated and less biased datasets to ensure long-term fairness. AI systems should be adaptive and regularly refined to align with evolving diversity and inclusion standards.

By integrating these strategies, organizations can significantly reduce bias in AI-driven HR systems, fostering a more equitable and inclusive workplace environment.

Transparency Tools

To enhance explainability in AI-powered HR systems, organizations should adopt robust interpretability techniques:

- Local Interpretable Model-Agnostic Explanations (LIME): Generates locally faithful explanations for individual AI predictions, making model outputs more comprehensible to users.
- SHapley Additive exPlanations (SHAP): A game-theoretic approach that assigns contribution scores to different input features, illustrating how AI models reach specific conclusions.

- Algorithmic Audits and Documentation: Implementing documentation protocols, such as model cards and data sheets, to ensure AI decision-making processes remain transparent and accountable.

Establishing accountability mechanisms and ethical oversight

AI governance and oversight structures play a critical role in ensuring that AI applications align with ethical principles and regulatory frameworks. Organizations must implement accountability mechanisms that include:

- Ethical AI Committees: Establishing interdisciplinary teams responsible for monitoring AI system development, deployment, and impact on HR decisions.
- Regulatory Compliance: Adhering to legal standards such as the General Data Protection Regulation (GDPR) and Equal Employment Opportunity (EEO) laws to prevent discrimination.
- Continuous Monitoring and Auditing: Conducting regular assessments of AI system performance, fairness, and compliance to detect and rectify emerging biases.

Ethical AI implementation in HR requires a multi-faceted approach encompassing data fairness, algorithmic transparency, and organizational accountability. By integrating robust audit mechanisms, deploying fairness-aware models, and fostering an ethical AI governance framework, organizations can harness AI's potential while ensuring equitable and non-discriminatory HR practices. The commitment to ethical AI principles will not only enhance decision-making quality but also promote trust and inclusivity in the workforce.

ROLE OF HR LEADERS IN PROMOTING ETHICAL AI

The growing reliance on AI in recruitment, performance management, employee engagement, and workforce planning necessitates a commitment to fairness, transparency, and accountability. HR professionals are uniquely positioned to advocate for responsible AI practices, ensuring that these technologies align with organizational values and ethical standards.

Advocating for Responsible AI Practices

HR leaders play a critical role in promoting responsible AI adoption within organizations. They must ensure that AI-driven HR technologies adhere to principles of fairness, non-discrimination, and transparency. To achieve this, HR professionals can undertake several key actions:

1. Establishing Ethical AI Guidelines: HR leaders should develop and enforce ethical guidelines specific to AI usage in HR processes. These guidelines should align with existing corporate policies, regulatory frameworks, and global ethical standards such as those proposed by the European Union's AI Act and the IEEE's Ethically Aligned Design framework.
2. Ensuring Transparency and Explainability: HR professionals should advocate for AI models that are interpretable and transparent. Black-box algorithms, which provide little insight into decision-making processes, can undermine trust and accountability. HR leaders should work with AI developers to ensure that automated decisions can be explained and justified to employees and other stakeholders.
3. Implementing Bias Audits and Fairness Assessments: AI systems can inadvertently reinforce biases present in historical data. HR leaders should mandate regular audits of AI tools to assess bias and ensure equitable outcomes. Implementing fairness metrics and impact assessments can help mitigate discriminatory practices and promote inclusivity.
4. Providing AI Ethics Training for HR Teams: To effectively manage AI-driven HR systems, HR professionals should undergo training on AI ethics, data privacy, and algorithmic bias. Organizations should invest in continuous learning programs to keep HR teams informed about emerging ethical challenges and regulatory developments.
5. Encouraging Employee Participation and Feedback: HR leaders should create channels for employees to voice concerns about AI-driven decisions. Transparency in AI implementation fosters trust and allows organizations to address unintended consequences before they escalate.

Collaborating with AI Developers, Legal Teams, and DEI Specialists

To ensure ethical AI implementation, HR leaders must collaborate closely with AI developers, legal teams, and diversity, equity, and inclusion (DEI) specialists. This cross-functional collaboration is essential in fostering responsible AI use within HR systems.

1. Working with AI Developers: HR leaders should engage AI developers in discussions about ethical considerations, ensuring that AI models used in HR functions are designed with fairness and inclusivity in mind. This includes defining ethical AI objectives, setting parameters for bias detection, and implementing human oversight mechanisms.
2. Engaging Legal and Compliance Teams: Given the evolving regulatory landscape surrounding AI, HR leaders must work with legal teams to ensure compliance with local and international data protection laws, such as the General Data Protection Regulation (GDPR). Legal teams can provide guidance on issues related to data privacy, algorithmic accountability, and employee rights in AI-driven HR decision-making.
3. Collaborating with DEI Specialists: Diversity, equity, and inclusion experts bring essential perspectives on mitigating bias in AI systems. HR leaders should incorporate DEI principles into AI governance strategies, ensuring that AI-driven HR tools support diverse hiring and career advancement opportunities rather than perpetuating historical biases.
4. Developing an AI Ethics Committee: Organizations should consider forming AI ethics committees that include representatives from HR, legal, DEI, and technology teams. Such committees can oversee AI implementation, conduct impact assessments, and provide recommendations to ensure ethical and responsible AI use in HR processes.

As AI continues to shape HR practices, HR leaders must take a proactive stance in promoting ethical AI usage. By advocating for transparency, fairness, and accountability, and fostering collaboration among key stakeholders, HR professionals can ensure that AI-powered HR systems contribute positively to workforce management and employee experience. Through structured ethical guidelines, cross-functional partnerships, and continuous oversight, HR leaders can play a pivotal role in mitigating AI biases and safeguarding organizational integrity.

RECENT DEVELOPMENTS IN AI GOVERNANCE AND EMERGING LEGAL AND ETHICAL STANDARDS

European Union

The EU Artificial Intelligence Act (April 2024) designates most HR applications—recruitment, promotion, performance monitoring—as "high-risk," imposing rigorous requirements on data quality, bias testing, documentation, and human oversight. Employers must notify workers before deploying AI, explain automated decisions on request, and may not use emotion- or intent-inference tools in employment contexts. (cliffordchance, 2024)

United States

No single U.S. AI-HR statute exists; instead, existing civil-rights laws (Title VII, ADA, ADEA) apply fully to AI tools. Both intentional discrimination and disparate-impact outcomes from algorithms are unlawful, and reasonable accommodations remain mandatory when AI is used in hiring or monitoring. Federal guidance has fluctuated, but EEOC fact sheets (Sept 2024) reaffirm that AI-driven decisions are subject to the same anti-bias standards as human ones. (commission, 2025)

State and Local Measures

New York City's Local Law 144 (effective Jan 2023) requires independent bias audits of any automated employment-decision tool (AEDT) and advance notice to applicants. (Council, 2021) Illinois HB 3773 and Colorado SB 24-205 (both effective 2026) similarly ban AI practices that yield discriminatory effects and obligate employers to notify employees when AI informs employment decisions. (Hilliard, 2023)

Asia–Pacific

Privacy-centric regimes in China (PIPL 2021 and algorithm-transparency rules) forbid unfair profiling and mandate disclosure of recommendation logic. Japan's 2022 Human Resource Tech Act bans biased AI hiring tools and requires disclosure of AI use in candidate evaluation. Singapore's Model AI Governance Framework (2020) and comparable guidelines in South Korea emphasize explainability, bias mitigation, and worker consultation. (OECD., 2024)

Industry Standards

The NIST AI Risk Management Framework (2023) and IEEE P7003 standardize bias-risk assessment, while ISO/IEC committees develop fairness (23894) and governance (42001) norms. (IEEE., n.d.) Common best practices include pre-deployment impact assessments, audit logging, human-in-the-loop controls, and transparent candidate notice measures reported by 89% of firms using algorithmic management to foster trust.

EMPLOYEE PERSPECTIVES: PERCEPTIONS, EXPERIENCES, AND CONCERNS REGARDING AI IN HR

As AI-powered tools become increasingly integrated into HRM, understanding employee perspectives is crucial for ethical deployment and long-term organizational trust. While much discourse focuses on the technological potential and legal responsibilities of AI in HR, the lived experiences and perceptions of employees who are subject to algorithmic decision-making remain underrepresented.

Transparency and Awareness

One of the most significant gaps in employee experience is awareness of when and how AI is used in HR processes. A 2021 Deloitte report revealed that nearly 65% of employees were unsure whether AI tools were being used in their hiring or performance evaluations (FIROZ M., 2024). This lack of transparency contributes to low trust and perceived procedural injustice.

Similarly, when employees were informed about algorithmic involvement, insufficient explanation of how AI systems operated (e.g., decision criteria, weighting mechanisms) contributed to feelings of opacity and helplessness. Employees expressed concerns about the "black box" nature of these systems, particularly when automated decisions appeared to lack nuance or context.

Concerns Over Fairness and Bias

Employee concerns about algorithmic bias are well documented. Studies have shown that employees, particularly those from historically marginalized groups, often perceive AI systems as amplifying existing workplace inequalities (Mergen, A., Çetin-Kılıç, N., & Özbilgin, M. F., 2025). Gender and racial bias in automated resume screening and video interviews raise concerns about discrimination without accountability. Similarly, employees assessed by AI performance tools report anxiety over constant monitoring and metrics that overlook context and emotional labor, especially in service or hybrid roles.

Privacy and Surveillance

The use of AI for monitoring productivity, behavior, and even emotional states in the workplace has raised significant privacy concerns among employees. In particular, the deployment of AI tools that track keystrokes, webcam usage, voice tone, or sentiment analysis in internal communication tools is often viewed as intrusive and dehumanizing.

A survey found that 60% of workers believed that AI-led surveillance could lead to increased stress and pressure, while 28% worried it might impact their mental health. Importantly, these concerns were not limited to blue-collar or gig workers white-collar employees also reported discomfort with the rise of "bossware" and algorithmic micromanagement. (Green, A., del Pero, A. S., & Verhagen, A., 2023). Employees have also expressed concern about how data collected through AI systems is stored, used, and shared—particularly in the absence of clear data governance policies or the right to opt out. These anxieties have direct implications for employee morale, workplace culture, and perceptions of psychological safety.

Perceived Benefits and Conditional Acceptance

Despite concerns, many employees recognize the potential benefits of AI in HR if used ethically with human oversight. The key condition for acceptance is human-in-the-loop oversight, ensuring AI augments rather than replaces human judgment. Employees are more receptive to AI in supportive roles (e.g., scheduling, training) than in evaluative or punitive functions (e.g., promotions, terminations) (Drewniak, Z., & Posadzinska, I., 2020)

Younger, digitally native employees tend to show higher acceptance rates, but even this group demands transparency and ethical assurance.

Implications for Ethical HR Practice

Transparent communication about the use, purpose, and limits of AI in HR decisions

Mechanisms for feedback and contestability, allowing employees to question and appeal AI-based outcomes

Collaborative governance models that include employee representatives in AI procurement, auditing, and review processes

Regular impact assessments that center employee experience and inclusivity

Incorporating employee voices into the design and evaluation of AI-powered HR systems is not only an ethical imperative but also a strategic necessity. Systems that fail to secure employee trust are less likely to achieve adoption or deliver fair outcomes.

BEST PRACTICES

The integration of AI in HR has revolutionized talent acquisition, performance management, and employee engagement. However, AI-powered HR systems are not devoid of ethical concerns and biases, which can significantly impact hiring decisions, promotions, and workplace inclusivity.

Successful Organizational Examples

1. Microsoft's AI Ethics Framework in HR

Microsoft has implemented a Responsible AI framework to ensure its AI-driven HR solutions uphold fairness and inclusivity. The company employs a fairness-aware machine learning approach, which helps in identifying potential biases in hiring algorithms. Furthermore, Microsoft has an internal AI Ethics Committee that oversees AI deployment, ensuring adherence to transparency and ethical standards. The company also prioritizes explainability by providing HR professionals with insights into how AI-based decisions are made. (Rao, S., & Zhao, T., 2025)

2. Johnson & Johnson's AI Recruitment Strategy

Johnson & Johnson leverages AI-powered tools to screen and assess job candidates while maintaining ethical integrity. The company collaborates with external AI ethics researchers to refine its algorithms, ensuring that they do not disproportionately disadvantage any group. To improve fairness, Johnson & Johnson regularly tests and updates its AI models with new datasets that reflect a diverse candidate pool. Additionally, the company ensures that recruiters receive AI ethics training to better understand and interpret AI-generated recommendations. (Kolmogorova, 2024)

3. Deloitte's Human-Centered AI in Workforce Analytics

Deloitte has adopted a human-centered approach to AI-driven workforce analytics. The company integrates AI with traditional HR processes to ensure that hiring and promotion decisions remain fair and unbiased. Deloitte employs bias-detection tools to audit its AI models continuously, and it uses ethics-driven guidelines to ensure compliance with regulatory requirements. The company also promotes transparency by providing employees with insights into how AI influences workforce decisions. (FIROZ, 2024)

4. LinkedIn's Bias Reduction in Talent Insights

LinkedIn, a platform widely used for recruitment, has developed AI-driven talent insights tools that prioritize fairness and inclusivity. The company implements bias-mitigation techniques by ensuring that job recommendations and candidate matching algorithms do not favor specific demographic groups unfairly. LinkedIn also engages in regular audits and collaborates with external AI ethics bodies to refine its algorithms and prevent unintentional discrimination. (Geyik, S. C., Ambler, S., & Kenthapadi, K., 2019)

5. Google's Inclusive AI for Hiring

Google has integrated inclusive AI strategies into its hiring processes, particularly through tools like Google Hire. The company focuses on designing AI models that emphasize fairness by training them on unbiased datasets. Google also has an internal AI ethics team that ensures the responsible deployment of AI in HR. Additionally, Google uses explainable AI techniques to provide recruiters with detailed insights into AI-driven hiring recommendations, enhancing trust and accountability. (Chi, N., Lurie, E., & Mulligan, D. K., 2021)

LESSONS LEARNED AND ACTIONABLE INSIGHTS

1. Transparency and Explainability

Organizations must prioritize transparency in AI-powered HR systems. Explainability frameworks enable HR professionals to understand AI decision-making processes, ensuring accountability. Providing clear documentation on how AI models function fosters trust among employees and job candidates.

2. Bias Detection and Continuous Auditing

AI models must undergo rigorous bias detection and auditing. Companies should implement fairness-testing tools, such as IBM's AI Fairness 360 or Google's What-If Tool, to identify potential biases. Regular audits of AI-driven HR processes help mitigate unintended discriminatory effects.

3. Diverse and Representative Training Data

Training AI models on diverse datasets minimizes biases and enhances fairness. Organizations should ensure that datasets reflect a wide range of demographics, backgrounds, and experiences to prevent skewed decision-making in hiring and performance evaluations.

4. Human-AI Collaboration

While AI enhances efficiency, human oversight remains critical. Organizations should adopt a hybrid approach where AI-driven recommendations are reviewed by HR professionals, ensuring that ethical considerations are incorporated into final decisions.

5. Ethical AI Governance and Compliance

Establishing AI ethics committees or governance boards helps organizations maintain ethical AI use. These bodies should oversee AI deployment in HR, ensuring adherence to ethical guidelines and legal frameworks, such as GDPR and EEOC regulations.

6. Employee and Candidate Awareness

Employees and job candidates should be informed about AI's role in HR processes. Transparent communication about how AI influences hiring, performance evaluations, and promotions fosters trust and engagement.

7. Collaboration with External AI Ethics Experts

Partnering with academic researchers, ethics committees, and AI watchdog organizations can provide companies with valuable external perspectives. This collaboration helps organizations refine their AI models and align them with ethical best practices.

8. Regular AI Model Updates and Improvements

AI models should be updated continuously to incorporate new findings in fairness and bias mitigation. Companies should establish regular review cycles to ensure AI-driven HR systems remain ethical and effective.

The responsible deployment of AI in HR requires a concerted effort to address ethical concerns and biases. By adopting best practices—such as transparency, continuous bias auditing, diverse data training, and human-AI collaboration—organizations can ensure that AI-powered HR systems contribute to fair and equitable workforce management. The lessons from leading companies like Microsoft, Johnson & Johnson, Deloitte, LinkedIn, and Google serve as a blueprint for HR leaders striving to balance AI-driven efficiency with ethical responsibility.

FUTURE DIRECTIONS AND RECOMMENDATIONS

Emerging Trends in Ethical AI Governance

As AI shapes HR management, ethical AI governance is crucial, focusing on fairness, transparency, and accountability. A key trend is the use of explainable AI (XAI), which enhances the transparency of AI decision-making. Fairness-aware machine learning also aims to identify and reduce biases, supported by fairness auditing tools to assess demographic impacts. Interdisciplinary collaboration between AI ethicists, HR professionals, and regulators ensures AI aligns with ethical and legal standards. The "human-in-the-loop" approach allows human oversight of AI decisions, while emerging ethical AI certifications standardize best practices for HR technologies.

Policy Recommendations for Regulating AI in HR

As AI increasingly shapes HR management, ethical AI governance has become crucial. Key trends include the adoption of explainable AI (XAI) for transparency in decision-making and fairness-aware machine learning to address biases. Fairness auditing tools help assess AI's impact on demographics, while interdisciplinary collaborations ensure compliance with ethical standards and laws. The "human-in-the-loop" approach combines human oversight with AI, allowing HR professionals to address biased outcomes. Industry-wide ethical AI certifications are also emerging to standardize best practices in HR AI technologies.

Auditing Complexity and Resource Constraints

Thorough algorithmic audits require deep technical expertise, sophisticated tooling, and significant time. Many HR teams lack dedicated data-science or AI-governance specialists, and external audits can be costly. Organizations should therefore budget explicitly for both internal up-skilling (e.g. training HR staff in basic model-audit techniques) and where needed, engage experts on a periodic basis to validate fairness and transparency claims.

Ensuring and Measuring Data Diversity

While fairness-aware ML and bias-mitigation protocols depend on rich, representative datasets, assembling and continuously refreshing such datasets is nontrivial. Data may be siloed across geographies, subject to privacy constraints, or simply unavailable for certain demographic groups. To address this, organizations should invest in data-governance frameworks that:

Map existing data sources and identify gaps in representation.

Define clear metrics for "diversity" in each HR context (e.g. applicant pools, performance reviews).

Partner with external data providers or academic institutions when internal data are insufficient.

Fostering Sustainable Interdisciplinary Collaboration

Bringing together AI engineers, ethicists, legal counsel, and HR practitioners often runs into cultural and language barriers—each discipline has its own jargon, priorities, and risk-tolerances. To overcome this, firms should:

Establish a standing "AI Ethics in HR" working group with rotating membership drawn from all relevant functions.

Use structured collaboration rituals (e.g. joint "bias-blast" workshops, cross-functional code reviews) to surface concerns.

Create shared documentation glossaries, decision-logs, playbooks that bridge terminological gaps and institutionalize lessons learned.

CALL TO ACTION FOR HR PROFESSIONALS TO PRIORITIZE ETHICS IN AI ADOPTION

HR professionals play a crucial role in ensuring AI adoption aligns with ethical standards and organizational values. They should prioritize ethics throughout AI implementation by establishing AI ethics committees with HR, data science, and legal experts to oversee deployment and manage risks. Additionally, HR professionals must promote diversity in AI development, ensuring diverse training datasets to reduce biases and improve fairness. Collaborating with vendors to enforce bias-testing and ethical AI certifications is also key to maintaining accountability.

HR leaders should promote ethical AI awareness by offering training, workshops, and discussions on algorithmic decision-making and potential biases. Transparency should guide AI practices, ensuring HR departments communicate how AI systems operate and how employees can challenge decisions. Additionally, HR professionals must engage in policy discussions and collaborate with regulatory bodies, HR associations, and AI research institutions to shape ethical AI frameworks.

In conclusion, as AI continues to transform HR management, ethical governance must remain a top priority. Through proactive policy measures, interdisciplinary collaboration, and a commitment to transparency and fairness, HR professionals can ensure that AI-powered HR systems enhance workplace equity rather than exacerbate biases. The future of ethical AI in HR depends on a collective effort to align technological advancements with fundamental principles of fairness, accountability, and human dignity.

CONCLUSION

AI-powered HR systems have the potential to revolutionize workforce management, offering increased efficiency, data-driven decision-making, and enhanced employee experiences. However, their true value can only be realized when ethics, fairness, and transparency are at the core of their implementation. Without deliberate efforts to address bias and mitigate risks, AI can unintentionally reinforce systemic inequalities, leading to significant ethical and legal concerns.

This chapter serves as a guide for HR leaders, equipping them with the knowledge and strategies needed to identify biases, implement ethical safeguards, and foster trust in AI-driven HR practices. By taking a proactive approach to ethical AI governance, organizations can ensure that their HR systems promote equity and inclusivity rather than perpetuate discrimination or opacity.

Furthermore, this discussion aligns with the overarching mission of the book—exploring the intersection of technology and human resources to drive positive transformation. As AI continues to reshape the workplace, HR professionals must not only embrace innovation but also champion responsible AI use. By doing so, they can turn AI into a tool for empowerment, fairness, and long-term organizational success.

REFERENCES

Athanasiou, M. N. (2023). Automation of recruitment: Decision-making system design and review of legal implications.

Barrett, I. (2024). Human vs. machine: An empirical study of him professionals' perceptions of bias and fairness issues in AI-driven evaluations.

Chang, X. (2023). Gender Bias in Hiring: An Analysis of the Impact of Amazon's Recruiting Algorithm. Advances in Economics. *Management and Political Sciences*, *23*, 134–140.

Chi, N., Lurie, E., & Mulligan, D. K. (2021, July). Reconfiguring diversity and inclusion for AI ethics. In Proceedings of the 2021 AAAI/ACM Conference on AI, Ethics, and Society (pp. 447-457).

Clifford Chance. (2024). EU Artificial Intelligence Act: Implications for high-risk AI systems. https://www.cliffordchance.com/content/dam/cliffordchance/briefings/2024/08/what-does-the-eu-ai-act-mean-foremployers.pdf#:~:text=%E2%80%A2%20Strict%20obligations%20for%20AI,intended%20to%20be%20used%20for

De Villiers, C., Farooq, M. B., & Molinari, M. (2022). Qualitative research interviews using online video technology–challenges and opportunities. *Meditari Accountancy Research*, *30*(6), 1764–1782.

Deloitte. (2021). 2021 Global Human Capital Trends: Innovating with digital and human potential (PDF). Deloitte Insights. Retrieved from https://www2.deloitte.com

Drewniak, Z., & Posadzinska, I. (2020). Learning and development tools and the innovative potential of artificial intelligence companies.

Equal Employment Opportunity Commission. (2024, September). EEOC fact sheet: AI for workers. https://www.eeoc.gov/2024-annual-performance-report

Ferrara, E. (2024). The butterfly effect in artificial intelligence systems: Implications for AI bias and fairness. *Machine Learning with Applications*, *15*, 100525.

FIROZ, M. (2024). IT in HRM: Enhancing efficiency and employee engagement

Friedman, B., & Nissenbaum, H. (1996). Bias in computer systems. ACM Transactions on information systems (TOIS), 14(3), 330-347.

Geyik, S. C., Ambler, S., & Kenthapadi, K. (2019, July). Fairness-aware ranking in search & recommendation systems with application to linkedin talent search. In Proceedings of the 25th acm sigkdd international conference on knowledge discovery & data mining (pp. 2221-2231).

Goren, J. D. (2024). AI and the Future of Work: Legal Perspectives on Disability Acommodation and Employment Equity. *Ohio Northern University Law Review*, *50*(3), 3.

Green, A., del Pero, A. S., & Verhagen, A. (2023). Artificial intelligence, job quality and inclusiveness. OECD Employment Outlook, 128.

Hardesty, L. (2018). Study finds gender and skin-type bias in commercial artificial-intelligence systems. Retrieved April, 3, 2019.

IEEE. (n.d.). P7003: Algorithmic bias considerations. Institute of Electrical and Electronics Engineers. https://standards.ieee.org/

Irshad, S. (2024). Role of Human and Artificial Intelligence Biases on Organizational Performance, Efficiency, and Enhanced Productivity. In Human Perspectives of Industry 4.0 Organizations (pp. 111-130). CRC Press.

Kolmogorova, T. V. (2024). A sociological perspective on innovations in recruitment and retention of personnel. Scientific Review, (4), 201-210.</edb>

Madhumita, G., Diana, P. D., Neena, P. C., Kiran, P. N., Aggarwal, S., & Nargunde, A. S. (2024, April). AI-powered Performance Management: Driving Employee Success and Organizational

Marlowe, A. N. (2021). Robot Recruiters: How Employers & Governments Must Confront the Discriminatory Effects of AI Hiring. *J. High Tech. L.*, *22*, 274.

Mehrabi, N., Morstatter, F., Saxena, N., Lerman, K., & Galstyan, A. (2021). A survey on bias and fairness in machine learning. *ACM Computing Surveys*, *54*(6), 1–35.

Mergen, A., Çetin-Kılıç, N., & Özbilgin, M. F. (2025). Artificial Intelligence and Bias Towards Marginalised Groups: Theoretical Roots and Challenges. In AI and Diversity in a Datafied World of Work: Will the Future of Work be Inclusive? (Vol. 12, pp. 17-38). Emerald Publishing Limited.

OECD. (2024). Survey on algorithmic management governance measures. https://www.oecd.org/

Rao, S., & Zhao, T. (2025). Ethical AI in HR: A Case Study of Tech Hiring. *Journal of Computer Information Systems*, •••, 1–18.

Rietdijk, S. (2024). The Relationship Between AI Recruitment and Gender Bias: A Literature Review.

Rodgers, W., Murray, J. M., Stefanidis, A., Degbey, W. Y., & Tarba, S. Y. (2023). An artificial intelligence algorithmic approach to ethical decision-making in human resource management processes. *Human Resource Management Review*, *33*(1), 100925.

Scatiggio, V. (2020). Tackling the issue of bias in artificial intelligence to design ai-driven fair and inclusive service systems. How human biases are breaching into ai algorithms, with severe impacts on individuals and societies, and what designers can do to face this phenomenon and change for the better.

Schwartz, R., Schwartz, R., Vassilev, A., Greene, K., Perine, L., Burt, A., & Hall, P. (2022). Towards a standard for identifying and managing bias in artificial intelligence (Vol. 3, p. 00). Gaithersburg, MD: US Department of Commerce, National Institute of Standards and Technology.

Shahbazi, N., Lin, Y., Asudeh, A., & Jagadish, H. V. (2023). Representation bias in data: A survey on identification and resolution techniques. *ACM Computing Surveys*, *55*(13s), 1–39.

Shneiderman, B. (2020). Bridging the gap between ethics and practice: Guidelines for reliable, safe, and trustworthy human-centered AI systems. [TiiS]. *ACM Transactions on Interactive Intelligent Systems*, *10*(4), 1–31.

Sonderling, K. E., Kelley, B. J., & Casimir, L. (2022). The promise and the peril: Artificial intelligence and employment discrimination. *U. Miami L. Rev.*, *77*, 1.

Tilmes, N. (2022). Disability, fairness, and algorithmic bias in AI recruitment. *Ethics and Information Technology*, *24*(2), 21.

Vivek, R. (2023). Enhancing diversity and reducing bias in recruitment through AI: a review of strategies and challenges. Информатика. Экономика. Управление/ Informatics. Economics. Management, 2(4), 0101-0118.

Yanamala, K. K. R. (2023). Transparency, privacy, and accountability in AI-enhanced HR processes. *Journal of Advanced Computing Systems*, *3*(3), 10–18.

Zhang, H. (2024). Exploring the Impact of AI on Human Resource Management: A case study of organizational adaptation and employee dynamics. *IEEE Transactions on Engineering Management*.

Chapter 8
Exploring the Impact of AI on Employee Spirituality:
A Roadmap for Cultivating Employee Mindfulness

Mahak Garg
https://orcid.org/0009-0005-5548-8757
Guru Jambheshwar University of Science and Technology, Hisar, India

B. K. Punia
https://orcid.org/0000-0003-4199-610X
Guru Jambheshwar University of Science and Technology, Hisar, India

Garima Bansal
https://orcid.org/0009-0001-6890-6242
Guru Jambheshwar University of Science and Technology, Hisar, India

Vandana Punia
Guru Jambheshwar University of Science and Technology, Hisar, India

ABSTRACT

There is a growing need for permanent spiritual practices to help individuals navigate the demanding high-tech environment. Technological spirituality, where technology supports mindfulness, is emerging as a transformative approach to addressing spiritual dilemmas in cyberspace. The present paper explores the effect of artificial intelligence on employees' spirituality and provides a roadmap for cultivating mindful employees in organizations with special reference to the BFSI sector. The

DOI: 10.4018/979-8-3373-8612-6.ch008

study surveyed 501 BFSI (Banking, Financial Services, and Insurance) employees. The data was analyzed using AMOS 22. The study revealed that there is a positive and significant relationship between AI and spirituality among employees across the BFSI sector. This study uniquely applies artificial intelligence to spirituality by combining the technical accuracy with intuitive engagement. This study also explores how AI and spirituality synergize to enhance workplace mindfulness. The paper also discusses theoretical and practical implications, as well as limitations and future research.

1. INTRODUCTION

Human resource management (HRM) today monitors all employee aspects and strives to address them, a crucial requirement for any organization to perform well. Faultless, the COVID-19 pandemic led humans close to spirituality again and also revealed spirituality's significance and consequences. Human resource managers and practitioners undoubtedly encouraged the organization, particularly its employees, to embrace spirituality, a goal made possible by Artificial Intelligence's (AI) ability to maintain social distance. The change management is the glorifying part that would initiate the bit of stride. Ray Kurzweil poses the question, "Can an intelligence create another intelligence more intelligent than itself?" and then provides a potential response in his book The Age of Spiritual Machines (Kurzweil 1999). The idea of an evolutionary dynamic that drives human progress is a compelling way to look at the human mind that comes from thinking about the limits of science. This viewpoint regards artificial intelligence as essential for technological advancement and as a means to transcend certain constraints inherent in human intellect. Nonetheless, scientific speculation indicates that a considerable issue emerges when artificial intellect endeavours to replicate human intellect and maybe supplant it. The increasing sophistication of AI raises philosophical and ethical concerns, particularly regarding its implications for human identity and societal roles. As AI develops greater self-awareness, the boundary between human and machine becomes increasingly blurred. This ambiguity not only challenges our traditional understanding of intelligence but also sparks debates on autonomy, decision-making, mindfulness and accountability in AI-driven systems. Given that mindfulness is the fundamental concept of this paper, it is imperative to investigate its significance.

Being totally present and involved in the moment, mindfulness is the discipline of paying attention to ideas, emotions, and surroundings without any judgment (Bansal & Punia, 2023). Those who practice mindfulness in their workplace are known as mindful workers. This implies staff members being aware of their behaviour, controlling stress, and concentrating on clearly defined duties. The discussion will whirl mainly around spirituality and AI, which will not only be a roadmap to cultivate mindful employees but also the overall success at the workplace. Here's how mindful employees could act:

1. Focused and Present: Avoiding multitasking and distractions, they give the current work their whole concentration.
2. Stress Management: Their intelligent response to stress helps them to manage it better than their reactive one. When necessary, they pause; they also practice strategies to keep calm, do breathing exercises, or use pauses.
3. Emotional Awareness: Mindful workers are more aware of their emotions and how they influence their job. This awareness helps individuals to have a positive and balanced attitude.
4. Improved Communication: Mindful workers' pay close attention and react with compassion, therefore improving the bonds among colleagues in the workplace.
5. Enhanced Productivity: They often seem more efficient and productive as they ignore distractions and concentrate on the current moment.
6. Resilience: Mindful workers tackle difficulties with a calm and solution-oriented attitude, so they are frequently more flexible and robust to obstacles. Mindful workers help create a better workplace overall, lowering burnout and supporting a more friendly atmosphere.

Artificial intelligence offers enormous benefits in terms of automation and efficiency; its arrival into the workplace also begs issues about its impact on workers' spiritual and emotional well-being (Syahrial et al., 2024). As artificial intelligence systems assume more roles typically performed by humans, employees suffer rising stress, a sense of separation, and challenges with work-life balancing (Calderero Hernández, 2021). Pursuits of performance measurements, automation, and algorithm-driven decisions might result in an impersonal work atmosphere that would compromise people's sense of purpose and fulfilment. This shift may lead one to ignore important components of human growth like emotional intelligence, mindfulness, and spirituality (Bansal et al., 2025). While it is true that the world of humans has changed due to new technological advancements, spirituality challenges this notion in its unique context. The originality of the world is still a question for all, and each person on this Earth has their own perception. Against the global trend of AI systems augmenting the jobs that were initially carried out by human beings, one urgent question for HRM is whether robots could take the place of humans in HRM or if they could be the assisting hand for the employees to be mindful, and for the well-established organization (Vrontis, et al., 2023).

In the context of business, spirituality is a person's feeling of meaning, purpose, and connection within their profession. It covers traits like empathy, moral judgment, and consistency with one's inner ideals (Jackelén,2021). According to numerous studies, spirituality is the base for mindfulness, and AI is the assistant (or helping hand) for success. Particularly in the BFSI (Banking, Financial Services, and Insurance) sectors, the fast progress of Artificial Intelligence (AI) has brought about transforming changes throughout several businesses. The financial services sector is presently under substantial pressure to maintain its viability in this competitive era as a result of the rapid pace of change in the business environment. The firm's ability to acquire a larger share of the market and its challenge to provide better service to its consumers significantly influence its survival in the industry. In India, the field of the BFSI sector has been the main driver of economic growth. By use of infrastructure, networks, software, and computers, this industry uses information technology systems to increase efficiency and provide services involving the administration and processing of data. Included in the scope of this are hardware and software development, technical assistance, and systems management. Leading digital pioneers, these sectors have relied more on artificial intelligence technology to provide customer-centric solutions, increase productivity, and streamline procedures.

Maintaining a healthy, motivated, and mindful workforce depends on supporting workers' spiritual well-being in fields like BFSI, where the speed of work is typically fast. Encouragement of awareness and a feeling of purpose will enable staff members to negotiate the difficulties of AI integration and guarantee their worth and connection to the more general corporate goal (Raghav & Gulia, 2023). This review signals the appalling need for artificial intelligence (AI) and spirituality at any workplace and also provides significant insights for human resource managers as well as practitioners for the attainment of mindful employees. A rigorous analysis is needed to explore the relationship between artificial intelligence and spirituality. This is an unexplored zone that needs to be surveyed for mindful employees. It explains the pros of connecting the mindful employee's work to their spiritual values to attain a behaviouristic and peaceful workplace. Emphasizing the requirement of a roadmap to develop mindful workers, this article investigates how artificial intelligence influences employees' spirituality in the BFSI sectors. Organizations may establish a work environment that harmonizes technology with human values by including techniques for improving spiritual well-being, including mindfulness practices, reflecting spaces, and ethical leadership, therefore promoting a sustainable and emotionally rewarding workplace (Bansal et al., 2025).

In line with this, the study aimed to investigate the following objective:

- To study the effect of Artificial Intelligence on employee spirituality across BFSI sector employees, a roadmap for cultivating employee mindfulness

Figure 1. a roadmap for cultivating employee mindfulness

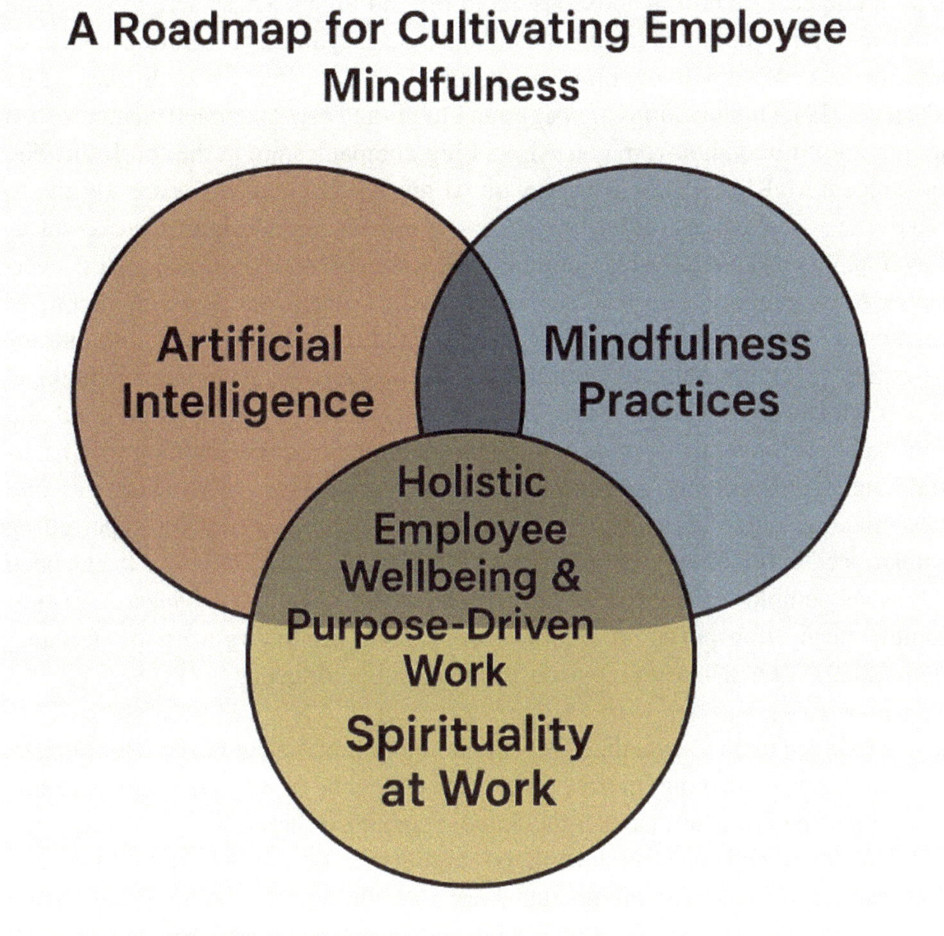

Source: The Author

2. LITERATURE REVIEW

2.1. Artificial Intelligence (AI)

Artificial intelligence (AI) is an emerging trend in Human Resource management (HRM) context. Authors and scientists discovered AI to be boon and bane for the society for the availability of service and also the misuse of it. HR managers and practitioners emerged in AI to enhance the corporate environment and to cope with the technological world. Artificial intelligence (AI) is the replication of human intellect in computers designed to think, learn, and carry out usually human intelligence-requiring activities under programming. These activities include problem-solving, comprehension of natural language, pattern recognition, decision-making, and even environmental perception—that is, vision, voice, or sensor data (Peters, 2019). Organizations are beginning to initiate organizational change aimed at creating future value from gen AI, and big companies are at the forefront. The most recent McKinsey Global Survey on AI reveals that companies are starting to make moves that drive bottom-line value—for instance, redesigning processes as they implement gen AI and placing senior leaders in pivotal positions, such as overseeing AI governance. The results also indicate that organizations are attempting to counteract an increasing number of gen-AI-related risks and are recruiting for new AI-related positions while they retrain staff to engage in AI deployment (Singla, et al., 2025). During the past decade, artificial intelligence has undergone rapid and remarkable advancements. AI technologies, including machine learning (ML), natural language processing, and computer vision, are progressively influencing and disseminating into a variety of fields and facets of our society. AI is superseding human decision-making and progressively taking over human tasks. It has been extensively employed in a diverse array of industries, including business, logistics, manufacturing, transportation, healthcare, education, and state governance (Huang, et al., 2022). Two primary groups define artificial intelligence:

- Designed to do a specialized job, including as translating, face recognition, or autonomous driving, narrow artificial intelligence (weak AI) It runs within a small spectrum and lacks broad intellect or self-awareness.
- Still hypothetical, general artificial intelligence (strong AI) is an AI system capable of doing any intellectual work a person could. Over a wide spectrum of activities, it would be able to reason, comprehend, and learn.

The trending ChatGPT, capacity to respond to follow-up inquiries that enables students to challenge and clarify information (Budhwar, et al., 2023). This fosters the integration of extant knowledge and fosters a more profound comprehension of multiple concepts and meanings (Rospigliosi, 2023). Practically, artificial intelligence sometimes consists of technologies like computer vision (which helps computers comprehend visual data), natural language processing (which lets machines understand and produce human language), and machine learning—where systems learn from data—whereby from banking and healthcare to entertainment and transportation, artificial intelligence is used in numerous sectors to improve efficiency, automate tasks, and solve difficult issues. It is anticipated that this generation will possess the ability to demonstrate scientific creativity and social skills. Leading platforms like Wysa, an AI-driven mental health chatbot, and Headspace, which provides guided meditations and mood monitoring, have found applications in both corporate and clinical environments. Wysa has been tested in various healthcare and financial companies for its mental well-being solutions, while Headspace for Work has been implemented by multinational organizations like Adobe and Unilever (Partal and Smirnova, 2021). Even with their increasing use, critics argue that they are not scalable across cultures and professions. For example, cultural constructions of mindfulness and mental health could impact participation levels, and the commercialization of spiritual practices might discourage employees looking for more authentic or non-commercial reflections (Kettle and Lee, 2024). A professionally specific and culture-based method is therefore crucial when embedding such tools in workplace spiritual systems. Wirth (2018) categorized AI into three categories: weak AI (AI that is specifically designed for specific tasks), hybrid AI (AI that can adapt to new tasks by combining numerous solutions), and strong AI (AI that is as intelligent as a human and can handle a variety of tasks). This classification is based on the extent of the tasks that AI is capable of performing. Additionally separating artificial intelligence (AI) into analytical, human-inspired, and humanized forms is Kaplan & Haenlein (2019). Analytical artificial intelligence has been used in many different contexts and guides future judgments by means of cognitive intelligence and learning—that is, prior data. Human inspired artificial intelligence has emotional as well as cognitive capacity. Human emotions may be sensed by an artificial intelligence system and included into decision-making process. Human-inspired artificial intelligence is reportedly growing in favour according to Kaplan & Haenlein (2019). For instance, Walmart used intervention—that is, open additional cashiers—by using face recognition technologies, which are human-inspired artificial intelligence, to detect disgruntled consumers waiting at check-outs. Humanized artificial intelligence is expected to have social, emotional, and cognitive intelligence as well as self-conscious awareness of their contacts with others. AI talks, necessitates to discuss about Robots which have transformed the human lives drastically. From chatbots such as Apple's Siri to humanoid robots such as Pepper and Mindar, AI has increasingly taken over the functions of humans in various professions (Dignum, 2018; Sharkey, 2019; Tamatea, 2010; Van Wynsberghe & Robbins, 2019). According to 2016 report of the International Federation for Robotics, the total number of professional service robots sold in 2015 has increased by 25%, particularly for service robots in defence applications and medical robots (Van Wynsberghe & Robbins, 2019). As mentioned by various researchers, people now-a-days are most dependent on technologies and leaving their own intelligence far behind. Initially, the absence of a precise definition of AI complicates the process of evaluating various AI systems and developing policies and regulations to address them. Secondly, the AI community is also harmed by the lack of consensus, as it makes it difficult for different groups to communicate and collaborate. This, in turn, will result in a lack of evaluation criteria, benchmark tests, milestones, and other essential elements for the healthy development of the AI community. (Lyu and Liu, 2021) It wouldn't be wrong to say "Humans are going to be stupid, not AI be smarter."

What will happen when a computing brain will become smarter than human brain. One of the authors writes, "Nowadays in the information age, it is hard to imagine how the world would be without computers and the internet. Turing's work, especially the core concept of Turing machine at the heart of every computer, mobile phone and microchip today, so many things on which we are so dependent would be impossible (this be the common issue regarding AI). There is no doubt that, in time, being a man-made creation, the AI entities might surely be able to match our abilities and surpass (almost) any of the human feature, even any Turing-like test. Although computer will be able to do everything, they can't be everything, (Popoveniuc, 2015). On the one hand, there are obstacles associated with the capacity of organizations and individuals to utilize these tools, such as a dearth of skills to work with or alongside AI, inadequate digital infrastructure and data, and management culture and staff resistance (Broecke, 2023). Together, the AI dimensions capture workers' impressions on artificial intelligence quality. According to past studies, these aspects of information and system quality may lead to people's favourable opinions of technology and help workers to produce job-related results (e.g., Forsgren et al., 2016; Wixom & Todd, 2005). Since Mark Zuckerberg's announcement in October 2021 that Facebook would be rebranded as Meta, the remarkable concept of the new name has become a popular topic on social media and has garnered significant attention and discussion from a variety of communities, including academia and industry (Huynh-The, et al., 2023). By analyzing consumer inquiries (e.g., language translation), exploring corporate knowledge systems, and crafting human-friendly solutions (Kirkpatrick, 2017), artificial intelligence may help workers do their jobs. While AI-driven mindfulness apps gain popularity, there are a number of negative factors that need to be scrutinized. Such technologies have the potential to commodify spirituality by making profound introspective practices mere routine metrics or corporate wellness objectives, which could translate into shallow involvement (Saisubramanian, et al., 2022). Algorithmic personalization also threatens spiritual autonomy by influencing users subtly towards predetermined behaviours that could be incongruent with their personal beliefs or cultural norms. Additionally, the gathering of intimate emotional information creates concerns about privacy and surveillance, especially in professional settings where involvement can be perceived as compulsory. AI technologies tend to be exclusive, excluding neurodivergent individuals and individuals from non-Western spiritual perspectives based on biased design and poor cultural versatility (Ipek, et al., 2023). The article (Prentice et al., 2020) is the source of the components of Artificial Intelligence, which are thoroughly examined in this paper.

Components of Artificial Intelligence (AI)

"**Accuracy**" is the measurement of the extent to which a machine learning model accurately predicts or classifies instances based on the total number of instances it has been tested on in the context of Artificial Intelligence (AI). In supervised learning tasks, where the model's predictions can be contrasted against known ground truth labels, it is a fundamental metric used to evaluate the efficacy of AI models.

In artificial intelligence (AI), **"Accessibility"** is the degree to which, independent of cognitive, physical, or technical capacity, people can use AI technology, applications, and systems. It comprises many key elements necessary to ensure that artificial intelligence is inclusive and advantageous to all users. It means the creation of interfaces, tools, and gadgets fit for disabilities such restricted mobility, hearing loss, or visual handicap. For consumers with vision or mobility problems, for example, voice assistants driven by artificial intelligence may improve accessibility by letting them engage with gadgets using voice commands.

In artificial intelligence (AI), **"Flexibility"** is the ability of AI systems to change and expand their knowledge, behaviours, or responses to different environments, tasks, or circumstances. It is a major factor influencing the adaptability and value of artificial intelligence technology in many uses. Artificial intelligence systems should be able to learn and modify their behaviour in response to changes in the environment or fresh data. This covers their ongoing knowledge base update, improvement of their decision-making process, or modification of their outputs in response to comments or changing conditions. Using its learned knowledge or skills, an adaptive artificial intelligence system may engage in a variety of tasks or scenarios outside of the ones it was specifically instructed on. This ability lets artificial intelligence solve fresh problems or iterations of existing ones without much retraining or change needed. It is of great relevance in using the great ability of artificial intelligence to solve complex issues and provide innovative ideas in various fields like healthcare, finance, robotics, IT/ITES and more.

In the context of artificial intelligence (AI), **"Currency"** describes the timeliness or relevance of the data utilized for training and operation of AI models. This fundamental component greatly affects the performance, accuracy, and usefulness of artificial intelligence systems in practical settings. Artificial intelligence's data currency emphasizes the requirement of using current and relevant data for both inference operations and training. As data ages, changes in the surroundings, user behaviour, or outside factors might reduce its usefulness and quality.

In the context of artificial intelligence (AI), **"Reliability"** refers to the congruity and believability of AI systems in delivering exact results and rendering accurate decisions. For many applications, it is a key factor influencing usability, efficiency, and acceptance of artificial intelligence technology. Reliable artificial intelligence systems often provide precise and accurate results depending on many inputs and conditions. The aim of this work is error, bias, and uncertainty minimizing in forecasts, classifications, or recommendations. Preserving trust in the functioning of the system and guaranteeing consistent judgments in regular operations or important applications relies on stability being maintained.

"**Comprehensiveness**" in the context of Artificial Intelligence (AI) refers to the extent and thoroughness of knowledge, understanding, or skills that an AI system has in a certain field or job. Comprehensiveness in artificial intelligence refers to the degree to which an AI system understands and incorporates a broad spectrum of relevant information, ideas, and situations into its realm of functioning. This involves accurately representing a wide range of viewpoints, subtleties, and intricacies related to the issue area. AI systems with extensive domain expertise are highly knowledgeable in the fundamental concepts, theories, norms, and optimal methods that are pertinent to their specific field of expertise. By skilfully managing complex intricacies, exceptions, and edge situations, they exhibit a profound comprehension of the subject matter.

2.2 Spirituality

Discovery of spirituality is in moments when an individual arises a meaning of personal existence question and attempts to place the self within a broader ontological context. Spirituality is not with a different person but a person with contrasting personality characteristics which gives an inner subjective and motivating experience that urges us to feel the strong interest in understanding the meaning of life (Frunză, 2023). From the sociological perspective, spirituality is a cultural fact, "the search for sacred" where sacred is not only for the god or spirit or the divine spirit or supernatural, but it is an extremely broad concept. Sacred do include all the things as a rock, flower, tree, a spring, wood, uttered word, a piece of pebble or wood or anything (Dubey and Bedi, 2024). Spirituality has been defined by various authors from decades as "inner consciousness ", "a process of self- enlightenment ", "the unique inner search for the fullest personal development ", "feeling of being connected with one's complete self, others and entire universe ", "journey to find a sustainable, authentic, meaningful, holistic and profound meaning of self". Some researchers found people to have positive and negative views of spirituality as mostly people find spirituality as our base of life and rest find it anti-materialist (Garg et al., 2022).

Spirituality is clearly a broader construct than religion. Spirituality allows a person to have a sense of the sacred without the institutional practices and limitations that are associated with traditional religions (Zinnbauer et al, 1999). Spirituality should not be confused with religion as some of the authors explain how people be spiritual but not religious for further exploration. For a person who adopted a certain conception of what it is to be spiritual, it means they can be escorted by this idea in their practice, through others so they are stable with their rules and thinking of spirituality. Virtue is goodness, morality which are attitudes, dispositions or character traits that enable us to righteous and to act in ways that allow us to grasp our basic prospective for moral excellence (Frunză, 2023). A virtuous person has a habit of truthfulness in all the circumstances; all his acts and activities are irrespective of bias and are followed towards truth. The virtuous agent has come to recognise the value of virtue and view it as the appropriate response in a given situation. Spirituality is self-creation, self- exploration by understanding our self which is the base for human being's existence. A spiritual person's internal harmony and peace will radiate for and wide reaching from his oneself to family, society to the state, nation and to the heavenly. Spirituality is grounded in morality and moral culture, which is the lacking factor from the life of the majority. The literature has emphasized the importance of compliance in order to uphold social norms, as well as the advantages of a positive relationship for workplace spirituality values. Despite the evident presence of deviant practices, there is also a lack of clarity regarding employees' perceptions when personal values and organizational procedures conflict. In order to further investigate the reactions of UK employees when their personal values did not align with those of the workplace, the perceptions of individuals from a variety of religious and generational backgrounds were sought (Jolliffe and Foster, 2022). The article (Singhn & Makkar, 2015) has been consulted to extract the components of spirituality, which are then elaborated upon in this paper.

Components of Spirituality

Self-awareness, as a component of spirituality, encompasses a profound comprehension and deliberate observation of one's own being in connection to the world, the cosmos, and beyond. Contemplation and self-examination are the first stages of spiritual self-awareness. Cognitive introspection is the process of examining one's own thoughts, feelings, beliefs, and motives.

As a component of spirituality, **Belief in Life** refers to the fundamental idea that existence itself has a deep sense of meaning, purpose, and connectivity. This conviction is fundamental to many spiritual traditions and belief systems, influencing how people interpret and interact with the surrounding environment. Spirituality is characterized by the fundamental belief that life has deep significance, purpose, and connectivity.

Spiritual Practices refer to essential actions or rituals which people participate in to foster a more profound connection with themselves, others, and the spiritual aspect of life. These practices are essential to many spiritual traditions and have a vital function in moulding and fostering one's spiritual development. Often, spiritual activities are specifically crafted to cultivate a feeling of connection and contact with a higher power, divine presence, or spiritual essence. The pursuit of transcending egoic tendencies, cultivating heightened self-awareness, and aligning oneself with spiritual principles to assist inner change is undertaken by people via the use of techniques like as meditation, prayer, or contemplation.

Spiritual requirements are fundamental aspects of the human experience that seek fulfilment and expression through **Spiritual Needs**. These requirements are inherent to the human condition and significantly influence the beliefs, values, and behaviours associated with spirituality. The significance and purpose of human existence are deeply ingrained in the human psyche. This necessity compels individuals to pursue answers to existential questions and to identify significance in their lives that transcends mere Existence. A desire for connection and belonging—to oneself, to others, and to a larger whole or spiritual community—is frequently a component of spiritual requirements.

The concept of **Spirit at Work** is the incorporation of spiritual values, principles, and practices into the work environment, with an emphasis on the development of meaningful connections among individuals, purpose-driven work, and holistic well-being. This concept recognizes that work is not solely a means of generating income; it can also serve as a platform for personal development, ethical conduct, and the promotion of the common good. It entails the identification of significance in one's contributions and the perception that employment serves a more significant, meaningful objective than financial gain. Organizational culture and individual behaviours are infused with spiritual principles, including integrity, compassion, honesty, and fairness. Employees are motivated to make decisions that prioritize stakeholders' welfare and ethical implications.

2.3. Hypothesis (H_1)- "Artificial Intelligence has positive effect on Spirituality among BFSI employees".

Cultural Intelligence and Spiritual Intelligence have emerged as essential instruments in global connections, presenting both possibilities and problems for humans in the digital age. In the era of Artificial Intelligence and digital globalization, it is essential to foster connections grounded in Cultural Intelligence and Spiritual Intelligence, both at the individual and institutional levels (Raghav & Gulia, 2023). One might see man as an individual who embodies a presence in his own existence. This involves scrutinizing all aspects of life that contribute to comprehending the human condition in the world. Existential considerations are pertinent in this context (Deurzen, 2021). The COVID-19 pandemic has revealed the high level of dissatisfaction that is prevalent among the working population worldwide, prompting employees to reconsider their expectations of their employment (Dubey and Bedi, 2024). The Catholic Church underscores the significance of education and spiritual development concerning AI technology. It cultivates a profound comprehension of the Catholic faith and promotes a measured spiritual practice in the context of technological advancement (Lektawan, 2024). Contemporary technology may be used to augment spiritual endeavours. As technology advances, spiritual practices like as prayer, recorded liturgy, and online forums may enhance an individual's connection with the Holy Spirit and foster a religious community. Technology may serve as an instrument to facilitate prayer, foster spiritual development, and promote meditation (Council, 2009). Digital technology establishes novel environments for individuals to engage with one another, cultivate their personal growth, and execute their obligations. Nevertheless, the new private and work-related platforms are not merely instruments; they are new spaces that modern individuals inhabit, resulting in the fact that they are inhabited for numerous hours each day. This is not a physical occurrence; rather, it is a mental one. Consequently, the digital environments that organizations construct become mental habitats in which we begin to feel at ease (Walter, 2024). The Church encourages individuals to use AI judiciously, considering its effects on human dignity, the common good, and human accountability as creations of God (Francis, 2023). The ethical dilemmas stemming from AI development may be surmounted by following the lead of the Holy Spirit and adhering to Catholic doctrine. In the era of AI technology, who possess a profound spiritual and theological heritage, confront the problems and possibilities of engaging with the Supreme power (Tan, 2020). Artificial Intelligence has introduced several intricate challenges concerning spiritual aspects. Catholic doctrine offers an ethical framework for technological use, highlighting moral principles, social equity, and the safeguarding of human rights (Lektawan, 2024). Simultaneously, digital spirituality facilitates the enhancement of religious practices via prayer applications, spiritual social media platforms, and virtual communities. By merging Catholic principles with technological innovation, adherents may judiciously incorporate their religion, enhance spiritual ties, and adapt to the changing dynamics of contemporary society (Tan, 2020). A study by Lektawan supports the current paper which exclaims Catholic dogma asserts that God the Holy Spirit is coequal with God the Father and the Son as the third member of the Trinity. The early Christian community grappled with understanding God's oneness with their impression of the triadic nature of their religious experience. The concept of the Holy Spirit as a heavenly presence raises questions about the role of artificial intelligence (AI), a technology created by humans, within this paradigm (Lektawan, 2024). The amalgamation of spirituality and technology will allow individuals to recognize and use chances for diverse development, especially in spiritual activities (Syahrial, et al., 2024). Various modalities of spiritual education and development include the following (Council, 2009):

1. Convenient access to Spiritual Formation resources: The internet era facilitates convenient access to resources for spiritual development. Websites and programs provide spiritual resources like as prayers, devotionals, and catechetical materials. This fosters self-directed study and facilitates individual spiritual development.
2. Social media and spiritual blogging facilitate online engagement. This website is created to facilitate connections among those who appreciate spirituality and can engage online.

Spirituality and artificial intelligence (AI) produce a unique and fascinating confluence of human existence and technology. While spirituality addresses many aspects of life, like purpose, meaning, and connection to something greater, artificial intelligence largely addresses automating tasks and solving challenging problems. One of the key realms in which these two fields interact is ethical ones. Often promoting ideas like compassion, empathy, and interconnectedness—which might guide the ethical development of artificial intelligence—are spiritual beliefs. Combining these ideas will enable artificial intelligence to be developed to promote justice and human well-being, therefore ensuring that technology advances humanity in a responsible and compassionate way. Still another junction falls within human meaning and purpose (Peters, 2019). As technology takes over more regular and monotonous tasks, artificial intelligence may free individuals to focus on personal growth, creativity, and spiritual development, therefore allowing them more time to participate in significant events outside of the workplace (Popkova, 2024). But the development of artificial intelligence begs issues of whether individuals would have existential crises or alienation, in which case they would doubt their value in a society becoming increasingly automated. In a society shaped by artificial intelligence, spirituality offers a mechanism to navigate challenges and help individuals to find meaning and maintain their sense of self-worth. The question of consciousness adds additional philosophical element to the interplay between artificial intelligence and spirituality. According to spiritual traditions, awareness is an essential quality of existence and that technology cannot replicate it. about the other side, artificial intelligence raises the possibility of machines developing a form of consciousness, which fuels debates about the core of human existence and the viability of AI to have any spiritual or conscious quality. This ongoing research challenges our consciousness, life, knowledge, and understanding of what it means to be human. The rising presence of artificial intelligence in daily life also requires emotional intelligence and awareness. Even while AI can do tasks rapidly, it lacks the emotional depth and understanding that humans possess. Mindfulness and meditation among other spiritual practices provide means for people to develop emotional intelligence and remain anchored in a society progressively shaped by technology (Garg et al., 2022). As artificial intelligence shapes the workplace and society, these techniques might enable individuals to control the emotional issues and stress that can result. At last, artificial intelligence may itself be a tool for spiritual development. Already helping individuals interact with their spiritual practices in fresh and easily available ways are AI-powered meditation applications, virtual spiritual advisors, and customized well-being programs. These instruments may provide customized advice, therefore enabling individuals in their spiritual development by making spirituality more approachable and fit to their particular circumstances.

Thomas Donaldson said that, despite the cultural disparities between the West and non-Western societies, we may distil some perspectives about the essence of humanity. Individuals must not see others only as instruments; rather, they should acknowledge each person's intrinsic worth as a human being. Subsequently, individuals and communities must respect and uphold the fundamental rights of others. Ultimately, community members must collaborate to enhance and sustain the institutions upon which the community relies. Those three principles are called as "good citizenship," "respect for basic rights," and "respect for human dignity." (Donaldson, 2016). In essence, even if spirituality and artificial intelligence appear to have nothing in common, they are in many respects quite closely. Society must make sure that technical developments complement human values and ethical standards as artificial intelligence develops so as to promote well-being, balance, and purpose. Spirituality may give vital direction in negotiating these changes and ideas into how we could include artificial intelligence into our life without sacrificing our humanity or connection to the more profound sides of life. Combining the best aspects of both disciplines will help us to build a more harmonic, caring, and conscious future.

3. PROPOSED RESEARCH MODEL

Figure 2. Proposed Research Model

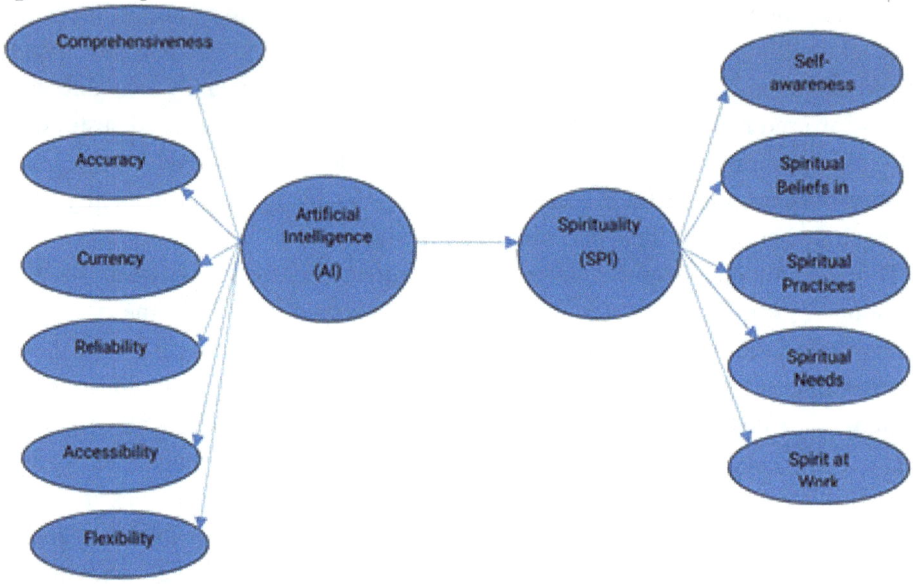

The hypothetical/ proposed Research Model represents all the variables that will be used in this particular research study.

4. RESEARCH METHODOLOGY

4.1. Measurement development

The study employed a quantitative research design to collect data from employees in the service sector. Our research instrument consisted of two sections. The first section of the survey had demographic questions, i.e., gender, age, place of birth, marital status, education, academic qualification, level of management, place of work, total years of service, average daily work hours, type of family, and type of company/organization. The second section comprised the statements to measure the study constructs: Artificial Intelligence (AI) and spirituality (SPI). These statements were measured using a 5-point Likert scale, with 1 denoting strongly disagree and 5 denoting strongly agree.

Artificial Intelligence (AI)

We accessed Artificial Intelligence, dividing its six dimensions adapted from Wixom and Todd (2005), i.e., comprehensiveness (3 items), accuracy (3 items), currency (3 items), reliability (3 items), accessibility (3 items), and flexibility (3 items) into an 18-item scale. The sample items are: "AI tools provide me with all the information I need", "Information provided by AI tools is accurate", "AI tools give the most current and recent information", "Work performed and operated by AI tools are reliable", "AI tools make it easy to access information for all my work", and "AI tools can flexibly adjust to new demands or conditions according to my need".

Spirituality

We adapted 20 statements from Singh & Makkar 2015 for measuring spirituality, which involves five dimensions: Self- awareness (5 items), Spiritual beliefs in life (5 items), Spiritual practice (3 items), Spiritual needs (3 items), and Spirit at work (4 items). The sample statements include: " Spirituality helps in maintaining positive attitude", " Spirituality helps me to be a better person", " Meditation helps in achieving inner peace and enhance spirituality", "I find my life is beautiful, purposeful and developing", and "I experience joy and feel motivated toward my work".

4.2. Population and Sample Selected for the Study

The demographic profile of respondents has been analysed using descriptive frequency analysis (refer to Table 1).

The sample consists predominantly of male employees (62.08%), followed by female employees (37.72%), with a minimal representation of other gender identities (0.19%). As per the age distribution, the majority of BFSI employees fall within the 30 to 40 years age bracket (46.11%), followed by those below 30 years (35.13%). Employees aged 40 to 50 years constitute 11.78%, while only 6.99% are over 50 years old. A significant proportion of employees were born in urban areas (74.65%), followed by suburban regions (18.36%) and rural areas (6.99%). In terms of marital status, most respondents are married (65.07%), with a notable proportion being unmarried (27.15%), while 7.78% belong to other categories. In education, a large majority of employees hold postgraduate degrees (59.68%), followed by undergraduates (19.16%) and those with higher degrees or vocational diplomas (18.96%). In the context of the level of management, the workforce is primarily concentrated at the middle management level (51.10%), followed by higher management (29.54%) and supervisory roles (9.78%). Employees at the top management level comprise 7.78%, while lower-level employees make up just 1.80%. Data on place of work shows that the majority of respondents work in urban areas (83.23%), with fewer in suburban areas (15.57%) and a minimal presence in rural locations (1.20%). In terms of total years of service, most employees have between 6 to 10 years of experience (43.11%), followed by those with up to 5 years (35.73%). Employees with 11 to 15 years (11.98%) and more than 15 years (9.18%) of experience form a smaller portion of the workforce. For average daily working hours, the majority of employees work 8 to 10 hours per day (55.49%), with 37.13% working up to 8 hours and 7.39% working more than 10 hours daily. Considering the type of family, the workforce is almost evenly split between nuclear families (51.10%) and joint families (48.90%). In terms of companies and organizations, the sample is primarily composed of banking sector employees (57.88%), followed by insurance (25.94%) and other financial services (16.17%).

Table 1. Sample profile

Variables	Categories	Frequency	%
Gender			
	Male	311	62.08%
	Female	189	37.72%
	Others	1	0.19%
Age (In Years)			
	Below 30 years	176	35.13%
	From 30 to 40 years	231	46.11%
	From 40 to 50 years	59	11.78%
	Above 50 years	35	6.99%
Place of Birth			
	Urban	374	74.65%
	Sub-Urban	92	18.36%
	Rural	35	6.99%
Marital Status			
	Married	326	65.07%
	Unmarried	136	27.15%
	Other	39	7.78%
Academic Qualification			
	Secondary	1	.20%
	Senior Secondary	10	2.00%
	Under Graduate	96	19.16%

continued on following page

Table 1. Continued

Variables	Categories	Frequency	%
	Post Graduate	299	59.68%
	Higher Degree and Vocational Diploma	95	18.96%
Level of Management			
	Lower	9	1.80%
	Supervisory	49	9.78%
	Middle	256	51.10%
	Higher	148	29.54%
	Top	39	7.78%
Place of Work			
	Urban	417	83.23%
	Sub-Urban	78	15.57%
	Rural	6	1.20%
Total Years of Services			
	Upto 5 years	179	35.73%
	From 6 to10 years	216	43.11%
	From 11 to 15 years	60	11.98%
	More than 15 years	46	9.18%
Average Daily Working Hour			
	Up to 8 Hours	186	37.13%
	From 8 to 10 Hours	278	55.49%
	More than 10 Hours	37	7.39%
Type of Family			
	Joint	245	48.90%
	Nuclear	256	51.10%
Type of Company/Organization			
	Banking	290	57.88%
	Insurance	130	25.94%
	Other Financial Services	81	16.17%

Source: The authors.

4.3. Descriptive Statistics for the AI-Related Constructs and the spirituality-Related Constructs:

The average score that respondents gave for the different aspects of AI (comprehensiveness, accuracy, currency, reliability, accessibility, and flexibility) was moderate to slightly higher than average, especially for AI reliability and flexibility. In general, variability is moderate in its degree, randomized, with the distributions (in terms of skewness and kurtosis) mostly proving to be substantially normal shape distribution--a few maybe slightly positively skewed. Yet spirituality-related items receive higher means—especially spiritual beliefs in life and spiritual needs--thus, these dimensions are much endorsed. The self-awareness dimension shows moderate ratings but greater spread concerning its respondents. Total statements of spirituality yield an approach showing a somewhat clear wider scope for negative skewness in many and some with a leptokurtic distribution where clusters are thinner.

Table 2. Descriptive Statistics

Statements	Mean	SD	Skewness	Kurtosis
AI_COMP1	3.24	.831	-.031	-.122
AI_COMP2	3.20	.827	-.216	.062
AI_COMP3	3.15	.825	-.267	.029
AI_ACCU1	3.39	.833	-.380	.207
AI_ACCU2	3.47	.791	-.257	.144
AI_ACCU3	3.48	.831	-.299	.127
AI_CUR1	3.32	.940	-.003	-.503
AI_CUR2	3.31	.969	-.122	-.480
AI_CUR3	3.31	.970	-.133	-.448
AI_REL1	3.61	.723	-.695	1.026
AI_REL2	3.60	.730	-.757	1.299
AI_REL3	3.53	.833	-.686	.951
AI_ACCES1	3.22	1.044	.072	-.713
AI_ACCES2	3.29	1.020	.098	-.744
AI_ACCES3	3.28	1.035	-.006	-.660
AI_FLEX1	3.56	.726	-.528	.599
AI_FLEX2	3.59	.717	-1.040	1.544
AI_FLEX3	3.58	.810	-.735	.924
SLF_AW1	3.12	1.216	-.164	-.963
SLF_AW2	3.07	1.211	-.159	-1.011
SLF_AW3	3.11	1.166	-.067	-.956
SLF_AW4	3.09	1.152	-.133	-.869
SLF_AW5	3.15	1.119	-.161	-.776
SPI_BLF1	4.21	.821	-1.167	1.682

continued on following page

Table 2. Continued

Statements	Mean	SD	Skewness	Kurtosis
SPI_BLF2	4.23	.830	-1.019	.916
SPI_BLF3	4.16	.891	-1.033	.848
SPI_BLF4	4.19	.827	-.976	1.036
SPI_BLF5	4.15	.918	-1.265	1.614
SPI_PRAC1	3.81	.729	-.372	.094
SPI_PRAC2	3.84	.762	-.488	.288
SPI_PRAC3	3.77	.813	-.453	.073
SPI_NEED1	4.10	1.046	-1.273	1.110
SPI_NEED2	4.00	1.060	-1.021	.439
SPI_NEED3	4.00	1.056	-1.020	.420
SPI_WORK1	3.77	.841	-.489	.172
SPI_WORK2	3.91	.866	-.679	.329
SPI_WORK3	3.74	.901	-.492	-.083
SPI_WORK4	3.84	.842	-.470	.038

Note(s): COMP=Comprehensiveness, ACCU=Accuracy, CUR=Currency, REL=Reliability, ACCES=Accessibility, and FLEX=Flexibility, AI=Artificial Intelligence, SLF_AWR= Self-awareness, SPI_BLF= Spiritual Beliefs in life, SPI_PRAC= Spiritual Practices, SPI_NEED= Spiritual Needs, SPI_WORK= Spirit at Work, SPI= Spirituality

Source: The authors.

4.4. Data Collection

The study focused on employees within the Indian BFSI (Banking, Financial Services, and Insurance) sector for data collection. A convenience sampling method was employed to select participants, ensuring ease of access and efficient data gathering. Primary data were collected using a structured survey questionnaire comprising validated scales and items adapted from previous research. Researchers designed the items to measure the employees' perception of artificial intelligence and spirituality in the workplace, specifically how artificial intelligence contributes to their spirituality. The data collection process involved both online and offline methods to accommodate respondents' preferences. The data collection process was initiated by seeking permission from managers of the targeted service organizations. The online approach included distributing the questionnaire via email, while the offline method involved direct, face-to-face interactions with employees. Over a six-month period, from June 2024 to Nov. 2024, researchers distributed 600 questionnaires through these channels. Researchers returned a total of 600 completed questionnaires, achieving an impressive response rate of 83.33%.

5. ANALYSIS AND RESULTS

Researchers developed a structural equation model (SEM) using SPSS AMOS 24.0. This is a specialised tool that includes confirmatory factor analysis (CFA) to measure the model's fitness to the data and path analysis to validate the study's assumptions and investigate the relationships between the constructs.

5.1. Reliability and Validity

To assess the validity and reliability of the scale and to evaluate how well the measurement model fits, confirmatory factor analysis (CFA) was conducted. Looking at the results in Table 3, the CFA outputs revealed that all factor loading values are in the range of 0.69-0.84, values that certainly surpass the suggested threshold of 0.6 (Chin et al., 1997). To assess the reliability of the scale, the researchers employed internal consistency measures—Cronbach's alpha (α) and composite reliability (CR). All α and CR values exceeded the threshold of 0.7 (Hair et al., 1986), as indicated in Table 3. Therefore, the study established the reliability of the measurement model for each construct. To check the validity of the scale, convergent and discriminant validity were measured for the scale. The average variance extracted (AVE) was then used as a measure of convergent validity. Again, the AVE values for each construct shown in Table 3 were above the suggested value of 0.5 (Hair et al., 1986). The scales used in this study then undoubtedly passed the convergent validity test.

Table 3. Construct's Reliability and Validity

Variables/Factors	Constructs	Loadings	CA	(α)	AVE
Artificial Intelligence	AI_COMP1	0.784	0.791	0.791	0.557
Comprehensiveness	AI_COMP2	0.732			
	AI_COMP3	0.723			
Artificial Intelligence	AI_ACCU1	0.802	0.824	0.824	0.61
Accuracy	AI_ACCU2	0.780			
	AI_ACCU3	0.760			
Artificial Intelligence	AI_CUR1	0.791	0.807	0.807	0.583
Currency	AI_CUR2	0.739			
	AI_CUR3	0.760			

continued on following page

Table 3. Continued

Variables/Factors	Constructs	Loadings	CA	(α)	AVE
Artificial Intelligence	AI_REL1	0.798	0.791	0.794	0.563
Reliability	AI_REL2	0.745			
	AI_REL3	0.705			
Artificial Intelligence	AI_ACCES1	0.799	0.819	0.819	0.602
Accessibility	AI_ACCES2	0.770			
	AI_ACCES3	0.758			
Artificial Intelligence	AI_FLEX1	0.841	0.818	0.823	0.609
Flexibility	AI_FLEX2	0.773			
	AI_FLEX3	0.723			
Spirituality	SLF_AW1	0.790	0.881	0.882	0.598
Self-Awareness	SLF_AW2	0.726			
	SLF_AW3	0.756			
	SLF_AW4	0.797			
	SLF_AW5	0.796			
Spirituality	SPI_BLF1	0.769	0.879	0.881	0.596
Spiritual Beliefs in Life	SPI_BLF2	0.767			
	SPI_BLF3	0.745			
	SPI_BLF4	0.798			
	SPI_BLF5	0.781			
Spirituality	SPI_PRAC1	0.809	0.819	0.821	0.605
Spiritual Practices	SPI_PRAC2	0.771			
	SPI_PRAC3	0.753			
Spirituality	SPI_NEED1	0.696	0.802	0.804	0.578
Spiritual Needs	SPI_NEED2	0.773			
	SPI_NEED3	0.808			
Spirituality	SPI_WORK1	0.765	0.859	0.859	0.604

continued on following page

Table 3. Continued

Variables/Factors	Constructs	Loadings	CA	(α)	AVE
Spirit at Work	SPI_WORK2	0.775			
	SPI_WORK3	0.764			
	SPI_WORK4	0.804			

Source: The authors.

Further, the researchers investigated the discriminant validity of the measurement model using the Fornell and Larcker criteria (1981). As per the Fornell and Larcker criterion (1981), the scale is discriminately valid when the square root of AVE for given constructs exceeds its correlation with inter-construct values. The results of the study, as referred to in Tables 4 demonstrated adequate discriminant validity for all constructs.

Table 4. Discriminant Validity using the Fornell-Larcker Criterion

Variables	1	2	3	4	5	6	7	8	9	10	11
1. SPI_BLF	**0.772**										
2. SLF_AW	0.162**	**0.774**									
3. SPI_WORK	0.518***	0.172**	**0.777**								
4. AI_ACCU	0.111*	0.071	0.013	**0.781**							
5. AI_ACCES	0.077	0.166**	0.058	0.220***	**0.776**						
6. AI_FLEX	0.330***	0.092†	0.116*	0.124*	0.159**	**0.78**					
7. AI_REL	0.369***	-0.028	0.150**	0.226***	0.196***	0.381***	**0.75**				
8. AI_CUR	0.112*	0.167**	0.005	0.131*	0.189***	0.191***	0.225***	**0.764**			
9. SPI_NEED	0.201***	0.213***	0.041	0.071	0.007	0.109*	0.06	0.184**	**0.76**		
10. AI_COMP	0.105†	0.439***	0.047	0.250***	0.309***	0.094†	0.121*	0.202***	0.072	**0.747**	
11. SPI_PRAC	0.471***	0.407***	0.463***	0.015	0.274***	0.128*	0.149**	0.092†	0.073	0.138*	**0.778**

Note(s): COMP=Comprehensiveness, ACCU=Accuracy, CUR=Currency, REL=Reliability, ACCES=Accessibility, and FLEX=Flexibility, AI=Artificial Intelligence, SLF_AWR= Self-awareness, SPI_BLF= Spiritual beliefs in life, SPI_PRAC= Spiritual Practices, SPI_NEED= Spiritual Needs, SPI_WORK= Spirit at Work, SPI= Spirituality

Source: The authors.

5.2. Fit Indices of Measurement Model

Further checks on the quality of the measurement model were made through the assessment of various other fit indices, such as CMIN/DF, SRMR, CFI, and RMESA, with all values being within their common acceptance level (Hu & Bentler,

1998). The two-factor model of artificial intelligence and spirituality here gives an acceptable fit, as shown in Table 5.

Table 5. Fit Indices of Measurement Model

Measure	CMIN	DF	CMIN/DF	CFI	SRMR	RMSEA	*P*-Close
Estimate	754.533	610	1.237	0.982	0.034	0.022	1
Threshold	--	--	Between 1 and 3	>0.95	<0.08	<0.06	>0.05
Interpretation	--	--	Excellent	Excellent	Excellent	Excellent	Excellent

Source: The authors.

5.3. Hypothesis Testing

Researchers performed path analysis to conduct hypothesis testing. We further applied the bootstrapping method at 5000 subsamples in order to examine the significance of path coefficients (Hu & Wang, 2010). Our study's main hypothesis (H1) posited that there is a positive effect of artificial intelligence on spirituality among BFSI sector employees. The standardized path coefficient for this relationship is ($\beta = 0.494$, $p < 0.05$), indicating that there is a moderately strong effect of AI on spirituality. This means that employees' spiritual health seems to improve as they use AI more or interact with it more, i.e., automation reducing cognitive load, data-driven insights for ethical decision-making, AI as a tool for encouraging self-discovery, and a culture of innovation and purpose.

Also, $p < 0.05$ means that the connection between these two variables is statistically significant, which shows that the effect seen is not likely to happen by chance. These results, therefore, lead one to suggest that AI plays a crucial role in cultivating or influencing the spiritual experiences of BFSI employees. Thus, this growth in spirituality promotes mindfulness within the workplace, ensuring that employees are focused, self-aware, and emotionally balanced, thereby making the working environment healthy and productive. Table 6 displays the results of the hypothesis.

Table 6. Structural Model Assessment

Hypothesis	Hypothesized Relationships	Estimate (β)	SE	Lower Bound (95%)	Upper Bound (95%)	P-values	Remarks
H1	AI→ SPI	0.494	0.082	0.322	0.640	0.009 (< 0.05)	**Hypothesis Supported**

Note(s): AI=Artificial Intelligence, SPI= Spirituality
Source: The authors.

6. DISCUSSION

It is increasingly imperative to consider the impact of artificial intelligence and digital communication on our ability to engage with the supreme power and cultivate spiritual growth. To navigate this junction and its many consequences for believers in the digital era, it compels us to examine the doctrines of spirituality and the implications of AI on our comprehension of the spiritual person in this inquiry (Coghill, 2023). Is the advancement of artificial intelligence making it more difficult or easier for humans to converse with the supreme power? The Catholic Church underscores the need for balancing technology and religion, necessitating careful consideration and discernment about the issues. The author employs a literary approach in this work. The author aims to emphasize how employees may mindfully connect traditional legacy with digital realities. The evolution in how individuals pursue, investigate, and engage with their religion necessitates a profound comprehension of the equilibrium between technology and spirituality (Garg et al., 2022). All the aforementioned issues are addressed in this study, along with further contributions to the current research.

The hypothesis *(H1)— "Artificial Intelligence has a positive effect on spirituality among BFSI employees"*—is strongly supported as the literature suggests artificial intelligence may improve spiritual well-being for mindfulness among employees in the workplace. Workers who are self-aware and driven toward personal development might find use for AI solutions meant to assist in their spiritual path. For example, personalized advice may meet workers' particular spiritual requirements, while AI-powered meditation applications can help them to enhance their mindfulness practices. AI may raise self-awareness—another vital component of spirituality—by providing insights into habits and mental processes. In this sense, artificial intelligence may provide conscientious workers tools encouraging emotional, mental, and spiritual development. The production of digital religious music and artwork has been driven by artificial intelligence (Schwarz, 2019) for the spiritual enhancement and mindfulness among employees. Voice assistants and interactive chatbots might be friends for conversation during introspection and the search for meaning. Consequently, artificial intelligence may assist in lowering stress and enhancing emotional control, which is essential for spiritual development—a need much sought for in the BFSI sectors. Notwithstanding the benefits of AI in enhancing spirituality, Herzfeld (2022) warns against the dangers of reductionism and manipulation. These concerns are particularly relevant to economic losses, such as the diminished economic worth of users caused by overly personified artificial intelligence. Examining the literature provides deeper insight into the complex relationship between AI and human spiritual values, especially in light of the ethical challenges associated with integrating AI into spirituality. It looks at the ethical and philosophical consequences of developments in artificial intelligence, therefore inspiring thought on how using AI shapes human morality; in other words, this phrase shows a focus on the moral and philosophical implications of artificial intelligence instead of just its technological features (Mitchell, 2020). The research by Floridi and Cowls identified ideas that comprise ethical guidelines meant to ensure that developments in artificial intelligence follow ethical standards and human spirituality so that the AI does not erode or influence one's spirituality and instead promotes employee mindfulness in a business. (Floridi and Cowls, 2019). Various websites provide a broad perspective on the moral consequences of integrating artificial intelligence into spirituality. This article guides readers to explore the ethical consequences and obligations connected with the fast development of artificial intelligence technology with respect to spiritual and moral values in contemporary society by including philosophical viewpoints and practical recommendations for employees to enhance their mindfulness. AI-based mindfulness interventions, no matter how good their intentions are, can stall or even derail in some contexts. For example, when excessively used, staff might suffer "mindfulness fatigue" whereby the continuous reminders to unwind or to introspect grow counterproductive and stressful. Imperfect personalization—e.g., suggesting common meditation scripts amidst peak distress or culturally insensitive materials—can precipitate frustration, disengagement, or worse, emotional harm. In strict work cultures, required or ill-contextualized AI mindfulness programs could be seen as performative or invasive and thus meet with resistance or scepticism. Additionally, AI reliance without human input could miss complex affective states requiring empathy, subtlety, or professional mental health intervention and lead to suboptimal or even deleterious advice. As technology continues to extend the limits of human experience, it encounters inherent limits when dealing with spirituality, which is inherently subjective, experiential, and routinely transcendent in nature (Bankins and Formosa, 2023). Algorithms can mimic religious rituals or even create spiritual material, but they can't comprehend or reproduce the lived, internal aspects of faith, consciousness, or moral awakening. Ethical limits also arise as technology threatens to commodify or distort religious traditions, inviting issues of authenticity, cultural appropriation, and the flattening of spiritual depth into data-driven results (Haenlein, et al., 2022). These limits call for discernment and respect in bringing technology into spiritual life.

Nicholas Carr argues that the steady advancement of AI poses a challenge to maintaining spiritual awareness and the recognition of God's presence amidst the allure of technology (Carr, 2011). Conversely, heightened dependence on technology may obscure the boundary between the holy and the profane (Havens, 2021). The detrimental impact of AI developments on spiritual well-being is evident here. Excessive use might impair spiritual and mental well-being, leading to worry or feelings of inadequacy (Twenge, 2017). Yuval contends that "this challenge entails the peril of forfeiting the freedom of independent thought and ethical accountability in the discernment of spiritual information" (Harari, 2018). It is vital to ensure that the incorporation of artificial intelligence augments and facilitates the spiritual journey as individuals navigate the implications of AI in their lives. Discusses the potential impact of the rapid advancement of AI technology on spiritual practices and the depth of one's connection with the Supreme power (Burdett, 2023). Lastly, excessive dependence on AI for emotional care disengages one from real human relations, sacrificing the social and relational nature of spirituality. These difficulties illustrate the imperative to have ethically sound, culture-sensitive, and human-centric approaches to embedding AI in employee mindfulness programs (Ipek, et al., 2023). While some see AI as a means to enhance their religious experiences via novel avenues for prayer, meditation, and education, others express concern over the potential erosion of genuine spiritual connections and the inherent authenticity of religious experiences (Graves, 2017).

6.1 Identified Risks

The application of AI to workplace spirituality also provokes a number of important ethical issues. To begin, commodification of spirituality can happen as companies implement mindfulness and wellness initiatives for the sole purpose of increasing productivity, with the result of shallow, performative practices that degrade authenticity and destroy employee trust. Second, there is a potential for loss of spiritual autonomy since AI technologies like wellness bots and behaviour trackers can subtly shape or normalize individual beliefs without considering the cultural or individual variances. This can lead to spirituality being organizationally proscribed instead of personally cultivated. Third, there are regulatory issues since these devices tend to gather sensitive information—emotional, biometric, or even spiritual—and which entail threats of nonadherence to data protection regulations like GDPR. Insufficient consent structures and transparency about AI decision-making processes further intensify these legal and ethical exposures. Combined, these risks demonstrate the necessity of prudent, ethics-based deployment of AI in staff wellbeing programs.

AI application in simulating spirituality—e.g., via chatbots or virtual mindfulness coaches—is psychologically risky, specifically emotional dependence on non-human systems. This can destabilize authentic human connection and impair personal development since workers can confuse algorithmic outputs with real empathy. To resolve this, companies must recognize the limitations of AI, refrain from using it for tasks that necessitate actual emotional or spiritual guidance, and define ethical limits to avoid deceptive or immersive experiences. Encouraging human-centred substitutes such as peer support and reflective practice guarantees an equilibrium, accountable integration of AI in spiritual wellbeing.

7. IMPLICATIONS

Examining how mindfulness and spiritual development tools combined into the workplace could improve employee well-being, the study looks at personalized advice and AI-powered applications that might help workers become more self-aware, emotionally regulated, and thoughtful, thereby strengthening their feeling of balance and purpose. Though it might affect employee trust, autonomy, and decision-making, the ethical ramifications of AI providing tailored spiritual or psychological guidance must also be carefully thought out. Though they could subvert conventional ideas of free will, AI technologies might also let workers—especially via mindfulness or meditation—achieve emotional emancipation or spiritual enlightenment. Furthermore, surroundings powered by artificial intelligence might support collective mindfulness techniques and workplace community-building, therefore enhancing company culture. The function of artificial intelligence in mental health support emphasizes even more its ability to improve psychological and spiritual well-being; therefore, it provides a whole strategy for employee mindfulness and well-being in the contemporary workplace.

7.1. Concerning Practical Implications

- AI-driven mindfulness tools may be included in workplace wellness initiatives to assist staff members in controlling stress, enhancing attention, and supporting emotional well-being, thus generating a better work environment.
- Organizations will have to create explicit ethical rules for the use of artificial intelligence in offering psychological or spiritual assistance, thereby guaranteeing that AI tools respect employee autonomy, privacy, and mental health requirements.
- Using AI technologies for collective mindfulness activities might help promote team cohesiveness and enhance company culture, thereby fostering a sense of belonging and shared goals among staff members.
- AI can provide customized mindfulness and meditation techniques, enabling workers to participate in self-care fit for their particular requirements, thus increasing job happiness and productivity.

7.2. Theoretical Connotations

- Redefining spirituality at work, for example, by combining AI with mindfulness and spiritual practices, we could come up with new theories about how technology affects human growth and spiritual evolution, which would go against what most people think about workplace spirituality.
- The use of artificial intelligence in directing workers' mindfulness practices begs issues of free will and decision-making. Understanding how artificial intelligence could affect spiritual autonomy or support reliance on technology for personal growth calls for theoretical study.
- Intersection of Technology and Consciousness by the existence of artificial intelligence, encouraging awareness might cause one to reevaluate consciousness in the workplace. Theoretical research might look at how artificial intelligence affects workers in a professional context's consciousness, presence, and spiritual awakening.
- The use of artificial intelligence in spiritual and mental health interventions may be different depending on the culture and ethical considerations. This raises theoretical questions about how different cultural views on spirituality affect how well and how widely AI tools are accepted in the workplace to promote mindfulness.

8. CONCLUSION AND FUTURE RESEARCH AVENUES

As AI continues to evolve, the relationship between AI and spirituality will likely become a central topic in philosophy, theology, psychology, and technology studies. Future research will need to address not only the opportunities AI presents for spiritual growth and exploration but also the ethical, psychological, and existential challenges it brings. There's immense potential to deepen our understanding of the human spirit, consciousness, and the evolving role of technology in our quest for the meaning of life.

Finally, the integration of artificial intelligence (AI) into the BFSI industries has surely changed the workplace and improved efficiency and creativity. This research might be quite beneficial for fostering mindful employees in the BFSI industry. The findings indicate a favourable trend for AI in enterprises to promote spirituality among employees and increase mindfulness. It is legitimate to assert that personnel in banking, insurance, and other financial institutions need more spirituality and mindfulness owing to the demands imposed by superiors, colleagues, and consumers; hence, it demonstrates that AI might be very beneficial in this context. For staff members, it has, however, also created challenges in terms of spirituality, mental health, and sense of duty. Artificial intelligence may unintentionally result in a more impersonal workplace, therefore restricting opportunities for emotional interactions and reflection even when it helps to streamline tasks. Techniques focusing on worker spirituality and mindfulness will assist in reducing these effects. Encouragement of meditation, mindfulness training, and self-reflection areas helps employees grow in a sense of purpose, balance, and well-being (Garg et al., 2022; Bansal & Punia, 2023). Companies should also invest in artificial intelligence technology supporting human-centred decision-making, collaboration, and meaningful work instead of just automation (Frunză, 2023). Leaders in the BFSI sectors have to realize the importance of spirituality in maintaining a good, efficient staff and implement a complete plan involving both technological improvements and human-centred values. By producing aware employees who feel connected to their inner selves and to the greater objective of their job, organizations may not only enhance their economic performance but also benefit the general well-being of their employees (Syahrial et al., 2024). A mixed approach integrating artificial intelligence with human values, mindfulness, and spirituality will finally provide a more sustainable and fulfilling workplace for employees in these fast-changing fields (Bansal & Punia, 2023).

Future research in this field could investigate many aspects, from theological and philosophical questions to technological and ethical issues. The junction of artificial intelligence and spirituality offers a rich ground for multidisciplinary study. Future studies on "Exploring the Impact of AI on Employee Spirituality: A Roadmap for Cultivating Employee Mindfulness" may probe numerous important directions.

- First, it would be imperative to look at the moral limits of artificial intelligence in offering staff members spiritual direction as well as its possible effects on autonomy and trust. Particularly in varied corporate environments, research might also look at how effectively AI-driven mindfulness tools support long-term employee well-being and spiritual development.
- Future research may also concentrate on how artificial intelligence shapes corporate culture and on the part, it plays in promoting collective mindfulness practices and community-building within the company. More research on how artificial intelligence may strike a balance between spiritual practices and mental health assistance as well as on how it affects employee behaviour and decision-making would be rather insightful.
- Cross-cultural research might lastly investigate how various spiritual and cultural backgrounds affect workers' adoption of mindfulness and spiritual tools derived from artificial intelligence.
- Carry out longitudinal research to measure the long-term spiritual impact of AI integration within the workplace. This research should look at how extended exposure to AI tools—especially those that are meant to enhance

mindfulness, decision-making, or emotional well-being—impacts employees' spiritual growth over the long term. This involves measuring shifts in purpose, connectedness, inner peace, and ethical alignment. Monitoring these aspects longitudinally will give greater depth to whether or not AI accelerates or arrests genuine spiritual growth, enabling firms to further enhance strategies that coalesce technological integration with comprehensive well-being among workers.

- The current research is on the Indian BFSI industry, as it is the sector that is increasingly embracing digital well-being solutions. Yet, mindfulness and spirituality are culturally situated practices. Thus, while in U.S.-based technology companies' mindfulness is secularized and framed as a productivity paradigm, in Japan Zen-based rituals will be woven into corporate culture, and in Scandinavian nations work-life integration is itself treated as a spiritual pursuit. Subsequent studies need to investigate how AI-facilitated mindfulness platforms are translated—or resisted—around the world.
- Comparative analysis would shed light on whether these platforms reinforce Western-driven conceptions of mindfulness or truly support a range of spiritual frameworks. There is a built-in conflict between the individually tailored nudging potential of AI and the deeply individualistic essence of spirituality. Algorithms can recommend guided meditations, contemplative prompts, or emotion-monitoring exercises based on collective user information. Helpful as they might be, these nudges threaten to commodify spirituality—reducing introspection into a series of optimized actions. This provokes the ethical issue of spiritual agency: How much control do workers exercise when their inner lives are organized by algorithmic recommendations? More philosophical engagement with digital ethics is required to ensure that AI serves as an organ for enabling spiritual development, not as the director of it.

REFERENCES

Bankins, S., & Formosa, P. (2023). The ethical implications of artificial intelligence (AI) for meaningful work. *Journal of Business Ethics, 185*(4), 725–740.

Bansal, G., & Punia, B. K. (2023). Precursors of workplace mindfulness: An exploration & conceptual modelling. In Narwal, K., Bhisnoi, V. K., Bhaker, S. K., & Saini, V. P. (Eds.), *Florilegium: Management theory, research and practices* (pp. 174–184). Arihant Books.

Bansal, G., Punia, B. K., Girdhar, R., & Punia, V. (2025). Mindfulness, Organizational Identification, Work-Life Balance, and Family Support in Female Happiness. In Tran, M. (Ed.), *Harnessing Happiness and Wisdom for Organizational Well-Being* (pp. 427–464). IGI Global Scientific Publishing.

Broecke, S. (2023). Artificial intelligence and labour market matching. *OECD Social, Employment and Migration Working Papers*, (284).

Budhwar, P., Chowdhury, S., Wood, G., Aguinis, H., Bamber, G. J., Beltran, J. R., & Varma, A. (2023). Human resource management in the age of generative artificial intelligence: Perspectives and research directions on ChatGPT. *Human Resource Management Journal, 33*(3), 606–659.

Burdett, M. (2023). Proximate and Ultimate Concerns in Christian Ethical Responses to Artificial Intelligence. *Studies in Christian Ethics, 36*(3), 620–641.

Calderero Hernández, J. F. (2021). Artificial intelligence and spirituality. *International Journal of Interactive Multimedia and Artificial Intelligence, 7*(1), 34–43.

Carr, N. (2011). *The Shallows: What the Internet Is Doing to Our Brains*. W. W. Norton & Company.

Chin, W. W., Gopal, A., & Salisbury, W. D. (1997). Advancing the theory of adaptive structuration: The development of a scale to measure faithfulness of appropriation. *Information Systems Research, 8*(4), 342–367.

Coghill, G. M. (2023). Artificial Intelligence (and Christianity): Who? What? Where? When? Why? and How? *Studies in Christian Ethics, 36*(3), 604–619.

Deurzen, E. (2021). Rising from Existential Crisis. Life Beyond Calamity. Monmouth: PCCS Books.

Dignum, V. (2018). Ethics in artificial intelligence: introduction to the special issue.

Donaldson, T. (2016). Values in Tension. Ethics Away from Home. In *HBR's 10 Must Reads on Managing Across Cultures* (pp. 123–148). Harvard Business School Publishing.

Dubey, S., & Bedi, S. S. (2024). Workplace spirituality: A systematic review and future research agenda. *Journal of Management, Spirituality & Religion, 21*(1), 83–128.

Floridi, L., & Cowls, J. (2019). A Unified Framework of Five Principles for AI in Society. *Harvard Data Science Review, 1*(1), 2–15. https://doi.org/https:// doi.org/ 10.1162/99608f92.8cd550d1

Fornell, C., & Larcker, D. F. (1981). Evaluating structural equation models with unobservable variables and measurement error. *JMR, Journal of Marketing Research, 18*(1), 39–50.

Forsgren, N., Durcikova, A., Clay, P. F., & Wang, X. (2016). The Integrated user satisfaction model: Assessing information quality and system quality as second-order constructs in system administration. *Communications of the Association for Information Systems, 38*, 803–839. DOI: 10.17705/1cais

Francis, P. (2023). LVII World Day of Peace 2024 - Artificial Intelligence and Peace Francis. en/messages/peace https://www.vatican.va/ content/francesco/ / documents/20231208-messaggio-57giornatamondiale pace2024.html

Frunză, S. (2023). Cultural intelligence, spiritual intelligence and counseling in the age of artificial intelligence. *Journal for the Study of Religions and Ideologies, 22*(64), 80–95.

Garg, M., Punia, B. K., Garg, N., & Punia, V. (2022). Spiritual leadership and well-being in the context of the modern workplace. In *Handbook of Research on Integrating Spirituality in Modern Workplaces* (pp. 170–185). IGI Global Scientific Publishing.

Garg, M., Punia, V., & Punia, B. K. (2022). Will Artificial Intelligence (AI) Overpower Human Intelligence (HI)? A Peep into Future Business and Education. *Amity Management Analyst, 9*(1), 5–16.

Graves, M. (2017). Shared Moral and Spiritual Development Among Human Persons and Artificially Intelligent Agents. *Theology and Science, 15*(3), 333–351.

Haenlein, M., Huang, M. H., & Kaplan, A. (2022). Guest editorial: Business ethics in the era of artificial intelligence. *Journal of Business Ethics, 178*(4), 867–869.

Hair, J., Anderson, R., & Tatham, R. (1986). *Multivariate Data Analysis with Readings*. MaCmillan Publishing Company.

Harari, Y. N. (2018). *21 Lessons for the 21st Century*. Random House.

Havens, J. C. (2021). Approaches to Spiritual Care for Artificially Intelligent Robots. *Pastoral Psychology*, *70*(5), 615–632.

Herzfeld, N. (2022). Artificial Intelligence and Theology. *Theology Today (Princeton, N.J.)*, *79*(2), 103–115.

Hu, C., & Wang, Y. (2010). Bootstrapping in AMOS. *Powerpoint. Consultéle*, 23-02.

Hu, L. T., & Bentler, P. M. (1998). Fit indices in covariance structure modeling: Sensitivity to underparameterized model misspecification. *Psychological Methods*, *3*(4), 424–453.

Huang, C., Zhang, Z., Mao, B., & Yao, X. (2022). An overview of artificial intelligence ethics. *IEEE Transactions on Artificial Intelligence*, *4*(4), 799–819.

Huynh-The, T., Pham, Q. V., Pham, X. Q., Nguyen, T. T., Han, Z., & Kim, D. S. (2023). Artificial intelligence for the metaverse: A survey. *Engineering Applications of Artificial Intelligence*, *117*, 105581.

Jackelén, A. (2021). Technology, theology, and spirituality in the digital age. *Zygon*, *56*(1), 6–18.

Jolliffe, P., & Foster, S. (2022). Different reality? Generations' and religious groups' views of spirituality policies in the workplace. *Journal of Business Ethics*, *181*(2), 451–470.

Kaplan, A., & Haenlein, M. (2019). Siri, Siri, in my hand: Who's the fairest in the land? On the interpretations, illustrations, and implications of artificial intelligence. *Business Horizons*, *62*, 15–25.

Kettle, L., & Lee, Y. C. (2024). User experiences of well-being chatbots. *Human Factors*, *66*(6), 1703–1723. PMID: 36916743

Kirkpatrick, K. (2017). AI in Contact Centers. *Communications of the ACM*, *60*(8), 18–19.

Kurzweil, R. (1999). *The Age of Spiritual Machines. When Computers Exceed Human Intelligence*. Viking.

Lektawan, F. K. (2024). Communicating with the Holy Spirit in the Age of AI Technology: Catholic. *Stipas Tahasak Danum Pambelum Keuskupan Palangkaraya*, 88-99.

Lyu, W., & Liu, J. (2021). Artificial Intelligence and emerging digital technologies in the energy sector. *Applied Energy*, *303*, 117615.

Mitchell, M. (2020). *Artificial Intelligence: A Guide for Thinking Humans*. Picador.

Partal, S., & Smirnova, S. (2021). It's Time to Relax: The Critical Importance of Digital Mental Health Products in the Context of Surveillance Capitalism. *Temes de Disseny*, (37), 38–59.

Peters, T. (2019, September). Artificial Intelligence versus Agape Love: Spirituality in a Posthuman Age. *In Forum Philosophicum, 24*(2), 259-278.

Popkova, E. G. (2024). Spirituality in the realities of digitalization of society in the era of intelligent machines development. *RUDN Journal of Economics*, *32*(1), 170–186.

Popoveniuc, B. (2015). Spiritual intelligence and artifactualness. *European Journal of Science and Theology*, *11*(1), 59–74.

Prentice, C., Dominique Lopes, S., & Wang, X. (2020). Emotional intelligence or artificial intelligence–an employee perspective. *Journal of Hospitality Marketing & Management*, *29*(4), 377–403.

Raghav, Y. Y., & Gulia, S. (2023). The rise of artificial intelligence and its implications on spirituality. In *Investigating the Impact of AI on Ethics and Spirituality* (pp. 165–178). IGI Global.

Rospigliosi, P. A. (2023). Artificial intelligence in teaching and learning: What questions should we ask of ChatGPT? *Interactive Learning Environments*, *31*(1), 1–3.

Saisubramanian, S., Zilberstein, S., & Kamar, E. (2022). Avoiding negative side effects due to incomplete knowledge of AI systems. *AI Magazine*, *42*(4), 62–71.

Schwarz, H. (2019). Theology in the Age of Artificial Intelligence: Embedding Grace in a Godlike Technology. *Theology Today (Princeton, N.J.)*, *76*(2), 107–120. DOI: 10.1177/0040573619847219

Sharkey, A. (2019). Autonomous weapons systems, killer robots and human dignity. *Ethics and Information Technology*, *21*(2), 75–87.

Singh, A. K., & Makkar, S. (2015). Measurement of spirituality: Development and validation of a questionnaire. *XVI Annual Proceedings*, (January), 806–847.

Singla, A., Sukharevsky, A., Yee, L., Chui, M., & Hall, B. (2025, March 12). *The state of AI: How organizations are rewiring to capture value*. McKinsey & Company. https://www.mckinsey.com/capabilities/quantumblack/our-insights/the-state-of-ai

Syahrial, A., Lubis, S., Pradana, H., & Farhani, F. (2024). The Importance of Spiritual Values in Religious Community Welcoming the Arrival of Artificial Intelligence Technology to Maintain the Balance of Faith and Piety with Sufism Learning. *International Conferance Of Digital Sciences And Engineering Technology*, *1*(1), 448–457.

Tamatea, L. (2010). Online Buddhist and Christian responses to artificial intelligence. *Zygon*, *45*(4), 979–1002.

Tan, C. (2020). Digital Confucius? Exploring the implications of artificial intelligence in spiritual education. *Connection Science*, *32*(3), 280–291.

Twenge, J. M. (2017). iGen: Why Today's Super-Connected Kids Are Growing Up Less Rebellious, More Tolerant, Less Happy--and Completely Unprepared for Adulthood. Atria Books.

Van Wynsberghe, A., & Robbins, S. (2019). Critiquing the reasons for making artificial moral agents. *Science and Engineering Ethics*, *25*(3), 719–735. PMID: 29460081

Vrontis, D., Christofi, M., Pereira, V., Tarba, S., Makrides, A., & Trichina, E. (2023). Artificial intelligence, robotics, advanced technologies and human resource management: a systematic review. *Artificial intelligence and international HRM*, 172-201.

Walter, Y. (2024). The digital transformation in the psychology of workplace spirituality. *Digital Transformation and Society*, *3*(1), 23–49.

Wirth, N. (2018). Hello marketing, what can artificial intelligence help you with? *International Journal of Market Research*, *60*(5), 435–438.

Wixom, B. H., & Todd, P. A. (2005). A theoretical integration of user satisfaction and technology acceptance. *Information Systems Research*, *16*(1), 85–102.

Zinnbauer, B. J., Pargament, K. I., & Scott, A. B. (1999). The emerging meanings of religiousness and spirituality: Problems and prospects. *Journal of Personality*, *67*(6), 889–919.

Chapter 9

Organizational and Methodological Conditions for the Design and Implementation of Personalized Training Programs Through HCI in Corporate Training

Evgenii Alexandrovich Makarenko
https://orcid.org/0000-0003-3461-3166
St. Petersburg Polytechnic University of Peter the Great, Russia

Vyacheslav Samorukov
https://orcid.org/0000-0001-9152-953X
St. Petersburg State Agrarian University, Russia

Dmitry Samorukov
https://orcid.org/0000-0002-7894-4955
St. Petersburg State University of Industrial Technologies and Design, Russia

Geetha Devi
https://orcid.org/0000-0001-9541-1985
College of Engineering, National University, Oman

DOI: 10.4018/979-8-3373-8612-6.ch009

ABSTRACT

Companies actively use interactive training materials in electronic format in corporate training to help employees acquire new knowledge, skills and abilities. Various formats of electronic courses, from presentations and educational screenshots to interactive videos, help not only to reduce the number of errors, but also to reduce training costs. However, quite often courses are presented with a large number of "small pieces" of content, often without disciplinary connections and sound technology for the formation and development of professional competencies. As a result, the fundamental principles of the continuous education system are blurred, acquiring at best intuitive, and often flawed forms, dressed in newfangled trends. Based on scientific research and practical experience in implementing additional educational programs for corporate customers, the authors identified organizational and methodological conditions and proposed models, methods and methodological tools for designing and implementing personalized training programs through corporate HCI in ate training.

1. INTRODUCTION

We are witnessing the traditional approaches to making business and organizing labor process undergo transformation in the context of globalization and swift technological changes. Work strategies tend to be more adaptive and corporate structures tend to becoming less hierarchical. The ability to learn quickly, think critically and creatively together with skills and knowledge are forming the most important resources.

Under the conditions of developing digital technologies the communicative sphere is undergoing dramatic fundamental changes, i.e. social networks, messengers and collaboration platforms are enabling new horizons of interaction. Nowadays professionals at all levels can easily share experiences and ideas, which draws a basis for not only individual growth, but for the formation of global communities.

According to experts from Class Central, HolonIQ, Gartner, Coursera for Business, Course Report, Gallup & Coursera, Data Insight, hh.ru, TAdviser, RBC, and others:

- The number of learners on online courses and MOOCs (Coursera, edX, Udemy) increased 2–3 times during 2020–2021. Coursera reached 100 million users by 2023. In 2024, the global online education market was estimated at $400 billion, with around 30% accounted for by professional courses. In Russia, platforms like Netology, Skillbox, GeekBrains, and Yandex.

Practicum increased their audiences 3–5 times since 2020. In 2024, around 2 million Russian citizens completed paid professional courses.

- In corporate training, companies are increasingly replacing traditional programs with online courses and microdegrees. By 2023, 70% of large corporations (Google, Amazon, Microsoft) were using platforms such as Coursera for Business. The global corporate e-learning market reached $50 billion in 2024. In Russia, Sberbank, Tinkoff, and VK actively utilize internal educational platforms. In 2023, 45% of Russian companies implemented digital training courses for employees (according to hh.ru).
- Bootcamps are experiencing growth. As of 2023, over 1,000 bootcamps (e.g., General Assembly, Le Wagon, SkillFactory) operated worldwide. Graduates of such IT programs found employment in about 60% of cases (data from Course Report).
- Platforms like Udacity, Coursera, and LinkedIn Learning offer short-term programs (3–12 months), resulting in microdegrees and nanodegrees. In 2024, 42% of U.S. employers considered such certificates during hiring (Gallup data).

Forecast for 2025:

- The share of alternative professional education (courses, bootcamps) in the overall learning landscape is expected to rise to 25–30% (compared to about 5% in 2020);
- AI courses (generative AI, machine learning) will become the fastest-growing segment.

Thus, a modern employee faces the necessity of constant self-study and involvement into the process of innovations. Being flexible, open-minded and apt to find a variety of approaches is a cornerstone of successful professional activity in a rapidly changing world.

Smart economy involves the integration of industrial and information and communication technologies to optimize all processes from planning production processes to product distribution. These technologies do not only increase effectiveness but also decrease negative impact on the environment, promoting production methods of higher sustainability. Under the conditions of global changes in technological processes, the development of adaptive strategies aimed at helping to cope with changes in both industrial production and consumer demand becomes a necessity.

Moreover, modern technologies allow real time collecting and analyzing data, which shows up new horizons for scientific research and finding practical solutions.

Combining advanced technologies and scientific approaches, one can not only increase productivity, but also create a more sustainable welfare assurance system for future generations.

These phenomena impose new requirements on the professional competencies of qualified personnel. Encouraging their employees to acquire new knowledge, skills and abilities, organizations actively use interactive formats in corporate training. They do not only help to decrease the number of mistakes made at workplaces, but also to reduce personnel training expenditures. Still, the active dissemination of university education into non-systemic education, presented as some newfangled trends, often provides controversial results.

The mentioned aspects emphasize the necessity to transform the educational system, which, in turn, raises questions about the prospects for introducing innovative forms of training. The relevance of flexible and adaptive educational programs is stipulated by the desire to ensure that qualifications meet modern labor market requirements. That is why it is important to develop modular courses that allow specialists to quickly acquire new knowledge and skills in accordance with changing conditions, including through the "design, qualitative assessment and implementation of interactive computing systems for human use, as well as studying the main phenomena surrounding them" (HCI — Human-Computer Interaction) (Carroll, 2002)(Cox, 1999)(Dix et al., 2003)(Erickson & McDonald, 2008).

We stand on the point that scientifically based organizational and methodological conditions for the interaction of students in interactive computing systems and transparent mechanisms for assessing the quality of specialist training will help to enhance confidence in non-systemic educational training programs (Pankova et al., 2015).

In our opinion, the National Qualifications Framework of the Russian Federation (NQF) in a safe a connecting basis for the interaction between university science and corporate training structures. The indicators of specialist qualifications used by NQF, such as: "breadth of powers and responsibilities" (general competence), "complexity of activity" (nature of skills) and "scientific intensity of activity" (nature of knowledge), are identical to international descriptors, for example, those of the European Framework of qualifications.

The successful implementation of the National Qualifications Framework will be the key factor for improving the competitiveness of both domestic specialists and the economic system of the state as a whole. Still, NQF cannot be treated as a panacea for all the diseases of virtual civilization, beginning with the disharmony and imbalance in movement towards a person's individual pattern of personal and professional growth (Samorukov, 2015).

Based on the scientific approaches of cognitive psychology and human factor engineering, pedagogical methods and tools of modern didactic technologies, as well as on the achievements in computer science and interaction design, software testing data and e-learning, organizational and methodological conditions should be created for the formation of an individual educational pattern of specialists applicable to both systemic education and non-formal training.

The lack of consensus among scholars and practitioners regarding the learning process through HCI (Human-Computer Interaction) is primarily due to the fact that this subject is often viewed from the perspective of integrating technological advancements into the educational system. Meanwhile, within the educational system itself—as an object of pedagogical research—the challenges of teaching through HCI represent an independent field of inquiry.

The specificity of the didactic (D) perspective lies in the fact that, from this standpoint, the researcher's focus is primarily directed toward the interaction between "teacher and student." At the same time, systemic education has accumulated extensive experience in the use of modern information technologies. Widely adopted tools include MOOC platforms (Coursera, edX, Stepik, Uchi.ru), Learning Management Systems (Moodle, Blackboard, Canvas), and virtual classrooms (Zoom, Google Meet, Microsoft Teams).

In 2020–2021, due to the pandemic, over 80% of school students temporarily transitioned to remote learning. By 2024, up to 45% of children were using online platforms (Skyeng, Uchi.ru, Foxford, Algorithmics) as a supplement to traditional schooling. The share of hybrid learning models (school + online) and the number of alternative educational initiatives is expected to grow.

According to official statistics from educational institutions, by 2024, 40% of university students worldwide had taken at least one online course. Artificial intelligence is actively applied in education in the form of adaptive learning (personalized materials tailored to learners), AI tutors (ChatGPT, Khanmigo by Khan Academy), and automated assessment tools (Grammarly, Gradescope). Virtual and augmented reality (VR/AR) is being developed in the form of VR labs (for chemistry, medicine, engineering), medical simulators (Osso VR for surgeons), AR textbooks (3D visualization of anatomy and physics), and electronic learning programs. The VR/AR market in education reached $12 billion in 2024 (Statista). Cloud technologies and 5G ensure global access to educational resources and online laboratories (Google Cloud Labs, AWS Educate). According to researchers from the University of Colorado, gamification (Duolingo, Minecraft: Education Edition) increases learner engagement by 60%. As of 2024, 90% of universities utilize cloud storage (McKinsey).

It is forecasted that by 2026, 20% of universities will use blockchain and digital NFT diplomas, and by 2030, traditional and digital education will fully converge into a hybrid model.

Written by an interuniversity team of authors, this work contains the results of practical educational activities, research and experimental work in designing and implementing personalized training programs through HCI in corporate training.

2. METHODOLOGY OF RESEARCH AND EXPERIMENTAL WORK

The authors define methodology as "a set of research techniques and methods, the procedure for applying them and interpreting the results obtained with the help of them" (International Yearbook of Technology of Education and Training, 1978) (Bespalko & Tatur, 1989)(Subbetto, 1994).

The organization and content of research and experimental work is based on the requirements of the principles of phased and comprehensive consideration of the problem, science and objectivity, determinism and the relationship between the main causes, the unity of external and internal conditions for the effectiveness of the training process. The need to ensure the consistency and complexity of the study and to ensure the reliability of the results obtained predetermined the development and use of special research methods.

The work was carried out in three stages: the preparatory, the main and the final ones (Figure 1).

Figure 1. Arrangement of research and experimental work

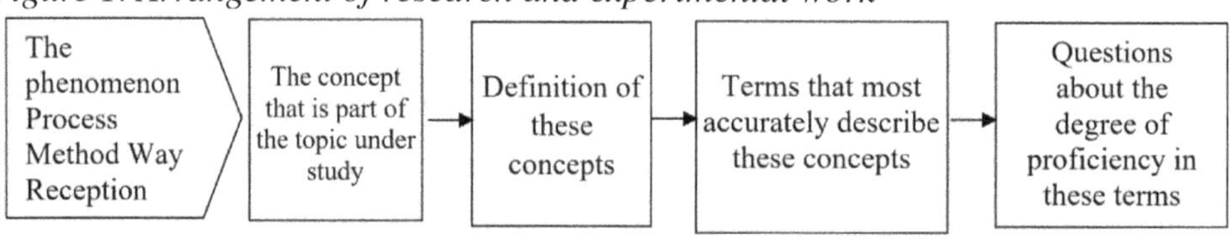

The organization and content of research and experimental work is inclusively based on the requirements of the principles of comprehensive consideration of the problem, science and objectivity, determinism and the relationship between the main causes, the unity of external and internal conditions for the effectiveness of the educational process. The need to ensure the consistency and complexity of the study and to ensure the reliability of the results obtained predetermined the development and use of special research methods.

The results of the comparative pedagogical study enabled to identify specific organizational measures and substantive areas of research and experimental work by the research team.

We appreciate the experience of solving similar problems in some foreign countries and advanced domestic practices (CEDEFOP, 2008)(Litvinova & Samorukov, 2015).

At the same time, one should focus on solving the perspective tasks of developing the continuous education system in the Russian Federation and integrating it into the international educational space when providing organizational and methodological support for the design and implementation of personalized training programs through HCI in corporate training.

Based on existing scientific recommendations the methodology for carrying out the research and experimental work was chosen in order to clarify and verify the validity of the theoretical and empirical provisions of the problem under study.

The basis for organizing research and experimental work was the Time Series Plan. The essence of the studies carried out according to the model of D. Campbell, consists in the targeted and phased introduction of certain research influences into the learning process and the subsequent series of psychological and pedagogical diagnostics (Campbell, 1980).

The purpose of the experimental work was to study the real level of training of qualified personnel, to test the effectiveness of the integrated training model and tools by introducing a targeted organizational and methodological support program for both individual original courses and various types of personalized training programs through HCI in corporate training based on the use of specific technology for implementing professional-oriented programs.

In keeping with this goal, during the pedagogical experiment, the following specific tasks were solved:

- studying and analyzing the practice of systematic and methodological support for the process of qualified personnel training;
- harmonizing the experimental factors used in experimental and control groups based on introducing a comprehensive targeted program for organizational and methodological support for the design and implementation of personalized training programs through HCI in corporate training;
- organizing a continuous and consistent impact on the condition of the learning process in experimental groups;
- interaction detection between the design measures taken and the effectiveness of implementing personalized training programs through HCI in corporate training;
- intermediate and final results analysis, conclusions formulation, practical recommendations development.

The research hypothesis reflected the assumption of the authoring team that the integrated model enables the usage of the effective methods of structuring content and teaching methods in the private method of designing original courses to achieve the goals of the training process as a whole. The description of the psychological and pedagogical determinants of training qualified personnel in interrelated didactic processes is determined by the quality of organizational and methodological support for personalized training programs through HCI. Training technology, based on formation of the level of didactic readiness and reflection on personal and situational factors of interaction, in the up-to date conditions of realistic environment stimulates professional self-improvement and contributes to the development of learning motivation.

Some particular elements of technology and their reproducibility were developed under the natural conditions of the learning process.

For to assess the quality of personalized training programs through HCI higher education teaching personnel, college teachers, representatives of federal and regional government organizations and large municipalities, and enterprises in the real sector of the Russian economy were involved as experts. Their composition was based on the procedures of competence of experts evaluation.

The assessment was carried out on the basis of the five levels of mastership (skills), defined by N. C. Kuzmina, that, in our opinion, are relevant to the research we have recently been carrying out: reproductive, adaptive, local modeling, system modeling knowledge, and system-modeling activities (Kuzmina & Rean, 1993).

During the preparatory period, the experts assisted in identifying the levels, criteria and indicators for assessing the effectiveness of personalized training programs through HCI. Methods for assessing the quality of training have been tested. These methods are used to collect, process, store and use various diagnostic information. Typical mistakes made by observers during the assessment of the activities of students have been identified. Together with experts and teachers, electronic educational and methodological complexes and electronic computer programs have been developed. The participants are familiar with the requirements for organizing experimental work. The structure and content of organizational, administrative, educational and methodological documents have been clarified, didactic materials have been developed, a representative sample of research objects has been identified, and an ascertaining experiment has been carried out.

During the ascertaining experiment, the main methods for determining the efficiency of personalized training programs through HCI were the following: expert assessment, analysis of objective results, analysis of the quantitative characteristics of the processes under consideration. The first stage of the formative experiment finished by the assessment of the efficiency of organizational and methodological support for personalized training programs through HCI, which was based on the use of structural elements of an integrated model of the corporate training process.

At this stage, private methods and tools for developing original courses were developed and selected for conducting the second stage of a formative experiment during training through HCI.

On the one hand, the systematic and methodological support of original courses made it possible to test the capabilities of the designed integrated corporate training model based on the proposed tools. On the other hand, it was to ensure that the conditions for conducting the second stage of the formative experiment are adequate when introducing design technology and implementing personalized training programs through HCI.

The main stage of experimental work is meaningfully aimed at optimizing and testing the efficiency of technology for implementing an integrated corporate training model, designing and implementing personalized training programs through HCI (Table 1).

Table 1. A Complex of Programs within the Formative Experiment

The object of influence	Number of programs	Number of people
Production specialists	6	74
Heads of the production sector	3	56
Administrative Management specialists	4	34
Teachers of educational organizations	2	48

The main stage included the alternations to the program of the formative experiment and to the specific methods for designing and implementing personalized training programs through HCI, as well as the criteria for assessing their efficiency were determined.

At the stage of the ascertaining experiment, based on the specialist's regulatory model, the aims of the integrated corporate training system were defined and described in detail in accordance with the requirements of the Federal State Educational Standard and professional standards and qualification requirements.

Thus, conditions have been created under which the regulatory effectiveness in control (EnC) and experimental groups (EnE) is equal:

$$EnC = EnE \tag{1}$$

Economic effectiveness in control and experimental groups (given the financial and economic expenditures are specified by the indicators) depends on the results achieved *(RA)*.

The economic efficiency of the model proposed is achieved provided that:

$$RAc < RAe \tag{2}$$

Therefore, by the stipulations of the experiment, a comprehensive assessment of the effectiveness of technology for implementing an integrated corporate training model is determined by functional efficiency indicators, while the determining factor is the results achieved (RA) while targets and regulatory indicators (TI), as well as financial and economic costs (FEE), are constant.

In accordance with the basic principles of a humanitarian and holistic strategy, when assessing effectiveness within the learning process, it is necessary to take into account the indicators of the social responsibility of an organization, the formative goal of learning and the social responsibility of students.

The integral qualitative indicator of an organization's social responsibility is assessed by the formula made by N. A. Krichevsky (Krichevsky & Goncharov, 2008).

$$П_к = \frac{1}{i}\sum_{1}^{i} П_i \tag{3}$$

where:

- Pi — i th qualitative indicator;
- $\sum^{i} П_i$ — the sum of quality indicators.
- $Pi = 1$, if this indicator exists;
- $Pi = 0$ if this indicator does not exist.

It is suggested to calculate an integral qualitative indicator of the development of social responsibility (SR) for students of additional professional education programs using the following formula:

$$C^{\Sigma} = \sum_{i=1}^{n} C_i \tag{4}$$

where:

- C_i stands for the qualitative indicators for calculating the development of students' social responsibility;
- i stands for the index of the evaluation indicator (i = 1, 2,..., n is the number of indicators);
- n is the number of indicators.

Based on previously mentioned factors, a set of efficiency criteria was determined, that could fully cover the substantive and effective characteristics of designing and implementing personalized training programs through HCI (Table 2).

Table 2. Compliance of Assessment Methods with the Requirements for Performance Criteria

Assessment methods	**Criterion number**													
	1	**2**	**3**	**4**	**5**	**6**	**7**	**8**	**9**	**10**	**11**	**12**	**13**	**14**
Self-reports	-	-	+	+	-	+	-	-	+	+	-	+	-	+
Expertise	+	+	+	-	+	+	-	+	-	+	+	-	+	+
Tests	+	-	-	+	-	+	+	+	+	+	+	-	+	+
Evaluation of results	+	+	-	-	+	+	-	+	+	-	+	+	+	+

Note: The list of effectiveness criteria was established by M. Blam and D. Naylor (Blum & Naylor, 1968)

At the final stage, a comprehensive review of the work done was carried out, conclusions and recommendations were drawn up.

The results of the research and experimental work were discussed with representatives of employers and professional and public community. They are also revealed in scientific reports and presentations at conferences and forums of various levels.

Thus, in order to successfully carry out research and experimental work, a comprehensive methodology was developed that stipulates a certain sequence of work on organizational and methodological support for the design and implementation of personalized training programs through HCI, which makes it possible to obtain reliable results in the introduction of technology in corporate training.

The logical foundation of the research and experimental work was based on the study of scientific and organizational-practical prerequisites for the institutional transformation of corporate training through the use of personalized learning programs via HCI (Human-Computer Interaction).

3. SCIENTIFIC, ORGANIZATIONAL AND PRACTICAL PREREQUISITES FOR THE INSTITUTIONAL TRANSFORMATION OF CORPORATE TRAINING USING PERSONALIZED TRAINING PROGRAMS THROUGH HCI

Ancient Greece and Sparta revealed to the world two fundamentally different ideas in the field of education and training. Since then, the search for a fundamental training model hardly has changed.

Two opposing philosophical approaches related to the development and formation of a person's personality are still evident in solving these problems.

It goes about contrasting rational and sensory ways of understanding the world around us. This pair means opposite but dialectically interrelated processes — the use and creation of significant values (Table 3).

Table 3. Characteristics of the Main Pedagogical Concepts

The concept	The essence of the concept
Didactic encyclopedism	The main goal is to provide students with an extremely large amount of knowledge and life experience
Didactic formalism	Learning is a means of developing students' abilities and cognitive interests, and therefore a preference for instrumental subjects
Didactic pragmatism	A continuous process of "reconstructing the student's experience" through practical exercises
Functional materialism	Integral connection of cognition with activity, criterion for building academic disciplines "leading idea"
Paradigmatic	The material should be presented not systematically, but "focused", "instantiated" — the content
Cybernetic	The process of information transfer and processing, the role of information and its processing is being absolutized
Associative reflex	The main task is to enrich the student's consciousness with images and representations. The simplest connection is a reflex
Step – by - step formation of mental actions	Managing the learning process through the interrelated stages of familiarization, formation, execution, and transition into convoluted processes of thinking and action
The management model	Training is considered as a process of implementing interrelated stages and management functions
Integrative and pedagogical concepts	Integrative pedagogical activity, at one or another level of implementation of educational goals and objective

Depending on the predominance of one or another component, the following initial differences between the two training models are given:

- knowledge transfer models (or translational models);

- production (creative) model.

Modern research in the field of cyberphysical systems does not fundamentally change historical approaches, but only raises the currently insoluble ethical problem of using technological solutions. According to the relevant and up-to-date D. Shell's expression that has not lost its aptness: "training contains a remarkable paradox: it has confidently established its existence, but is unable to determine what it is" (Shale, 2005).

Thus, the analysis of the historical experience, theory and practice of higher education shows that the current system of professional training is diverse. The educational environment is being overwhelmed by classical ideas about education and training along with the innovations that aim at renewal for the sake of renewal. At the same time, the question is "How to teach?" is often screened or substituted by some more obvious questions "What should I teach?" and "Why should I teach teach?"

We are convinced that the following principles should be taken into account when developing and implementing innovations in education:

1. *Maintaining best practices* First of all, it is necessary to determine which time proved methods and approaches are still relevant and effective. The traditional teaching methods that have proven effective over the years are included here.
2. *Flexibility and adaptability* The introduction of innovations should be flexible and adaptive to new social and economic trends. This requires constant analysis and evaluation of new approaches and their integration into the educational system.
3. *Innovation in response to social needs* Innovations should meet the current and future needs of society and economy. This includes new competencies and skills development, those demanded at the labor market.
4. *The quality of education* The implementations of innovations should not lead to the decrease of quality of education. New methods and technologies should be thoroughly tested and imploded into the educational process, taking into account their impact on the quality of education and student development.
5. *Cooperation with interested parties.* Innovation implementation demands that teachers and students collaborate with employers and other interested parties. This helps to consider different points of view and ensures more effective implementation and adaptation of innovations.
6. *Monitoring and evaluation.* It is necessary to monitor and evaluate their effectiveness regularly once the innovations are implemented. This provides the opportunity to make adjustments and improvements to the educational process based on the data obtained.

We consider the approach formulated by K.D. Ushinsky to be relevant nowadays: "Pedagogics cannot make pretense to be as independent as the sciences that discover the laws of nature, history, and human spirit. This subject only uses all these discoveries to achieve its own educational goal. Physiology, psychology, philosophy, and history provide laws to pedagogics: it also expresses these laws in the form of pedagogical theories and rules and finds ways to apply them to human education at this time and in this society" (Ushinsky, 1990).

The formation of a systematic outlook became one of the characteristic features of the XX-th century, which created the prerequisites for educology. It is one of the systemic disciplines using the most common method of natural science research.

The term *educology* was introduced in 1964, when it was "the first time for the object of study to become an educational system and processes in general in their interaction with society and human education" (Spitsnadel, 2000).

According to the domestic authors who used this methodology (A.I. Subetto, 1994; B.S. Gershunsky, 1998; E.N. Gusinsky, 1994; V.I. Prokoptseva, 1997; N.P. Litvinova, 1997, etc.), when analyzing the approaches to training, general systems theory can be used in the following three main qualities:

1. Analysis of opportunities for developing an integrated educational system:
    - identifying means to enhance the main useful function. Systems theory helps to determine which elements and processes in the education system are the key ones to fulfil its main function, that is of training highly qualified specialists. This includes assessing the interaction between students and teachers, educational structures and forms and the labor market.
    - analysis of the ambient environment. Systems theory makes it possible to consider the influence of such external factors as economic, social and technological changes on innovative changes in the education system. It helps to develop adaptation and sustainable development strategies.
2. Analysis and improvement of the education process:
    - the structure and content of training courses (disciplines). A systematic approach makes it possible to consider academic disciplines and training courses as part of a broader educational system. This helps optimize the course structure, ensuring that they are consistent and logically consistent.
    - teaching methods. Systems theory suggests a whole row of tools for analyzing and improving teaching methods. It helps to identify the most effective methods that contribute to the active involvement of students in the educational process and the development of their critical thinking.
3. Formation and development of specialists creative thinking:

- systematic thinking. Systems theory helps specialists to develop the ability of systematic thinking, which allows them to see complex relationships and patterns in various fields of knowledge. This contributes to more profound understanding of the subject and the development of analytical skills.
- solving complex problems. The use of a systematic approach to learning helps one to learn to solve complex problems that require considering many factors and relationships. This develops creative and innovative thinking skills.

Based on the upper mentioned, we stick to the point that the development of scientific and methodological apparatus for modeling educational processes requires an interdisciplinary approach.

Previously, in order to resolve certain elements of contradictions in educational practice, we suggested that we proceed from the principles of "the uncertainty of humanitarian systems", the "complementarity" and "pedagogical feasibility" of the use of teaching methods, and "the diagnosability of the results of psychological and pedagogical influence".

Having developed a systematic-situational model of educational process management as a basic one we have shown that the interrelated scientific and practical approaches to training can be efficiently used, taking in mind either of them prevail at a certain stage of training.

Bearing in mind the fact that the domestic practice has created appropriate regulatory conditions, and there is a tendency for sectors of the economy to create their own corporate training entities, the attention should be focused on using them and designing and implementing personalized training programs through HCI.

It is necessary to follow the mentioned prospective aims for training systems when forming innovative models of systematic methodological provision of individual educational pattern:

- developing the modular principle of individual educational patterns design;
- forming certification modules for awarding qualifications based on the requirements of relevant standards;
- expanding the professional competencies acquired by students by integrating training programs with HCI;
- using independent public and professional accreditation of HCI programs at their utmost;
- full-scale introduction of public and professional certification of qualifications.

Over the years, HCI has incorporated numerous theories originated from various disciplines and has significantly enriched each of them. HCI has introduced new aspects and in-depth insights into these spheres, beginning with Paul Fitts' law on sensory-motor processes, proceeding with mental models, activity theory, and distributed cognition. As a result, UX-HCI (User Experience Human-Computer Interaction) has become a comprehensive and interdisciplinary field that comprises the best anthropological and technical practices in designing user experience (Martin, 2003).

It should be mentioned that general scientific modeling methods are a powerful tool for resolving internal contradictions and increasing the efficiency of designing and implementing personalized training programs through HCI. Based on this conclusion, the authors have proposed a scientific and methodological framework for modeling integrated training programs.

4. SCIENTIFIC AND METHODOLOGICAL FRAMEWORK FOR MODELING INTEGRATED TRAINING PROGRAMS

A paradigm is defined as a combination of theoretical provisions, methodological foundations, concepts and value criteria. It should be noted that training and education activities are changing and are even forced to change in line with socio-cultural conditions. In this area, as well as in the development of the economy as a whole, there is an active introduction of the project approach and risk-based thinking.

The project method as an idea in Logical Science and Theory of Knowledge. Methodology and practice take us back to the first third of the twentieth century, connecting today's research and experiments with that time. This method reflected the approach of the American philosopher and teacher, educational reformer J. Dewey (Fitts, 1954).

The project paradigm "and the integration of upbringing and education with work" by A.S. Makarenko and other educational organizers of the 1920s and 1930s acts as a guideline for the new Russian pedagogy (Makarenko, 2003).

Just like HCI, the methodology of pedagogical design has technical roots. However, pedagogy as a science remains within the pedagogical system being the format of its object and subject of study . The pedagogical process is the way of life of pedagogical systems and therefore the main object of study. These systems are designed exactly to create favorable conditions for personal development and the implementation of pedagogical processes.

Therefore, when designing personalized training programs through HCI, a systematic approach should analyze all the elements of the system under study, their internal and external relations, the level and quality of goal achievement, and identify contradictions, reserves and development limits of individual components and the system as a whole.

The pedagogical origins of scientific design include forecasting, which plays a key role in planning and developing educational systems. The main goal of forecasting is to describe the characteristics of the future object, while design is aimed at its specific, detailed construction. The forecast is evaluated on the basis of compliance with reality, and the project is evaluated for compliance with the intended goal.

Scientists are ambitiously studying the design as a manifestation of creativity in pedagogical activity, but there still exist some contradictions in the terminology and content of this problem. The analysis of theory and practice of designing pedagogical systems, processes and situations reveals that this is a complex, multi-stage innovative activity that requires continuous diagnosis, analysis and adjustment of work under strict restrictions on expenditures, terms and quality.

Project innovation management when designing personalized training programs through HCI can be represented by a delimited set of interrelated elements (Figure 2).

Figure 2. Structural diagram of project management of personalized training programs through HCI

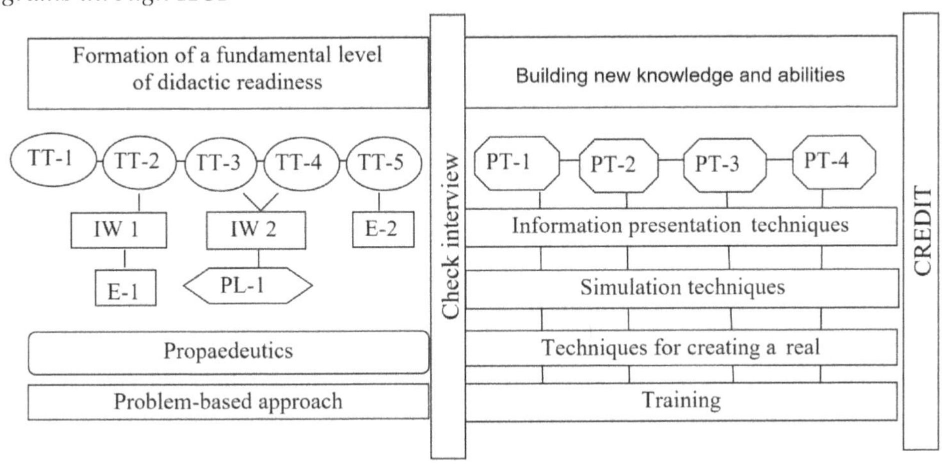

The criteria for training effectiveness can be the content and level of students' basic management functions, acting, in their sustainable forms, as socially and professionally significant qualities. At the same time, the social and professional development of an individual is considered a form of mental development.

With organizational theory the concept of project management stands for the management of important activities that require constant guidance under strict restrictions on expenditures, timing and quality of work. Thus, based on the management model, bearing in mind the criteria of adequacy, it is possible to identify paradigms and interrelated types of innovative activities, while certain ones of these predominate at an appropriate stage of designing process with personalized training programs through HCI.

The training process is a way of life of training systems and therefore the main object of study. These systems are designed specifically for the purpose of implementing these processes. In its most vague form, training modeling reproduces a multi-level process of mental activity, including conceptualization, programming and planning of the original idea:

- conceptualization presupposes going beyond subject sciences through the general theory of activity and the methodological foundations of research;
- programming involves the use of educational theory and practice;
- planning is based on taking into account the requirements of teaching specific disciplines and training courses.

Today it is lain down as an axiom that, as part of the competence approach, the previously presented training models and interactive computer systems cannot be absolutized. However, in our opinion, we should not depreciate their importance.

Each of the previously developed scientific and practical approaches has a predominant area of applicability, and under certain conditions they complement each other.

Practice shows that when switching from a knowledge-based to a competency-based approach, nothing changed in the essential nature of planning learning outcomes. One can only talk about the adequacy and optimization of models of training systems based on the needs of continuous personal and professional development of a person at a specific stage of life.

Despite the heterogeneity and variability of factors affecting a person's personal and professional development, they can be identified, ranged and studied, and combined into a sustainable combination. At the same time, the fundamental principles for creating the content of personalized training programs through HCI are science, continuity, compatibility, and advanced training.

The training system can be studied both statically and dynamically. Statically, it is sufficient to identify the main interrelated elements: developers (teachers) and students, training content and material resources.

The scientists have not reached the agreement on the issue of the component composition of training systems. The model simplifies the modelling process and cannot cover all the elements and connections of reality. Based on the optimality requirement, the model being developed should present only those components and properties, the functional relationship of which determines the pedagogical process.

But this does not exclude the requirement of system stability. Having identified the characteristics and features of existing phenomena and educational practice, we should begin searching for a new layout and combination of leading subsystems, modeling a fundamentally new state of personal and professional development.

The learning process can be represented by a regressive model of the following form:

$$S1 = f(So, P, F, L, C, Y) \quad (5)$$

where:

- S_0 is a vector characterizing students' initial level of knowledge and their individual development;
- S_1 is a vector of the same dimension that characterizes the level of education achieved;
- *P, F, L, C, Y* — stands for the criteria for assessing the main process indicators;
- the *f* function is linear in terms of regression rates.

Each of the *P, F, L, C, Y* estimates is represented as a linear regression function of the components, which, in turn, are written as linear regression functions from the corresponding parameters.

A complete mathematical model of training process was not implemented due to the complexity of the system of equations. However, the value of this model is determined by the fact that the methodological basis for the mathematical apparatus for modeling educational processes has been developed. It is important for us that, using this model we can scientifically approach the substantiation of an integrated model of organizational and methodological support, technology and methodology for corporate training based on a description of the education system with the following causal relationship.

Thus, *the model of the training process* is quite adequately described by the model on sets:

$$Mtp = \{Mt, Msms, Mtt, Mmlp\} I^1 s, \ldots, I^n s\} \quad (6)$$

where:

- *Mtp* is the model of the training process;
- *Mt* stands for the teachers with knowledge of the subject having mastered the teaching methods;

- *Msms* stands for the systematic and methodological support for the training of specialists;
- *Mtt* is for the training tools;
- *Mmlp* stands for organizing and managing the learning process;
- $I^1 s - I^n s$ stands for the students.

Aiming at design personalized programs in an integrated system of organizational and methodological support for corporate training, a set of competencies characterizing the level of qualification of a specialist can be presented in the form of:

$$Mrpp = \{M^1_{rpp}, M^2_{rpp}, M^3_{rpp}\} \quad (7)$$

where:

- *Mrpp* is a set of psychological and pedagogical requirements in the reference model of a specialist's personality;
- M^1_{rpp} stands for personality traits, knowledge and skills that should be developed by a specialist in any field;
- M^2_{rpp} stands for professional qualities, knowledge, skills and abilities, based on the characteristics of professional activity;
- M^3_{rpp} stands for personality traits, knowledge and skills that determine activities within the framework of specialization (labor functions).

Along with a set of competencies, requirements for students are also regulatory. They are determined by the level of education and the stages of procedures for admission to the profession (level of qualification, certification). We believe that input control plays an independent role in the system of continuing education at the postgraduate stage.

Input control is understood as an element of an integrated training system, during the implementation of which the student's degree of didactic readiness for the next stage of educational activities is established and ways to manage the learning process are determined. At the same time, input control functions are not considered in the format of qualifying events. They are reduced to comparative analysis with the minimum level of readiness for training and are corrected by information and communication mechanisms.

The input control is aimed at providing the management subsystem with information about the current state of the object not only on the motivational and/or cognitive component, but also on work experience and/or official purpose.

Thus, the control circuit is closed, and the target setting is formed to the appropriate level (sublevel) of qualification. In this case, designing personalized training programs through HCI will have a number of qualitative characteristics that distinguish it from other activities:

1. Multiplicity of elements and their dialectical relationship:
   - design includes many components: aims, objectives, methods, tools, forms, resources, etc.;
   - the elements are in constant interaction, which allows the system to function and develop.
2. Compatibility of elements:
   - all elements must be compatible for the efficiency of the system;
   - incompatibility leads to failures and a decrease in the quality of results.
3. Interconnection of the elements makes it possible to obtain a new systemic quality:
   - the elements interact in such a way that a new quality arises that is not inherent in each element separately;
   - quality ensures the efficiency and effectiveness of the system.
4. Internal integrity of the system:
   - the system has an internal structure and organization that ensures its functioning as a whole;
   - all the elements are matching to achieve a common goal.
5. Relative limitations from other systems:
   - the HCI training system has its own boundaries and operates within a specific educational environment;
   - it interacts with other systems (for example, social, economic, cultural ones) but it remains relatively independent.
6. Involvement of each element of the system in obtaining the final result makes the regulating factor:
   - each element of the system contributes to the achievement of the common aim;
   - design success depends on how effectively all the elements interact.

The proposed scientific and methodological modeling framework enabled the development of an original authorial technology for designing and implementing professionally oriented educational programs.

5. TECHNOLOGY FOR THE DEVELOPMENT AND IMPLEMENTATION OF PROFESSIONALLY-ORIENTED TRAINING PROGRAMS

The interconnected processes of designing and implementing personalized training programs through HCI determine the choice of appropriate technology. At the same time, the concept of technology is currently not generally accepted in traditional teaching practice. UNESCO documents consider the concept of "learning technology" as a systematic method of creating, applying and defining the entire process of teaching and learning, taking into account technical and human resources and their interaction, aimed at optimizing forms of education (Samygin, 1998).

On the one hand, training technology is a combination of methods and tools for processing, presenting, modifying and presenting educational information, on the other hand, it is the science of methods to pedagogically influence students during the learning process using the necessary technical or informational tools. In teaching technology, the content, methods and tools of training are interrelated and interdependent. The problem of learning through HCI is to select the right content, apply optimal teaching methods and tools in accordance with the program and the objectives of personal and professional development.

For the concept of "technology", a term that has become quite popular in the past decade there are a lot of interesting classifications and definitions as well. We adhere to the point of view of those authors who understand technology in the learning process, first of all, as the generalized practice of successfully implementing methods of education and training, based on the system of developing and using an extensive and sustainable set of scientifically based organizational and methodological tools (Zinchenko, 2002).

Consideration of organizational and methodological tools as a project of a materialized form of training makes it possible to consolidate designing and implementing personalized programs through HCI in corporate training the stable features of classical pedagogical practice (technology) in the technological scheme of the process. At the same time, the capabilities of such technology are closely related to the model of the educational system and the pedagogical process as a whole.

The integrative model of organizational and methodological support for corporate training makes it possible to combine learning strategies in various educational situations, based on the living knowledge concept.

V. P. Zinchenko considers developing knowledge to be the subject of activity of subjects of pedagogical interaction the main source of educational dynamism. The main difference between the "living knowledge" from the "dead" one is that it cannot be learned, it must be built. In the proposed integrative model of organizational and methodological support for corporate training, living knowledge does not present an opposition to scientific and program knowledge, but being based on them, it serves as a prerequisite for their development in quasi-professional activities and the result of the development of a specialist's professional potential.

Let us refer to the main components that determine the professional potential of a specialist:

$$PPS = Punp + Ppvp + Past + Papa, \quad (8)$$

where:

- *PPS* stands for the professional potential of a specialist:
- *Punp* is an unchangeable part of potential due to the general innate abilities of the individual;
- *Ppvp* is a partially variable (progressive) part of the potential due to the natural special abilities of the individual, their development during his/her professional training and practical activities;
- *Past* stands for the capacity component added by training (special one);
- *Papa* is a part of the potential, the result of training distributed over time, acquired through practical activity.

Obviously, there exists a "direct contradiction with the existing model of the classical educational process" which is objectively due to:

- on the one hand, the focus of the educational environment on developing the professional competencies of a specialist, mainly on the basis of didactic readiness and quasi-professional activities;
- on the other hand, a manifestation of the progressive part of the potential and the time-spaced result of training in the process of real activity.

This provision, fundamental for the team of authors, was implemented in the course of solving interrelated problems:

- testing models, methods and tools, designing and implementing personalized training programs through HCI;
- systematization and standardization of organizational and methodological support for the design and implementation of personalized training programs through HCI.

At the same time, we proceeded from the fact that the conceptual aspects of the development of basic educational programs are determined by the Federal State Educational Standards. In turn, the quality of education in basic educational programs is confirmed by state accreditation procedures.

At the same time, when developing and implementing personalized training programs, HCI provides greater autonomy for educational entities.

Based on this, we believe that it is advisable to present the technological aspects of designing and implementing personalized training programs through HCI in the form of an appropriate quality management system standard.

Being based on the proposed model of organizational and methodological support for the design and implementation of personalized training programs through HCI, the technology involves using the situation as an initial level of analysis of appropriate activities.

The structure of a single technological act of the training process includes the subjects, the purpose, the means of influence, ways to use these tools in organizing interaction, and the final result of the activity (Figure 3).

Figure 3. The structure of the technological act of training

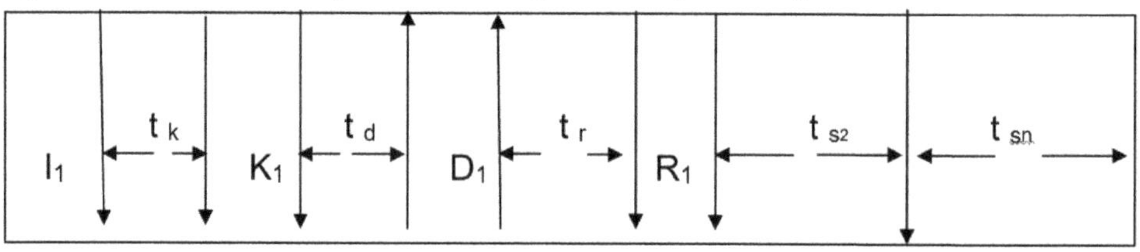

With regard to organizational and methodological support for the design and implementation of personalized training programs through HCI, one can mention the following technological types of actions:

- clarifying the aims of specific activities;
- identifying significant didactic characteristics of students as objects of influence;
- selecting and refining training tools;
- implementing the teaching methods and techniques;
- evaluating the results of the learning process.

In accordance with the ways of materializing information, the following types of methodological tools can be identified:

- oral speech and non-verbal means of expression;
- material objects of educational activities;

- educational texts (questions, cases, tasks);
- visual aids, manuals, tables, graphics charts;
- handouts;
- technical media of educational information;
- virtual training tools.

The practice of testing models, methods and tools in the process of implementing educational programs makes it possible to identify the main technological features of increasing the effectiveness of the learning process:

- lawfulness, scientific validity and focus on solving didactic problems;
- comfortable interaction, increased motivation of listeners;
- increasing the informative capacity of special courses;
- priority use of active forms and methods of training;
- widespread use of modern training tools through HCI;
- reliability and guarantee of result, clarity and certainty in recording it;
- a designed, step-by-step and formalized structure of the activities of training subjects, which determines the planning, tolerability and repeatability (reproducibility) of training experience.

The following requirements are imposed on system-situational analysis:

- consistent aims and performance results;
- the continuity of study of activities;
- situation is the unit of analysis.

Within the method of consistent dynamic assessment of the situation, the technical act of training usually begins with the student being informed of certain new material, the informational content of which is called an educational dose of information. Let's denote it by *I*. Then, after a certain time period $t_{k,}$ to make sure that the student has mastered the proposed training dose, the student is given a test task, the content of which will be denoted by the letter *K*. After that, after a period of time t_d, the student gives his solution *D* to the offered task. After the t_r time for the analysis, the student is given an evaluation of the effectiveness of his answer, analyzing the mistakes made and being rewarded for the correct and, especially, for creative decisions. The informational content of this analysis is indicated by *R*. Let us assume that the optimal *K* ratios are: *I* and *D: K* exist, then one can accept the appropriate designations for them:

- $K: I = n_k$ is control rate;

- $D: K = n_d$ is the assimilation rate.

When these rates are multiplied, we get:

$$D{:}I = n_k n_d = n_r. \quad (9)$$

Ratio $D: I$ is the feedback rate n_r.

Thus, the amount of the training dose in an optimized process is determined by the information content of the decision issued for the test task of the educational step. This ratio is valid for any training case. Deviations from it should be considered deviations from the optimal conditions of the educational process.

A sequence of four elements of scheme *I, K, D,* and *R* constitutes one step of learning *A*. After the first step has passed through t_s, the second one begins and the training process is systematic.

A schematic diagram of the learning process is shown in Figure 4.

Figure 4. Schematic diagram of the training process

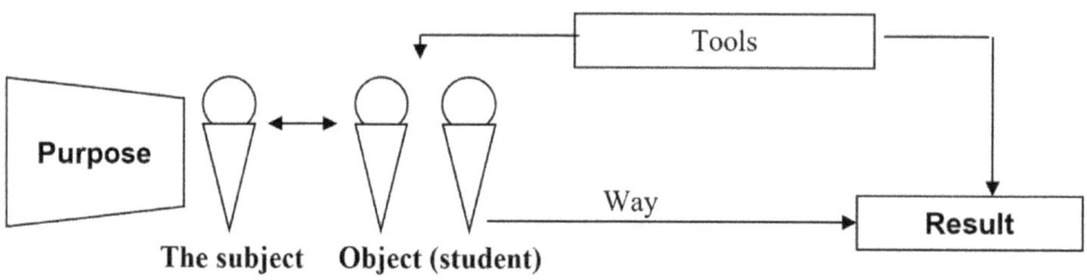

The number of educational steps in the training process as a whole may vary and is determined by a number of factors, which include:

- the level of preparedness of students;
- the complexity of educational issues and their specific features;
- time spent on the learning process;
- teaching methods accepted;
- technical means, etc.

Within the model, identifying the situation as a systematic unit of analysis of the set of conditions and circumstances, in which the student is actively involved, makes it possible to use the two extreme methods of conducting an educational step.

In the first case, the training process takes place at the maximum training dose

$I = max$. According to the method of using the information acquired, the student's activity is reproductive. In this case, control task K and reinforcement R characterize the fundamental level of didactic readiness.

Carrying out the training process at a training dose of $I = min$ is a prerequisite for productive activity. With this method, the student is constantly active, his attention is sharpened from start to finish, and logical thought is active. With a properly developed private teaching method, this provides not only solid knowledge, but also emotional satisfaction from constant success in learning.

The structuring of the abstract provisions of the theory, on the one hand, and the generalization of specific knowledge within the framework of quasi-professional activities, on the other hand, create the basis for a qualitative leap in the learning process. Such a synthesis is provided by the scientific thesis of operations research based on a figurative and conceptual model of expedient activity. However, the formal model of operations research considers a person participating in an operation as a person endowed with a cold mind but devoid of feelings. As a result, the student personality traits are ignored. They often determine the way and outcome of training activities.

In order to ensure high efficiency in solving didactic problems based on the technological features of the learning process, the study developed electronic computer training programs that comply with the "Standard for the Development of Educational and Methodological Materials (Complexes)", with the implementation of procedures for their state registration by the Federal Service for Intellectual Property of the Russian Federation.

During the testing of teaching materials in the process of implementing basic additional professional retraining and advanced training programs, and vocational training according to an individual plan, e-learning programs have received the highest expert rating among the teaching staff (0.92) and students (0.96).

As an example, the Original training course "Business Communication" Figure 5 is presented.

Figure 5. E-learning program

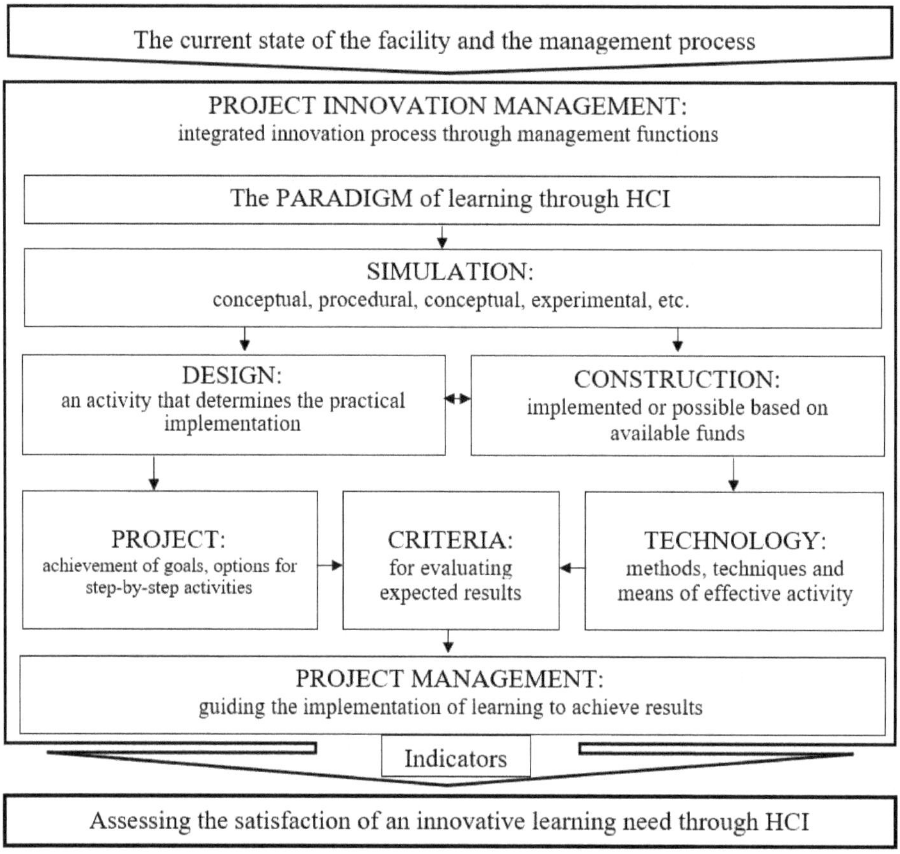

(Programming language: Html, CSS, JavaScript)

The humanistic paradigm and modern scientific and practical approaches to organizing the training process have determined the choice of logical structuring of sections, topics and training sessions within the thematic plan of the discipline. The course of the academic discipline is divided into two sections:

1. Theoretical bases of rhetoric, discussion and communication.
2. Communicative competence training.

The structural and logical scheme of the training course is shown in Figure 6.
The learning step on $J = max$ he learning step on a $J = \min$

Figure 6. Structural and logical diagram of the training course

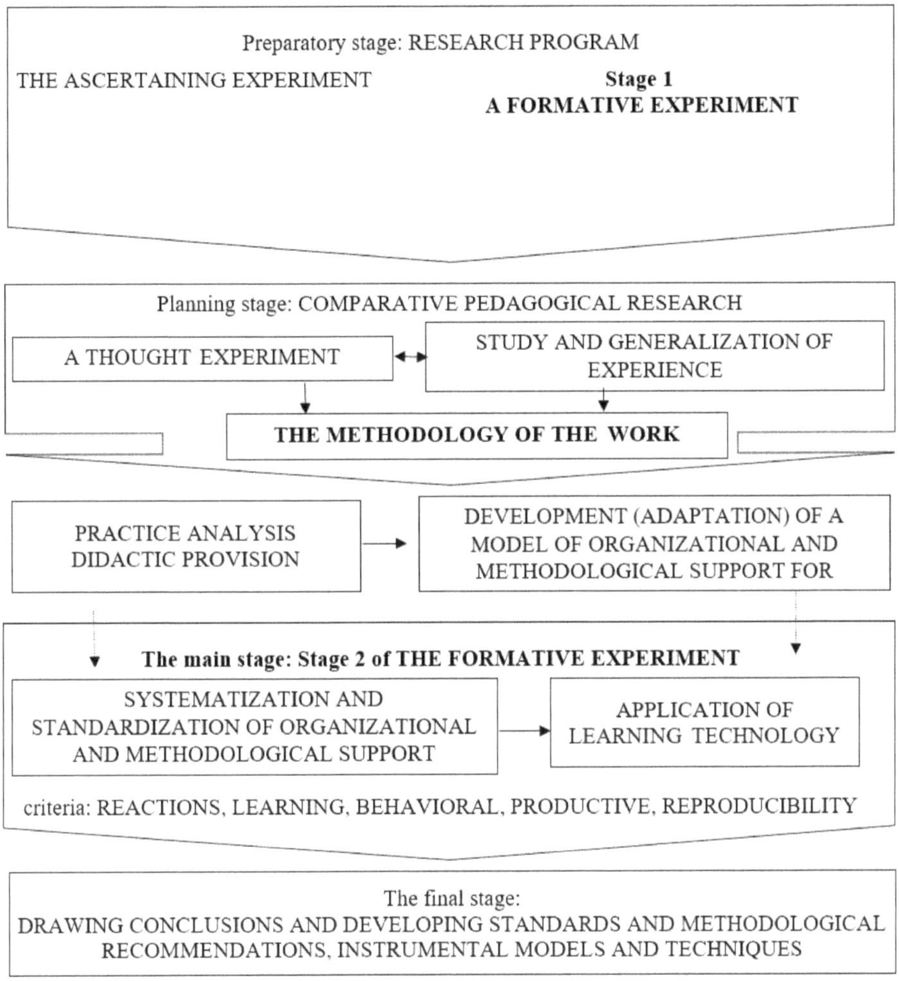

This approach is justified by the results of a study on the effectiveness of learning educational information (Table 4).

Table 4. The effectiveness of learning educational material

Survey method	**Amount of updated material, %**		
	after the lecture	**a month from now**	**practical action**
Essay	18.8	6.1	61.8
Designed answers	45.3	13.6	87.9
Selective answers	80.7	42.1	98.9

The basis for for determining the amount of material learned were methods developed by I. A. Kulak and A. I. Kulak (Kulak & Kulak, 1988).

Using the method of "composing", the necessary material is randomly produced in memory by remembering irrelative to any specific activity. Immediately after mastering the theoretical material the results are less than 20%, and after a month they decrease by more than half. When performing some practical action, the updated material appears on average rate of more than 60%. The "constructed answers" method helps to find the corresponding information block in memory. The results of reproducing material immediately after the lecture and in a month, as compared to the essay, are more than double, but do not reach 50%.

The "multiple choice" method helps to connect the learning process to mental activity and gives the best results. The trend of reducing the reproducibility of the material by half, a month after presentation remains, but in practical action it gives optimal results.

The first section presents independent work, essays and practical classes as practical training in the process of educational activities.

During independent work (IW), students learn to actively perceive, understand and deepen the information received, solve practical problems, and acquire skills necessary for professional activity. Independent work includes various forms of organization, maintaining the focus on developing students' self-improvement skills. Along with working on information sources and rhetorical development of public activities, special attention is paid to self-diagnostic skills, personal qualities and education. Didactic readiness is monitored and self-training tasks are individualized according to the quality of work and the completeness of the workbook.

The essay is aimed at implementing a partial exploratory and research method of teaching, organizing mental interaction in solving problem situations. Students act as trainers. Didactic readiness monitoring involves assessing not only substantive knowledge, but also organizing interpersonal feedback using a methodology for assessing the quality of public speaking.

A practical lesson within a theoretical course is a kind of "bridge" for introduction to programmed training based on the integration of interdisciplinary knowledge.

During IW2, which precedes the practical lesson, students systematize knowledge about the structure of professional activity, the management of psychological and pedagogical variables of individuals and groups, and factors in the living environment. By expert means, using professional methods, they form a list of professionally important communicative qualities.

The practical lesson is designed to develop abilities, evaluate personal potentials, predict and regulate self-government. The actual level of didactic readiness is assessed by the quality of the list of professionally important qualities and objective professional diagnostic data.

The theoretical section of the course ends *with a test survey* (in writing) and provides control over the level of development: “have ideas”, “know”, “be able to”. The initial level of didactic readiness is evaluated based on the structuring of fundamental scientific knowledge in the theoretical course (Figure 7).

Figure 7. The logical sequence of the test survey

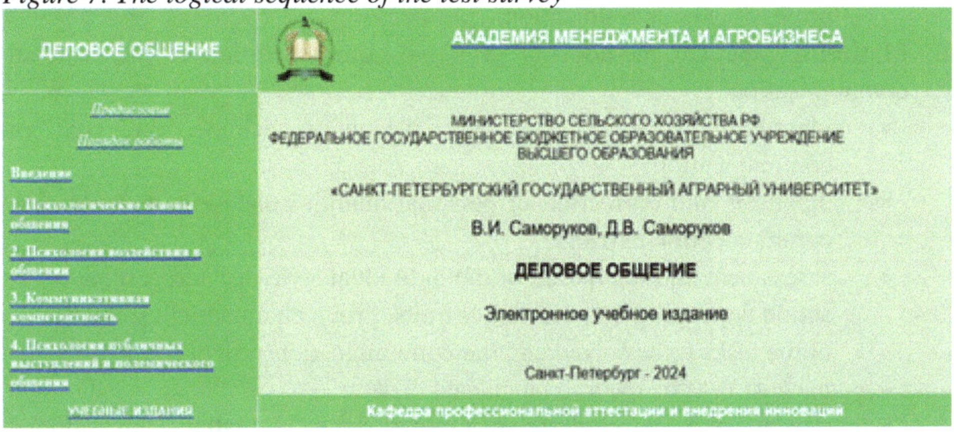

A test survey task is a propaedeutic tool in case of a significant discrepancy between the required and actual level of didactic readiness to build new knowledge and abilities. The answers to the questions make it possible to assess the initial level of didactic readiness quite accurately using the formula:

$$IDG = \frac{\text{number of correct answers}}{\text{total number of questions}} \qquad (9)$$

If the assimilation rate is below 0.7, the question arises about additional propaedeutics of this topic or section when preparing and during programmed training (required J = min).

The requirements for the development of communication skills are materialized by setting educational and programmed training objectives.

1. Improving communication skills:
    - analysis and evaluation of the efficiency of subject-oriented communication;
    - analysis of interpersonal relationships and interaction in given situations of professionally oriented communication;
    - skills and abilities for constructive dialogue in professional activities;

- skills necessary to rhetorically develop the idea and composition of public speech, present substantive material in the interaction of text and illustrations, and influence people with their speech;
- the ability to objectively assess partners in official communication and audience diagnostics in the process of public activities;
- self-control skills, adequate self-esteem and the level of ambition in professional communication.

2. Mastering practical methods of effective communication in professional communication:
   - identifying optimal ways and means to achieve the goal of communication;
   - diagnosis and correction of personal qualities and skills to overcome communication barriers;
   - assessment and regulation of the individual style of interpersonal interaction depending on personality traits, group characteristics, the nature of the tasks to be solved and the communication situation;
   - management of specific language barriers;
   - ethical and psychological protection in situations of official communication;
   - principles and rules for preparing and conducting discussions;
   - behavioral skills and rhetorical response to a specific situation.
3. Creating motivation for self-improvement:
   - an attitude towards the fullest possible knowledge of oneself and others;
   - positive self-attitude;
   - strive for interpersonal reflection and empathy;
   - self-confidence in the performance of official duties.

To implement the program, the main pedagogical tasks of the subjects of interaction have been formulated.

The task of creating the content of programmed training:

- provide an opportunity to get acquainted with the nature, characteristics and organization of training elements;
- to motivate self-exploration and active interaction;
- create conditions for increasing students' motivation to make constructive changes through adequate feedback, showing productive personal and professional manifestations, testing new options and methods of professional activity, forming and developing the necessary skills and abilities;

- create situations of professional communication that reveal personal qualities, characteristics of types of communication, and contribute to improving professional skills and personal growth;
- organize a discussion of psychological phenomena that occur during the training.

Pedagogical Task for Students:

Carry out self-diagnosis of personal characteristics. Based on its results, make an adequate volitional effort to improve communication skills and correct (bringing the development to the average of population norm) psychological qualities through psychogymnastic exercises.

Teaching methods are used on the basis of principles that involve the systematic determination of students' psychological and pedagogical variables, taking into account the characteristics, needs and aims of subsequent professional activity. The leading methods for solving the problems of developing communicative competence are methods of modeling professional situations with the predominance of active educational forms and teaching aids.

In the process of student-centered learning, individual behavioral patterns and performance results are constantly correlated with learning goals and criteria for the success of professional-oriented communication. The goals of the personal and content plan are specified based on the degree of achievement of the result. Students receive the information necessary for developing communication skills from the teacher or independently on based on the teacher's instructions from textbooks and teaching documents.

The methodological aspects of managing the learning process are determined by the schematic scheme of aim-setting, diagnosis, behavior, and pedagogical techniques (Figure 8).

Figure 8. Training management model

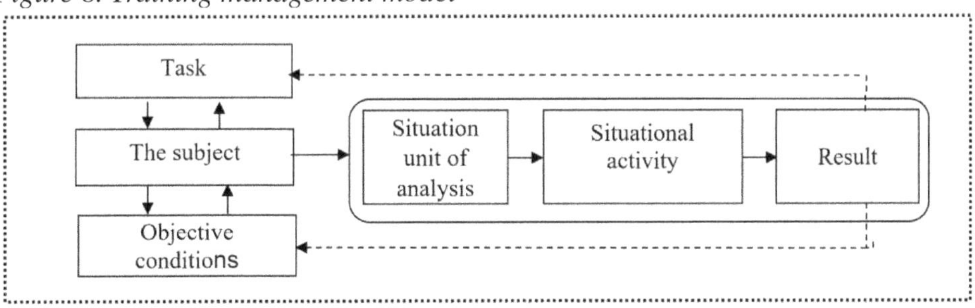

In addition to passive control methods, this model offers opportunities for active action. It can be predictive, that is, it solves the issue of anticipating, predicting and taking into account the impact of psychological and pedagogical dominants on the quality of activity.

The model has a retrospective mechanism that assesses the student's training and activities, establishes the influence of general factors in the productivity of the training process, the need for pedagogical influence and self-improvement.

The proposed learning technology is specified through a methodology for developing an original course tailored to personalized learning programs via HCI (Human-Computer Interaction).

6. METHODOLOGY FOR DEVELOPING AN ORIGINAL COURSE FOR PERSONALIZED TRAINING PROGRAMS THROUGH HCI

In the corporate training system, through HCI, information content is presented mainly on the basis of original courses, with the mandatory provision of practical tools for personal development and/or subsequent professional activities for the students. As a result of the research and experimental work, the authors have tested and proposed a methodology for developing an original course for personalized training programs through HCI.

The methodological requirements for developing original courses regulate the necessity for:

- take into account the features and peculiarities of a specific personalized training program through HCI;
- provide for the specifics of the relevant science, its conceptual framework, and the peculiarities of methods for studying its patterns;
- the preferential use of active learning methods to implement modern methods of information processing through HCI.

The mechanism for structuring the fundamental provisions of scientific knowledge and reflecting personal experience in the learning process in the instrumental model of managing the learning process through HCI is reflected in Figure 9.

Figure 9. Methodological scheme for implementing the author's training course

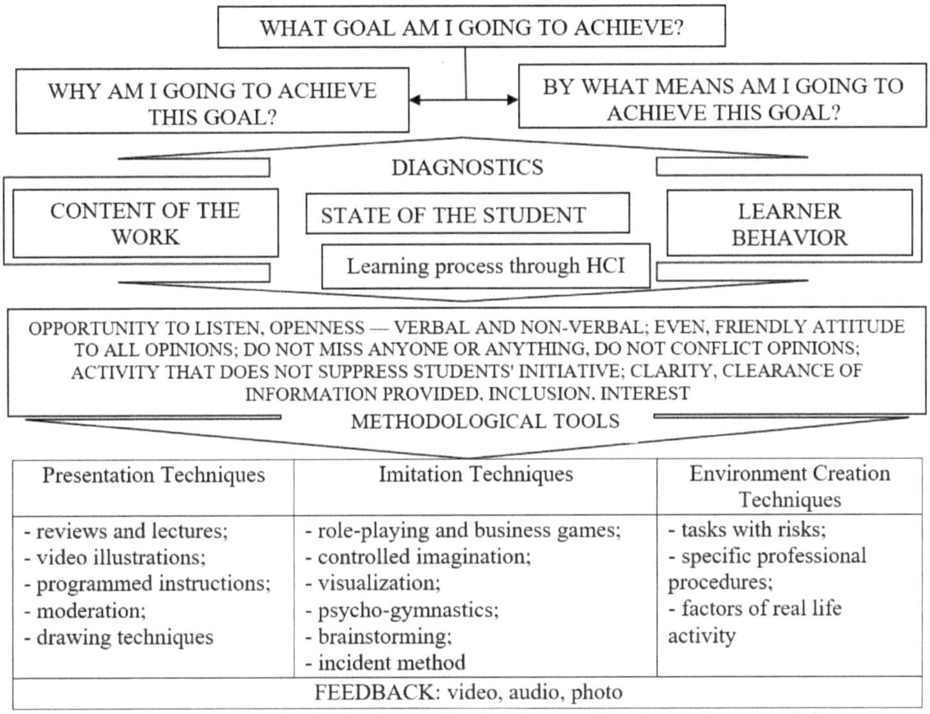

The technique of developing skills for operating practical tools is based on the method of sequential dynamic evaluation of a specific practical situation and is shown in Figure 10.

Figure 10. Technique for developing proficiency skills

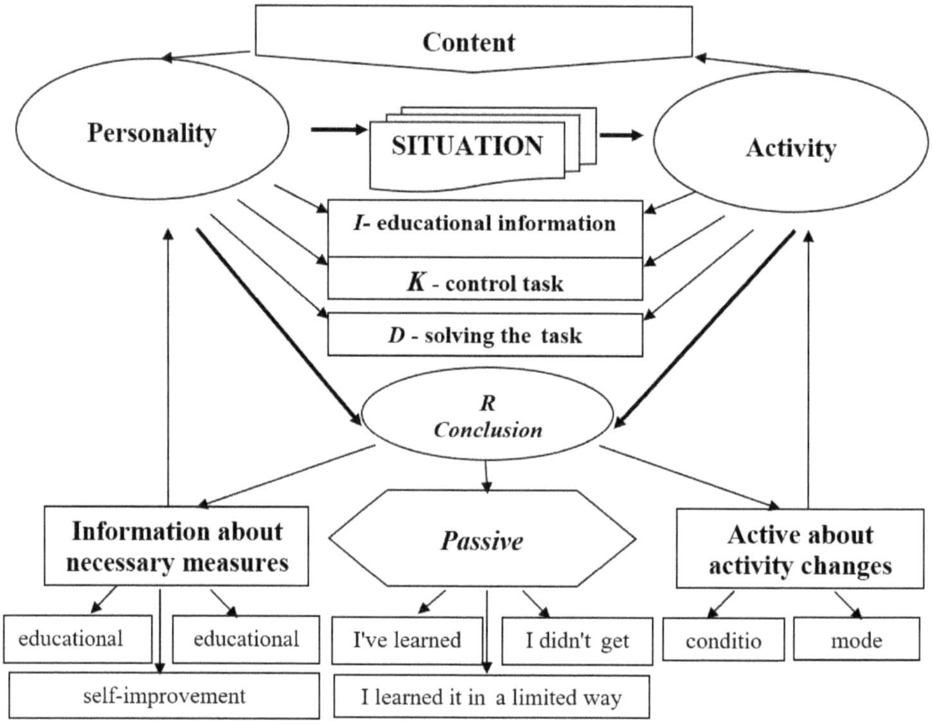

The methodological aspects of diagnosing the development of an indicative basis of activity during learning when developing and implementing the content of the author's training course (presented educational information through HCI) are based on a level assessment of the solution to the tests presented:

- Level I *a 1:* algorithmic activity with an externally defined algorithmic description ("on a hint");
- Level II *a 2:* reproductive effect (knowledge is a copy) by reproducing information from memory and using information on a previously learned indicative basis for performing a typical activity, i.e. algorithmic activity from memory;
- Level III *a 3:* productive activity carried out over a number of objects similar to the educational elements studied. Heuristic activity performed not according to a ready-made algorithm, but a new algorithm being created.
- Level IV *a 4:* productive activity performed by independently constructing an objectively new indicative basis for activity — creative (research) activity.

Table 5. Level Evaluation of Test Solutions

		à1	à2	à3	à4
Control of assimilation	up to 0.7	0.7-0.8 0.8-0.9 0.9-1.0	0.7-0.8 0.8-0.9 0.9-1.0	0.7-0.8 0.8-0.9 0.9-1.0	0.7-0.8 0.8-0.9 0.9-1.0
Score in points	*0*	*1 23*	*4 5 6*	*7 8 9*	*10 11 12*
Assessment of the development of OOD	Unsatis-factory	Satisfactory	Good	Excellent	Profes-sionally
Qualitative assessment of the author's course development	Unsatis-factory	*2*	*3*	*5*	Ready, Ñapable

Training is carried out on the basis of the development of teaching materials for each lesson. The lesson plan for a lesson is developed in a form convenient for provision an individual educational pattern through HCI.

The multimedia (OHR) presentation of educational material is being developed based on the requirements to implement the principle of visualized educational information as harmonized with the artistic and informational components of the digital environment.

The structure of a multimedia (OHR) presentation is as follows:

- the number of slides corresponds to the content of the educational information presented and to the duration of training through HCI;
- the first slide provides the following information: course title, lesson topic, first name, patronymic and last name of the content developer;
- the structure (contents) of the presentation is revealed on the second slide (using the "Final Slide" option);
- the penultimate slide (or after each quote and photo) contains links to all sources used;
- the last slide contains literature used.

The content of the multimedia (OHR) presentation is consistent with the goals and organizational form of the learning process through HCI.

Text on the slides:

- the text on the slide is a reference note (keywords, bulleted or numbered list), without complete sentences;
- the volume of the text on the slide is no more than 7 lines;
- the bulleted/numbered list contains no more than 7 items;
- there are no errors or typos;
- there are no punctuation marks at the end of lines in bulleted and numbered lists.

- the most important information is highlighted by color, the body of a letter size, animation effects, etc.

Illustrations on the slides:

- illustrations serve as an appropriate and sufficient means of illustration, help to fully reveal the content of the learning process through HCI and do not distract attention from it;
- high-resolution illustrations with a clear image are used.

Infographics on the slides:

The selected visualization tools (tables, diagrams, graphs, etc.) correspond to the content of the HCI learning process and the level of training of students.

Design and customization:

- the slide design corresponds to the topic, audience and purpose of training through HCI; it does not interfere with the perception of the content of the speech;
- whenever it is possible, the same design template is used for all presentation slides;
- a the body of a letter is no less than 18-20 points;
- the background and font colors are contrasting (mostly the background is light);
- the font is easy to read (no narrow font, serif font, etc.);
- slides are shown at the click of the mouse or keyboard (not automatically);
- the presentation is not overloaded with animation effects.

Training information requirements:

- the presentation serves as an illustration to the educational information presented, but does not replace it;
- the process of learning through HCI is not limited to reading text from slides;
- meaningful content does not compete with illustrative material (enough time is allocated to perceive the information on the slides);
- visual contact is provided;
- attention to the most important parts of the content is drawn in various ways (verbally, using animation effects, the pointer option, the mouse cursor, etc.);
- the presentation file is saved in the PowerPoint Demo mode (slideshow) *.pps
- if necessary, the student can easily get on to any presentation slide;

- the student is given the opportunity to print handouts before, during or after the HCI training process.

Requirements for handouts prepared on the basis of an electronic presentation:

- MS PowerPoint format (output is no more than 4 slides per A-4 sheet);
- the body of a letter size is no less than 12 points;
- headers and footers (name and surname of the educational information developer; topic; date of development; page numbers) are designed in the same language as the electronic presentation itself.

The volume, content and design of the handouts correspond to the didactic task solved during the learning process through HCI and the requirement to provide students with practical tools for further professional activities.

Illustrative materials containing a large amount of information, such as complex tables, diagrams, bibliography, examples of text fragments or calculations, are prepared using other programs (MS Word, MS Excel, etc.).

Original courses that are integrated into the formal education system through the exercise of the right to transfer learning outcomes through HCI are usually provided with the Original Course Workbook.

A workbook is a multifunctional didactic tool for designing a learning environment. It is developed in accordance with the established form (developing didactic tools, a set of tasks for independent work that differ in the level of complexity, independence, nature of activity, development of criteria for completing tasks) (Bordovskaya, 2007).

The structure of the workbook:

- the title reflects: logos, full name of the educational institution, name of the structural unit, affiliation with the educational program, surname and initials, academic degree, academic title of developer (s), title of bibliographic material (Workbook), title of the original course, bold font.
- content that corresponds to the list of topics of the re-credited curriculum, topics and educational questions in full scale.
- bibliography;
- test questions and assignments;
- enclosures.

The text of the workbook content:

- the text is a reference note for increasing productivity and enhancing students' learning activities;
- the volume, content and design of the educational material correspond to the didactic task solved during the learning process;
- material that forms the degree of training to "have an idea of", reference data and conditions for solving a practical problem and illustrations can be revealed in a full scale.
- the form of presenting a categorical apparatus, generalizing conclusions, and material for developing the degree of training to "know" and "be able" provides an indispensable element for activating motor memory and internal speaking (filled in during learning through HCI using the indicated stimuli).
- the ratio of fully elaborated material and prepared structured forms for completion depends on the method of organizing the learning process through HCI, but does not exceed 60% to 40% compliance.

Practical tools:

- to develop professional skills during the learning process, HC is posted after outlining the content of the issue under study (revealing mechanisms for solving professional problems);
- it is posted in enclosures for self-study and subsequent professional activities.

Formatting text in a workbook:

Page format A-4; left — 2, right — 2; top — 2; bottom — 2.

Times New Roman font, size 14 for the main text (10-12 for tables, diagrams, illustrations, reference and additional material), line spacing — 1.5 lines (single for tables, diagrams, illustrations, reference and additional material), paragraph — indent 1.25.

Thus, the description of specific methods, approaches, and techniques of pedagogical practice contributes to enhancing the effectiveness of the learning process through HCI.

7. CONCLUSION

A task on improvement of organization and methodological provision for the development and implementation of personalized training programs through HCI in the framework of corporate training has been solved in the result of the scientific and experimental activity carried out..

An analysis of the status and problems, the existing scientific approaches and solutions, organizational and practical prerequisites for the institutional transformation of corporate training using personalized training programs through HCI was carried out, taking into account the transfer of the results of their development in the formal education system. The scientific and methodological apparatus for modeling integrated training programs, mechanisms for managing the design and implementation of personalized training programs through HCI in corporate training are presented.

To ensure the effective functioning of the proposed integrated model of organizational and methodological support, a mechanism has been developed to deploy an indivisible part of system-organized activities according to tasks, objects and processes in a specific situation in order to manage the learning process through HCI: "Task" — "Subject of activity" — "Objective conditions" — "Normative description of the situation" — "Situational activity" — "Solution".

The introduction of the mentioned solutions based on the methodology of system-situational analysis made it possible to adapt the method of consistent dynamic assessment of organizational and methodological conditions by designing and implementing personalized training programs, to use Situational awareness and "e-Terravision" technologies, which are becoming the most important condition for supporting the learning process through HCI.

As a result of the research and experimental work, the authors have tested and suggested a methodology for developing an original course for personalized training programs through HCI. A methodological scheme for implementing the original training course, tools for supporting the learning process through HCI based on the multifunctional didactic tool "Workbook" have been proposed.

The methodological aspects of diagnosing the development of an indicative basis of activity in the development and implementation of the content of the original training course (educational information presented through HCI) are based on a level evaluation of the solution to the tests presented.

REFERENCES

Bespalko, V. P., & Tatur, Y. G. (1989). *Systematic and methodological support of the educational process of training specialists*. High School.

Blum, M. L., & Naylor, J. C. (1968). *Industrial psychology: Its theoretical and social foundations*. No Title.

Bordovskaya, N. V. (2007). *Humanitarian technologies in university educational practice: theory and methodology of design*. Book House.

Campbell, D. T. (1980). Models of experiments in special psychology and applied research/translated from English, edited by M.I. Bobneva, M.: Progress. – 389 p.

Carroll, J. M. (Ed.). (2002). *Human-Computer Interaction in the New Millennium*. ACM Press.

Cox, G. (1999). The Digital Crowd: Some Questions on Globalization and Agency. *Design Issues*, *15*(1), 16–25.

Dix, A., Finlay, J., Abowd, G., & Beale, R. (2003). *Human-Computer Interaction* (3rd ed.). Prentice Hall.

Erickson, T., & McDonald, D. W. (2008). *HCI Remixed. Reflections on Works That Have Influenced the HCI Community*. MIT Press.

Fitts, P. M. (1954). The information capacity of discrete motorresponses. *Journal of Experimental Psychology*, *47*, 381–391. PMID: 13174710

International Yearbook of Technology of Education and Training. (1978).

Krichevsky, N. A., & Goncharov, S. F. (2008). Corporate social responsibility. M.: Yzdat.-bid. corporation" Dashkov & Co", 2007.-216 p.

Kulak I.A. (1988). Methodology for identifying the fixation of educational material in memory traces of different fixation. // Pedagogy of higher and secondary special schools: Interdepartmental. collection. – Minsk, 1988. – Issue. 2 (21) (2-19), pp. 143-154.

Kuzmina, N. V., & Rean, A. A. (1993). Professionalism of pedagogical activity. St. Petersburg.; Rybinsk. – 54 p.

Litvinova, N. P., & Samorukov, V. I. (2015). The experience of recognizing competencies acquired in non-formal and informal education in foreign countries//Modern education. — No. 4. – pp. 17-35.

Makarenko, A. S. (2003). *Pedagogical poem*. ITRK.

Martin, J. (2003). *The Education of John Dewey*. Columbia University Press.

Pankova, N. V., Evdokimov, K. V., & Samorukov, V. I. (2015). *Scientific and methodological support for the development of the system of training, retraining and advanced training of personnel in priority sectors of the economy in the context of Russia's membership in the WTO* [monograph]. St. Petersburg State Technical University.

Samorukov, V. I. (2015) Organizational and pedagogical conditions for managing innovative processes in the educational system//Innovative and information technologies in education: proceedings of the III All- Russian Scientific and Practical Conference. St. Petersburg: Publishing house LEMA, pp. 25-28.

Shale D.G. (2005) Toward a reconception of distance education//The American Journal of Distance Education. No. 5.

Spitsnadel, V. N. (2000). *Fundamentals of system analysis: Textbook. allowance. SPb*. Publishing House. Business Press House.

Subbetto, A. I. (1994). *Systemological foundations of educational systems. Part 2*. Research Center for Quality Problems in Specialist Training.

Ushinsky, K. D. (1990). *Pedagogical works: In 6 volumes* (Vol. 1). Pedagogika.

Zinchenko, V. P. (2002). Psychological foundations of pedagogy (Psychological and pedagogical foundations of building a system of developing learning by D.B. Elkonin – V. V. Davydov). – M. – 431 p.

Chapter 10
Robotic Process Automation (RPA) in HR Operations

Natalia Khazieva
https://orcid.org/0000-0002-8726-6842
HSE University, Russia

Andrei Ternikov
https://orcid.org/0000-0003-2354-0109
HSE University, Russia

ABSTRACT

This chapter delves into the transformative impact of Robotic Process Automation (RPA) in Human Resources (HR) operations, illustrating how digital transformation is essential for maintaining competitiveness in contemporary business environments. Despite the proven benefits of RPA in other sectors, its integration in HR remains limited but promising. The chapter discusses the significant role of RPA and HR in optimizing organizational performance through enhanced data utilization and automation. It highlights how AI-driven data analytics can provide actionable insights into employee performance and decision-making processes. The chapter identifies challenges in adopting RPA and proposes solutions to transform HR departments to make them more effective. Key areas for RPA application in HR include recruitment, onboarding, data management, payroll, and compliance. The overarching theme is that RPA can significantly automate routine tasks, provide strategic insights, and enhance overall organizational efficiency, making HR teams more agile and evidence-based.

DOI: 10.4018/979-8-3373-8612-6.ch010

INTRODUCTION

In today's business landscape, companies regard digital transformation as a cornerstone for remaining competitive. According to Li (2022), digitalization has become a global phenomenon, commemorating the Fourth Industrial Revolution. Nevertheless, despite the widespread push toward digitalization, many companies struggle to embrace a new paradigm (Loebbecke & Picot, 2015).

A common strategy in digital transformation is the adoption of various digital technologies to help organisations achieve their goals. These technologies range from big data and robotic process automation (RPA), to other specialised tools and platforms. RPA brings notable benefits to businesses, as it addresses some common issues such as cost reduction, improved quality and faster processes. This trend is particularly relevant in the context of shared service centres (SSCs) and business process outsourcing (BPOs), which cover a wide range of sectors such as finance, supply chain, and human resources (Anagnoste, 2017; 2018). Importantly, these technologies have applications beyond production processes: integrating technology across different departments is a way to achieve better organisational efficiency. Robotic process automation is expected to have an economic impact of almost $6.7 trillion worldwide by the end of 2025, according to a McKinsey analysis on emerging and disruptive technologies. However, the automated process of RPA in human resources (HR) is not well spread as other tools, even though it can improve the daily activities of employees and give them time to develop their skills. Thus, the main objectives are:

- to overview the nature and current position of RPA across countries and industries;
- to identify the ways how Human Resources might be optimize through the RPA;
- to determine the challenges while implementing RPA in HR;
- to distinguish main players of RPA sector and future trends

THE STATE OF ROBOTIC PROCESS AUTOMATION (RPA) IN CURRENT DOMAIN

In the field of human resource management, the integration of artificial intelligence (AI) and HR analytics has emerged as a transformative approach, offering the potential to enhance organisational performance and secure a competitive advantage from the outset by optimising data utilisation (Arora et al., 2021). Data analytics plays a pivotal role in this regard, as it furnishes managers with actionable insights pertaining to employee performance, decision-making processes, and engagement levels. This, in turn, facilitates the dissemination of information in a more efficient manner, in line with the human resources strategy (Bandi et al., 2021). In the healthcare and pharmaceutical sectors, for instance, the convergence of RPA and machine learning has been shown to facilitate the analysis of voluminous data sets, the streamlining of administrative tasks, and the enhancement of service delivery (Bhatnagar, 2020). Despite the significant digitalization initiatives, many companies encounter challenges in adopting a transformative mindset. The integration of workforce analytics, predictive analytics, and the implementation of novel technologies is instrumental in transforming HR departments from cost centres into strategic profit centres. The utilisation of tools enables organisations to leverage data for the purpose of formulating strategic decisions and enhancing outcomes (DiClaudio, 2019). Notwithstanding the challenges associated with digitalization, such impediments have already been identified and solutions devised to rectify these issues. (Fernandez & Gallardo-Gallardo, 2021).

The Fourth Industrial Revolution commands a new understanding of employee engagement through the use of HR analytics frameworks, which in turn leads to increased employee trust and experience in performance management (Gaur, 2020). The data-driven nature of people analytics and its impact on better individual and organisational outcomes is in line with the advancements in HR practices to promote evidence-based decisions (Gupta & Shaikh, 2018). RPA is one of the most popular tools used by organisations during digital transformation, mainly to optimise repetitive but complicated activities. In its embedded version, RPA is a robotic process that takes over the repetitive tasks, thus saving employees' efforts and time while helping them to be more accurate. At the same time, big data analytics offers not only opportunities to effectively manage human capital, but also challenges that need to be addressed to fully reap its benefits (Hamilton & Sodeman, 2020). For example, RPA, together with AI, chatbots and intelligent optical character recognition (IOCR), not only increases the automation of various business processes, but also dramatically increases overall operational efficiency (Ansari et al., 2019).

RPA is a technology that organizations leverage during digital transformation to optimize monotonous but still sophisticated processes (Van Der Aalst et al., 2018). As an integrated robotic system, RPA automates repetitive tasks to help employees work with fewer resources and greater accuracy (Mamede et al., 2023). Van Der Aalst et al. (2018) note that RPA can perform tasks previously completed manually by humans, simulating human activities (Moreira et al., 2023). Many industries implement RPA at varying levels of operation (Moreira et al., 2023). It relies on specialized software that precisely executes repetitive tasks once handled by employees. In addition, RPA can integrate seamlessly with other systems, embedding automated workflows within employees' daily responsibilities (Ribeiro et al., 2021). The RPA market reached a size of $22.79 billion in 2024, and by 2030, it is projected to expand at a 43.9% CAGR, according to Statista. The Precedence Research supports the estimation and expects to grow at a compound annual growth rate (CAGR) of 25.01% from 2025 to 2034, reaching around USD 211.06 billion (Robotic Process Automation Market Size, Share, and Trends 2025 to 2034, n.d.).

Because of variations in market maturity and technology infrastructure, RPA adoption varies greatly among regions (see Figure 1). Due to early adoption in sectors including banking, healthcare, and manufacturing, North America holds a significant market share and leads the worldwide RPA industry. The United States continues to be the biggest contributor in this region owing to its sophisticated IT ecosystem. RPA is expanding quickly in Europe. For predictive decision-making and customer experience optimization, nations like Germany, the UK, and France are utilizing AI-integrated RPA systems. As more nations like China and India undertake digital transformation projects, Asia-Pacific is becoming a major player in the global RPA industry.

Figure 1. Robotic Process Automation Market share, by Region, 2024 (%)

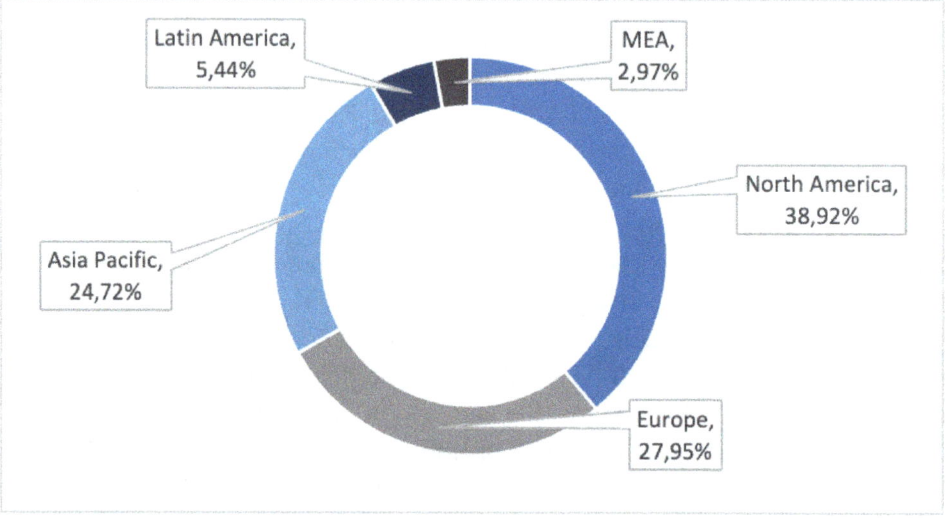

Source: https://www.precedenceresearch.com/robotic-process-automation-market

The growth trajectory of the global RPA market highlights its potential to revolutionize various geographical areas and industries (see Table 1). Top-three industries of RPA implementation based on market revenue are banking, financial services and insurance (BFSI), pharma and healthcare, and manufacturing. BFSI demonstrates the significant growth in terms or revenue from 2022 till 2024 (increase by 66.5%) and the trend will continue. Organizations within each industry use automation to improve efficiency, lower costs, and simplify processes. The requirement for high-volume, repetitive operations like data input, compliance checks, and fraud detection has made the banking and financial services industry a leader in RPA adoption. By automating administrative processes like patient data management, billing, and appointment scheduling, RPA also revolutionizes the healthcare sector. In order to enhance production lines and supply chain management, the manufacturing industry is utilizing RPA for smart factory solutions, integrating bots alongside human labor. RPA is being used more and more in the retail and telecommunications industries to improve customer experiences and expedite backend processes.

Table 1. Global Robotic Automation Market Revenue, by Industry (USD Billion), 2022-2024

Industry	2022	2023	2024
BFSI	5.535	6.778	8.325
Pharma & Healthcare	3.036	3.823	4.827
Manufacturing	2.731	3.384	4.207
Retail & Consumer Goods	1.413	1.726	2.117
Information Technology (IT) & Telecom	1.064	1.297	1.588
Communication and Media & Education	0.408	0.499	0.612
Logistics and Energy & Utilities	0.315	0.381	0.463
Construction	0.158	0.189	0.227

Source: https://www.precedenceresearch.com/robotic-process-automation-market

As the adoption of RPA continues to grow, organisational workflow and employee productivity are coming under increased scrutiny. Productivity is a key metric for assessing the overall performance of an organisation. The digital transformation of organisations is changing the traditional business models, which means that the assessment of productivity is completely different. Therefore, when focusing on employee productivity, two important ideas - effectiveness and efficiency - are the most suitable measurements. Employee effectiveness examines the calibre of work done, while efficiency measures the number of jobs done with the available resources (Hess et al., 2020). Dakhoul (2018) states that the inroads of digital transformation in the form of easier analysis of existing information, faster problem solving and fewer errors have a positive impact on employee productivity. Syed et al. (2020) identified twelve factors affecting both the introduction and continued use of RPA. Among those factors, "Social-technical implementations" and "Comprehensive metrics for benefits" illustrate the importance of employees' and the organization's readiness, as well as the need to alter performance metrics in response to new technology (Syed et al., 2020).

OPTIMIZING HUMAN RESOURCE (HR) BY ROBOTIC PROCESS AUTOMATION (RPA)

One of the famous consulting agencies McKinsey & Company showed that more than half (77%) of HR functions has a potential for automation using proven technologies, meaning an increasing amount of the work done by people will be transferred to bots and various algorithms (Edlich, Ip, & Whiteman, 2018). The efficacy of RPA in Human Resource Management Systems (HRMS) has been demonstrated on numerous occasions when compared to traditional methods, leading to substantial improvements in efficiency and accuracy (Mohamed et al., 2022). Specifically, HR analytics and machine learning have been shown to facilitate the development of predictive models capable of anticipating employee turnover and retention (Pandey & Mehta, 2022). These models, in turn, have been identified as a foundation for proactive workforce management strategies (Leshob et al., 2018). A process-focused analysis of business processes is an effective way of identifying those processes that are most conducive to RPA implementation and thus enhancing HR functions (Leshob et al., 2018). The digital transformation of HR processes with the help of RPA is of particular value to SMEs, thus improving their position in an increasingly digital marketplace (Turcu & Turcu, 2021). The integration of RPA within HR departments, specifically in activities such as candidate screening, payroll processing, and compliance reporting, has been shown to yield numerous advantages, including enhanced operational efficiencies and increased employee satisfaction (Vijai & Mariyappan, 2023).

The rise of HR analytics has been well documented, with bibliometric studies marking the growth and intellectual benefits in the field (Bonilla-Chaves & Palos-Sánchez, 2023). ROI-centred assessments and frameworks stand by the leaders in the use of HR analytics, ensuring that these technologies are adopted according to business objectives, thereby maximising the return on investment (Chalutz Ben-Gal, 2019). In addition, RPA, along with AI and data analytics, is transforming HR functions by automating routine tasks, providing strategic insights, and making HR teams nimbler and more fact-based. Due to the rapid advancement of technology, the organizations that are able to absorb these tools will be more capable of navigating through the challenges of workforce management and maintain distinct competitive advantages (Willcocks, Lacity, & Craig, 2017; Yoon, Han, & Chae, 2024).

In light of these insights, RPA may be integrated in HR in several ways. The main possibilities for RPA in HR are expansive and presented in Figure 2.

Figure 2. Directions of RPA implementation in HR

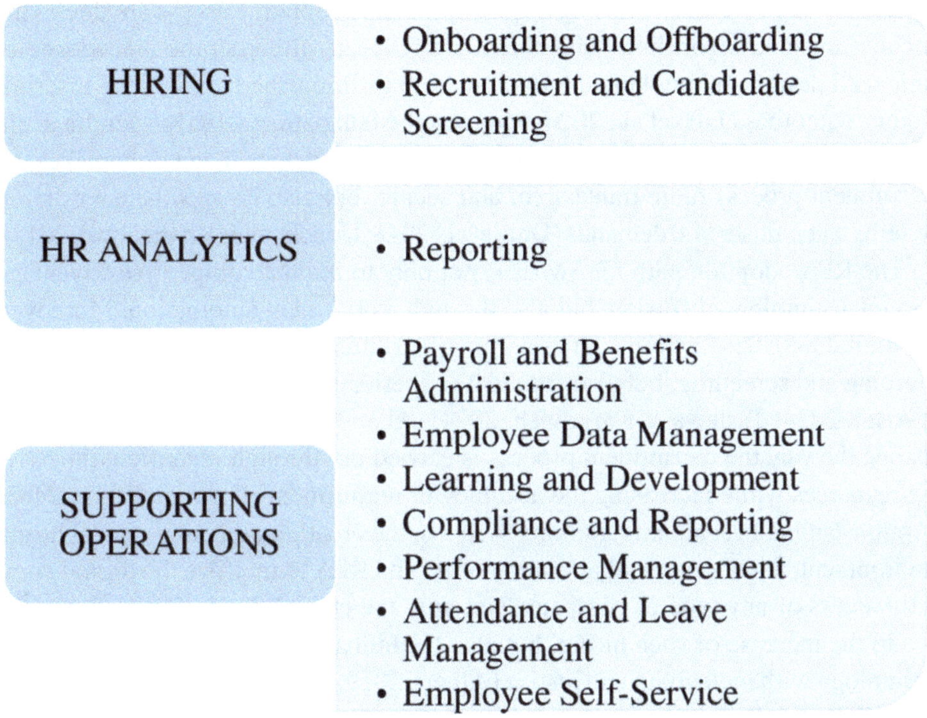

Recruitment and Candidate Screening

AI and RPA have been a great help in changing the whole recruitment and selection process by making the work easier with the help of automation, such as that used in CV screening, candidate matching, etc. AI systems that work with machine learning and natural language processing (NLP) automatically extract, analyse and rank candidate profiles extremely well, leading to shorter time to hire and higher quality of decisions made by recruiters (Azzou & Talei, 2024; Kinge et al., 2022). RPA reduces activities such as CV screening, interview scheduling and candidate communication, thereby increasing the efficiency of recruitment operations (Khatal et al., 2022; Roopesh & Babu, 2021). At the same time, these technologies are making HR departments more strategic and less distracting by taking away administrative tasks (Leong, 2018; Saad et al., 2021).

In addition, the use of integrated artificial intelligence capabilities such as personality mining systems and candidate ranking platforms improve the accuracy of pre-selection and also predict candidate performance, through applications such as

PROSPECT and integrated e-recruitment systems (Faliagka et al., 2012; Singh et al., 2010). The outcomes of using digital systems to support fairness are due to the unconscious and algorithmic biases that are reduced, although the precedence of ethical AI design and implementation is in no way diminished to avoid the discriminatory outcomes (Jafri et al., 2024; Mujtaba & Mahapatra, 2019; Raveendra et al., 2020). Collaboration with new technologies such as blockchain not only makes the recruitment process more transparent and secure, but also creates the data-driven systems that Industry 4.0 demands (Onik et al., 2018; Upadhyay & Khandelwal, 2018).

The RPA adoption path for SMEs is not only to build a competitive advantage through technology diffusion, but also through recruitment automation. Moreover, the digital assistants and machine-learning recruitment systems not only improve sourcing and screening, but also candidate experience and engagement (Balcioğlu & Artar, 2024; Tasheva & Karpovich, 2024). AI and RPA methods fundamentally change the way the recruitment process is carried out through repetition, thus saving resources while increasing the accuracy of recruitment. Their application goes through candidate screening, ranking systems, the creation of a more ethical hiring environment, and also the collaboration of AI and RPA to improve the digital competitiveness of any type of company. Not only the ethical dimension is necessary due to the increase of such hiring, but also the human factor is still the balance of technology with inclusivity and justice (Albert, 2019; Tasheva & Karpovich, 2024).

Dell Technologies Inc. - an American multinational technology company - is a good example of implementing RPA for the recruitment process. Dell Technologies provides businesses with the necessary infrastructure to change IT, safeguard data, and create a digital future. With more than 160,000 workers, the firm develops technologies that advance humankind for customers in over 180 countries. By automating the hiring process, managers are now able to assign recruiters according to job requisitions. A bot was developed to use Workday data, compare it to a matrix of recruiters, and allocate recruiters according to predetermined criteria. Regional or national-level sheets were forwarded to a talent liaison if a match was discovered. Because of this system's mobility, agility, and flexibility, recruiters might be allocated more swiftly and fill vacancies more quickly (Dell Leverages RPA to Boost Enterprise HR Productivity with Workday by up to 85%, 2020).

Onboarding and Offboarding

RPA is a very effective tool that helps automate manual HR processes such as onboarding and offboarding, reducing errors and increasing efficiency, respectively. By automating tasks such as data entry, role assignment, and access provisioning, organisations using RPA technology can spend less time and money, in addition to allowing HR teams to focus on their strategic priorities (Anagnoste, 2017; Mohamed et al., 2022). The characteristics of improved employee onboarding platforms include further employee satisfaction and operational consistency, making RPA a strategic enabler for streamlined HR workflows (Sambare et al., 2022; Biswal et al., 2020).

For instance, Robotic Service Orchestration (RSO) and Smart HR 4.0 (utilising the Internet of Things and AI) have been integrated into RPA to enhance its capabilities. Consequently, the processes of onboarding and offboarding have become more reliable and efficient due to RPA. Such coordination is facilitated by RPA, which enables enhanced interactions between humans and machines (Šimek & Šperka, 2019; Sivathanu & Pillai, 2018). These approaches are not only advantageous for large enterprises, but also for SMEs, as they can achieve digital transformation and maintain competitiveness. For instance, the automation of role allocation and the configuration of the system for onboarding activities can mitigate the risk of new employees experiencing a loss of productivity on their first day, thereby enhancing their readiness (Anjana et al., 2022; Vijai & Mariyappan, 2023). It is evident that as businesses continue to expand the scope of RPA, it will profoundly transform conventional HR practices and enhance employee engagement within the organisation (Madakam et al., 2019; Zaharia-Ruddulescu et al., 2017).

Santander is an example of implementing RPA for the onboarding process. With 3.7 million clients, USD $11.6 billion in assets under management, and 8,200 employees, Santander is one of Argentina's top financial services companies. Its size demands an extensive staff to efficiently deliver all the services that its clients demand, but it was taking six weeks to onboard new employees after hiring them. Among the various duties the bank had to complete for hiring up and running a new person were account setup and IT setup, which involved input from multiple divisions. To solve this issue the digital workers were implemented. They handle the onboarding process immediately when an offer of employment is made. They create accounts, collect the necessary data, notify the appropriate departments automatically, and carry out the requisite compliance checks. Consequently, a procedure that previously took six weeks is now finished in two days (Santander Reduces Time to Onboard Newcomers by 85% with Blue Prism, n.d.).

Employee Data Management

RPA has successfully established itself as the most widely used tool for automating HR functions, particularly the handling of employee data. RPA helps to reduce errors, save time and improve business efficiency by automatically streamlining processes such as adding new employees, managing contracts and extracting data. This radical change, in turn, gives HR the opportunity to focus on more strategic goals by eliminating the need to perform repetitive and manual tasks (Anagnoste, 2017; Mohamed et al., 2022; Vijai & Mariyappan, 2023). Employee onboarding is an area that largely benefits from RPA, with studies showing that speed and accuracy have increased, while resource dependency has decreased and the likelihood of errors has also decreased (Biswal et al., 2020; Anjana et al., 2022). Moreover, the use of artificial intelligence in RPA applications leads to better data-driven decision making, thereby adding further value to HR operations (Nyathani, 2023; Šimek & Šperka, 2019).

RPA is the one that can automate the structured, rule-based processes, which is why it has the greatest impact on employee data management, reducing administrative costs and improving data accuracy. An example of this is the machine learning and RPA systems that have demonstrated not only the successful automation of contract worker management, but also tangible time and labour benefits (Parchande et al., 2019). Furthermore, the orchestration of robotic systems together with human inputs, such as RSO, is one of the factors facilitating the seamless integration of automation into the daily operations of HR (Šimek & Šperka, 2019). These capabilities are also found in small and medium-sized enterprises, where the digital transformation of HR workflows brings significant cost savings and competitive advantages.

RPA is predominantly employed to enhance productivity and operational efficiency within the domain of human resources and human resources employee data management. It accomplishes this by addressing time-consuming manual activities with a high degree of accuracy and expediency. Notwithstanding the de-humanisation and challenges associated with implementation, the application of RPA in onboarding, data management and resource orchestration underscores the transformative potential of automation for HR departments. Subsequent advancements in AI-integrated systems are poised to amplify these benefits, rendering RPA not only a desirable but a compulsory investment for all organisations, irrespective of their size (Madakam et al., 2019; Vijai & Mariyappan, 2023).

Payroll and Benefits Administration

RPA systems have revolutionised the work by freeing up HR departments and payroll and benefits administrators from repetitive tasks. By doing so, RPA not only increases the speed and accuracy of payroll processing, but also does so at a lower cost and with less human error (Anagnoste, 2017; Ansari et al., 2019). Organisations are embracing technology to make the HR department a change agent in the organisation, allowing management to focus on strategic and valuable activities rather than time-consuming manual tasks (Mohamed et al., 2022). Payroll processes where the programme has been used include salary calculations, tax deductions and compliance monitoring, all of which have become very good advanced operational transfers (Aguirre & Rodriguez, 2017; Vijai & Mariyappan, 2023). In addition, RPA has revealed the potential demand for a wider application in HR systems with artificial intelligence and cloud computing to further optimize workflows (Anagnoste, 2018; Willcocks et al., 2017). The fact of their coupling is that RPA has moved from simple execution to more complicated tasks, such as predictive analytics and improvements in workforce management. Although the majority, if not the only, key benefits, some studies have shown that the hurdle of RPA implementation in HR payroll is adapting old processes, securing data and managing employee resistance to automation (Pramod, 2022; Suswaram & Sekhara, 2021).

The crucial changes in its payroll systems were made by BAE Systems plc. BAE Systems plc. is a British multinational aerospace, military and information security company, that is located in London. The company employs 85,000 people in more than 40 countries. Its goods and services include the air, land, and naval sectors, as well as advanced electronics, security, information technology, and support, and it generates £18,400 million in revenue annually. The functions of HR and finance departments of BAE Systems are centralized by the Shared Services Team. This team includes 350 personnel who oversee the back-office operations for hiring and managing the 34,000 UK workers as well as the financial operations that span all business divisions, including expense and accounts payable. One of the first tasks to be automated inside the Shared Services team was payroll. As multiple business divisions joined to form BAE Systems, the Shared Services team absorbed numerous payroll cycles. Because of the processing's limitations, the team was frustrated because only one of the ten payroll clerks could access certain parts of the system to alter information at any moment. The payroll activities are now finished by a bot, which processes all the data files according to a schedule that the payroll team has established and overseen. The bot reports its progress each morning, freeing up the staff to concentrate on more important tasks like ensuring accuracy through data quality checks rather than the tedious process of uploading data. Additionally, this work can be done outside of office hours by using a bot. As a result of the implemented solution, 50 operations have been automated by BAE Systems, resulting in a 7 times faster transfer of payroll data and an annual savings of over 2,600 hours (Customer Story: BAE SYSTEMS, 2020).

Attendance and Leave Management

RPA is an emerging technology that is changing many business and HR functions by automating repetitive and routine tasks. In human resource management, the popularity of RPA is particularly beneficial for attendance and leave management as it promotes speed, accuracy, and efficiency, thereby reducing costs and errors that would occur with traditional manual methods (Ansari et al., 2019; Mohamed et al., 2022). The literature focuses on the area of RPA in facilitating payroll, recruitment and onboarding, which are located in human resources, in addition to attendance tracking, allowing organisations to focus on their strategic tasks (Madakam et al., 2019; Vijai & Mariyappan, 2023). Furthermore, the implementation of RPA in HR has led to the automation of attendance and leave management, among other employee-centric processes, making it an indispensable part of SMEs' digital transformation. This transformation brings benefits by both reducing administrative tasks and improving overall performance (Turcu & Turcu, 2021; Timbadia et al., 2020). RPA models tailored to HR functions have been shown to be more reliable and faster than traditional systems (Suswaram & Sekhara, 2021).

Nevertheless, the implementation of Robotic Process Automation (RPA) necessitates the resolution of issues such as process optimisation, employee training, and the alignment of technological systems with organisational objectives. Furthermore, studies have highlighted the increasing links of RPA with advanced analytics and AI to further enhance its impact on HR systems (Anagnoste, 2018; Willcocks et al., 2017). However, in cases where adoption and implementation difficulties arise, there is a clear need for systematic planning and technological adaptation to ensure the optimal benefits of these technologies can be reaped and their integration into existing human resources frameworks can be accomplished in an uninterruptible manner.

Convestro - a German company producing polyurethane and polycarbonate raw materials - was trying to figure out how to automate a typical HR procedure. Reading doctor-issued sick leave certificates for employees and entering the information into the internal system for sick leave submission is the primary responsibility. It typically takes up to seven minutes to handle each sick leave request by hand. Convestro adopted an AI-enhanced RPA solution for processing 500 sick leave certificates weekly, with 50% of documents going for straight-through processing with 95% accuracy (Covestro Leverages AI & RPA to Streamline Repetitive HR Processes, n.d.).

Performance Management

HR departments monitor the overall performance within the organisation. To provide an overview of employee performance, various KPI's and data are aggregated. RPA software captures actual data and makes reports to manage the employees' performance more efficiently and impartially and suggest the areas for professional development.

RPA in this regard automates performance appraisal processes, providing timely reminders, collecting feedback, and consolidating data. This simplifies the performance management cycle, increases transparency, and enables data-driven decision making for employee development and human resource planning.

Coca-cola company - the world's largest beverage company and one of the most valuable global brands with 130-years history - improved its performance and optimized its audit using RPA. Previously, the HR services unit conducted HR audits exclusively for Coca-Cola Refreshments. However, the organization was tasked with inspecting eight distinct sets of data as the franchising environment changed. Coca-Cola was running reports, having them audited, and investing time in preparing them so that errors and exceptions in the data could be examined. For instance, if there was a discrepancy in the data, it was impossible to analyze it. Now, Coca-Cola's human resources department uses an automation system to conduct HR audits. With more than 50 processes and interacting with numerous people, this automation has significantly reduced time and allowed to pay greater attention to the output data than previously possible. In order to balance the work, Coca-Cola can now deliver reports at different times, allowing them to manually handle exceptions when needed. Reports can be monitored in a management system to ascertain when items were delivered and handled, which was not feasible with the manual procedure. Since the solution was put into practice, it is possible for Coca-Cola to increase productivity by switching from an 8-hour workday to a 24-hour one. This was done without hiring more staff to manage the constantly growing workload. Additionally, current employees are free to concentrate on completing more worthwhile and interesting jobs, all the while improving the client experience (Coca-Cola extends business services capacity and improves performance with RPA, n.d.).

Learning and Development

RPA helps in selection, registration and tracking a study process and learning progress of employees. Based on the level of expertise and request of learning outcomes automation may be used in delivering online training materials. This leads to customized learning experience and targeted personnel development. RPA may also create a training schedule and select an appropriate trainer.

Employee Self-Service

Automation enables the use of employee self-service portals or HR chatbots, allowing employees to access and update their personal information, view payslips, submit leave requests, and obtain HR-related information. It empowers employees and reduces the administrative burden on HR.

Employees may find it inconvenient to report absences or log attendance, particularly if multiple forms must be filled out. RPA solves the problem by using software bots to automatically check absence reports with the times that employees log into the company system. If the information does not match, the bots will notify the employee and remind them to complete the required forms. Furthermore, RPA tools can be outfitted with machine learning-based biometric analysis and picture recognition features to automatically calculate and record clock-in and clock-out times.

Some companies use several tools in their daily activities and face difficulties in matching them. NGA Human Resources has been a top supplier of payroll and HR solutions for nearly 50 years which is based in the UK. They are acknowledged by prominent market watchers as a driving force for HR innovation. The multinational corporation offers incentives to 3 million workers across more than 100 nations. However, the initial automation solution in NGA Human Resources was not producing the desired results because it took a lot of technical expertise and training from the staff to automate procedures. For the urgent and repetitive procedures that took place 24/7, new automation was the ideal answer. The company now efficiently manages operations that affect 1,000 systems. For instance, an extensive employee access termination procedure and a huge volume of password resets are now automated. As a result of the implemented solution, 23 key processes were migrated into the new RPA in 4 months that helped to save 13 000 working hours annually and decrease the number of virtual machines by 50% (NGA HR Discovers Untapped Automation Potential by Switching to Automation Anywhere RPA, 2019).

Compliance and Reporting

HR departments have to provide accurate reports on regular bases that strongly respect the complex and frequently changing rules and norms. RPA software collects data about benefits, expenses, and performance of employees from various internal business systems that helps to minimize the errors in reviews and reports and accelerates operational performance. It can make compliance reports, track license and certification expirations, and ensure consistent HR policies are followed. RPA bots may put data into standard templates, providing the custom reports.

HR Analytics

Automation supports HR analytics. Data is not only collected automatically, but also integrated and analyzed. It provides reports and visual representations that provide insights in HR metrics such as trends in workforce, employee engagement, turnover rates, and others. The decisions are made based on a data-driven approach that is more argumented and proved.

Still, transitioning to digital technologies poses challenges, including training employees on new systems, which can initially diminish productivity (Alsufyani & Gill, 2022). However, Blanka et al. (2022), Guo et al. (2023), and others argue that this decrease is short-lived; following the adaptation and training period, digital tools typically boost both efficiency and effectiveness. In this context, digital technologies become supportive instruments, enabling tasks to be automated, reducing manual errors, increasing data-processing speed, and focusing employee attention on more strategic aspects of their work (Siraj & Hágen, 2023). Digital tools also improve employee effectiveness by facilitating more structured analysis, thereby enhancing decision-making quality (Davis, 1989; Siraj & Hágen, 2023).

MAIN CHALLENGES OF ROBOTIC PROCESS AUTOMATION (RPA) IMPLEMENTATION IN HUMAN RESOURCE (HR)

Despite the fact, the RPA has a great potential for implementation, a lot of RPA projects fail. According to a 2019 EY survey, between 30% and 50% of the initial RPA programs do not turn out as planned. For example, one of the top banks tried to use RPA to automate its customer onboarding procedure. But because of the lack of a comprehensive understanding of the process and poor communication between the business and IT teams, the RPA initiative resulted in inaccurate data entry, unhappy customers, and eventually project termination.

However, some potential issues around RPA in HR may occur in organizations on different stages of RPA implementation. Figure 3 represents the main challenges that the organizations usually face while implementing RPA in HR.

Figure 3. Challenges in implementing RPA in HR

Considering the technology's potential, adoption success may be severely impacted by employee worries about job security and workflow modifications. While some employees may feel fear about their replacement by digital tools, others may be skeptical about modern technologies and whether they can perform their work efficiently and in a short time. The lack of clear communication about the goals and objectives of automation leads to employees avoiding its use. Moreover, due to insufficient training and support from the IT department, employees often prefer to perform their task in a previous manner. HR professionals and employees need time to learn how to use digital tools and adapt to new approaches within their functionalities. Continually, some employees are not ready to change their traditional manual approaches to working processes and refuse to learn and use new.

RPA programs are successfully piloted by many organizations to automate processes, however expanding these initiatives throughout the workplace is a very different challenge. Processes and requirements in different departments may vary within the organization and implementation of any technologies and tools may require significant time. Lack of standardization across departments and infrastructure limitations reduce the number of processes that might automate or limit expansion potential. Additionally, some processes can not be fully automated due to their nature and complexity.

Implementing and running new digital tools may require specialized skills, knowledge and experience in technologies such as RPA, AI, and data analytics. Around 50% of all workers would require reskilling by 2025, according to a 2022 World Economic Forum report, especially in industries where technology and artificial intelligence have a significant impact.

Companies must make sure their RPA systems are scalable to accommodate increasing workload volumes and data flows, and that they have strong security features to prevent new vulnerabilities or compliance gaps from being introduced by their automation efforts. Insider risks via bot access, inadequate encryption of critical data, and unprotected bot credentials and access rights could lead to new issues and raise doubts about the necessity of using RPA. Collected and used data in the automation process is very sensitive because it includes personal information, payroll details and results of performing.

Any AI-driven decision-making tools or algorithms should be checked for compliance fairness and transparency. It might be challenging for certain multinational corporations to standardize their human resources procedures across many international marketplaces. They discovered that different regional compliance standards and older legacy systems made the automation process more difficult.

Despite the enormous cost savings that RPA offers, implementation issues and hidden expenses frequently prevent enterprises from seeing the anticipated returns. Unexpected infrastructure and license costs, longer than anticipated payback periods, unstated maintenance and support charges, etc., could require further expenditures and strain the company's financial stability. The connection between spendings on digital tools and approach and benefits of its implementation is obvious and not direct (Pramod, 2022).

To minimize the number of failures in the process of implementing digital tools such as RPA, companies must approach any changes consciously, as this will affect internal business processes and impact employee engagement and satisfaction. Organizations should analyze current internal processes thoroughly to find inefficiencies, bottlenecks, and areas for improvement before implementing RPA. Any identified issues help to clearly state aims and objectives of RPA implementations. Based on aims and objectives, the organizations may elaborate a solid change management strategy that minimizes resistance by addressing staff concerns, offering training, and emphasizing the advantages of automation. Having a plan makes it easier to gauge success and coordinate teamwork. At the same time, it is highly recommended to start with procedures that strike a balance between complexity and possible outcomes. Organizations should thoroughly test any RPA solution before deploying. Consistent cycles of feedback and communication among stakeholders of the process help avoid expectations that are not in line and test RPA solutions in a variety of scenarios. Staff members should receive the necessary training to operate with implemented tools to reduce errors and boost their RPA confidence.

MAIN PLAYERS OF ROBOTIC PROCESS AUTOMATION (RPA) SECTOR AND FUTURE TRENDS

The number of companies that offer solutions on RPA in various industries and for diverse functions increases each year. Their solutions not only solve the current issues but also aim to vision the future development of tools. A famous American research and advisory agency that focuses on business and technology topics, Gartner, developed the Magic Quadrant for RPA. The suggested quadrant highlights market trends, including direction, maturity, and participants, using exclusive qualitative data analysis techniques. Based on the ability to execute and completeness of vision it distinguishes four places among companies that operate in the RPA industry: challengers, leaders, visionaries and niche players. The "Leaders" quadrant has the greatest composite ratings because of their capacity to execute and comprehensive vision. To promote the adoption of new technologies, the Leaders possess the necessary market share, credibility, and marketing and sales skills. They are also innovators and leading thinkers who have a strong awareness of market needs. They have their operations in all five of the key geographic regions, consistently succeed financially, and offer a wide range of platform support. The "Challengers" are active players in the market and perform well enough to pose a significant risk to the Leaders. Along with having resources to support ongoing growth, they also have great products and a respectable enough market position. Although they are not as large or powerful as Leaders, Challengers are nevertheless financially viable. Although the "Visionaries" produce cutting-edge solutions that tackle significant end-user issues on a large scale from an operational or financial standpoint, they are still struggling to gain crucial market share or achieve long-term profitability. Often privately held, Visionaries are targets for acquisition by larger and well-developed corporations. The "Niche Players" are frequently strictly oriented towards particular vertical or market niches. Some of the companies struggling to develop and implement their vision may also be included in this quadrant, as may companies modifying their current products to enter the market under evaluation. The main players of the industry are presented in Figure 4 (Gartner Magic Quadrant for Robotic ProcessAutomation, 2024):

Figure 4. Main Representatives of Gartner Magic Quadrant for Robotic Process Automation

With $1.2 billion in funding, UiPath is the market leader with an AI-enhanced automation platform; Automation Anywhere has $840 million in funding for cloud-native RPA solutions; Blue Prism has $182 million in funding for enterprise-grade RPA with robust security features; and WorkFusion has $180 million in funding for AI-driven intelligent automation. These numbers highlight the significant investments and financial support that these RPA companies have received, reflecting the increasing significance and uptake of RPA across a range of industries.

Previously mentioned companies are famous and obtain significant market share meaning that they develop and implement new technologies (especially RPA) and the usage of RPA may be spread in different fields including HR operations. With several niche small-scale competitors and well-established large-scale manufacturers providing advanced robotic process automation systems, the industry is extremely competitive. Prominent rivals in the sector are offering advanced solutions that surpass rule-based automation. The major companies are focusing on offering more advanced solutions while specialized competitors with distinct solutions appear to compete in the global market. RPA's future will be characterized by a closer connection with developing technologies such as machine learning and artificial intelligence.

To strengthen their position on the market, some of the key players of the RPA sector actively participate in M&A deals and develop new products. For example, for $180 million, UiPath purchased Cloud Elements, a top API integration platform, at the beginning of 2023. The purpose of this acquisition is to improve UiPath's capacity to integrate RPA with different cloud services and apps. In a $1.3 billion merger, Blue Prism and SS&C Technologies merged in late 2023. By utilizing SS&C's experience, this deal is anticipated to increase Blue Prism's RPA offerings in the financial services industry. Microsoft released Power Automate Desktop in early 2024, democratizing automation by making it accessible to both technical and non-technical users. Automation Anywhere launched AARI 2.0 in mid-2023, an upgraded version of its digital assistant tailored to make automation easier for business users by offering a conversational interface and improved integration capabilities.

With the integration of AI and ML, Cognitive Automation is the next step up from RPA. It allows bots to evaluate unstructured data and generate automatic predictions. For more complicated workflows, cognitive automation gives bots human-like thinking capabilities, in contrast to standard RPA, which depends on rule-based tasks. Optical character recognition and natural language processing are two tools used by cognitive RPA to evaluate large, complicated datasets and extract useful information. Improved decision-making will increase productivity in the financial, healthcare, and other sectors by streamlining processes and minimizing manual involvement. By making RPA more intelligent, flexible, and able to manage complex business processes, cognitive automation is poised to revolutionize the technology.

Instead of automating discrete activities, hyperautomation combines RPA, AI, ML, and process mining to automate whole workflows. Through AI-driven analytics, it facilitates real-time decision-making and enables organizations to function with little assistance from humans. Without requiring significant infrastructure changes, customized solutions increase adaptability, lower costs, and improve efficiency. Cloud-based RPA as a service makes scalable, reasonably priced automation possible, particularly for SMEs. RPAɘs low-code or no-code platforms make it simple for non-technical people to create workflows. Industries are changing as a result of hyperautomation and customized RPA solutions, which increase automation's effect, intelligence, and accessibility.

CONCLUSION

Knowledge-based professional service tasks that don't need human interaction are actively automated by companies using RPA technology. RPA services will continue to be crucial in defining the course of business operations globally due to their rapid growth and wide range of applications in many industries. Ultimately, automation has proven transformative for the HR industry, modernizing how organizations manage their workforce and streamlining day-to-day functions. According to Flobotics, employees who use automation tools have more time to learn more skills, take a new challenging tasks, and deepen relations with customers and stakeholders. When properly implemented, RPA platforms help HR departments become more flexible, efficient, and effective, thus contributing to higher organizational performance. In our fast-evolving digital era, harnessing RPA in HR is necessary to gaining and maintaining a competitive edge. It is crucial for management to have a clear implementation plan and to inspire staff members by demonstrating the benefits of technological advancements in conjunction with prompt training program intervention.

Robotic Process Automation in HR increases productivity significantly, but it also presents serious ethical issues for businesses. Organizations must strike a balance between efficiency, accountability, fairness, and employee well-being in order to guarantee the ethical use of RPA in HR. Maximizing benefits and limiting harm can be achieved through the implementation of ethical principles, bias mitigation methods, and rigorous governance.

REFERENCES

Aguirre, S., & Rodriguez, A. (2017). Automation of a business process using robotic process automation (RPA): A case study. In Applied Computer Sciences in Engineering: 4th Workshop on Engineering Applications, WEA 2017, Cartagena, Colombia, September 27-29, 2017 [Springer International Publishing.]. *Proceedings*, *4*, 65–71.

Albert, E. T. (2019). AI in talent acquisition: A review of AI-applications used in recruitment and selection. *Strategic HR Review*, *18*(5), 215–221.

Alsufyani, N., & Gill, A. Q. (2022). Digitalisation performance assessment: A systematic review. *Technology in Society*, *68*, 101894.

Anagnoste, S. (2017, July). Robotic automation process-the next major revolution in terms of back office operations improvement. In Proceedings of the International Conference on Business Excellence (Vol. 11, No. 1, pp. 676-686). Sciendo.

Anagnoste, S. (2018, March). Robotic automation process–The operating system for the digital enterprise. In Proceedings of the International Conference on Business Excellence (Vol. 12, No. 1, pp. 54-69). Sciendo.

Anjana, S., Bhuvaneswaran, B., Sornashanthi, D., & Vijay, P. (2022). Employee onboarding automation. In *ICT Systems and Sustainability: Proceedings of ICT4SD 2022* (pp. 623–631). Springer Nature Singapore.

Ansari, W. A., Diya, P., Patil, S., & Patil, S. (2019, April). A review on robotic process automation-the future of business organizations. In *2nd International Conference on Advances in Science & Technology (ICAST).*

Arora, M., Prakash, A., Mittal, A., & Singh, S. (2021, December). HR analytics and artificial intelligence-transforming human resource management. In *2021 International Conference on Decision Aid Sciences and Application (DASA)* (pp. 288-293). IEEE.

Azzou, K. B., & Talei, H. (2024, October). A machine learning approach for automated CV data analysis and job profile identification. In *2024 Sixth International Conference on Intelligent Computing in Data Sciences (ICDS)* (pp. 1-7). IEEE.

Balcioğlu, Y. S., & Artar, M. (2024). Artificial intelligence in employee recruitment. *Global Business and Organizational Excellence*, *43*(5), 56–66.

Bandi, G. N. S., Rao, T. S., & Ali, S. S. (2021, January). Data analytics applications for human resource management. In *2021 International Conference on Computer Communication and Informatics (ICCCI)* (pp. 1-5). IEEE.

Bhatnagar, N. (2020). Role of robotic process automation in pharmaceutical industries. In The International Conference on Advanced Machine Learning Technologies and Applications (AMLTA2019) 4 (pp. 497-504). Springer International Publishing.

Biswal, S., Ganesh, A., & Madhavan, P. (2020). Robotic automation of employee onboarding using neural computing. *International Journal of Scientific and Technology Research*, *9*(4), 353–357.

Blanka, C., Krumay, B., & Rueckel, D. (2022). The interplay of digital transformation and employee competency: A design science approach. *Technological Forecasting and Social Change*, *178*, 121575.

Bonilla-Chaves, E. F., & Palos-Sánchez, P. R. (2023). Exploring the evolution of human resource analytics: A bibliometric study. *Behavioral Sciences (Basel, Switzerland)*, *13*(3), 244. PMID: 36975268

Chalutz Ben-Gal, H. (2019). An ROI-based review of HR analytics: Practical implementation tools. *Personnel Review*, *48*(6), 1429–1448.

Coca-Cola extends business services capacity and improves performance with RPA (n.d.). Retrieved from https://www.blueprism.com/uploads/resources/case-studies/blue-prism-cola-case-study.pdf

Covestro Leverages AI & RPA to Streamline Repetitive HR Processes (n.d.). Retrieved from https://www.uipath.com/resources/automation-case-studies/covestro-leverages-ai-to-streamline-repetitive-hr-processes

Customer Story. BAE SYSTEMS. BAE Systems shared services team soars to new performance heights with automation (2020). Retrieved from https://www.automationanywhere.com/resources/customer-stories/bae-systems-scales-processes-with-rpa

Dakhoul, Z. M. (2018). The determinants of employee performance in Jordanian organizations. Journal of Business. *Economics and Finance*, *5*(1), 11–17.

Davis, F. D. (1989). Perceived usefulness, perceived ease of use, and user acceptance of information technology. *Management Information Systems Quarterly*, •••, 319–340.

Dell Leverages RPA to Boost Enterprise HR Productivity with Workday by up to 85% (2020). Retrieved from https://www.automationanywhere.com/sites/default/files/internal-assets/casestudy/casestudy-dell_en.pdf

DiClaudio, M. (2019). People analytics and the rise of HR: How data, analytics and emerging technology can transform human resources (HR) into a profit center. *Strategic HR Review*, *18*(2), 42–46.

Edlich, A., Ip, F., & Whiteman, R. (2018). How bots, algorithms, and artificial intelligence are reshaping the future of corporate support functions. Retrieved from https://www.mckinsey.com/capabilities/mckinsey-digital/our-insights/how-bots-algorithms-and-artificial-intelligence-are-reshaping-the-future-of-corporate-support-functions#/

Faliagka, E., Tsakalidis, A., & Tzimas, G. (2012). An integrated e-recruitment system for automated personality mining and applicant ranking. *Internet Research*, *22*(5), 551–568.

Fernandez, V., & Gallardo-Gallardo, E. (2021). Tackling the HR digitalization challenge: Key factors and barriers to HR analytics adoption. *Competitiveness Review*, *31*(1), 162–187.

Gartner Magic Quadrant for Robotic ProcessAutomation, published at 7 August 2024, https://www.gartner.com/en/documents/5656223

Gaur, B. (2020, July). HR4.0: An analytics framework to redefine employee engagement in the Fourth Industrial Revolution. In 2020 11th International Conference on Computing, Communication and Networking Technologies (ICCCNT) (pp. 1-6). IEEE.

Guo, X., Li, M., Wang, Y., & Mardani, A. (2023). Does digital transformation improve the firm's performance? From the perspective of digitalization paradox and managerial myopia. *Journal of Business Research*, *163*, 113868. DOI: 10.1016/j.jbusres.2023.113868

Gupta, B. N., & Shaikh, M. S. (2018). People analytics: Novel approach to modern human resource management practice. *International Journal of Engineering Technologies and Management Research*, *5*(7), 78–83.

Hamilton, R. H., & Sodeman, W. A. (2020). The questions we ask: Opportunities and challenges for using big data analytics to strategically manage human capital resources. *Business Horizons*, *63*(1), 85–95.

Hess, T., Matt, C., Benlian, A., & Wiesböck, F. (2020). Options for formulating a digital transformation strategy. In *Strategic information management* (pp. 151–173). Routledge.

Jafri, S., Upreti, S., Saiyad, F. B. J., Madhukar, K. S., Chaturvedi, V. M., & Divakaran, P. (2024, March). Effectiveness of artificial intelligence for enhancing decision-making process of recruitment in HRM process. In 2024 IEEE International Conference on Contemporary Computing and Communications (InC4) (Vol. 1, pp. 1-6). IEEE.

Khatal, N., Chaughule, S., & Mangaonkar, N. (2022). Resume screening bot using RPA. In Soft Computing for Security Applications [Springer Singapore.]. *Proceedings of ICSCS, 2021*, 723–732.

Kinge, B., Mandhare, S., Chavan, P., & Chaware, S. M. (2022). Resume screening using machine learning and NLP: A proposed system. International Journal of Scientific Research in Computer Science. *Engineering and Information Technology*, *8*(2), 253–258.

Leong, C. (2018). Technology & recruiting 101: How it works and where it's going. *Strategic HR Review*, *17*(1), 50–52.

Leshob, A., Bourgouin, A., & Renard, L. (2018, October). Towards a process analysis approach to adopt robotic process automation. In 2018 IEEE 15th International Conference on e-Business Engineering (ICEBE) (pp. 46-53). IEEE.

Li, L. (2022). Digital transformation and sustainable performance: The moderating role of market turbulence. *Industrial Marketing Management*, *104*, 28–37. DOI: 10.1016/j.indmarman.2022.04.007

Loebbecke, C., & Picot, A. (2015). Reflections on societal and business model transformation arising from digitization and big data analytics: A research agenda. *The Journal of Strategic Information Systems*, *24*(3), 149–157.

Madakam, S., Holmukhe, R. M., & Jaiswal, D. K. (2019). The future digital work force: Robotic process automation (RPA). *JISTEM-Journal of Information Systems and Technology Management*, *16*, e201916001.

Mamede, H. S., Martins, C. M. G., & Da Silva, M. M. (2023). A lean approach to robotic process automation in banking. *Heliyon*, *9*(7), e18041. DOI: 10.1016/j.heliyon.2023.e18041 PMID: 37501980

Mohamed, S. A., Mahmoud, M. A., Mahdi, M. N., & Mostafa, S. A. (2022). Improving efficiency and effectiveness of robotic process automation in human resource management. *Sustainability*, *14*(7), 3920.

Moreira, S., Mamede, H. S., & Santos, A. (2023). Process automation using RPA–a literature review. *Procedia Computer Science*, *219*, 244–254.

Mujtaba, D. F., & Mahapatra, N. R. (2019, November). Ethical considerations in AI-based recruitment. In *2019 IEEE International Symposium on Technology and Society (ISTAS)* (pp. 1-7). IEEE.

NGA HR Discovers Untapped Automation Potential by Switching to Automation Anywhere RPA. (2019). Retrieved from https://www.automationanywhere.com/resources/asset-library/casestudy-nga-hr

Nyathani, R. (2023). AI-driven HR analytics: Unleashing the power of HR data management. *Journal of Technology and Systems*, *5*(2), 15–26.

Onik, M. M. H., Miraz, M. H., & Kim, C. S. (2018, April). A recruitment and human resource management technique using blockchain technology for Industry 4.0. In Smart Cities Symposium 2018 (pp. 1-6). IET.

Pandey, S., & Mehta, J. (2022, August). HRPA: Human resource prediction analytics. In *2022 Third International Conference on Intelligent Computing Instrumentation and Control Technologies (ICICICT)* (pp. 721-726). IEEE.

Parchande, S., Shahane, A., & Dhore, M. (2019, September). Contractual employee management system using machine learning and robotic process automation. In 2019 5th International Conference on Computing, Communication, Control And Automation (ICCUBEA) (pp. 1-5). IEEE.

Pramod, D. (2022). Robotic process automation for industry: Adoption status, benefits, challenges, and research agenda. *Benchmarking*, *29*(5), 1562–1586.

Raveendra, P. V., Satish, Y. M., & Singh, P. (2020). Changing landscape of recruitment industry: A study on the impact of artificial intelligence on eliminating hiring bias from recruitment and selection process. *Journal of Computational and Theoretical Nanoscience*, *17*(9-10), 4404–4407.

Ribeiro, J., Lima, R., Eckhardt, T., & Paiva, S. (2021). Robotic Process Automation and Artificial Intelligence in Industry 4.0 – A Literature review. *Procedia Computer Science*, *181*, 51–58. DOI: 10.1016/j.procs.2021.01.104

Robotic Process Automation Market Size, Share, and Trends 2025 to 2034 (n.d.). Retrieved from https://www.precedenceresearch.com/robotic-process-automation-market

Roopesh, N., & Babu, C. N. (2021, August). Robotic process automation for resume processing system. In *2021 International Conference on Recent Trends on Electronics, Information, Communication & Technology (RTEICT)* (pp. 180-184). IEEE.

Saad, M. F. M., Nugro, A. W. L., Thinakaran, R., & Baijed, M. (2021, December). A review of artificial intelligence-based platform in human resource recruitment process. In 2021 6th IEEE International Conference on Recent Advances and Innovations in Engineering (ICRAIE) (Vol. 6, pp. 1-5). IEEE.

Sambare, S. S., Singh, A., Kriplani, C., Kale, S., & Balkhande, T. (2022, August). Automated platform for onboarding employee. In 2022 6th International Conference on Computing, Communication, Control and Automation (ICCUBEA) (pp. 1-5). IEEE.

Santander Reduces Time to Onboard Newcomers by 85% with Blue Prism (n.d.). Retrieve from https://www.blueprism.com/resources/case-studies/santander-reduces-time-to-onboard-newcomers-by-85-with-blue-prism/

Šimek, D., & Šperka, R. (2019). How robot/human orchestration can help in an HR department: A case study from a pilot implementation. *Organizacija*, *52*(3), 204–217.

Singh, A., Rose, C., Visweswariah, K., Chenthamarakshan, V., & Kambhatla, N. (2010, October). PROSPECT: A system for screening candidates for recruitment. In *Proceedings of the 19th ACM International Conference on Information and Knowledge Management* (pp. 659-668).

Siraj, N., & Hágen, I. (2023). Performance management system and its role for employee performance: Evidence from Ethiopian SMEs. *Heliyon*, *9*(11), e21819. DOI: 10.1016/j.heliyon.2023.e21819 PMID: 38027983

Sivathanu, B., & Pillai, R. (2018). Smart HR 4.0–How Industry 4.0 is disrupting HR. *Human Resource Management International Digest*, *26*(4), 7–11.

Suswaram, S., & Sekhara, S. C. (2021). Study on role of robotics in digitalisation of human resource development: Impact and RPA implementation. International Journal of Creative Research Thoughts (IJCRT, 9(3), 1275-1288.

Syed, R., Suriadi, S., Adams, M., Bandara, W., Leemans, S. J., Ouyang, C., & Reijers, H. A. (2020). Robotic process automation: Contemporary themes and challenges. *Computers in Industry*, *115*, 103162.

Tasheva, Z., & Karpovich, V. (2024). Transformation of recruitment process through implementation of AI solutions. *Journal of Management and Economics*, *4*(02), 12–17.

Timbadia, D. H., Shah, P. J., Sudhanvan, S., & Agrawal, S. (2020, February). Robotic process automation through advance process analysis model. In *2020 International Conference on Inventive Computation Technologies (ICICT)* (pp. 953-959). IEEE.

Turcu, C. E., & Turcu, C. O. (2021). Digital transformation of human resource processes in small and medium sized enterprises using robotic process automation. *International Journal of Advanced Computer Science and Applications*, *12*(12).

Upadhyay, A. K., & Khandelwal, K. (2018). Applying artificial intelligence: Implications for recruitment. *Strategic HR Review*, *17*(5), 255–258.

Van Der Aalst, W. M. P., Bichler, M., & Heinzl, A. (2018). Robotic Process Automation. *Business & Information Systems Engineering*, *60*(4), 269–272. DOI: 10.1007/s12599-018-0542-4

Vijai, C., & Mariyappan, M. (2023). Robotic process automation (RPA) in human resource functions. *Advances in Management*, *2023*(16), 3.

Willcocks, L., Lacity, M., & Craig, A. (2017). Robotic process automation: Strategic transformation lever for global business services? *Journal of Information Technology Teaching Cases*, *7*(1), 17–28.

Yoon, S. W., Han, S. H., & Chae, C. (2024). People analytics and human resource development–Research landscape and future needs based on bibliometrics and scoping review. *Human Resource Development Review*, *23*(1), 30–57.

Zaharia-Rădulescu, A. M., Pricop, C. L., Shuleski, D., & Ioan, A. C. (2017). RPA and the future of workforce. In Proceedings of the 11th International Management Conference. The Role of Management in the Economic Paradigm of the XXIst Century (Vol. 11, No. 1, pp. 384-392).

Chapter 11

Unveiling the Transformative Power of AI in Recruitment

Monica Chaudhary
https://orcid.org/0000-0002-8344-1447
Melbourne Institute of Technology, Sydney, Australia

Kejal Jain
https://orcid.org/0009-0001-0160-2068
S.P. Jain School of Global Management, India

Aditya Narvekar
https://orcid.org/0000-0001-6686-6542
S.P. Jain School of Global Management, India

ABSTRACT

This chapter aims to examine the implications of the increasing influence of artificial intelligence on the recruitment market. This study examined the impact of artificial intelligence on employers and candidates particularly during the different phases of the hiring process. Given modest extent of academic study undertaken thus far, AI has been acknowledged by recruitment specialists as a transformative force in the field of human resources. The primary objective of this research is to propose improvements to recruitment processes in response to the implementation of AI technology. The recruitment landscape has always been influenced by technology which has resulted in cost reduction and improved effectiveness in candidate selection. The implementation of artificial intelligence presents the potential to obtain substantial

DOI: 10.4018/979-8-3373-8612-6.ch011

enhancements. According to bullhorn, the first enhancements are expected to impact the acquisition and evaluation of potential candidates through the only faces of the recruitment process.

INTRODUCTION

This Chapter looks at artificial intelligence on the significant role it is anticipated to play in the recruitment sector. Specifically analysing how the arrival of artificial intelligence will affect businesses and candidates for employment throughout the recruitment process. This encompasses the entire process starting from the first job advertising followed by the applicant search and concluding with the interviews and evaluation of candidates. The objective of this is to define the recommended approach for recruiters, both in house and consultancies, to make hairs following the inevitable changes in the industry that will be seen. This study concludes that a novel and recommended recruitment approach should be adhered to. The method necessitates substantial structural and technological modifications and recruitment procedures, empower teams to optimise the efficiency and efficacy of their talent acquisition initiatives. The standardised procedure of recruiting for vacancies should be inverted from a trial and error approach to a test for success model.

The recruiting sector has a notable challenge: the conventional hiring procedure which relies on CVS and interviews has been deemed unsuccessful. In order to address this risk, some organizations have implemented pre employment tests that require candidates to respond to a predetermined set of questions. These assessments are both reliable (constant across multiple administrations) and valid (accurately measuring work performance). However, they are excessively time consuming for candidates and consequently lead to lower completion rates due to the effort required to complete them. Consequently, organisations are missing out on highly skilled individuals in the market. This elucidates the reason why talent acquisition has been emphasised as the 3rd most significant obstacle that forms encounter with 81% of 10,000 participants indicating that it was either important or extremely important. According to Schwartz et al (2017), the analysis indicates that recruiting is currently in the initial phases of a revolution driven by technology. LinkedIn research on the global recruitment trends (2017) supports the claim that the biggest obstacle faced by recruiters is the intense competition for talent (57%).

The use of technology has consistently allowed recruiters to efficiently handle a large number of candidates and provide the superior more efficient service to both job searchers and companies. Artificial intelligence is anticipated to have the same effect. Do you recognition that AI has the potential to significantly impact HR implies that it may have both beneficial and detrimental consequences. The recruitment sector underwent significant transformation with the advent of the Internet specifically the worldwide web. This innovation enabled the implementation of global e recruitment techniques resulting in a widespread search in job applications. Company started gathering diverse data from personal sources like social media a practice that was not always welcomed by applicants who preferred to maintain a clear distinction between their professional and personal lives. The notion of artificial intelligence has existed for several decades, but it was only lately transitioned into a tangible reality. IBM's Watson and similar AI systems have demonstrated the capacity to challenge human cognitive abilities showcasing the potential of artificial intelligence to the public. The advancements in AI technologies have now entered a phase of rapid progress significantly influencing various industries by providing support and potentially substituting a range of tasks that require both physical and mental abilities (Ghouse & Chaudhary, 2024). They allow companies to eliminate repetitive and error prone tasks caused by ambiguity. Without data none of this would have been achievable. From 2013-2015 the amount of data generated surpassed the cumulative data created by the whole human population. Artificial intelligence encompasses various sub disciplines with machine learning being one of them. Machine learning involves analysing data sets and deriving insights by identifying patterns based on past behaviour. In recent times deep learning has replaced machine learning as it provides untrained intuition enabling the identification of patterns without explicit guidance from a human coder. This offers the chance to explode novel and thrilling alternatives and approaches in diverse range of jobs and decision-making processes. According to Matt Fisher the chief technology officer of bull horn, certain operations in the recruitment sector such as finding and evaluating candidates are expected to be automated in the near future.

From 2013-2015 the amount of data generated surpassed the cumulative data created by the whole human population. Machine learning is one of the many subdisciplines that make up artificial intelligence. Through the analysis of data sets and the identification of patterns based on historical behaviour, machine learning generates insights. Deep learning has supplanted machine learning in recent times because it offers untrained intuition that makes pattern recognition possible without the need for explicit direction from a human programmer. This is an opportunity to explore innovative and exciting options and strategies in a variety of roles and decision-making scenarios. Bullhorn's chief technology officer, Matt Fisher, predicts that in the near future, some recruitment-related tasks, like locating and assessing prospects, will be automated.

LITERATURE REVIEW

There is currently a dearth of academic research on the potential impact of AI on recruitment. New perspectives on the subject are produced via integrative reviews (Saunders et al., 2016). To increase the body of literature, academic and professional works have both been used. First, because AI is a rapidly evolving field, scholarly research has not kept up. Academics rarely study HR, thus professional reports are preferable.

Analysis was used to examine these sources qualitatively. The literature on AI's effects on hiring, specifically for candidates and employers, provided the inspiration for these themes.

These are the following:

1. Dangers and Boundaries
2. Inclusion and Bias
3. Difficulties and Possibilities

Risks and Limits

Raviprolu (2017) directly considers the role of AI in Human Resources (HR) and acknowledges that there are several barriers to adoption at this stage. First, AI requires a lot of accurate, complex data to understand candidate psychology. Without data, Yano (2017) says AI is useless. Campolo et al. (2017) warned that corporations may train AI programs with cheaper, non-representative, and less reliable data sets as data sets become more protected. Bafaro et al. (2017) further suggests that an ML program may need years of succession data to determine success variables, assuming reliable data. Wishkirchen et al. (2017) endorse AI in recruitment but acknowledge that even the most advanced AI technology can make blunders. GDPR is another data challenge, and 80% of recruitment organizations are not compliant, which will hurt the market (Chaker, 2018). However, IBM (2016) stated that AI's benefits outweigh its hazards. Raviprolu (2017) similarly argues AI has not yet developed robust communication abilities. Tandon et al. (2017) agrees that AI will not fully automate the process.

Okolie et al. (2017) deemed E-recruiting the last recruiting technology revolution. E-Recruitment first discriminated against non-internet users and impersonalized the process on both sides, according to the research. Human Capital Management (HCM) elements Schwartz et al. (2017) ranked ‘Robotics, Cognitive Computing and AI’ last (40%) and Talent Acquisition third (81%). AI is still developing in the HR market, and the workplace is trying to catch up (Francis et al., 2017). This is why recruitment and new technologies are disconnected. According to Frey et al.

(2013), AI could duplicate the human decision-making process, however Parnas (2017) warns that this could lead to untrustworthy and hazardous algorithms.

38% of organizations are currently utilizing AI in the workplace, and 62% anticipate that they will begin to do so in the near future, according to a recent study. According to the Deloitte report, 33% of employees anticipate that AI will be implemented in their workplaces in the near future. It would be more convenient for personnel to allocate more time to innovation and creativity if repetitive tasks could be facilitated by digital systems and automated software. IBM is interested in the implementation of an AI system that will address the most critical concerns for new employees, thereby enhancing their productivity. Statistically, an AI system can learn and anticipate certain potential outcomes, and subsequently make decisions based on a variety of criteria. AI can be incorporated with EI (Emotional Intelligence), in which a variety of robots utilize automated learning, reasoning, and structural programming capabilities to identify the emotions and feelings of humans. The information provided by these machines is also used to guide, direct, think, behave, and regulate emotions in accordance with the dynamic environment that is constantly changing. These contemporary systems are capable of digitally assisting and collaborating with humans to enable users to make logical and rational decisions. Routine duties are being replaced by AI automation, which requires minimal human intervention.AI assists in the screening of CVs, the creation of automated messaging, and the verification of references and backgrounds.

By 2025, it is anticipated that the global market for human resource management will exceed $30 billion. Technology advancements, artificial intelligence, and machine learning in HR functions are allowing professionals to execute traditional practices in a more efficient and straightforward manner. Many HR professionals are considering investments in automation processes, such as predictive analysis and artificial intelligence, over the next two years. The organization's onboarding process is facilitated by the time spent by the human resources in sifting CVs from thousands of applications on online portals for new employees. This process is non-biased and assists in the identification of technically qualified candidates for positions.

The traditional face-to-face interview has been replaced, migrated, or re-considered by video screening interviews as a result of the advancement of multimedia technology, including video capturing and audio recording features. AI-based platforms, such as Adnexio, X0PA AI, HireVue, Manatal, Harver, and Entelo, offer video screening interviews that incorporate facial recognition systems, vocal pattern analysis, and word choice analysis. Sree and Geetha have demonstrated that AI-based platforms are crucial for the selection of job candidates and the scheduling of job interviews.

Among the other AI features that can be leveraged in the recruitment process are the latest technology with intelligent algorithms for sentiment analysis and psychometrics, as featured in the X0PA AI platform. Additionally, an AI-based platform may facilitate engagement, re-building, and onboarding-related duties, thereby enhancing the employer's brand and reputation. Additionally, Sriram and Gandhi have proposed that an AI-based platform can be beneficial to HR management functions in the preparation and organization of job descriptions, specifications, job applicants, onboarding, learning and development, and compensation mapping for new employees.

E-recruitment is one of the most prevalent non-traditional recruitment methods for identifying and attracting potential job candidates, as per Dhamija (2012). Organizations opted to utilize online recruitment due to its expedited, cost-effective, and expedient process of identifying potential job candidates. The potential for discrimination between active internet users and non-internet users is a noteworthy drawback of online recruitment (Dhamija, 2012). It is crucial to consider the extensive scope of technological advancements in HRM, in addition to the numerous benefits that online recruitment offers. In addition to electronic job application forms, online recruitment encompasses a variety of recruitment components, including the announcement of available job positions on the Internet, the receipt of job applications online, and the utilization of various electronic recruitment tools. Recruitment banks and robots that scan online applications are among the electronic instruments (Panayotopoulou, Vakola, & Galanaki, 2007).

One of the most remarkable trends among recruitment professionals in 2018 was the implementation of AI in HRM, as per Upadhyay and Khandelwal (2018). Stuart and Norvig (2016) define information extraction as the process of collecting information and knowledge by scanning a text. Specifically, AI can be employed in the recruitment of new employees by employing information extraction techniques that automate the process of resume scanning and the extraction of pertinent information (Kaczmarek, Kowalkiewicz & Piskorski, 2005). In order to expedite the recruiting process, automated systems that rank job candidates have been introduced due to the surge in the number of job applications, which has the potential to overwhelm HR departments. The utilization of AI to develop applicant ranking systems can enhance the efficiency of recruiters' evaluation tasks, as the HR department typically conducts the evaluation of the received job applications manually (Faliagka, Ramantas, Tsakalidis & Tzimas, 2012). The candidate ranking system is powered by AI algorithms and human recruiters who provide training data to the AI algorithms, which enables them to learn the scoring function of applicants (Faliagka et al. 2012). Upadhyay and Khandelwal (2018) introduce chatbots, which are AI-driven recruitment assistants that facilitate personal and up-to-date connections with candidates through emails, text messages, or dialogue boxes. A variety of computer-supported job matchmaking techniques have been devised to alleviate the workload of recruiters. Software that classifies resumes is an example of such techniques, which can be implemented through the use of learning-based techniques and algorithms (Montuschi, Gatteschi, Lamberti, Sanna, & Demartini, 2014).

Despite the fact that there are studies that suggest that HRM is more efficient and accurate as a result of new technology and big data (Zang & Ye, 2015), there are those who believe that human resource analytics may only be a transient trend if the technology transformation fails to become a permanent component of management decision-making (Rasmussen & Ulrich, 2015). Personal privacy and the manner in which data is processed and analyzed are among the numerous obstacles that AI-based recruitment presents. This issue affects both HR professionals and online HRM users in terms of data analysis and the sharing of personal information (Bondarouk & Brewster, 2016). According to Martincevic and Kozina (2018), it is nearly impossible for organizations to function effectively without some degree of adaptation to new technologies. Organizations' market competitiveness is significantly influenced by their capacity to integrate new technology. Martincevic and Kozina (2018) have demonstrated that the implementation of new technology results in numerous advantages with regard to enhanced performance.

Bias, Inclusion

Campolo et al. (2017) analyzes AI's social and economic impacts and warns that ML programs employing existing data to make judgments could perpetuate cultural and gender-based discrimination. However, Wishkirchen et al. (2017) argue that AI will eliminate prejudice in recruitment by focusing on facts rather than emotions and sympathies. According to Randstad (2018), 70% of HR and recruitment departments say technology improves hiring decisions. Video analysis systems assist eliminate unconscious biases and increase diversity and inclusion by making judgments based on facts rather than opinion (Poitevin et al., 2017 & PwC, 2017). Bafaro et al. (2017) say data analytics techniques improve candidate decision-making and predictions.

Florentine (2016) demonstrated AI algorithm discrimination. An AI, machine learning algorithm that found that American Football quarterbacks had a statistical relationship with high sales performance based on mental skills, decision making, and leadership could eliminate all females from the process because they cannot play in the NFL. The report suggests humans may miss subtleties.

Technicalities and Chances

King et al. (2017) discusses AI's economic influence and capabilities. Deep Learning affects object recognition, NLP, and machine vision, according to King et al. (2017). Machines can digest data faster and find patterns in vast data sets that humans cannot. LeCun et al. (2015) emphasizes NLP's importance in Deep Learning. Deep Learning eats data in the environment programmers expose it to, and with large data available, it grows quicker than before. Frey et al. (2013) discuss the advances in 'Affective Computing' theories, which merge human social intelligence into technology. This allows real-time social tasks like negotiation, persuasion, and care, which is why over 85% of AI recruitment survey respondents believe assessment centres, interview scheduling, sourcing candidates, and on-boarding new employees could be automated (Pröhm et al., 2017). Recruitment firms and leadership are fundamentally adjusting their processes to meet the acceleration in AI capabilities (Chitkara et al., 2017 & CognitionX, 2017) to get a competitive advantage from first movers.

Frey et al. (2013) say AI is "spreading to domains commonly defined as non-routine" (p.17). The report also distinguishes cognitive and manual tasks and routine and non-routine responsibilities. Big data allows programs to perform cognitive tasks. Raviprolu (2017) expects that AI would save recruitment agencies time and money by providing more accurate candidate and company requirements analysis.

Okolie et al. (2017) reported lower expenses, more applicants, better candidate matching, a simpler application procedure, a wide variety of job options, and a higher employer feedback rate. Randstad (2018) estimates that poor hiring decisions cost $1.6 million per 1000 hires. Efficiency is one of two reasons Bullhorn (2018) suggests automating recruitment processes. The second objective is enhancing candidate engagement, which they say chatbots are best for. Based on their duties, recruiters spend 33% to 60% of their day sourcing and vetting applicants (de Lara et al., 2018; CognitionX, 2017). If AI removes this load (HRPA, 2017), hiring candidates might cost 71% less and recruiters could be three times more efficient (CognitionX, 2017). Faliagka et al. (2012) agree, adding that AI will speed up hiring and help recruiters rank candidates. AI is proposed as a way for recruiters to improve candidate experience despite the industry's administrative burden (May, 2016).

CONCEPTUAL FRAMEWORK

The literature review reveals 3 prominent themes that can be classified as risks and limitations, Bias and inclusion and technicalities and opportunities. The topic of bias and inclusion could be categorised and either risks and limitations or technicalities and opportunities. Nevertheless, this specific sector is a highly disputed domain in literature with an equitable distribution of both favorable and unfavorable viewpoints. Consequently, it has been allocated as a distinct subject.

The intricacies of artificial intelligence seem to be thoroughly documented in scholarly literature that specifically focuses on AI. Consequently, any primary study conducted will give minimal attention to the technical aspects of the technology and instead prioritise its applicability, potential benefits, and value in the recruitment process. The remaining categories will thus be the primary focal points in our research given there is extensive disagreement among academic and professional sources regarding these topics.

A conceptual framework (Figure 1) is developed with the help of literature review and four different theories.

The Technology Acceptance Model (TAM): It is a theoretical framework that examines the factors influencing the acceptance and adoption of technology. The TAM framework, developed by Davis in 1989 (Davis, 1989), can be utilized to comprehend the uptake and acceptance of AI-based recruitment tools by companies and candidates. Key drivers of technology acceptance include perceived utility and perceived ease of use. The adoption of AI in recruiting can be strongly influenced by employers and candidates' perceptions of its ability to improve efficiency and effectiveness, as well as the ease of integrating AI into their operations.

Resource Dependence Theory (RDT): Resource Dependence Theory (RDT) (Pfeffer & Salancik, 1978). examines the reliance of organizations on external resources to meet their requirements. When it comes to AI in recruiting, firms may rely on AI technology to make their hiring procedures more efficient, cut down on expenses, and gain a competitive advantage. Candidates, however, may rely on AI-powered platforms to connect them with appropriate employment prospects and offer valuable information about their career paths.

Social Exchange Theory (SET): Social Exchange Theory (SET) (Homans, 1958) is a theoretical framework that examines social interactions in terms of the exchange of resources and the costs and benefits associated with those exchanges. SET analyzes the connections between persons that are founded on reciprocal advantages. In the realm of AI in recruiting, employers and candidates participate in a social transaction where businesses present employment possibilities and candidates present their skills and knowledge. AI solutions streamline this interaction by pairing individuals with appropriate roles, thereby optimizing the effectiveness of the recruitment process and assuring a more compatible match for both parties.

Human Capital Theory: The theory of human capital (Schultz, 1961) highlights the significance of investing in human resources to improve productivity and organizational success. Within the realm of AI in recruiting, this idea can be utilized to comprehend how AI technologies enhance human abilities, allowing recruiters to concentrate on more valuable duties such as fostering relationships and making strategic decisions. In the same way, job seekers may utilize AI platforms to improve their job search abilities and gain access to possibilities that match their talents and career objectives.

Figure 1. Conceptual Model

RESEARCH OBJECTIVES

The aim of the current study is to explore the forthcoming effects of AI on the recruitment market over the next 5 years with a particular emphasis on how this technology will shape the experience of employers and candidates. Consequently, generating recommendations for a novel recruitment procedure.

There is currently a dearth of academic research on the potential impact of AI on recruitment. New perspectives on the subject are produced via integrative reviews (Saunders et al., 2016). To increase the body of literature, academic and professional works have both been used. First, because AI is a rapidly evolving field, scholarly research has not kept up. Academics rarely study HR, thus professional reports are preferable.

1. To examine the probable influence of artificial intelligence on the employer and candidates separately and determine the favourable and unfavourable consequences for both entities.
2. To observe relevant activities to gather current and focus research on the subject of AI and recruitment with a specific focus on risk and limitations, bias and inclusion, and opportunity.
3. Provide valuable tips to recruiters who are contemplating the integration of AI technology into their current processes empowering readers to make informed assessments on the feasibility of implementing AI in the recruiting process

RESEARCH METHODOLOGY

The first research phase included desk research with document analysis. Several research papers and articles from google scholar, research gate and from other publications were reviewed to get a proper insight on how AI is a developing tool in the process of learning the future of work and people management. Semi-structured interview (which is commonly used in qualitative studies) was used and an Interview guide was formulated and divided into three main topics namely general information, current overview in recruitment practices, and AI in recruitment. An expert was recruited for this interview process, him being an International Human Resources expert (his identity remains anonymous for privacy purposes as asked by the interviewee) and the interview was conducted in an offline setting.

An online survey was also conducted which targeted various employees, people looking for jobs, students and retirees. approach is good. Since this area is still in nascent stage, the sample size is small, primary purpose being to understand what a candidate thinks about the AI and recruitment, an online survey was conducted. The online survey facilitated by Google forms, allowed for a substantial sample size and a data set that was geographically diversified. The survey of 12 questions was designed with the particular purpose of obtaining insights from candidates regarding their perspectives on the job application process. In order to gain a better understanding, inquiries were made on candidates' perspectives on the automation and computerization of the recruitment process. Inquiries were also made regarding the current challenges experienced by candidates. The sample size comprised of 30 candidates using random sampling.

DATA ANALYSIS

Correlation

All the questions have favourable sentiment scores on average (0.22). This implies that the survey was well-received by the participants overall. On the other hand, the sentiment scores for each question vary widely. For instance, the average sentiment score for the question "Would you recommend this company to a friend?" is 0.40, whereas the average sentiment score for the question "Would you be willing to work extra hours for this company?" is -0.14.

The sentiment scores for each respondent are also displayed in the table. This can help you comprehend why a given question has a favourable or negative average sentiment score. For instance, a lot of respondents answered the question "Would you recommend this company to a friend?" a score of 1, which gives it a high sentiment score Figure 1). A small percentage of respondents, meanwhile, gave it a score of -1. All things considered; the data offers insightful information on the attitudes of survey participants. It can be applied to pinpoint both the company's strong points and places for improvement.

Figure 2. Sentiment score

	Age	ployment	stated to a job	employer hinde	company cultu	a decision	tions about tu	rather than	man or a	comber a 1 or 2	for computer	rs you actively dislike
Age	1											
Employment	0.72129112	1										
Have you eve	0.12991877	0.15369134	1									
Would a slow	0.1366341	0.0568717	0.08365704	1								
Is hearing ab	0.15174175	0.24239801	0.1233978	0.22220367	1							
Do you think	0.1854906	0.0772074	0.1761501	0.24314721	0.01668152	1						
Would you re	0.36263249	0.34736852	0.2302717	0.1823263	0.05003519	0.0808232	1					
If the majorit	0.07464286	0.40001181	0.1599557	0.10599803	0.27997858	0.12018017	0.2418964	1				
Would you ra	-0.0442086	0.1104066	0.1546721	0.0772667	0.01855355	0.05994009	0.13483997	0.27436909	1			
Would you ra	0.280351	0.187845	0.291866	-0.095608	0.2094892	0.00927106	0.06256793	0.1599557	0.40214735	1		
Would you ra	0.281351	-0.1984497	0.3186603	0.1560805	0.2094892	0.09271057	0.05256793	0.1699557	0.40214735	0.46178335	1	
Process you :	0.0446756	0.11901126	0.2250809	0.04684984	0.24749428	0.07268804	0.21802331	0.25593953	0.1940285	0.075027	0.40214735	1

Capabilities, Constraints & Obstacles

The impact of AI on recruitment is highly debated. The opinions put forth by the interviewees were very consistent within their respect to domains of expertise. Bradshaw and Hulme, both renowned AI specialists formally advocate for the widespread implementation of artificial intelligence in recruitment across various scenarios. Francis and Doyle highlighted the existing disparity between the capacity and the present condition of the recruitment business which is expected to grow until perceptions are harmonised. Candidates must comprehend the manner in which a computer program enhances fairness and transparency as emphasised by many recruiting professionals. AI powered chat bots can provide feedback to both successful and unsuccessful candidates a task that was previously not feasible in positions that receive a large number of applications (Bullhorn, 2022) .

This has the potential to alter the prevailing negative opinions of candidates. Consensus exists in the study that currently and in the foreseeable future the involvement of a human recruiter is indispensable for hiring middle management a senior management positions (Tandon et al,2017). Those who currently harbour apprehensions towards AI seem to possess just a limited comprehension of the potential and constraints of the technology. The reports findings indicate that the largest obstacle to adaptation at present is closely followed by data quality.

CONCLUSION & RECOMMENDATIONS

In decades, the recruitment procedure has barely changed. Introduction of AI requires modifications to maximise benefits and minimise drawbacks. This research has led to a new recruitment strategy. The augmented intelligence recruitment processes a new approach proposed for inhouse and agency recruiters before each recruitment recommends the level of AI to add at each stage.

Company profile: Reports show that company consideration is low while recruiting. Job descriptions may provide some context in history, but recruiters failed to critically evaluate the organization. This should be prioritised utilising data analytics from the operations database. Additionally essential staff who will engage with the winning applicant should be interviewed in detail. This allows to design a matrix for the role to determine the ideal candidate. The findings through radically changed job descriptions and who to advertise to. To weigh the matrix, consider company ambitions for the future.

Market mapping: The increasing adoption of AI in recruitment is expected to rapidly devalue recruitment agency cv databases. Legal limits on data management and public data protection will further reduce the incentive to reserve larger data collections. Thus, recruiting teams will likely engage considerably in marketing and candidate outreach using targeted ads and chatbots to expand their candidate pool. Intelligent AI chat bots that talk to candidates evaluate their suitability and guide them through the application process will result in more diverse and high-quality applicant pool and higher likelihood of matrices matching between the company and the applicants.

In person: Undoubtedly face to face encounters are valuable regardless of AI. It allows the recruiter and the form to see if the candidate is a good fit as the algorithms predict and it allows the candidate to tour the office and meet their future coworkers. Without interview pressure this lets the candidate act spontaneously. This leads the candidate experience the company culture which should suit them if the algorithm works. This strategy increases applicant acceptance and retention rates by setting realistic expectations for both parties.

AI will revolutionise the entire HR process starting with recruitment. In the next 5 years considerable structural changes will be needed to implement the above recommendations resulting in better hiring results, lower daily costs and the competitive advantage over rival recruitment teams.

REFERENCES

Bafaro, C., Ellsworth, D., Gandhi, S., & Kindig, S. (2017). *The CEO's guide to competing through HR*. McKinsey & Company. https://www.mckinsey.com/capabilities/people-and-organizational-performance/our-insights/the-ceos-guide-to-competing-through-hr (Note: This is the most likely source for the 2017 Bafaro et al. succession-planning reference)

Bondarouk, T., & Brewster, C. (2016). Conceptualising the future of HRM and technology research. *International Journal of Human Resource Management*, *27*(21), 2652–2671. DOI: 10.1080/09585192.2016.1232296

Bullhorn, U. K. (2022, September 16). *Ready to redeploy: Tips to get the most out of your candidate pool*. https://www.bullhorn.com/uk/resources/ready-to-redeploy-tips-to-get-the-most-out-of-your-candidate-pool-2/

Campolo, A., Sanfilippo, M., Whittaker, M., & Crawford, K. (2017). *AI Now 2017 report*. AI Now Institute. https://ainowinstitute.org/AI_Now_2017_Report.pdf

Chaker, M. (2018). *GDPR compliance challenges in recruitment: A market analysis* [Industry report]. (Original source not located; cited in multiple recruitment blogs)

Dhamija, P. (2012). E-recruitment: A roadmap towards e-human resource management. *Research World*, *3*(3), 33–39.

Faliagka, E., Ramantas, K., Tsakalidis, A., & Tzimas, G. (2012). Application of machine learning algorithms to an online recruitment system. In *Proceedings of the International Conference on Internet and Web Applications and Services* (pp. 1033–1039). ACM. https://doi.org/DOI: 10.1145/2345396.2345570

Francis, H., Parkes, C., & Reddington, M. (2017). *The future of HR: Emerging trends in AI adoption* [Report]. Likely a CIPD or similar industry report; exact source not located.

Frey, C. B., & Osborne, M. A. (2013). *The future of employment: How susceptible are jobs to computerisation?* (Oxford Martin School Working Paper). University of Oxford. https://doi.org/DOI: 10.2139/ssrn.2557564

Geetha, R., & Bhanu Sree Reddy, D. (2018). Recruitment through artificial intelligence: A conceptual study. *International Journal of Mechanical Engineering and Technology*, *9*(7), 63–70.

Ghouse, S. M., & Chaudhary, M. (2024). Artificial intelligence (AI) for tourism start-ups. In Kaur, A., & Singh, A. (Eds.), *Innovative technologies for increasing service productivity* (pp. 161–178). IGI Global., DOI: 10.4018/979-8-3693-2297-4.ch010

Homans, G. C. (1958). Social behavior as exchange. *American Journal of Sociology*, *63*(6), 597–606. DOI: 10.1086/222355

IBM. (2016). *Cognitive computing in HR: The benefits outweigh the hazards* [White paper]. IBM Institute for Business Value.

Kaczmarek, T., Kowalkiewicz, M., & Piskorski, J. (2005). Information extraction from CV. In *Proceedings of the 8th International Conference on Business Information Systems (BIS 2005)* (pp. 185–192).

Martincevic, I., & Kozina, G. (2018). The relationship between technological dynamics of new technologies and absorptive capacity of export companies of the Republic of Croatia. *Economic Research-Ekonomska Istraživanja*, *31*(1), 425–448. DOI: 10.1080/1331677X.2018.1431042

Montuschi, P., Gatteschi, V., Lamberti, F., Sanna, A., & Demartini, C. (2014). Job recruitment and job seeking processes: How technology can help. *IT Professional*, *16*(3), 41–49. DOI: 10.1109/MITP.2014.40

Okolie, U. C., & Irabor, I. E. (2017). E-recruiting: Practices, benefits and challenges to job seekers. *International Journal of Advanced Engineering. Management and Education Research*, *3*(1), 1–9.

Panayotopoulou, L., Vakola, M., & Galanaki, E. (2007). E-HR adoption and the role of HRM: Evidence from Greece. *Personnel Review*, *36*(2), 277–294. DOI: 10.1108/00483480710726190

Parnas, D. L. (2017). The real risks of artificial intelligence. *Communications of the ACM*, *60*(10), 29–31. DOI: 10.1145/3128739

Pfeffer, J., & Salancik, G. R. (1978). *The external control of organizations: A resource dependence perspective*. Harper & Row. (Reprinted as Classics of Organization Theory, pp. 521–532)

Rasmussen, T., & Ulrich, D. (2015). Learning from practice: How HR analytics avoids being a management fad. *Organizational Dynamics*, *44*(3), 236–242. DOI: 10.1016/j.orgdyn.2015.05.008

Raviprolu, T. (2017). *The role of AI in human resources: Barriers to adoption*

Schultz, T. W. (1961). Investment in human capital. *The American Economic Review*, *51*(1), 1–17.

Schwartz, J., Liakopoulos, A., Woetzel, J., & Dobbs, R. (2017). *Rewriting the rules for the digital age: 2017 Deloitte global human capital trends*. Deloitte University Press.

Sriram, D., & Gandhi, G. M. (2017). *AI-based platforms for HR management*

Tandon, A., et al. (2017). *AI in recruitment: Limitations to full automation*

Upadhyay, A. K., & Khandelwal, K. (2018). Applying artificial intelligence: Implications for recruitment. *Strategic HR Review*, *17*(5), 255–258. DOI: 10.1108/SHR-07-2018-0051

Yano, Y. (2017). *AI without data: Useless in practice* [Technical report; exact source not located].

Zang, Y., & Ye, M. (2015). Big data and human resource management: Efficiency and accuracy through analytics. *Journal of Management Analytics*, *2*(1), 1–18.

APPENDIX

Expert interview

Q1. Thank you for joining us today. Could you please introduce yourself and your expertise in AI in recruitment?

ANSWER: Of course. I have extensive knowledge of artificial intelligence (AI) and how it applies to hiring. Having worked with a variety of firms for more than ten years, I have direct knowledge of the revolutionary potential of AI to improve recruiting outcomes overall, streamline the recruitment process, and improve candidate experiences.

Q2. What are some key ways in which AI is transforming the recruitment process, both for employers and candidates?

ANSWER: AI is transforming hiring in a lot of ways. AI-powered solutions help companies find, filter, and match candidates more quickly and efficiently. This saves time and money while guaranteeing better hire quality. By concentrating just on the qualifications and performance indicators of candidates, these technologies can also aid in the reduction of prejudice in the hiring process. Furthermore, AI improves the candidate experience by offering tailored interactions, prompt feedback, and smooth communication all along the hiring process, all of which raise candidate satisfaction levels.

Q3. How can employers ensure that AI-driven recruitment processes are fair and unbiased?

ANSWER: It is critical to maintain equity and reduce prejudice in AI-driven hiring procedures. Employers can avoid algorithmic biases during the training phase by using varied datasets. It is also important to regularly audit AI algorithms in order to find and fix any biases that might develop over time. Furthermore, in order to verify AI-driven choices, step in when needed, and uphold responsibility, human oversight is crucial at every stage of the hiring process.

Q4. What challenges do employers face when implementing AI in recruitment, and how can they overcome these challenges?

ANSWER: Concern that AI would eventually replace human recruiters is one of the biggest obstacles. However, rather than taking the place of human skill, AI should be seen as an enhancement tool. Data security and privacy issues present another difficulty, particularly in light of the large amount of sensitive candidate data at stake. Employers can overcome these obstacles by providing adequate training to HR staff members on how to use AI tools, setting explicit policies for data usage and security, and cultivating an environment where candidates feel transparent and trusted when AI is used in the hiring process.

Q5. How can candidates leverage AI in their job search efforts?

ANSWER: There are various ways in which candidates might use AI to improve their job hunt. They can get tailored job recommendations based on their preferences, experience, and skill set by using AI-powered job search sites. AI can also assist applicants in optimizing their web profiles and resumes to increase their visibility to employers and application tracking systems. In order to make their job search more informed and effective, candidates can also interact with AI-powered chatbots to learn more about the corporate culture, job requirements, and application status.

Q6. What advice would you give to employers and candidates looking to embrace AI in recruitment?

ANSWER: My recommendation to businesses would be to systematically approach the implementation of AI in recruiting, beginning with a clear grasp of organizational goals and objectives. Throughout the implementation process, give ethical considerations top priority and make investments in reliable AI tools and technologies that support your recruitment objectives and beliefs. In order to stand out in a crowded job market, candidates should embrace AI as a useful tool in their toolkit and remember to augment AI-driven insights with human networking, research, and communication abilities.

Questionnaire Data Responses

Figure 3. Age

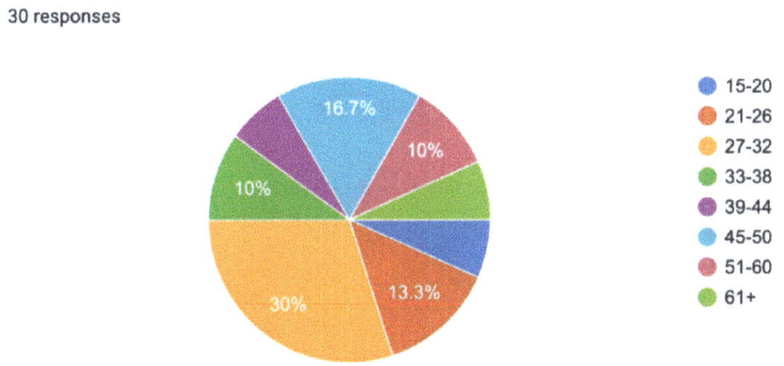

Figure 4. Employment status

30 responses

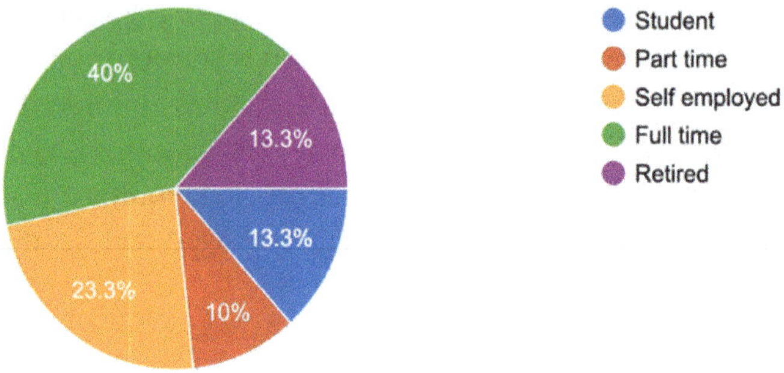

Figure 5. Have you ever applied to a hob and not heard back?

30 responses

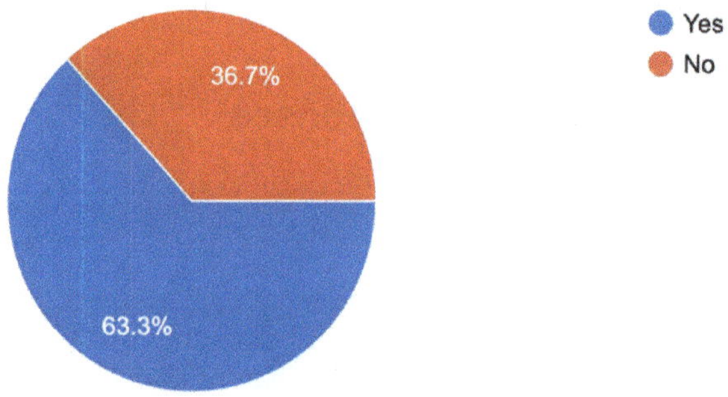

Figure 6. Would a slow reply from your employer hinder your decision on joining them?

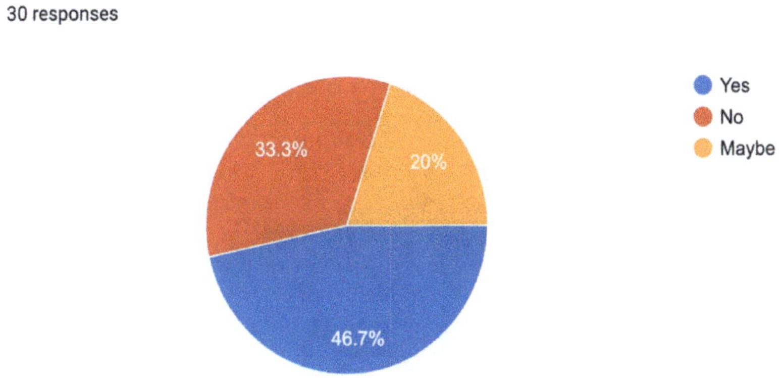

Figure 7. Is hearing about the company culture important to you?

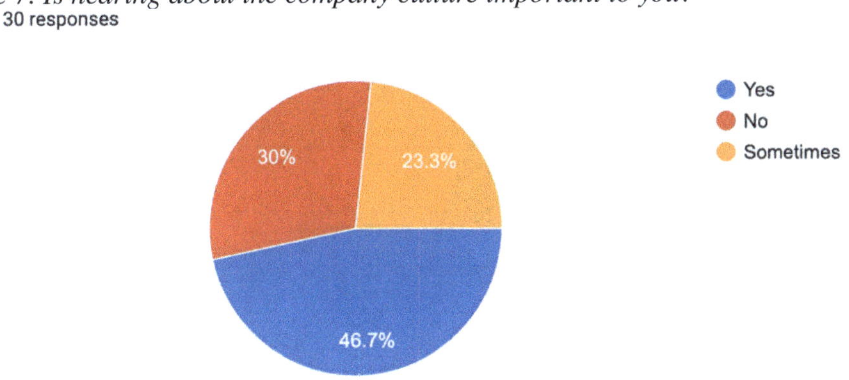

Figure 8. Do you it is fair for a company to make a decision on your suitability based solely on your CV?

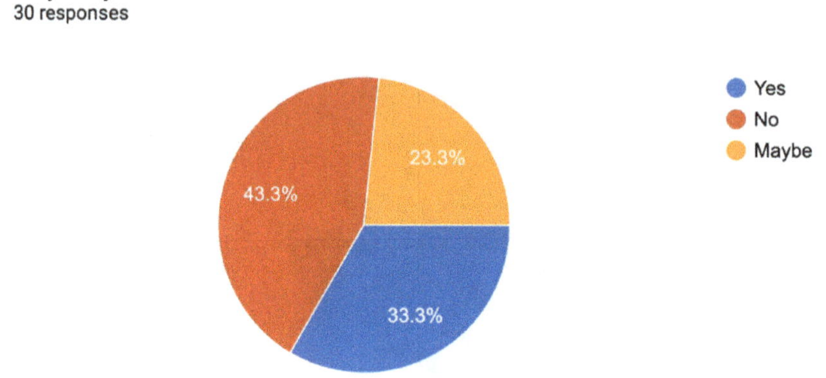

Figure 9. Would you normally ask questions about the company in your interview?

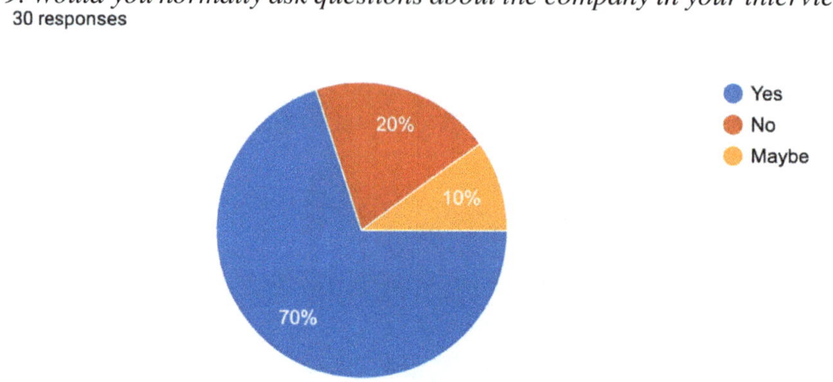

Figure 10. If the majority of an interview was delivered by a computer program instead of a human recruiter, how would it change your perception of the company?

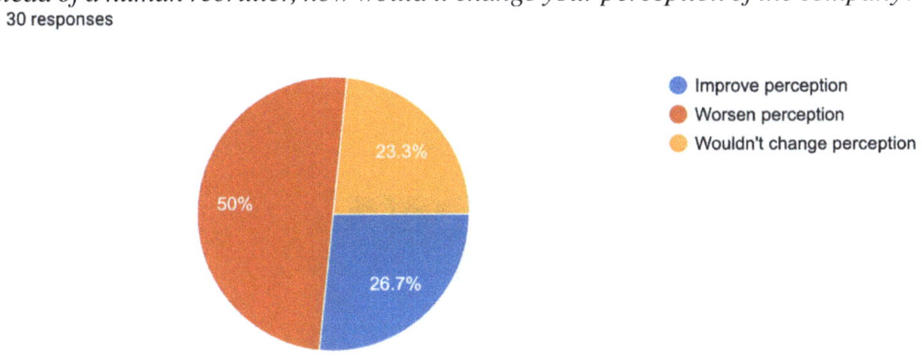

Figure 11. Would you rather a computer or a human look at your CV?

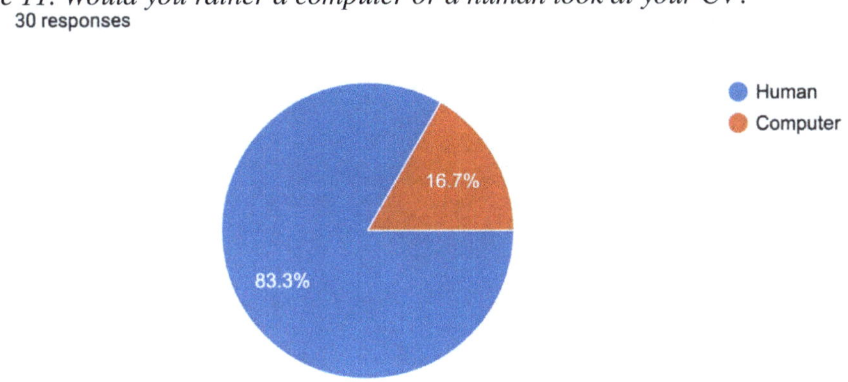

Figure 12. Would your rather a computer or a human interview you?

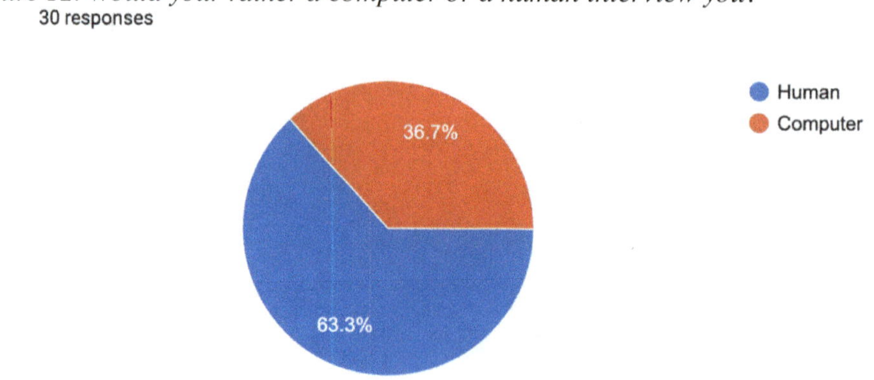

Figure 13. Would you rather a human or a computer negotiate your salary?

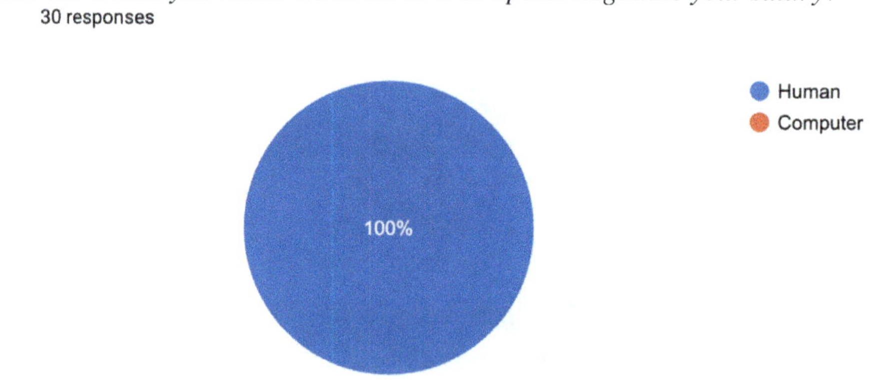

Figure 14. Process you actively dislike

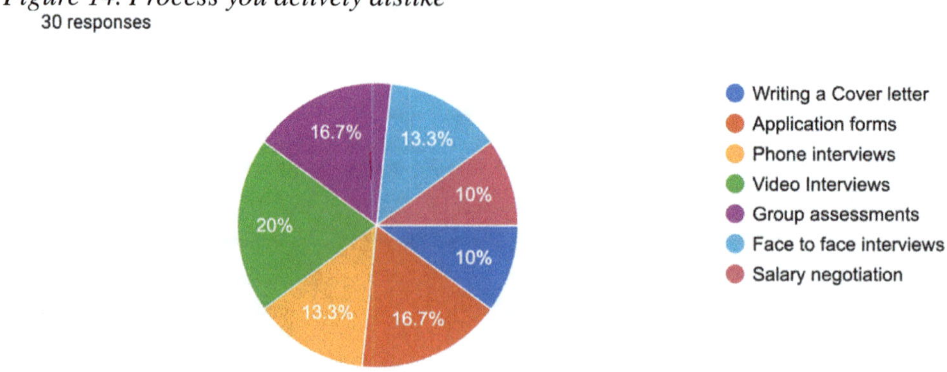

Regression Analysis

Here are some of the key findings:

Multiple R: 0.653 this statistic measures the strength of the relationship between all of the independent variables and the dependent variable. A value of 0.653 indicates a moderate to strong relationship.

R square: 0.236 this statistic measures the proportion of the variance in the dependent variable that is explained by the independent variables. Value of 0.236 indicates that 23.6% of the variance is explained by the model.

Adjusted r square: 1.111 this statistic is an adjusted version of r square that takes into account the number of independent variables in the model. It is often used to compare models with different number of variables. Value of 1.111 is unusual and suggests that that model may be overfitting the data.

Standard error: 1.243 this statistic measures the average distance between the predicted values and the actual values. A lower standard error indicates a better fit.

The ANOVA table shows the results of a test of the alternate hypothesis that there is a relationship between the Independent and dependent variable. The F statistic is 0.677 and the pH value is 0.0417. Since the p value is lesser than 0.05 we reject the null hypothesis. This means that there is a statistically significant relationship between the independent variables and the dependent variable.

The coefficient table shows the estimated coefficients for each of the independent variables. The coefficient for the intercept is 2.770 and the pH value is 0.036. This means that the intercept is statistically significant.

Compilation of References

Abramov, A. (2023). A Neural Network Wrote a Thesis for a Russian Student in One Evening. Teachers are Shocked – How to Check Knowledge now? https://www.msk.kp.ru/daily/27460/4714947/

Aguirre, S., & Rodriguez, A. (2017). Automation of a business process using robotic process automation (RPA): A case study. In Applied Computer Sciences in Engineering: 4th Workshop on Engineering Applications, WEA 2017, Cartagena, Colombia, September 27-29, 2017 [Springer International Publishing.]. *Proceedings*, *4*, 65–71.

Ahmad, S. F., Han, H., Alam, M. M., Rehmat, M. K., Irshad, M., Arraño-Muñoz, M., & Ariza-Montes, A. (2023). Impact of artificial intelligence on human loss in decision making, laziness and safety in education. *Humanities & Social Sciences Communications*, *10*(1), 1–14. DOI: 10.1057/s41599-023-01787-8 PMID: 37325188

Albert, E. T. (2019). AI in talent acquisition: A review of AI-applications used in recruitment and selection. *Strategic HR Review*, *18*(5), 215–221.

Aleshkovsky, I. A., Gasparishvili, A. T., Narbut, N. P., Kruhmaleva, O. V., & Savina, N. E. (2025). Russian Students on the Possibilities and Limitations of Using Artificial Intelligence in Education. *Bulletin of Peoples' Friendship University of Russia. Series. Sociology*, *24*(2), 335–353. DOI: 10.22363/2313-2272-2024-24-2-335-353

Alexandrova, E. (2024). Artificial Intelligence in Education: Good or Bad? *The World of Robotics*. https://roboticsworld.ru/it-ai/iskusstvennyy-intellekt-v-uchebe-blago-ili-zlo/

Ali, F. (2023). GPT-1 to GPT-4: Each of OpenAI's GPT Models Explained and Compared. *MUO*. https://www.makeuseof.com/gpt-models-explained-and-compared/

Alnsour, A. S., Kanaan, O. A., Salah, M., Alfayyad, L., Hijazi, Y., & Alsharif, D. (2024). The impact of implementing AI in recruitment on human resource management efficiency and organizational development effectiveness. Journal of Infrastructure. *Policy and Development*, *8*(8), 6186. DOI: 10.24294/jipd.v8i8.6186

Alsufyani, N., & Gill, A. Q. (2022). Digitalisation performance assessment: A systematic review. *Technology in Society*, *68*, 101894.

Al-Surmi, A., Bashiri, M., & Koliousis, I. (2022). AI based decision making: Combining strategies to improve operational performance. *International Journal of Production Research*, *60*(14), 4464–4486. DOI: 10.1080/00207543.2021.1966540

Aluwala, A. (2023). Optimizing IT Operations with AI-Driven Application Performance Management. *Journal of Artificial Intelligence & Cloud Computing*, *2*(2), 1–6. DOI: 10.47363/JAICC/2023(2)355

Alyushin, M. V., Kolobashkina, L. V., Golov, P. V., & Nikishov, K. S. (2020). Adaptive Behavioral Model of the Electricity Object Management Operator for Intelligent Current Personnel Condition Monitoring Systems. *Advanced Technologies in Robotics and Intelligent Systems.*, (502). Advance online publication. DOI: 10.1007/978-3-030-33491-8_38

Alzoubi, H. M., & Aziz, R. (2021). Does emotional intelligence contribute to quality of strategic decisions? The mediating role of open innovation. *Journal of Open Innovation*, *7*(130). Advance online publication. DOI: 10.3390/joitmc7020130

Amar, S., & Benchouk, K. (2024). The Role of Generative AI in Higher Education: Fostering Teamwork and Interaction as a Virtual Teaching Assistance. In Lahby, M., Maleh, Y., Bucchiarone, A., & Schaeffer, S. E. (Eds.), *General Aspects of Applying Generative AI in Higher Education*. Springer., DOI: 10.1007/978-3-031-65691-0_3

Aminov, K. A., & Lyandau, Yu. V. (2023). Digital transformation of the oil and gas complex as a way to increase the efficiency of production processes in the fuel and energy sector [in Russ.]. *Innovation and investment.*, (1), 258–261.

Anagnoste, S. (2017, July). Robotic automation process-the next major revolution in terms of back office operations improvement. In Proceedings of the International Conference on Business Excellence (Vol. 11, No. 1, pp. 676-686). Sciendo.

Anagnoste, S. (2018, March). Robotic automation process–The operating system for the digital enterprise. In Proceedings of the International Conference on Business Excellence (Vol. 12, No. 1, pp. 54-69). Sciendo.

Anjana, S., Bhuvaneswaran, B., Sornashanthi, D., & Vijay, P. (2022). Employee onboarding automation. In *ICT Systems and Sustainability: Proceedings of ICT4SD 2022* (pp. 623–631). Springer Nature Singapore.

Ansari, W. A., Diya, P., Patil, S., & Patil, S. (2019, April). A review on robotic process automation-the future of business organizations. In *2nd International Conference on Advances in Science & Technology (ICAST).*

Apple has won a major patent relating to real-time Acoustical Ray Tracing that takes Spatial Audio to new dimensions for VR Environments. (2021) https://www.patentlyapple.com

Arora, M., Prakash, A., Mittal, A., & Singh, S. (2021, December). HR analytics and artificial intelligence-transforming human resource management. In *2021 International Conference on Decision Aid Sciences and Application (DASA)* (pp. 288-293). IEEE.

Arora, S. S., Chaudhary, P., & Singh, R. K. (2024). Adoption of HR analytics for future-proof decision making: Role of attitude toward artificial intelligence as a moderator. *The International Journal of Organizational Analysis*. Advance online publication. DOI: 10.1108/ijoa-03-2024-4392

Ashabokov, B. A., Tashilova, A. A., Kesheva, L. A., Teunova, N. V. (2025). Implementation of a neural network model in the Statistica 12 for mudflow frequency forecasting. *Nauka Innovatsii Tekhnologii*. doi: .DOI: 10.37493/2308-4758.2025.1.2

Ashrafuzzaman, M., Prince, K. B., & Rahman, A. (2024). INTEGRATING ARTIFICIAL INTELLIGENCE IN HRM: THE ROLE OF MANAGEMENT INFORMATION SYSTEMS IN ENHANCING DECISION-MAKING PROCESSES. *GLOBAL MAINSTREAM JOURNAL*, *1*(4), 1–16. DOI: 10.62304/ijmisds.v1i04.177

Athanasiou, M. N. (2023). Automation of recruitment: Decision-making system design and review of legal implications.

Audrin, C., & Audrin, B. (2023). More than just emotional intelligence online: Introducing "digital emotional intelligence.". *Frontiers in Psychology*, *14*(1). Advance online publication. DOI: 10.3389/fpsyg.2023.1154355 PMID: 37205063

Audrin, C., & Audrin, B. (2024). Emotional intelligence in digital interactions – A call for renewed assessments. *Personality and Individual Differences*, *223*, 112613. https://doi.org/https://doi.org/10.1016/j.paid.2024.112613

Avdyushkin, V. V. (2023). Digital technologies in education // Pedagogy: current issues of theory and practice. Collection of articles of the III International Scientific and Practical Conference. Penza: Science and Education. pp. 20-22. (in Russ.)

Azzou, K. B., & Talei, H. (2024, October). A machine learning approach for automated CV data analysis and job profile identification. In *2024 Sixth International Conference on Intelligent Computing in Data Sciences (ICDS)* (pp. 1-7). IEEE.

Baabdullah, A. M. (2024). The precursors of AI adoption in business: Towards an efficient decision-making and functional performance. *International Journal of Information Management*, *75*, 102745. DOI: 10.1016/j.ijinfomgt.2023.102745

Badhurunnisa, M., & Dass, V. S. (2023). Challenges and opportunities involved in implementing AI in Workplace. International Journal For Multidisciplinary Research, 5(6).

Bafaro, C., Ellsworth, D., Gandhi, S., & Kindig, S. (2017). *The CEO's guide to competing through HR*. McKinsey & Company. https://www.mckinsey.com/capabilities/people-and-organizational-performance/our-insights/the-ceos-guide-to-competing-through-hr (Note: This is the most likely source for the 2017 Bafaro et al. succession-planning reference)

Bakar, A., Albadry, S. A., Jessika, S., & Sunaryo, J. (2024). Analysis of the Use of Artificial Intelligence (AI) in Human Resources Management (HR): Study at PT Semen Baturaja Persero (SMBR). *Enigma in Economics*, *2*(1), 59–62.

Balcioğlu, Y. S., & Artar, M. (2024). Artificial intelligence in employee recruitment. *Global Business and Organizational Excellence*, *43*(5), 56–66.

Bandi, G. N. S., Rao, T. S., & Ali, S. S. (2021, January). Data analytics applications for human resource management. In *2021 International Conference on Computer Communication and Informatics (ICCCI)* (pp. 1-5). IEEE.

Bankins, S., & Formosa, P. (2023). The ethical implications of artificial intelligence (AI) for meaningful work. *Journal of Business Ethics*, *185*(4), 725–740.

Bano, M., Zowghi, D., Mourão, F., Kaur, S., & Zhang, T. (2024). *Diversity and Inclusion in AI for Recruitment: Lessons from Industry Workshop*. /arxiv.2411.06066DOI: 10.48550

Bansal, G., & Punia, B. K. (2023). Precursors of workplace mindfulness: An exploration & conceptual modelling. In Narwal, K., Bhisnoi, V. K., Bhaker, S. K., & Saini, V. P. (Eds.), *Florilegium: Management theory, research and practices* (pp. 174–184). Arihant Books.

Bansal, G., Punia, B. K., Girdhar, R., & Punia, V. (2025). Mindfulness, Organizational Identification, Work-Life Balance, and Family Support in Female Happiness. In Tran, M. (Ed.), *Harnessing Happiness and Wisdom for Organizational Well-Being* (pp. 427–464). IGI Global Scientific Publishing.

Bansal, S., Agarwal, M., Bansal, D., & Narayanan, S. (2022). *Artificial Intelligence Inroads Into HR*., DOI: 10.4018/978-1-7998-8497-2.ch016

Baratelli, G., & Colleoni, E. (2022). Does Artificial Intelligence (AI) Enabled Recruitment Improve Employer Branding? *International Journal of Business and Management*, *17*(2), 45. DOI: 10.5539/ijbm.v17n2p45

Bar-Gil, O., Ron, T., & Czerniak, O. (2024). AI for the people? Embedding AI ethics in HR and people analytics projects. *Technology in Society*, *77*, 102527. DOI: 10.1016/j.techsoc.2024.102527

Barrett, I. (2024). Human vs. machine: An empirical study of him professionals' perceptions of bias and fairness issues in AI-driven evaluations.

Basnet, S. (2024). The Impact of AI-Driven Predictive Analytics on Employee Retention Strategies. *International Journal of Research and Review*, *11*(9), 50–65. DOI: 10.52403/ijrr.20240906

Basu, S., Majumdar, B., Mukherjee, K., Munjal, S., & Palaksha, C. (2023). Artificial Intelligence–HRM Interactions and Outcomes: A Systematic Review and Causal Configurational Explanation. *Human Resource Management Review*, *33*(1), 100893. DOI: 10.1016/j.hrmr.2022.100893

Bergalieva, A. N., & Keulimzhaeva, A. Zh. (2024) The Influence of Artificial Intelligence on Disease Diagnosis. *Science Bulletin* 12 (81), Vol. 1, 1586–1593. https://www.vestnik-nauki.com/article/19367

Bespalko, V. P., & Tatur, Y. G. (1989). *Systematic and methodological support of the educational process of training specialists*. High School.

Bhalke, V., Satanure, D., Ghabade, P. S., & Vedalankar, A. (2024).. . *AI-Driven Transformation of HR: Enhancing Recruitment, Training, and Employee Retention, 1–5*. Advance online publication. DOI: 10.1109/asiancon62057.2024.10837981

Bharadwaj, V. (2024). Integrating artificial intelligence in human resource management: A comprehensive overview. *Journal of Management*, *11*(3), 71–78. DOI: 10.34218/jom_11_03_006

Bhatnagar, N. (2020). Role of robotic process automation in pharmaceutical industries. In The International Conference on Advanced Machine Learning Technologies and Applications (AMLTA2019) 4 (pp. 497-504). Springer International Publishing.

Bhattacharya, S. (2023b). The Future of HR: Embracing AI for Smarter and More Human Workplaces. [IJSR]. *International Journal of Scientific Research*, *12*(5), 457–459. DOI: 10.21275/SR23423182128

Bhattacharya, S., Bhattacharya, S., Vallabh, V., Marzo, R. R., Juyal, R., & Gokdemir, O. (2023). Digital Well-being Through the Use of Technology-A Perspective. *International Journal of MCH and AIDS*, *12*(1), e588. DOI: 10.21106/ijma.588 PMID: 36683649

Biswal, S., Ganesh, A., & Madhavan, P. (2020). Robotic automation of employee onboarding using neural computing. *International Journal of Scientific and Technology Research*, *9*(4), 353–357.

Biswas, A., & Dutta, P. K. (2021). *Novel Approach of Automation to Risk Management: The Reduction in Human Errors*. EAI/Springer Innovations in Communication and Computing., DOI: 10.1007/978-3-030-49795-8_65

Blanka, C., Krumay, B., & Rueckel, D. (2022). The interplay of digital transformation and employee competency: A design science approach. *Technological Forecasting and Social Change*, *178*, 121575.

Blum, M. L., & Naylor, J. C. (1968). *Industrial psychology: Its theoretical and social foundations*. No Title.

Bobylev, S. N.. (2018). Indicators for digitalization of sustainable development goals in PEEX program. *Geography, Environment, Sustainability*, *11*(1), 145–156. DOI: 10.24057/2071-9388-2018-11-1-145-156

Bodensteiner, W. D. (1970). *Information channel utilization under varying research and development project conditions: an aspect of inter-organizational communication channel usage.*

Boguslavsky, M. V., & Neborsky, E. V. (2023). Methodological approaches to digital transformation of education: risks and solutions // Conceptual framework of pedagogy and education: A collective monograph. Blagoveshchensk: BSPU Publishing. pp. 54-64. (in Russ.)

Bondarouk, T., & Brewster, C. (2016). Conceptualising the future of HRM and technology research. *International Journal of Human Resource Management*, *27*(21), 2652–2671. DOI: 10.1080/09585192.2016.1232296

Bonilla-Chaves, E. F., & Palos-Sánchez, P. R. (2023). Exploring the evolution of human resource analytics: A bibliometric study. *Behavioral Sciences (Basel, Switzerland)*, *13*(3), 244. PMID: 36975268

Bordovskaya, N. V. (2007). *Humanitarian technologies in university educational practice: theory and methodology of design*. Book House.

Borowski, P. F. (2022). *Digital Transformation and Prosumers Activities in the Energy Sector. Intelligent Systems in Digital Transformation*. Springer International Publishing., DOI: 10.1007/978-3-031-16598-6_6

Borzykh A.K. (2001). Universal Self-Learning System from Matchboxes. *Computer Tools in Education*, 90–94.

Bouhsaien, L., & Azmani, A. (2024). The potential of artificial intelligence in human resource management. *Applied Computer Science*, *20*(3), 153–170. DOI: 10.35784/acs-2024-34

Bozkurt, A. (2024). Tell me Your Prompts and I will Make Them True: The Alchemy of Prompt Engineering and Generative AI. *Open Praxis*, *16*(2), 111–118. DOI: 10.55982/openpraxis.16.2.661

Bresler, M., Galiullina, S., & Gerasimova, D. (2020). Transformation of the values of Generation Z-Residents of the digital society of sustainable development. In *E3S Web of Conferences* (Vol. 208, p. 09043). EDP Sciences.

Brien, P. (2022). *Diversity and Inclusion in Artificial Intelligence* (pp. 109–134). T.M.C. Asser Press eBooks. DOI: 10.1007/978-94-6265-523-2_6

Broecke, S. (2023). Artificial intelligence and labour market matching. *OECD Social, Employment and Migration Working Papers*, (284).

Brynjolfsson, E., Li, D., & Raymond, L. (2023). Generative AI at Work. DOI: 10.3386/w31161

Budhwar, P., Chowdhury, S., Wood, G., Aguinis, H., Bamber, G. J., Beltran, J. R., & Varma, A. (2023). Human resource management in the age of generative artificial intelligence: Perspectives and research directions on ChatGPT. *Human Resource Management Journal*, *33*(3), 606–659.

Bullhorn, U. K. (2022, September 16). *Ready to redeploy: Tips to get the most out of your candidate pool*. https://www.bullhorn.com/uk/resources/ready-to-redeploy-tips-to-get-the-most-out-of-your-candidate-pool-2/

Burdett, M. (2023). Proximate and Ultimate Concerns in Christian Ethical Responses to Artificial Intelligence. *Studies in Christian Ethics*, *36*(3), 620–641.

Buyakova, K. I., Dmitriev, Y. A., Ivanova, A. S., Feshchenko, A. V., & Yakovleva, K. I. (2024). The Attitude of Students and Teachers Towards the Use of Tools with Generative Artificial Intelligence in the University. *Education in Science*, *26*(7). Advance online publication. https://cyberleninka.ru/article/n/otnoshenie-studentov-i-prepodavateley-k-ispolzovaniyu-instrumentov-s-generativnym-iskusstvennym-intellektom-v-vuze. DOI: 10.17853/1994-5639-2024-7-160-193

Büyüksomer, A. E., & Tekeoğlu, A. N. T. (2024). Enhancing Marketing Communications with Generative AI: A Systematic Literature Review. *Journal of Industrial Policy and Technology Management*. https://www.jipat.org/index.php/jipat/article/view/188

Cai, F., Zhang, J., & Zhang, L. (2024). The Impact of Artificial Intelligence Replacing Humans in Making Human Resource Management Decisions on Fairness: A Case of Resume Screening. *Sustainability*, *16*(9), 3840. DOI: 10.3390/su16093840

Calderero Hernández, J. F. (2021). Artificial intelligence and spirituality. *International Journal of Interactive Multimedia and Artificial Intelligence*, *7*(1), 34–43.

Campbell, D. T. (1980). Models of experiments in special psychology and applied research/translated from English, edited by M.I. Bobneva, M.: Progress. – 389 p.

Campolo, A., Sanfilippo, M., Whittaker, M., & Crawford, K. (2017). *AI Now 2017 report*. AI Now Institute. https://ainowinstitute.org/AI_Now_2017_Report.pdf

Cao, S., & Li, H. (2023). A Scoping Review of Digital Well-Being in Early Childhood: Definitions, Measurements, Contributors, and Interventions. *International Journal of Environmental Research and Public Health*, *20*(4), 1–20. DOI: 10.3390/ijerph20043510 PMID: 36834204

Capasso, M., Arora, P., Sharma, D., & Tacconi, C. (2024). On the Right to Work in the Age of Artificial Intelligence: Ethical Safeguards in Algorithmic Human Resource Management. *Business and Human Rights Journal*, *9*(3), 346–360. DOI: 10.1017/bhj.2024.26

Carr, N. (2011). *The Shallows: What the Internet Is Doing to Our Brains*. W. W. Norton & Company.

Carroll, J. M. (Ed.). (2002). *Human-Computer Interaction in the New Millennium*. ACM Press.

Caudell Thomas, P., & David, W. Mizell. (1992) Augmented reality: An application of heads-up display technology to manual manufacturing processes. Proceedings of the Twenty-Fifth Hawaii International Conference on. 2. IEEE.

Cavalcante, A. M.. (2021). 5G for remote areas: Challenges, opportunities and business modeling for Brazil. *IEEE Access : Practical Innovations, Open Solutions*, *9*, 10829–10843. DOI: 10.1109/ACCESS.2021.3050742

Cenzharik, M. K., Krylova, Yu. V., & Steshenko, V. I. (2020). Digital transformation of companies: Strategic analysis, influencing factors and models [in Russ.]. *Bulletin of St. Petersburg University. Economy.*, *36*, 390–420. DOI: 10.21638/spbu05.2020.303

Chaker, M. (2018). *GDPR compliance challenges in recruitment: A market analysis* [Industry report]. (Original source not located; cited in multiple recruitment blogs)

Chalutz Ben-Gal, H. (2019). An ROI-based review of HR analytics: Practical implementation tools. *Personnel Review*, *48*(6), 1429–1448.

Chan, C. K. Y., & Hu, W. (2023). Students' Voices on Generative AI: Perceptions, Benefits, and Challenges in Higher Education. *International Journal of Educational Technology in Higher Education, 20*(1). Advance online publication. DOI: 10.1186/s41239-023-00411-8

Chandrasekaran, A. (2024). Gartner Hype CycleTM for Emerging Technologies. Gartner. https://www.gartner.com/en/articles/hype-cycle-for-emerging-technologies

Chandratreya, A. (2024). AI in HR: A Comprehensive Analysis and Framework for Success. INTERANTIONAL JOURNAL OF SCIENTIFIC RESEARCH IN ENGINEERING AND MANAGEMENT, 08(008), 1–11. DOI: 10.55041/IJSREM37020

Chang, X. (2023). Gender Bias in Hiring: An Analysis of the Impact of Amazon's Recruiting Algorithm. Advances in Economics. *Management and Political Sciences, 23*, 134–140.

Charlwood, A., & Guenole, N. (2022). Can HR adapt to the paradoxes of artificial intelligence? *Human Resource Management Journal, 32*(4), 729–742. DOI: 10.1111/1748-8583.12433

Chen, N., Li, Z., & Tang, B. (2022). Can digital skill protect against job displacement risk caused by artificial intelligence? Empirical evidence from 701 detailed occupations. *PLoS One, 17*(11), e0277280. DOI: 10.1371/journal.pone.0277280 PMID: 36346798

Cherbonnier, A., & Michinov, N. (2021). The recognition of emotions beyond facial expressions: Comparing emoticons specifically designed to convey basic emotions with other modes of expression. *Computers in Human Behavior, 118*. Advance online publication. DOI: 10.1016/j.chb.2021.106689

Cherep, A., Voronkova, V., & Androsova, O. (2022). Transformational changes in organizational management and human resources in the digital age. Baltic journal of economic studies, 8(3), 210-219.

Chi, N., Lurie, E., & Mulligan, D. K. (2021, July). Reconfiguring diversity and inclusion for AI ethics. In Proceedings of the 2021 AAAI/ACM Conference on AI, Ethics, and Society (pp. 447-457).

Chichulin, A. (2023). *AI operator*. Guide for the Artificial Intelligence Operator. Publishing Solutions.

Chin, W. W., Gopal, A., & Salisbury, W. D. (1997). Advancing the theory of adaptive structuration: The development of a scale to measure faithfulness of appropriation. *Information Systems Research, 8*(4), 342–367.

Cipresso, P., Giglioli, I., Raya, M. A., & Riva, G. (2018). The Past, Present, and Future of Virtual and Augmented Reality Research: A Network and Cluster Analysis of the Literature. *Frontiers in Psychology*, *9*, 2086. DOI: 10.3389/fpsyg.2018.02086 PMID: 30459681

Clifford Chance. (2024). EU Artificial Intelligence Act: Implications for high-risk AI systems. https://www.cliffordchance.com/content/dam/cliffordchance/briefings/2024/08/what-does-the-eu-ai-act-mean-foremployers.pdf#:~:text=%E2%80%A2%20Strict%20obligations%20for%20AI,intended%20to%20be%20used%20for

Coca-Cola extends business services capacity and improves performance with RPA (n.d.). Retrieved from https://www.blueprism.com/uploads/resources/case-studies/blue-prism-cola-case-study.pdf

Coghill, G. M. (2023). Artificial Intelligence (and Christianity): Who? What? Where? When? Why? and How? *Studies in Christian Ethics*, *36*(3), 604–619.

Covestro Leverages AI & RPA to Streamline Repetitive HR Processes (n.d.). Retrieved from https://www.uipath.com/resources/automation-case-studies/covestro-leverages-ai-to-streamline-repetitive-hr-processes

Cox, G. (1999). The Digital Crowd: Some Questions on Globalization and Agency. *Design Issues*, *15*(1), 16–25.

Customer Story. BAE SYSTEMS. BAE Systems shared services team soars to new performance heights with automation (2020). Retrieved from https://www.automationanywhere.com/resources/customer-stories/bae-systems-scales-processes-with-rpa

D'Cruze, D. (2025). GPT-5 Launch Plan Revealed: All ChatGPT Users to get Free Access, but Plus, Pro Users to get More. *Business Today*. https://www.businesstoday.in/technology/news/story/gpt-5-launch-plan-revealed-all-chatgpt-users-to-get-free-access-but-plus-pro-users-to-get-more-464449-2025-02-13

Daft, R., & Lengel, R. (1983). Information Richness. A New Approach to Managerial Behavior and Organization Design. *Research in Organizational Behavior*, *6*, 73.

Daft, R., & Lengel, R. (1986). Organizational Information Requirements, Media Richness and Structural Design. *Management Science*, *32*, 554–571. DOI: 10.1287/mnsc.32.5.554

Dakhoul, Z. M. (2018). The determinants of employee performance in Jordanian organizations. Journal of Business. *Economics and Finance*, *5*(1), 11–17.

Dane, E., & Pratt, M. G. (2007). Exploring Intuition and its Role in Managerial Decision Making. *Academy of Management Review*, *32*(1), 33–54. DOI: 10.5465/amr.2007.23463682

DĂNILOAIA, D.-F. (2024). EXPLORING THE LANDSCAPE: A LITERATURE REVIEW OF AI'S IMPACT ON HUMAN RESOURCE MANAGEMENT. *European Journal of Public Administration Research*, *3*, 15–22. DOI: 10.47743/ejpar.2024-3-6

Davalos, J., & Yin, L. (2024). Do AI Detectors Work? Students Face False Cheating Accusations. Bloomberg.com. https://www.bloomberg.com/news/features/2024-10-18/do-ai-detectors-work-students-face-false-cheating-accusations

Davide, S., Sciannamè, M., & Ceconello, M. (2024). *User Experience + Artificial Intelligence*. Springer Nature., DOI: 10.1007/978-3-031-77521-5

Davis, F. D. (1989). Perceived usefulness, perceived ease of use, and user acceptance of information technology. *Management Information Systems Quarterly*, •••, 319–340.

De Villiers, C., Farooq, M. B., & Molinari, M. (2022). Qualitative research interviews using online video technology–challenges and opportunities. *Meditari Accountancy Research*, *30*(6), 1764–1782.

Dell Leverages RPA to Boost Enterprise HR Productivity with Workday by up to 85% (2020). Retrieved from https://www.automationanywhere.com/sites/default/files/internal-assets/casestudy/casestudy-dell_en.pdf

Deloitte. (2021). 2021 Global Human Capital Trends: Innovating with digital and human potential (PDF). Deloitte Insights. Retrieved from https://www2.deloitte.com

Deschenes, A., & McMahon, M. (2024). A Survey on Student Use of Generative AI Chatbots for Academic Research. *Evidence Based Library and Information Practice*, *19*(2), 2–22. DOI: 10.18438/eblip30512

Deurzen, E. (2021). Rising from Existential Crisis. Life Beyond Calamity. Monmouth: PCCS Books.

Dhamija, P. (2012). E-recruitment: A roadmap towards e-human resource management. *Research World*, *3*(3), 33–39.

DiClaudio, M. (2019). People analytics and the rise of HR: How data, analytics and emerging technology can transform human resources (HR) into a profit center. *Strategic HR Review*, *18*(2), 42–46.

Dignum, V. (2018). Ethics in artificial intelligence: introduction to the special issue.

Dix, A., Finlay, J., Abowd, G., & Beale, R. (2003). *Human-Computer Interaction* (3rd ed.). Prentice Hall.

Donaldson, T. (2016). Values in Tension. Ethics Away from Home. In *HBR's 10 Must Reads on Managing Across Cultures* (pp. 123–148). Harvard Business School Publishing.

Drewniak, Z., & Posadzinska, I. (2020). Learning and development tools and the innovative potential of artificial intelligence companies.

Dubey, S., & Bedi, S. S. (2024). Workplace spirituality: A systematic review and future research agenda. *Journal of Management, Spirituality & Religion*, *21*(1), 83–128.

Du, J. (2024a). Do Humans Trust AI in HRM? Why Do? Why Not? — Insights from a Decade of Research. *Journal of Research in Social Science and Humanities*, *3*(7), 20–48. DOI: 10.56397/JRSSH.2024.07.04

Du, J. (2024b). Ethical and Legal Challenges of AI in Human Resource Management. *Journal of Computing and Electronic Information Management*, *13*(2), 71–77. DOI: 10.54097/83j64ub9

Du, J. (2024c). Exploring Gender Bias and Algorithm Transparency: Ethical Considerations of AI in HRM. *Journal of Theory and Practice of Management Science*, *4*(03), 36–43. DOI: 10.53469/jtpms.2024.04(03).06

Duke, T., & Giudici, P. (2025). *Responsible AI in Practice: A Practical Guide to Safe and Human AI. Apress eBooks*. Apress., DOI: 10.1007/979-8-8688-1166-1

Dwi, M., & Hidayatullah, A. N. A. (2024). Exploring AI's Role in Supporting Diversity and Inclusion Initiatives in Multicultural Marketplaces. *International Journal of Religion*, *5*(10), 5549–5582. DOI: 10.61707/apmwg008

Dyachkova, M. A., & Tomyuk, O. N. (2017). Social networks as an educational resource. *Pedagogical education in Russia.*, (12), 141–146.

Dzwigol, H.. (2024). Digitalization and energy in attaining sustainable development: Impact on energy consumption, energy structure, and energy intensity. *Energies*, *17*(5). Advance online publication. DOI: 10.3390/en17051213

Edlich, A., Ip, F., & Whiteman, R. (2018). How bots, algorithms, and artificial intelligence are reshaping the future of corporate support functions. Retrieved from https://www.mckinsey.com/capabilities/mckinsey-digital/our-insights/how-bots-algorithms-and-artificial-intelligence-are-reshaping-the-future-of-corporate-support-functions#/

Efremov, A. A., & Kovalev, I. L. (2023). Overview of trends in the digital transformation of agricultural production [in Russ.]. *Agricultural Economics*, (1), 50–57. DOI: 10.29235/1818-9806-2023-1-50-57

Ekman, P. (1992). An argument for basic emotions. *Cognition and Emotion*, *6*(3–4), 169–200. DOI: 10.1080/02699939208411068

El Bouti, M. Y., & Allouch, M. (2020). Analysis of human factors for enhancing safety and security management system in fossil and renewable power plants. *International Journal of Safety and Security Engineering*, *10*(4), 491–500.

Equal Employment Opportunity Commission. (2024, September). EEOC fact sheet: AI for workers. https://www.eeoc.gov/2024-annual-performance-report

Erickson, T., & McDonald, D. W. (2008). *HCI Remixed. Reflections on Works That Have Influenced the HCI Community*. MIT Press.

Estrada, F. J. R., George-Reyes, C. E., & Glasserman-Morales, L. D. (2022). Security as an emerging dimension of Digital Literacy for education: A systematic literature review. *Journal of E-Learning and Knowledge Society*, *18*(2), 22–33. DOI: 10.20368/1971-8829/1135440

Eubanks, B. (2022). *Artificial Intelligence for HR: Use AI to Support and Develop a Successful Workforce* (2nd, illustr ed.). Kogan Page. https://books.google.nl/books?id=NGBuzgEACAAJ

European Commission. (2024). Regulatory Framework on AI *Shaping Europe's digital future*. European Commission. https://digital-strategy.ec.europa.eu/en/policies/regulatory-framework-ai

Faliagka, E., Ramantas, K., Tsakalidis, A., & Tzimas, G. (2012). Application of machine learning algorithms to an online recruitment system. In *Proceedings of the International Conference on Internet and Web Applications and Services* (pp. 1033–1039). ACM. https://doi.org/DOI: 10.1145/2345396.2345570

Faliagka, E., Tsakalidis, A., & Tzimas, G. (2012). An integrated e-recruitment system for automated personality mining and applicant ranking. *Internet Research*, *22*(5), 551–568.

Faqihi, A., & Miah, S. J. (2023). Artificial Intelligence-Driven Talent Management System: Exploring the Risks and Options for Constructing a Theoretical Foundation. *Journal of Risk and Financial Management*, *16*(1), 31. DOI: 10.3390/jrfm16010031

Faqih, M., Sukistini, A. S., Asrianto, A., Siri, A., & Nggandung, Y. (2024). The Impact of AI on Talent Acquisition: Opportunities and Challenges in Modern HR Practices. *Global International Journal of Innovative Research*, *2*(11), 2626–2638. DOI: 10.59613/global.v2i11.365

Fedeshchenko, A. V. (2012). Social networks in education: Analysis of experience and prospects of development. *Humanitarian informatics. Tomsk.*, (6), 124–134.

Felzmann, H., Villaronga, E. F., Lutz, C., & Tamò-Larrieux, A. (2019). Transparency you can trust: Transparency requirements for artificial intelligence between legal norms and contextual concerns. *Big Data & Society*, *6*(1). Advance online publication. DOI: 10.1177/2053951719860542

Fernandez, V., & Gallardo-Gallardo, E. (2021). Tackling the HR digitalization challenge: Key factors and barriers to HR analytics adoption. *Competitiveness Review*, *31*(1), 162–187.

Ferrara, E. (2024). The butterfly effect in artificial intelligence systems: Implications for AI bias and fairness. *Machine Learning with Applications*, *15*, 100525.

Feuerriegel, S., Hartmann, J., Janiesch, C., & Zschech, P. (2023). Generative AI. *Business & Information Systems Engineering*, *66*(1), 111–126. DOI: 10.1007/s12599-023-00834-7

FIROZ, M. (2024). IT in HRM: Enhancing efficiency and employee engagement

Fitts, P. M. (1954). The information capacity of discrete motorresponses. *Journal of Experimental Psychology*, *47*, 381–391. PMID: 13174710

Floridi, L., & Cowls, J. (2019). A Unified Framework of Five Principles for AI in Society. *Harvard Data Science Review*, *1*(1), 2–15. https://doi.org/https:// doi.org/10.1162/99608f92.8cd550d1

Fomude, A. H., Yang, C., Agordzo, G. K., Serwah, A. V., & Abangbila, L. (2023a). AI Model to Improve HR Decision-Making with Machine Learning Predictions Algorithm. 2023 25th International Conference on Advanced Communication Technology (ICACT), 206–212. DOI: 10.23919/ICACT56868.2023.10079282

Fornell, C., & Larcker, D. F. (1981). Evaluating structural equation models with unobservable variables and measurement error. *JMR, Journal of Marketing Research*, *18*(1), 39–50.

Forsgren, N., Durcikova, A., Clay, P. F., & Wang, X. (2016). The Integrated user satisfaction model: Assessing information quality and system quality as second-order constructs in system administration. *Communications of the Association for Information Systems*, *38*, 803–839. DOI: 10.17705/1cais

Francis, H., Parkes, C., & Reddington, M. (2017). *The future of HR: Emerging trends in AI adoption* [Report]. Likely a CIPD or similar industry report; exact source not located.

Francis, P. (2023). LVII World Day of Peace 2024 - Artificial Intelligence and Peace Francis. en/messages/peace https://www.vatican.va/ content/francesco/ / documents/20231208-messaggio-57giornatamondiale pace2024.html

Frey, C. B., & Osborne, M. A. (2013). *The future of employment: How susceptible are jobs to computerisation?* (Oxford Martin School Working Paper). University of Oxford. https://doi.org/DOI: 10.2139/ssrn.2557564

Friedman, B., & Nissenbaum, H. (1996). Bias in computer systems. ACM Transactions on information systems (TOIS), 14(3), 330-347.

Frunză, S. (2023). Cultural intelligence, spiritual intelligence and counseling in the age of artificial intelligence. *Journal for the Study of Religions and Ideologies*, *22*(64), 80–95.

Fuller, R. M., & Dennis, A. R. (2009). Does fit matter? The impact of task-technology fit and appropriation on team performance in repeated tasks. *Information Systems Research*, *20*(1), 2–17. DOI: 10.1287/isre.1070.0167

Ganagi, M. C., & Rotti, A. A. (2024). A study on Pursuit of Artificial Intelligence in Human Resource Management: A Narrative view. *ITM Web of Conferences, 68*, 01005. DOI: 10.1051/itmconf/20246801005

Ganatra, N. J. (2024). A research paper on how Artificial Intelligence changes the Human Resource Activities inside the organization and provides the significant improvement in workforce working environment for various day to day decisions making along with their efficiency and their productivity. *Journal of Management Research and Analysis*, *11*(3), 182–184. DOI: 10.18231/j.jmra.2024.030

Ganatra, N. J., & Pandya, J. D. (2023). The transformative impact of artificial intelligence on hr practices and employee experience: A review. *Journal of Management Research and Analysis*, *10*(2), 106–111. DOI: 10.18231/j.jmra.2023.018

Garg, M., Punia, B. K., Garg, N., & Punia, V. (2022). Spiritual leadership and well-being in the context of the modern workplace. In *Handbook of Research on Integrating Spirituality in Modern Workplaces* (pp. 170–185). IGI Global Scientific Publishing.

Garg, M., Punia, V., & Punia, B. K. (2022). Will Artificial Intelligence (AI) Overpower Human Intelligence (HI)? A Peep into Future Business and Education. *Amity Management Analyst*, *9*(1), 5–16.

Garkusha, N., & Gorodove, Ju. (2023). Pedagogical Opportunities of ChatGPT for Developing Cognitive Activity of Students. *Vocational Education and Labour Market*, *1*(52), 6–23. DOI: 10.52944/port.2023.52.1.001

Gartner Magic Quadrant for Robotic ProcessAutomation, published at 7 August 2024, https://www.gartner.com/en/documents/5656223

Gaur, B. (2020, July). HR4.0: An analytics framework to redefine employee engagement in the Fourth Industrial Revolution. In 2020 11th International Conference on Computing, Communication and Networking Technologies (ICCCNT) (pp. 1-6). IEEE.

Geetha, R., & Bhanu Sree Reddy, D. (2018). Recruitment through artificial intelligence: A conceptual study. *International Journal of Mechanical Engineering and Technology*, *9*(7), 63–70.

George, A. S., George, A., & Baskar, D. (2023). Emoji Unite: Examining the Rise of Emoji as an International Language Bridging Cultural and Generational Divides. *Partners Universal International Innovation Journal*, *01*(4), 183–204. DOI: 10.5281/zenodo.8280356

Geyik, S. C., Ambler, S., & Kenthapadi, K. (2019, July). Fairness-aware ranking in search & recommendation systems with application to linkedin talent search. In Proceedings of the 25th acm sigkdd international conference on knowledge discovery & data mining (pp. 2221-2231).

Ghezelseflou, H. (2023). Investigating the Challenges and Opportunities of Using Artificial Intelligence in Human Resource Management. *Journal of Technology in Entrepreneurship and Strategic Management*, *2*(2), 28–36. DOI: 10.61838/kman.jtesm.2.2.4

Ghosh, B., Wilson, J. H., Burden, A., & Daugherty, P. H. (2019). *Taking a Systems Approach to Adopting AI*. Harvard Business Review. https://hbr.org/2019/05/taking-a-systems-approach-to-adopting-ai

Ghouse, S. M., & Chaudhary, M. (2024). Artificial intelligence (AI) for tourism start-ups. In Kaur, A., & Singh, A. (Eds.), *Innovative technologies for increasing service productivity* (pp. 161–178). IGI Global., DOI: 10.4018/979-8-3693-2297-4.ch010

Goldenberg, A., & Gross, J. J. (2020). Digital Emotion Contagion. *Trends in Cognitive Sciences*, *24*(4), 316–328. https://doi.org/https://doi.org/10.1016/j.tics.2020.01.009 PMID: 32160568

Goodhue, D. L. (1998). Development and Measurement Validity of a Task-Technology Fit Instrument for User Evaluations of Information System. *Decision Sciences*, *29*(1), 105–138. https://doi.org/https://doi.org/10.1111/j.1540-5915.1998.tb01346.x

Goodhue, D. L., & Thompson, R. L. (1995). Task-Technology Fit and Individual Performance. *Management Information Systems Quarterly*, *19*(2), 213–236. DOI: 10.2307/249689

Goodhue, D., Klein, B., & March, S. (2000). User evaluation of IS as surrogates for objective performance. *Information & Management*, *38*(2), 87–101. DOI: 10.1016/S0378-7206(00)00057-4

Goren, J. D. (2024). AI and the Future of Work: Legal Perspectives on Disability Acommodation and Employment Equity. *Ohio Northern University Law Review*, *50*(3), 3.

Graves, M. (2017). Shared Moral and Spiritual Development Among Human Persons and Artificially Intelligent Agents. *Theology and Science*, *15*(3), 333–351.

Greceva, I. (2024). How to Write a Diploma or Term Paper Using a Neural Network. *Softline.ru*. https://softline.ru/about/blog/kak-napisat-diplom-ili-kursovuyu-s-pomoshyu-nejroseti

Green, A., del Pero, A. S., & Verhagen, A. (2023). Artificial intelligence, job quality and inclusiveness. OECD Employment Outlook, 128.

Guo, X., Li, M., Wang, Y., & Mardani, A. (2023). Does digital transformation improve the firm's performance? From the perspective of digitalization paradox and managerial myopia. *Journal of Business Research*, *163*, 113868. DOI: 10.1016/j.jbusres.2023.113868

Gupta, A., & Mishra, M. (2022). Ethical Concerns While Using Artificial Intelligence in Recruitment of Employees. *Business Ethics and Leadership*, *6*(2), 6–11. DOI: 10.21272/bel.6(2).6-11.2022

Gupta, B. N., & Shaikh, M. S. (2018). People analytics: Novel approach to modern human resource management practice. *International Journal of Engineering Technologies and Management Research*, *5*(7), 78–83.

Gupta, R. (2024). Impact of Artificial Intelligence (AI) on Human Resource Management (HRM). *International Journal For Multidisciplinary Research*, *6*(3). Advance online publication. DOI: 10.36948/ijfmr.2024.v06i03.21444

Gutorova N.A. (2019). Features of teacher-student communication in social networks: an ethical aspect // The sign: the problematic field of media education. No.2(32). pp.7-16.

Guzhova I. V. (2020). Problems of formation of digital literacy of youth in social networks // Sign: problematic field of media education . No. 4(38). pp.14-25.

Haenlein, M., Huang, M. H., & Kaplan, A. (2022). Guest editorial: Business ethics in the era of artificial intelligence. *Journal of Business Ethics*, *178*(4), 867–869.

Hair, J., Anderson, R., & Tatham, R. (1986). *Multivariate Data Analysis with Readings*. MaCmillan Publishing Company.

Hamilton, R. H., & Sodeman, W. A. (2020). The questions we ask: Opportunities and challenges for using big data analytics to strategically manage human capital resources. *Business Horizons*, *63*(1), 85–95.

Harari, Y. N. (2018). *21 Lessons for the 21st Century*. Random House.

Hardesty, L. (2018). Study finds gender and skin-type bias in commercial artificial-intelligence systems. Retrieved April, 3, 2019.

Havens, J. C. (2021). Approaches to Spiritual Care for Artificially Intelligent Robots. *Pastoral Psychology*, *70*(5), 615–632.

Herzfeld, N. (2022). Artificial Intelligence and Theology. *Theology Today (Princeton, N.J.)*, *79*(2), 103–115.

Hess, T., Matt, C., Benlian, A., & Wiesböck, F. (2020). Options for formulating a digital transformation strategy. In *Strategic information management* (pp. 151–173). Routledge.

Heyder, T., Passlack, N., & Posegga, O. (2023): Ethical Management of Human-AI Interaction : Theory Development Review, in: *The Journal of Strategic Information Systems : Incorporating International Information Systems*, Amsterdam: Elsevier, Jg. 32, Nr. 3, S. 101772, 1–50, doi: DOI: 10.1016/j.jsis.2023.101772

Homans, G. C. (1958). Social behavior as exchange. *American Journal of Sociology*, *63*(6), 597–606. DOI: 10.1086/222355

Howarth, J. (2024). Languages Supported by ChatGPT. Exploding Topics. https://explodingtopics.com/blog/chatgpt-supported-languages

Hu, C., & Wang, Y. (2010). Bootstrapping in AMOS. *Powerpoint. Consultéle*, 23-02.

Huang, C., Zhang, Z., Mao, B., & Yao, X. (2022). An overview of artificial intelligence ethics. *IEEE Transactions on Artificial Intelligence*, *4*(4), 799–819.

Huang, C., Zhang, Z., Mao, B., & Yao, X. (2023). An Overview of Artificial Intelligence Ethics. *IEEE Transactions on Artificial Intelligence*, *4*(4), 799–819. DOI: 10.1109/TAI.2022.3194503

Hu, L. T., & Bentler, P. M. (1998). Fit indices in covariance structure modeling: Sensitivity to underparameterized model misspecification. *Psychological Methods*, *3*(4), 424–453.

Hu, Q. (2023). Unilever's Practice on AI-based Recruitment. Highlights in Business. *Economics and Management*, *16*, 256–263. DOI: 10.54097/hbem.v16i.10565

Huynh-The, T., Pham, Q. V., Pham, X. Q., Nguyen, T. T., Han, Z., & Kim, D. S. (2023). Artificial intelligence for the metaverse: A survey. *Engineering Applications of Artificial Intelligence*, *117*, 105581.

IBM. (2016). *Cognitive computing in HR: The benefits outweigh the hazards* [White paper]. IBM Institute for Business Value.

IEEE. (n.d.). P7003: Algorithmic bias considerations. Institute of Electrical and Electronics Engineers. https://standards.ieee.org/

International Yearbook of Technology of Education and Training. (1978).

Irshad, S. (2024). Role of Human and Artificial Intelligence Biases on Organizational Performance, Efficiency, and Enhanced Productivity. In Human Perspectives of Industry 4.0 Organizations (pp. 111-130). CRC Press.

Israfilzade, K. (2025). Benefits and Risks of Generative AI in content marketing. *Adauniversity*. https://www.academia.edu/123673514/Benefits_and_Risks_of_Generative_AI_in_Content_Marketing. doi: DOI: 10.5281/ZENODO.13731679

Ivanko, A. F., & Ushenko, G. V. (2015). Educational opportunities of Facebook // Bulletin of MGUP. No.6. Access mode: https://cyberleninka.ru/article/n/obrazovatelnye-vozmozhnosti-facebook (date of application: 07.11.2017)

Jackelén, A. (2021). Technology, theology, and spirituality in the digital age. *Zygon*, *56*(1), 6–18.

Jafri, S., Upreti, S., Saiyad, F. B. J., Madhukar, K. S., Chaturvedi, V. M., & Divakaran, P. (2024, March). Effectiveness of artificial intelligence for enhancing decision-making process of recruitment in HRM process. In 2024 IEEE International Conference on Contemporary Computing and Communications (InC4) (Vol. 1, pp. 1-6). IEEE.

Jafri, S., Upreti, S., Saiyad, F. B. J., Madhukar, K. S., Chaturvedi, V. M., & Divakaran, P. (2024a). Effectiveness of Artificial Intelligence for Enhancing Decision-Making Process of Recruitment in HRM Process. 2024 IEEE International Conference on Contemporary Computing and Communications (InC4), 1–6. DOI: 10.1109/InC460750.2024.10649327

Jain, A. (2023). Job Displacement Due to Artificial Intelligence and Machine Learning – A Review. *International Journal For Multidisciplinary Research*, *5*(6). Advance online publication. DOI: 10.36948/ijfmr.2023.v05i06.10958

Jarrahi, M. H. (2018). Artificial intelligence and the future of work: Human-AI symbiosis in organizational decision making. *Business Horizons*, *61*(4), 577–586. https://doi.org/https://doi.org/10.1016/j.bushor.2018.03.007

Jiaping, Y. (2022). Enterprise Human Resource Management Model by Artificial Intelligence Digital Technology. *Computational Intelligence and Neuroscience*, *2022*, 1–9. DOI: 10.1155/2022/6186811 PMID: 36479021

Johnson, P. C., Laurell, C., Ots, M., & Sandström, C. (2022). Digital innovation and the effects of artificial intelligence on firms' research and development – Automation or augmentation, exploration or exploitation? *Technological Forecasting and Social Change*, *179*. Advance online publication. DOI: 10.1016/j.techfore.2022.121636

Jolliffe, P., & Foster, S. (2022). Different reality? Generations' and religious groups' views of spirituality policies in the workplace. *Journal of Business Ethics*, *181*(2), 451–470.

Kaczmarek, T., Kowalkiewicz, M., & Piskorski, J. (2005). Information extraction from CV. In *Proceedings of the 8th International Conference on Business Information Systems (BIS 2005)* (pp. 185–192).

Kadirov, A., Shakirova, Y., Ismoilova, G., & Makhmudova, N. (2024a). AI in Human Resource Management: Reimagining Talent Acquisition, Development, and Retention. *2024 International Conference on Knowledge Engineering and Communication Systems (ICKECS)*, 1–8. DOI: 10.1109/ICKECS61492.2024.10617231

Kaggwa, S., Eleogu, T. F., Okonkwo, F., Farayola, O. A., Uwaoma, P. U., & Akinoso, A. (2024). AI in Decision Making: Transforming Business Strategies. *International Journal of Research and Scientific Innovation*, *X*(XII), 423–444. DOI: 10.51244/IJRSI.2023.1012032

Kaplan, A., & Haenlein, M. (2019). Siri, Siri, in my hand: Who's the fairest in the land? On the interpretations, illustrations, and implications of artificial intelligence. *Business Horizons*, *62*, 15–25.

Karakulin, A. Yu. (2019). Foreign experience in the use and development of human resources // Bulletin of the Altai Academy of Economics and Law. No. 12-3. pp. 176-182. (in Russ.)

Karangutkar, A. A. (2023). The Impact of Artificial Intelligence on Job Displacement and the Future of Work. *International Journal of Advanced Research in Science. Tongxin Jishu, 635–638*. Advance online publication. DOI: 10.48175/IJARSCT-12096

Kaur, S., & Sharma, R. (2021). Emotion AI: Integrating Emotional Intelligence with Artificial Intelligence in the Digital Workplace. In P. K. Singh, Z. Polkowski, S. Tanwar, S. K. Pandey, G. Matei, & D. Pirvu (Eds.), *Innovations in Information and Communication Technologies (IICT-2020)* (pp. 337–343). Springer International Publishing. https://doi.org/https://doi.org/10.1007/978-3-030-66218-9_39

Kaur, S., Katoch, G., & Zahidi, F. (2024). A Bibliometric Review on Technostress : Performance and Scientific Approach. *Prestige International Journal of Management & IT- Sanchayan, 13*(1), 21–40.

Keffer, L. (2023). Minister of Education and Science Falkov Urged not to Punish a Graduate who Wrote his Thesis Using ChatGPT. *Kommersant*. https://www.kommersant.ru/doc/5812075

Kelan, E. K. (2023). Algorithmic inclusion: Shaping the predictive algorithms of artificial intelligence in hiring. *Human Resource Management Journal*. Advance online publication. DOI: 10.1111/1748-8583.12511

Kergilova, N. V., & Sazonova, O. K. (2017). The use of social networks in the educational process of a university (on the example of the VKontakte group "Pedagogy and not only"). *Siberian Pedagogical Journal.*, (6), 87–92.

Kettle, L., & Lee, Y. C. (2024). User experiences of well-being chatbots. *Human Factors*, *66*(6), 1703–1723. PMID: 36916743

Khadzakos, N. (2024). 21st Century Student: How to Use AI in the Learning Process? *Habr*. https://habr.com/ru/articles/820375/

Khair, M. A., Mahadasa, R., Tuli, F. A., & Ande, J. R. P. K. (2020). Beyond Human Judgment: Exploring the Impact of Artificial Intelligence on HR Decision-Making Efficiency and Fairness. *Global Disclosure of Economics and Business*, *9*(2), 163–176. DOI: 10.18034/gdeb.v9i2.730

Khan, M., Parahyanti, E., & Hussain, S. M. A. M. (2024). The Role Generative AI in Human Resource Management: Enhancing Operational Efficiency, Decision-Making, and Addressing Ethical Challenges. *Asian Journal of Logistics Management*, *3*(2), 104–125. DOI: 10.14710/ajlm.2024.24671

Khan, S., Faisal, S., & Thomas, G. (2024). Exploring the nexus of artificial intelligence in talent acquisition: Unravelling cost-benefit dynamics, seizing opportunities, and mitigating risks. *Problems and Perspectives in Management*, *22*(1), 462–476. DOI: 10.21511/ppm.22(1).2024.37

Khatal, N., Chaughule, S., & Mangaonkar, N. (2022). Resume screening bot using RPA. In Soft Computing for Security Applications [Springer Singapore.]. *Proceedings of ICSCS, 2021*, 723–732.

Khrennikov, A. Yu., & Lyubarsky, Yu. Ya. (2022). Principles of building artificial intelligence systems and their application in the electric power industry [in Russ.]. *Power Engineering*, (3), 22–30.

Kim, S. (2024). Developing AI literacy in HRD: Competencies, approaches, and implications. *Human Resource Development International.* Advance online publication. DOI: 10.1080/13678868.2024.2337962

Kinge, B., Mandhare, S., Chavan, P., & Chaware, S. M. (2022). Resume screening using machine learning and NLP: A proposed system. International Journal of Scientific Research in Computer Science. *Engineering and Information Technology*, *8*(2), 253–258.

Kinyashina, Yu. B. (2021). Features of the use of social networks in the process of studying at a university. *Izvestiya Tula State University. Humanities*, (2), 126–133.

Kiritsi, A., & Adamantidis, V. (2024). Recruitment and Talent Management in the Modern World Using AI. International Journal of Management. *Knowledge and Learning*, *13*. Advance online publication. DOI: 10.53615/2232-5697.13.151-157

Kirkpatrick, K. (2017). AI in Contact Centers. *Communications of the ACM*, *60*(8), 18–19.

Koch I. A., Melnik A.V. (2019). Social networks as a means of communication in the educational environment of the university // Society and power. N° 1 (75). C. 31-41

Kolmogorova, T. V. (2024). A sociological perspective on innovations in recruitment and retention of personnel. Scientific Review, (4), 201-210.</edb>

Koroleva, D., Pivovarova, X., Zagranichmy, A., Kolabinova, A., Andreeva, A., Podlipskaya, Y., Arzumanyan, M., & Ronanchenko, A. (2025). *Global Education Trends in the Russian Context* – 2025. Ioe.hse.ru. https://ioe.hse.ru/edu_global_trends/2025/

Kotler, P., Kartajaya, H., & Setiawan, I. (2023). *Marketing 6.0*. Wiley.

Kozlov, D. I. (2024). Competence of a teacher in the field of using social networks in the educational process of a university / Scientific notes. electronic scientific journal of Kursk State University. N° 1 (69). Access mode: http:// api-mag.kursksu .ru/api/v1/get_pdf/5219 / (date of reference 03/31/2024)

Kramer, A. D. I., Guillory, J. E., & Hancock, J. T. (2014). Experimental evidence of massive-scale emotional contagion through social networks. *Proceedings of the National Academy of Sciences of the United States of America*, *111*(24), 8788–8790. DOI: 10.1073/pnas.1320040111 PMID: 24889601

Krichevsky, N. A., & Goncharov, S. F. (2008). Corporate social responsibility. M.: Yzdat.-bid. corporation" Dashkov & Co", 2007.-216 p.

Kukitz, P. (2024). Challenges and Prospects of Implementing Generative Artificial Intelligence Tools in Business Marketing Activities. *Economic Development Research Journal*. 22–30.

Kulak I.A. (1988). Methodology for identifying the fixation of educational material in memory traces of different fixation. // Pedagogy of higher and secondary special schools: Interdepartmental. collection. – Minsk, 1988. – Issue. 2 (21) (2-19), pp. 143-154.

Kumar Tyagi, P., Jit Singh, V., Kumar Singh, A., Saxena, A., Tyagi, P., & Mehta, P. (2023). The Impact of Artificial Intelligence-Based Human Resource Management Systems on Organizational Efficiency. 2023 10th IEEE Uttar Pradesh Section International Conference on Electrical, Electronics and Computer Engineering (UPCON), 1727–1731. DOI: 10.1109/UPCON59197.2023.10434792

KUMAR, A. (2024). An Analysis of Artificial Intelligence Adoption in the Human Resource Management. INTERANTIONAL JOURNAL OF SCIENTIFIC RESEARCH IN ENGINEERING AND MANAGEMENT, 08(04), 1–5. DOI: 10.55041/IJSREM32681

Kumar, M. R., Sharma, A., Bhargavi, Y. K., & Ramesh, G. (2022). Human Resource Management Using Machine Learning-Based Solutions. 2022 3rd International Conference on Electronics and Sustainable Communication Systems (ICESC), 801–806. DOI: 10.1109/ICESC54411.2022.9885526

Kumar, H., & Martin, A. (2023). Artificial Emotional Intelligence: Conventional and deep learning approach. *Expert Systems with Applications*, *212*, 118651. https://doi.org/https://doi.org/10.1016/j.eswa.2022.118651

Kumari, D. A., Karim Shaikh, I. A., Gangadharan, S., Narendra Kiran, P. B., Ramya, S. R., & Nargunde, A. S. (2024). Machine Learning for Diversity and Inclusion: Addressing Biases in HR Practices. 2024 5th International Conference on Recent Trends in Computer Science and Technology (ICRTCST), 182–187. DOI: 10.1109/ICRTCST61793.2024.10578442

Kumari, M. (2024a). The Effects and Functionality of Artificial Intelligence in Human Resource Management. *INTERANTIONAL JOURNAL OF SCIENTIFIC RESEARCH IN ENGINEERING AND MANAGEMENT*, *08*(04), 1–5. DOI: 10.55041/IJSREM31091

Kumar, S. (2024). Risks from Generative AI. https://ssrn.com/abstract=4858973 or http://dx.doi.org/DOI: 10.2139/ssrn.4858973

Kurzweil, R. (1999). *The Age of Spiritual Machines. When Computers Exceed Human Intelligence*. Viking.

Kuzmina, N. V., & Rean, A. A. (1993). Professionalism of pedagogical activity. St. Petersburg.; Rybinsk. – 54 p.

Kuznetsova, N., & Konovalov, Y. (2020). Enhancing the Safety of Energy Systems Functioning at Their Digitalization // E3S Web of Conferences. Vol. 209. https://doi.org/DOI: 10.1051/e3sconf/ 202020906017

Kuźniarska, A., & Stańczyk, I. (2024). *Artificial Intelligence in HR*. Informa., DOI: 10.4324/9781032678719-6

Lafferly, J. (2025). Generative AI Regulations – What Your Business Needs To Know for 2025. https://www.salesforce.com/blog/generative-ai-regulations/

Lahby, M. (Ed.). (2024a). Empowering Digital Education with ChatGPT. *CRC Press is*. doi: DOI: 10.1201/9781032716350

Lanier, J. (2018). Virtual Reality: The Promise of the Future. *Interactive Learning International*, *8*(4), 275–279.

Lazarus, R. S., & Folkman, S. (1984). *Stress, Appraisal, and Coping*. Springer Publishing Company. https://books.google.nl/books?id=i-ySQQuUpr8C

Leeuw, R. T., & Joseph, N. (2023). Reciprocal Influence between Digital Emotional Intelligence and Agile Mindset in an Agile Environment. *Administrative Sciences*, *13*(11). Advance online publication. DOI: 10.3390/admsci13110228

Lektawan, F. K. (2024). Communicating with the Holy Spirit in the Age of AI Technology: Catholic. *Stipas Tahasak Danum Pambelum Keuskupan Palangkaraya*, 88-99.

Lem, S. (1978). *Summa Technologiae*. Insel Verlag.

Lengel, R. H., & Daft, R. L. (1988). The Selection of Communication Media as an Executive Skill. *The Academy of Management Perspectives*, *2*(3), 225–232. DOI: 10.5465/ame.1988.4277259

Leong, C. (2018). Technology & recruiting 101: How it works and where it's going. *Strategic HR Review*, *17*(1), 50–52.

Leshob, A., Bourgouin, A., & Renard, L. (2018, October). Towards a process analysis approach to adopt robotic process automation. In 2018 IEEE 15th International Conference on e-Business Engineering (ICEBE) (pp. 46-53). IEEE.

Li, X. (2018). New thinking of human resource management in the age of artificial intelligence. In 2nd International Proceedings on International Conference on Systems, Computing, and Applications, Francis Academic Press, UK (pp. 133-136).

Li, Y. (2024). Security and Privacy of Artificial Intelligence with Ethical Concerns. *2024 IEEE 9th International Conference on Data Science in Cyberspace (DSC)*, 660–667. DOI: 10.1109/DSC63484.2024.00098

Li, L. (2022). Digital transformation and sustainable performance: The moderating role of market turbulence. *Industrial Marketing Management*, *104*, 28–37. DOI: 10.1016/j.indmarman.2022.04.007

Litvinova, N. P., & Samorukov, V. I. (2015). The experience of recognizing competencies acquired in non-formal and informal education in foreign countries//Modern education. — No. 4. – pp. 17-35.

Loebbecke, C., & Picot, A. (2015). Reflections on societal and business model transformation arising from digitization and big data analytics: A research agenda. *The Journal of Strategic Information Systems*, *24*(3), 149–157.

Lu, D. (2025). We Tried out DeepSeek. It Worked Well, Until we Asked it about Tiananmen Square and Taiwan. *The Guardian*; The Guardian. https://www.theguardian.com/technology/2025/jan/28/we-tried-out-deepseek-it-works-well-until-we-asked-it-about-tiananmen-square-and-taiwan

Lukaszewski, K. M., & Stone, D. L. (2024). Will the use of AI in human resources create a digital Frankenstein? *Organizational Dynamics*, *53*(1), 101033. DOI: 10.1016/j.orgdyn.2024.101033

Luo, Y., & Dan, X. (2025). China Releases New Labeling Requirements for AI-Generated Content. *Lexology*. https://www.lexology.com/library/detail.aspx?g=1e66cce9-1936-4e63-96f0-5fdf378a8a04

Lyu, W., & Liu, J. (2021). Artificial Intelligence and emerging digital technologies in the energy sector. *Applied Energy*, *303*, 117615.

Madakam, S., Holmukhe, R. M., & Jaiswal, D. K. (2019). The future digital work force: Robotic process automation (RPA). *JISTEM-Journal of Information Systems and Technology Management*, *16*, e201916001.

Madanchian, M. (2024). From Recruitment to Retention: AI Tools for Human Resource Decision-Making. *Applied Sciences (Basel, Switzerland)*, *14*(24), 11750. DOI: 10.3390/app142411750

Madhumita, G., & Dolly Diana, P. PC, N., Narendra Kiran, P. B., Aggarwal, S., & Satish Nargunde, A. (2024). AI-powered Performance Management: Driving Employee Success and Organizational Growth. 2024 5th International Conference on Recent Trends in Computer Science and Technology (ICRTCST), 204–209. DOI: 10.1109/ICRTCST61793.2024.10578371

Madhumita, G., Diana, P. D., Neena, P. C., Kiran, P. N., Aggarwal, S., & Nargunde, A. S. (2024, April). AI-powered Performance Management: Driving Employee Success and Organizational

Maiorov, S. A. (2022). Development of the ecosystem of SberBank PJSC [in Russ.]. *Integral International Journal of Applied Sciences and Technologies.*, (1), 111–117. DOI: 10.55186/02357801-2022-7-1-3

Makarenko, A. S. (2003). *Pedagogical poem*. ITRK.

Malik, A., Budhwar, P., & Kazmi, B. A. (2023). Artificial intelligence (AI)-assisted HRM: Towards an extended strategic framework. *Human Resource Management Review*, *33*(1), 100940. DOI: 10.1016/j.hrmr.2022.100940

Malik, A., Budhwar, P., Patel, C., & Srikanth, N. R. (2022). May the bots be with you! Delivering HR cost-effectiveness and individualised employee experiences in an MNE. *International Journal of Human Resource Management, 33*(6), 1148–1178. DOI: 10.1080/09585192.2020.1859582

Malysheva, N. A. (2013). The role of social networks in the model of distance learning for students of art specialties // Scientific journal of KubGAU. No.86. Access mode: https://cyberleninka.ru/article/n/rol-sotsialnyh-setey-vmodeli-distantsionnogo-obucheniya-studentov-hudozhestvennyh-spetsialnostey (Date of reference: 03/31/2024)

Malyshev, I. O. (2024). Overview of Modern Generative Neural Networks: Domestic and Foreign Practice. *International Journal of Humanities and Natural Sciences, 1-2*(88), 168–171. https://cyberleninka.ru/article/n/obzor-sovremennyh-generativnyh-neyrosetey-otechestvennaya-i-zarubezhnaya-praktika. DOI: 10.24412/2500-1000-2024-1-2-168-171

Mamede, H. S., Martins, C. M. G., & Da Silva, M. M. (2023). A lean approach to robotic process automation in banking. *Heliyon, 9*(7), e18041. DOI: 10.1016/j.heliyon.2023.e18041 PMID: 37501980

Mamikonyan, O. (2023). Half of Russian Students Use Neural Networks in Their Studies. *Forbes.ru.* https://www.forbes.ru/forbeslife/495175-polovina-rossijskih-studentov-ispol-zuut-nejroseti-v-ucebe

Manoharan, P. (2024). A Review on AI Driven HR Systems: Revolutionizing HR Systems and Talent Management. *Scholars Journal of Engineering and Technology, 12*(06), 179–184. DOI: 10.36347/sjet.2024.v12i06.001

Manyaev, A. G., & Shipitsin, A. I. (2018). Prospects of using social network technology in university education. *Innovación Educativa (México, D.F.)*, (5), 148–157.

Marín Díaz, G., Galán Hernández, J. J., & Galdón Salvador, J. L. (2023). Analyzing Employee Attrition Using Explainable AI for Strategic HR Decision-Making. *Mathematics, 11*(22), 4677. DOI: 10.3390/math11224677

Marlowe, A. N. (2021). Robot Recruiters: How Employers & Governments Must Confront the Discriminatory Effects of AI Hiring. *J. High Tech. L., 22*, 274.

Martincevic, I., & Kozina, G. (2018). The relationship between technological dynamics of new technologies and absorptive capacity of export companies of the Republic of Croatia. *Economic Research-Ekonomska Istraživanja, 31*(1), 425–448. DOI: 10.1080/1331677X.2018.1431042

Martin, J. (2003). *The Education of John Dewey*. Columbia University Press.

McCulloch, W. S., & Pitts, W. (1943). A Logical Calculus of the Ideas Immanent in Nervous Activity. *The Bulletin of Mathematical Biophysics*, *5*(4), 115–133. DOI: 10.1007/bf02478259

Mehrabi, N., Morstatter, F., Saxena, N., Lerman, K., & Galstyan, A. (2021). A survey on bias and fairness in machine learning. *ACM Computing Surveys*, *54*(6), 1–35.

Mergen, A., Çetin-Kılıç, N., & Özbilgin, M. F. (2025). Artificial Intelligence and Bias Towards Marginalised Groups: Theoretical Roots and Challenges. In AI and Diversity in a Datafied World of Work: Will the Future of Work be Inclusive? (Vol. 12, pp. 17-38). Emerald Publishing Limited.

Miao, C., Humphrey, R., & Qian, S. (2017). A meta-analysis of emotional intelligence and work attitudes. *Journal of Occupational and Organizational Psychology*, *90*(2), 177–202. DOI: 10.1111/joop.12167

Mikhailov, E. (2023). Students Cheat From ChatGPT. Is Education Under Threat? (It's Not That Simple). *Afisha Daily*. https://daily.afisha.ru/culture/25132-studenty-spisyvayut-u-chatgpt-obrazovanie-pod-ugrozoy-vse-ne-tak-prosto/

Mikhalev, M. (2020). Individualization is Useless if the University Thinks in the Old Way. *RBC Trends*. https://trends.rbc.ru/trends/education/cmrm/5fe06c989a794774a4861cd3?from=copy

Mitchell, M. (2020). *Artificial Intelligence: A Guide for Thinking Humans*. Picador.

Mohamed, S. A., Mahmoud, M. A., Mahdi, M. N., & Mostafa, S. A. (2022). Improving efficiency and effectiveness of robotic process automation in human resource management. *Sustainability*, *14*(7), 3920.

Mollay, M. H., Sharma, D. S., Kale, A. P., Anawade, P., & Gahane, S. (2024). *Smart Hiring: Leveraging AI for Effective Employee Selection*. 1–6. DOI: 10.1109/idicaiei61867.2024.10842754

Montuschi, P., Gatteschi, V., Lamberti, F., Sanna, A., & Demartini, C. (2014). Job recruitment and job seeking processes: How technology can help. *IT Professional*, *16*(3), 41–49. DOI: 10.1109/MITP.2014.40

Moreira, S., Mamede, H. S., & Santos, A. (2023). Process automation using RPA–a literature review. *Procedia Computer Science*, *219*, 244–254.

Mujtaba, D. F., & Mahapatra, N. R. (2019, November). Ethical considerations in AI-based recruitment. In *2019 IEEE International Symposium on Technology and Society (ISTAS)* (pp. 1-7). IEEE.

Mustakrimov, V. (2023). GPT for Students. Publishing Solutions. https://mybook.ru/author/vyacheslav-mustakimov-2/gpt-studentam-580promptov-sposobnyh-reshit-lyubuyu/

Mylrea, M. (2025). The Generative AI Weapon of Mass Destruction: Evolving Disinformation Threats, Vulnerabilities, and Mitigation Frameworks. *Interdependent Human-Machine Teams*, 315–347). Academic Press. doi: .DOI: 10.1016/B978-0-443-29246-0.00007-9

Nasef Zaki, H., Saeed Ahmed Abd-Elrhaman, E., & Ghoneimy Hasanin Ghoneimy, A. (2018). The Effect of Emotional Intelligence Program on Decision Making Style. *American Journal of Nursing Research*, *6*(6), 524–532. DOI: 10.12691/ajnr-6-6-21

Nawaz, N., Arunachalam, H., Pathi, B. K., & Gajenderan, V. (2024). The adoption of artificial intelligence in human resources management practices. *International Journal of Information Management Data Insights*, *4*(1), 100208. DOI: 10.1016/j.jjimei.2023.100208

Nayak, A., Dr, S. S., & Choudhury, S. N. B. (2024). The Future of Performance Management: Leveraging Ai for Better Feedback and Coaching. *Journal of Informatics Education and Research*, *4*(2). Advance online publication. DOI: 10.52783/jier.v4i2.649

Nazarova, A. N., & Treiman, M. G. (2023). Digital transformation of logistics activities in the implementation of freight transportation by rail // Current issues of modern scientific research. International scientific and practical conference. pp. 13-15. (in Russ.)

Neural Networks for Writing a Thesis (2024). giga.chat. https://giga.chat/help/articles/ai-for-diploma.

NGA HR Discovers Untapped Automation Potential by Switching to Automation Anywhere RPA. (2019). Retrieved from https://www.automationanywhere.com/resources/asset-library/casestudy-nga-hr

Nikonova, Ya. I., & Ivasenko, A. G. (2023). Digital transformation of the financial sector of the Russian economy // International Scientific Research Journal. No. 1(127). pp. 1-8. https://doi.org/ (in Russ.)DOI: 10.23670/IRJ.2023.127.82

Ningsih, W., & Lahby, M. (2024). The Potential of GPT in Education. *Chapman and Hall/CRC eBooks*, 247–263. doi: .DOI: 10.1201/9781032716350-17

Norman, E., & Pahlawati, E. (2024). Peran Artificial Intelligence dalam Rekrutmen dan Seleksi: Meningkatkan Efisiensi dan Akurasi dalam MSDM. *Sci-Tech Journal*, *3*(1), 45–59. DOI: 10.56709/stj.v3i1.320

Nyathani, R. (2023). AI in Performance Management: Redefining Performance Appraisals in the Digital Age. *Journal of Artificial Intelligence & Cloud Computing, 1–5*. Advance online publication. DOI: 10.47363/JAICC/2023(2)134

Nyathani, R. (2023). AI-driven HR analytics: Unleashing the power of HR data management. *Journal of Technology and Systems*, *5*(2), 15–26.

O, Y.-L. (2004). Intelligent Information Systems for Decision Support. *International Conference on Artificial Intelligence, IC-AI, 1*, 326–332.

OECD. (2024). Survey on algorithmic management governance measures. https://www.oecd.org/

Okatta, C. G., Ajayi, F. A., & Olawale, O. (2024). NAVIGATING THE FUTURE: INTEGRATING AI AND MACHINE LEARNING IN HR PRACTICES FOR A DIGITAL WORKFORCE. *Computer Science & IT Research Journal*, *5*(4), 1008–1030. DOI: 10.51594/csitrj.v5i4.1085

Okolie, U. C., & Irabor, I. E. (2017). E-recruiting: Practices, benefits and challenges to job seekers. *International Journal of Advanced Engineering. Management and Education Research*, *3*(1), 1–9.

Okorokov, R. V., & Timofeeva, A. A. (2020). Formation of key competencies of specialists in the era of digitalization // Russia, Europe, Asia: digitalization of the global space. Collection of scientific papers of the III International Scientific and Practical Forum. Nevinnomyssk: SEQUOIA LLC. pp. 522-525. (in Russ.)

Okorokov, R. V., & Timofeeva, A. A. (2022). Improving human potential in the management of electric power systems in the context of digitalization // The role of innovation in the transformation and sustainable development of modern science: A collective monograph. Vol. 66. Ufa: Aeterna LLC. pp. 45-61. (in Russ.)

Okorokov, R. V., & Timofeeva, A. A. (2023). Industry specifics of digital transformation models // Global challenges of digital transformation of markets: A collective monograph. St. Petersburg: POLYTECH PRESS. pp. 681-703. (in Russ.)

Okorokov, R. V., Timofeeva, A. A., & Sapanova, R. (2024). *The role of the human factor in electric power systems in the context of digitalization // Navigating Digital Transformation: Original Research Across Smart Cities, Sustainable Development and Beyond*. Nova Science Publishers., DOI: 10.52305/YMXR0010

Omotunde, H., & Ahmed, M. (2023). *A Comprehensive Review of Security Measures in Database Systems: Assessing Authentication, Access Control, and Beyond*. Mesopotamian Journal of Cyber Security., DOI: 10.58496/mjcsc/ 2023/016

Onik, M. M. H., Miraz, M. H., & Kim, C. S. (2018, April). A recruitment and human resource management technique using blockchain technology for Industry 4.0. In Smart Cities Symposium 2018 (pp. 1-6). IET.

Onukwulu, E. C.. (2025). Integrating sustainability into procurement and supply chain processes in the energy sector. *Gulf Journal of Advance Business Research.*, *3*(1), 76–104. DOI: 10.51594/gjabr.v3i1.68

Osorio, M. L., & Madero, S. (2024). Explaining Gen Z's desire for hybrid work in corporate, family, and entrepreneurial settings. *Business Horizons*, •••. Advance online publication. DOI: 10.1016/j.bushor.2024.02.008

Othman, M. H. (2023). Students' Perceptions and Understanding of Elective Courses and Their Effects on Academic Performance. [MJSSH]. *Malaysian Journal of Social Sciences and Humanities*, *8*(3), e002171. DOI: 10.47405/mjssh.v8i3.2171

Page, M. J., McKenzie, J. E., Bossuyt, P. M., Boutron, I., Hoffmann, T. C., Mulrow, C. D., Shamseer, L., Tetzlaff, J. M., Akl, E. A., Brennan, S. E., Chou, R., Glanville, J., Grimshaw, J. M., Hróbjartsson, A., Lalu, M. M., Li, T., Loder, E. W., Mayo-Wilson, E., McDonald, S., & Moher, D. (2021). The PRISMA 2020 statement: An updated guideline for reporting systematic reviews. *BMJ (Clinical Research Ed.)*, *372*. Advance online publication. DOI: 10.1136/bmj.n71 PMID: 33782057

Paigude, S., Pangarkar, S. C., Hundekari, S., Mali, M., Wanjale, K., & Dongre, Y. (2023). Potential of Artificial Intelligence in Boosting Employee Retention in the Human Resource Industry. International Journal on Recent and Innovation Trends in Computing and Communication, 11(3s), 01–10. DOI: 10.17762/ijritcc.v11i3s.6149

Panayotopoulou, L., Vakola, M., & Galanaki, E. (2007). E-HR adoption and the role of HRM: Evidence from Greece. *Personnel Review*, *36*(2), 277–294. DOI: 10.1108/00483480710726190

Pandey, S., & Mehta, J. (2022, August). HRPA: Human resource prediction analytics. In *2022 Third International Conference on Intelligent Computing Instrumentation and Control Technologies (ICICICT)* (pp. 721-726). IEEE.

Pankova, N. V., Evdokimov, K. V., & Samorukov, V. I. (2015). *Scientific and methodological support for the development of the system of training, retraining and advanced training of personnel in priority sectors of the economy in the context of Russia's membership in the WTO* [monograph]. St. Petersburg State Technical University.

Pan, Y., & Froese, F. J. (2023). An interdisciplinary review of AI and HRM: Challenges and future directions. *Human Resource Management Review, 33*(1), 100924. DOI: 10.1016/j.hrmr.2022.100924

Paramita, D., Okwir, S., & Nuur, C. (2024). Artificial intelligence in talent acquisition: Exploring organisational and operational dimensions. *The International Journal of Organizational Analysis, 32*(11), 108–131. DOI: 10.1108/IJOA-09-2023-3992

Parchande, S., Shahane, A., & Dhore, M. (2019, September). Contractual employee management system using machine learning and robotic process automation. In 2019 5th International Conference on Computing, Communication, Control And Automation (ICCUBEA) (pp. 1-5). IEEE.

Parnas, D. L. (2017). The real risks of artificial intelligence. *Communications of the ACM, 60*(10), 29–31. DOI: 10.1145/3128739

Partal, S., & Smirnova, S. (2021). It's Time to Relax: The Critical Importance of Digital Mental Health Products in the Context of Surveillance Capitalism. *Temes de Disseny*, (37), 38–59.

Patrecia, M. (2025). The Future of Marketing: AI Transformations by 2025. *ContentGrip*. https://www.contentgrip.com/future-ai-marketing/ or DOI: 10.61796/ijaifd.v1i4.185

Pavlidis, E. (2025). The Good, the Bad, and the Ugly: Generative AI in Marketing in 2025. *SIXGUN*. https://sixgun.com.au/insights/the-good-the-bad-and-the-ugly-generative-ai-in-marketing-in-2025/

Perkins, M. (2023). Academic Integrity considerations of AI Large Language Models in the post-pandemic era: ChatGPT and beyond. *Journal of University Teaching & Learning Practice, 20*(2). Advance online publication. DOI: 10.53761/1.20.02.07

Perov, R. (2024). How to Use the GigaChat Neural Network in 2025. *Hi-Tech Mail*. https://hi-tech.mail.ru/review/109793-kak-polzovatsya-nejrosetyu-gigachat/#anchor17157754334643962

Peters, T. (2019, September). Artificial Intelligence versus Agape Love: Spirituality in a Posthuman Age. *In Forum Philosophicum, 24*(2), 259-278.

Petrov, D. (2023). How Artificial Intelligence is Changing the Future of Medicine. *Forbes.ru*. https://www.forbes.ru/mneniya/488597-kak-iskusstvennyj-intellekt-menaet-budusee-mediciny?utm_source=yandex.ru&utm_medium=organic&utm_campaign=yandex.ru&utm_referrer=yandex.ru

Pfeffer, J., & Salancik, G. R. (1978). *The external control of organizations: A resource dependence perspective*. Harper & Row. (Reprinted as Classics of Organization Theory, pp. 521–532)

Pitts, V. E., Wright, N. A., & Harkabus, L. C. (2012). Communication in Virtual Teams : The Role of Emotional Intelligence. *Journal of Organizational Psychology*, *12*(3/4), 21–34. DOI: 10.1016/j.chb.2012.06.001%5Cnhttp://

Pivotto, I., Matias, V., & William de Paula, F. (2024). CAVE automatic virtual environment technology to enhance social participation of autistic people: A classification and literature review. *Research in Autism Spectrum Disorders*, *117*, 1–21.

Podchalimova G.N., Belova S.N. Digital transformation of the system of additional professional education at the university // Human capital. 2021. No. S5-3 (149). pp. 78-85.

Popkova, E. G. (2024). Spirituality in the realities of digitalization of society in the era of intelligent machines development. *RUDN Journal of Economics*, *32*(1), 170–186.

Popo-Olaniyan, O., James, O. O., Udeh, C. A., Daraojimba, R. E., & Ogedengbe, D. E. (2022). FUTURE-PROOFING HUMAN RESOURCES IN THE U.S. WITH AI: A REVIEW OF TRENDS AND IMPLICATIONS. *International Journal of Management & Entrepreneurship Research*, *4*(12), 641–658. DOI: 10.51594/ijmer.v4i12.676

Popoveniuc, B. (2015). Spiritual intelligence and artifactualness. *European Journal of Science and Theology*, *11*(1), 59–74.

Porkodi, S., & Cedro, T. L. (2025). The Ethical Role of Generative Artificial Intelligence in Modern HR Decision-Making: A Systematic Literature Review. *European Journal of Business and Management Research*, *10*(1), 44–55. DOI: 10.24018/ejbmr.2025.10.1.2535

Pramod, D. (2022). Robotic process automation for industry: Adoption status, benefits, challenges, and research agenda. *Benchmarking*, *29*(5), 1562–1586.

Prasad, Prof. Dr. S. (2024). AI-Powered Talent Acquisition: Enhancing Recruitment Processes in the Digital Age. INTERANTIONAL JOURNAL OF SCIENTIFIC RESEARCH IN ENGINEERING AND MANAGEMENT, 08(06), 1–5. DOI: 10.55041/IJSREM35619

Prentice, C., Dominique Lopes, S., & Wang, X. (2020). Emotional intelligence or artificial intelligence–an employee perspective. *Journal of Hospitality Marketing & Management*, *29*(4), 377–403.

Prithu Sarkar, R. B. N. K., & Sreenivasulu Arigela, P. S. A. K. G. (2024). Ethical Implications of AI Adoption in HRM: Balancing Automation with Human Values. *Journal of Informatics Education and Research*, *4*(3). Advance online publication. DOI: 10.52783/jier.v4i3.1337

Proskuryakov, A. S. (2014). Education in the context of globalization. The use of social networks in the educational process // Bulletin of the Voronezh State Technical University. No.3-2. T10. Access mode: https://cyberleninka.ru/article/n/obrazovanie-v-usloviyah-globalizatsii-ispolzovanie-sotsialnyh-setey-v-obrazovatelnom-protsesse (Date of application: 03/31/2024)

Prostejovsky, A. M., Brosinsky, C., Heussen, K., Westermann, D., Kreusel, J., & Marinelli, M. (2019). The future role of human operators in highly automated electric power systems. *Electric Power Systems Research*, *175*, 105883.

Pyankova, S. G., Ergunova, O. T., & Dudnikov, T. E. (2024). Trends in the development of the theory of noonomics: Artificial intelligence as a tool for the transition to a new industrial society [in Russ.]. *Ufa Humanitarian Scientific Forum.*, (2), 156–174. DOI: 10.47309/2713-2358-2024-2-156-174

Quillian, C. (2025). *AI for Life*. Adams Media.

Raghav, Y. Y., & Gulia, S. (2023). The rise of artificial intelligence and its implications on spirituality. In *Investigating the Impact of AI on Ethics and Spirituality* (pp. 165–178). IGI Global.

Rami, K. (2024). AI in Human Resource Marketing and Its Influence on Recruitment Efficiency. *Journal of Global Economy. Business and Finance*, *6*(12), 7–10. DOI: 10.53469/jgebf.2024.06(12).02

Ramli, R., Wida'atullah, M. R., & Rahayu, Y. S., Rahmat, & Ramly, A. T. (2024). Leadership and Decision-Making to Strengthen HR Competency in AI Emergence. Diversity. *Jurnal Ilmiah Pascasarjana*, *4*(2), 88–103. DOI: 10.32832/djip-uika.v14i2.17024

Randieri, C. (2024). Council Post: Personalized Learning And AI: Revolutionizing Education. *Forbes*, *12*(Aug). https://www.forbes.com/councils/forbestechcouncil/2024/07/22/personalized-learning-and-ai-revolutionizing-education/

Ranjan, J., & Foropon, C. (2021). Big Data Analytics in Building the Competitive Intelligence of Organizations. *International Journal of Information Management*, •••. Advance online publication. DOI: 10.1016/j.ijinfomgt.2020.102231

Rao, S., & Zhao, T. (2025). Ethical AI in HR: A Case Study of Tech Hiring. *Journal of Computer Information Systems*, •••, 1–18.

Rasmussen, T., & Ulrich, D. (2015). Learning from practice: How HR analytics avoids being a management fad. *Organizational Dynamics*, *44*(3), 236–242. DOI: 10.1016/j.orgdyn.2015.05.008

Raveendra, P. V., Satish, Y. M., & Singh, P. (2020). Changing landscape of recruitment industry: A study on the impact of artificial intelligence on eliminating hiring bias from recruitment and selection process. *Journal of Computational and Theoretical Nanoscience*, *17*(9-10), 4404–4407.

Raviprolu, T. (2017). *The role of AI in human resources: Barriers to adoption*

Rechetnikova, M. (2025). What is the DeepSeek Neural Network: a Chatbot with an Internet Search Option. *RBC TrendS*. https://trends.rbc.ru/trends/industry/67920b739a794768fab8fe92

Reddy, K. S., Kethan, M., Mahabub Basha, S., Singh, A., Kumar, P., & Ashalatha, D. (2024). Ethical and Legal Implications of AI on Business and Employment: Privacy, Bias, and Accountability. *2024 International Conference on Knowledge Engineering and Communication Systems (ICKECS)*, 1–6. DOI: 10.1109/ICKECS61492.2024.10616875

Rêgo, B. S., Lourenço, D., Moreira, F., & Pereira, C. S. (2024). Digital transformation, skills and education: A systematic literature review. *Industry and Higher Education*, *38*(4), 336–349.

Resnyanskaya, M. A., & Kuzmina, S. V. (2016). The influence of social networks on the worldview of students. *Young Scientist.*, *4*(9), 61–63.

Rezgui, Y. (2007). Exploring virtual team-working effectiveness in the construction sector. *Interacting with Computers*, *19*(1), 96–112. https://doi.org/https://doi.org/10.1016/j.intcom.2006.07.002

Rhinehart, R. R. (2018). Genetic Algorithms and Evolutionary Computation. *ASME Press eBooks*, 243–252. doi: .DOI: 10.1115/1.861opt_ch14

Ribeiro, J., Lima, R., Eckhardt, T., & Paiva, S. (2021). Robotic Process Automation and Artificial Intelligence in Industry 4.0 – A Literature review. *Procedia Computer Science*, *181*, 51–58. DOI: 10.1016/j.procs.2021.01.104

Rice, R. E. (1992). Task Analyzability, Use of New Media, and Effectiveness: A Multi-Site Exploration of Media Richness. *Organization Science*, *3*(4), 475–500. DOI: 10.1287/orsc.3.4.475

Rice, R. E., Hughes, D., & Love, G. (1989). Usage and Outcomes of Electronic Messaging at an R&D Organization: Situational Constraints, Job Level, and Media Awareness Organization: Situational Constraints, Job Level, and Media Awareness. *Office Technology and People*, *5*(2), 141–161. DOI: 10.1108/EUM0000000003532

Rietdijk, S. (2024). The Relationship Between AI Recruitment and Gender Bias: A Literature Review.

Robotic Process Automation Market Size, Share, and Trends 2025 to 2034 (n.d.). Retrieved from https://www.precedenceresearch.com/robotic-process-automation-market

Rodgers, W., Murray, J. M., Stefanidis, A., Degbey, W. Y., & Tarba, S. Y. (2023). An artificial intelligence algorithmic approach to ethical decision-making in human resource management processes. *Human Resource Management Review*, *33*(1), 100925. DOI: 10.1016/j.hrmr.2022.100925

Roopesh, N., & Babu, C. N. (2021, August). Robotic process automation for resume processing system. In *2021 International Conference on Recent Trends on Electronics, Information, Communication & Technology (RTEICT)* (pp. 180-184). IEEE.

Rosenberg, L. (2023). Generative AI as a Dangerous New Form of Media. *Proceedings*, 165–170. doi: .DOI: 10.54808/imsci2023.01.165

Rospigliosi, P. A. (2023). Artificial intelligence in teaching and learning: What questions should we ask of ChatGPT? *Interactive Learning Environments*, *31*(1), 1–3.

Roy, M. (2021). AI-Powered Workforce Management and Its Future in India. DOI: 10.5772/intechopen.97817

S, S. (2024). Exploring an AI-Based Algorithmic Framework for Ethical Decision-Making in Human Resource Management Procedures. Shanlax International Journal of Management, 11(S1-Mar), 228–234. DOI: 10.34293/management.v11iS1-Mar.8110

Saad, M. F. M., Nugro, A. W. L., Thinakaran, R., & Baijed, M. (2021, December). A review of artificial intelligence-based platform in human resource recruitment process. In 2021 6th IEEE International Conference on Recent Advances and Innovations in Engineering (ICRAIE) (Vol. 6, pp. 1-5). IEEE.

Sahay, U., & Kaur, G. (2021). Leveraging AI to Drive Organizational Performance through Effective Performance. 2021 Fifth International Conference on I-SMAC (IoT in Social, Mobile, Analytics and Cloud) (I-SMAC), 584–588. DOI: 10.1109/I-SMAC52330.2021.9640761

Saini, A. (2023). AI-Intelligent Automation in Workforce Management: Enhancing the Hourly Work Experience. Journal of Artificial Intelligence & Cloud Computing, 1–13. DOI: 10.47363/JAICC/2023(2)E127

Saisubramanian, S., Zilberstein, S., & Kamar, E. (2022). Avoiding negative side effects due to incomplete knowledge of AI systems. *AI Magazine*, *42*(4), 62–71.

Salovey, P., & Mayer, J. D. (1989). Emotional intelligence. *Imagination, Cognition and Personality*, *9*(3), 185–211. DOI: 10.2190/DUGG-P24E-52WK-6CDG

Sambare, S. S., Singh, A., Kriplani, C., Kale, S., & Balkhande, T. (2022, August). Automated platform for onboarding employee. In 2022 6th International Conference on Computing, Communication, Control and Automation (ICCUBEA) (pp. 1-5). IEEE.

Sambunjak, D., Cumpston, M., & Watts, C. (2021). *Module 1: Introduction to conducting systematic reviews. In: Cochrane Interactive Learning: Conducting an intervention review. Cochrane*. Cochrane. https://training.cochrane.org/interactivelearning/module-1-introduction-conducting-systematic-reviews

Samorukov, V. I. (2015) Organizational and pedagogical conditions for managing innovative processes in the educational system//Innovative and information technologies in education: proceedings of the III All- Russian Scientific and Practical Conference. St. Petersburg: Publishing house LEMA, pp. 25-28.

Sampath, K., Devi, K., Ambuli, T. V., & Venkatesan, S. (2024). AI-Powered Employee Performance Evaluation Systems in HR Management. 2024 7th International Conference on Circuit Power and Computing Technologies (ICCPCT), 703–708. DOI: 10.1109/ICCPCT61902.2024.10673159

Sampath, K., Devi, K., Ambuli, T. V., & Venkatesan, S. (2024). *AI-Powered Employee Performance Evaluation Systems in HR Management*. 703–708. DOI: 10.1109/iccpct61902.2024.10673159

Samuel Olaoluwa Folorunsho, Olubunmi Adeolu Adenekan, Chinedu Ezeigweneme, Ike Chidiebere Somadina, & Patrick Azuka Okeleke. (2024). Optimizing network performance and quality of service with AI-driven solutions for future telecommunications. International Journal of Frontiers in Engineering and Technology Research, 7(1), 073–092. DOI: 10.53294/ijfetr.2024.7.1.0041

Sanjeev, N. (2019). Augmented Reality and Virtual Reality in Education. Myth or Reality. *International Journal of Emerging Technologies in Learning*, *14*(3), 203–228. DOI: 10.3991/IJET.V14I03.9289

Santana, M., & Díaz-Fernández, M. (2023). Competencies for the artificial intelligence age: visualisation of the state of the art and future perspectives. In *Review of Managerial Science* (Vol. 17, Issue 6). Springer Berlin Heidelberg. https://doi.org/ DOI: 10.1007/s11846-022-00613-w

Santander Reduces Time to Onboard Newcomers by 85% with Blue Prism (n.d.). Retrieve from https://www.blueprism.com/resources/case-studies/santander-reduces-time-to-onboard-newcomers-by-85-with-blue-prism/

Saraswathi, T., Karthikeyan, M., Balakrishnan, C., Nithya, T., Maheswari, B., & Subramanian, R. S. (2023). Artificial intelligence in human resource management: Advancements, implications and future prospects. *International Journal on Recent and Innovation Trends in Computing and Communication*, *11*(11), 266–281.

Sasi, K. P. (2024). Impact of AI in Recruitment and Talent Acquisition. *Human Resource and Leadership Journal*, *9*(3), 78–83. DOI: 10.47941/hrlj.2117

Sayfutdinova, G. B., Livshits, S. A., & Usachev, S. S. (2017). Information technologies and social networks as a means of improving the effectiveness of the educational process in universities // Problems of modern pedagogical education. No. 56-8. pp. 199-204.

Scatiggio, V. (2020). Tackling the issue of bias in artificial intelligence to design ai-driven fair and inclusive service systems. How human biases are breaching into ai algorithms, with severe impacts on individuals and societies, and what designers can do to face this phenomenon and change for the better.

Schultz, T. W. (1961). Investment in human capital. *The American Economic Review*, *51*(1), 1–17.

Schwartz, R., Schwartz, R., Vassilev, A., Greene, K., Perine, L., Burt, A., & Hall, P. (2022). Towards a standard for identifying and managing bias in artificial intelligence (Vol. 3, p. 00). Gaithersburg, MD: US Department of Commerce, National Institute of Standards and Technology.

Schwartz, J., Liakopoulos, A., Woetzel, J., & Dobbs, R. (2017). *Rewriting the rules for the digital age: 2017 Deloitte global human capital trends*. Deloitte University Press.

Schwarz, H. (2019). Theology in the Age of Artificial Intelligence: Embedding Grace in a Godlike Technology. *Theology Today (Princeton, N.J.)*, *76*(2), 107–120. DOI: 10.1177/0040573619847219

Selezenev R. S., Skripak E. I. (2013). Social networks as a phenomenon of information society and the specifics of social relations in their environment // Bulletin of KemSU. No. 2 (54). pp. 125-132.

Semenovskikh, T. V. (2014). The phenomenon of "Clip thinking" in the educational university environment // Bulletin of Eurasian science – No. 5 (24). Access mode: https://cyberleninka.ru/article/n/fenomen-klipovogo-myshleniya-v-obrazovatelnoy-vuzovskoy-srede/viewer (Accessed 04/01/2024)

Shahbazi, N., Lin, Y., Asudeh, A., & Jagadish, H. V. (2023). Representation bias in data: A survey on identification and resolution techniques. *ACM Computing Surveys*, *55*(13s), 1–39.

Shale D.G. (2005) Toward a reconception of distance education//The American Journal of Distance Education. No. 5.

Sharkey, A. (2019). Autonomous weapons systems, killer robots and human dignity. *Ethics and Information Technology*, *21*(2), 75–87.

Shcherbakova I. V., Timashova M. V. (2020). Vkontakte social network for teaching vocabulary and grammar of the German language // Baltic Humanitarian Journal. Vol. 9. No. 2(31). pp. 317-321

Sherman, N. (2024). AI Regulations Around the World. Mind Foundry. Acceptable at: https://www.mindfoundry.ai/blog/ai-regulations-around-the-world

Shneiderman, B. (2020). Bridging the gap between ethics and practice: Guidelines for reliable, safe, and trustworthy human-centered AI systems. [TiiS]. *ACM Transactions on Interactive Intelligent Systems*, *10*(4), 1–31.

Shouran, Z., & Ali, D. A. (2024). The Implementation of Artificial Intelligence in Human Resources Management. *Journal of International Conference Proceedings*, *7*(1), 244–258. DOI: 10.32535/jicp.v7i1.2993

Šimek, D., & Šperka, R. (2019). How robot/human orchestration can help in an HR department: A case study from a pilot implementation. *Organizacija*, *52*(3), 204–217.

Singh, A. K., & Makkar, S. (2015). Measurement of spirituality: Development and validation of a questionnaire. *XVI Annual Proceedings*, (January), 806–847.

Singh, A., Rose, C., Visweswariah, K., Chenthamarakshan, V., & Kambhatla, N. (2010, October). PROSPECT: A system for screening candidates for recruitment. In *Proceedings of the 19th ACM International Conference on Information and Knowledge Management* (pp. 659-668).

Singh, T. (2020). Fintech adoption: A critical appraisal of the strategies of Paytm in India. *IUP Journal of Management Research.*, *19*(4), 7–17.

Singla, A., Sukharevsky, A., Yee, L., & Chui, M. (2024). The State of AI in early 2024: Gen AI Adoption Spikes and Starts to Generate Value. *McKinsey & Company*. https://www.mckinsey.com/capabilities/quantumblack/our-insights/the-state-of-ai/

Singla, A., Sukharevsky, A., Yee, L., Chui, M., & Hall, B. (2025, March 12). *The state of AI: How organizations are rewiring to capture value*. McKinsey & Company. https://www.mckinsey.com/capabilities/quantumblack/our-insights/the-state-of-ai

Siraj, N., & Hágen, I. (2023). Performance management system and its role for employee performance: Evidence from Ethiopian SMEs. *Heliyon*, *9*(11), e21819. DOI: 10.1016/j.heliyon.2023.e21819 PMID: 38027983

Sivathanu, B., & Pillai, R. (2018). Smart HR 4.0–How Industry 4.0 is disrupting HR. *Human Resource Management International Digest*, *26*(4), 7–11.

Skarbez, R., Smith, M., & Whitton, M. C. (2021). Revisiting Milgram and Kishino's Reality-Virtuality Continuum. *Frontiers in Virtual Reality*. Advance online publication. DOI: 10.3389/frvir.2021.647997

SketchUp. (2025) URL: http://scirraconstruct.ru/news/vse-o-vozmozhnostyax-programmy-sketchup/

Sonderling, K. E., Kelley, B. J., & Casimir, L. (2022). The promise and the peril: Artificial intelligence and employment discrimination. *U. Miami L. Rev.*, *77*, 1.

Sorokin, V. (2024). How to Use YandexGPT in 2025. *Hi-Tech Mail*. https://hi-tech.mail.ru/review/109799-kak-polzovatsya-yandexgpt/#anchor171575595670418014

Spicer, D. P., & Sadler-Smith, E. (2005). An examination of the general decision making style questionnaire in two UK samples. *Journal of Managerial Psychology*, *20*(2), 137–149. DOI: 10.1108/02683940510579777

Spitsnadel, V. N. (2000). *Fundamentals of system analysis: Textbook. allowance. SPb*. Publishing House. Business Press House.

Sriram, D., & Gandhi, G. M. (2017). *AI-based platforms for HR management*

Srivastava, S. R. (2024). Transforming Talent Acquisition: How AI is shaping modern HRM. *International Journal of Science and Research Archive*, *13*(2), 1236–1244. DOI: 10.30574/ijsra.2024.13.2.2252

Starodubceva, A. S. (2021). Employee motivation for remote work // Digital economy: problems and prospects of development. Collection of scientific articles of the 3rd Interregional Scientific and Practical Conference. Kursk: South-Western State University. pp. 395-398. (in Russ.)

Steinert, S., & Dennis, M. J. (2022). Emotions and Digital Well-Being: On Social Media's Emotional Affordances. *Philosophy & Technology*, *35*(2), 36. DOI: 10.1007/s13347-022-00530-6 PMID: 35450167

Stone, D. L., Lukaszewski, K. M., & Johnson, R. D. (2024). Will artificial intelligence radically change human resource management processes? *Organizational Dynamics*, *53*(1), 101034. DOI: 10.1016/j.orgdyn.2024.101034

Subbaiah, D. S. N., & Rajalakshmi, M. (2024). AI-Powered Strategies for Talent Management Optimization. *Journal of Informatics Education and Research*, *4*(2). Advance online publication. DOI: 10.52783/jier.v4i2.848

Subbetto, A. I. (1994). *Systemological foundations of educational systems. Part 2*. Research Center for Quality Problems in Specialist Training.

Sulejmanov, A. V. (2024). Digital transformation of the Russian oil and gas industry: Status, prospects, systemic problems and ways to solve them [in Russ.]. *The scientific aspect.*, *27*(7), 3340–3345.

Sundari, S., Silalahi, V. A. J. M., Wardani, F. P., Siahaan, R. S., Sacha, S., Krismayanti, Y., & Anjarsari, N. (2024). Artificial Intelligence (AI) and Automation in Human Resources : Shifting the Focus from Routine Tasks to Strategic Initiatives for Improved Employee Engagement. *East Asian Journal of Multidisciplinary Research*, *3*(10), 4983–4996. DOI: 10.55927/eajmr.v3i10.11758

Suswaram, S., & Sekhara, S. C. (2021). Study on role of robotics in digitalisation of human resource development: Impact and RPA implementation. International Journal of Creative Research Thoughts (IJCRT, 9(3), 1275-1288.

Syahrial, A., Lubis, S., Pradana, H., & Farhani, F. (2024). The Importance of Spiritual Values in Religious Community Welcoming the Arrival of Artificial Intelligence Technology to Maintain the Balance of Faith and Piety with Sufism Learning. *International Conferance Of Digital Sciences And Engineering Technology*, *1*(1), 448–457.

Syed, R., Suriadi, S., Adams, M., Bandara, W., Leemans, S. J., Ouyang, C., & Reijers, H. A. (2020). Robotic process automation: Contemporary themes and challenges. *Computers in Industry*, *115*, 103162.

Szczygiel, D. D., & Mikolajczak, M. (2018). Emotional intelligence buffers the effects of negative emotions on job burnout in nursing. *Frontiers in Psychology, 9*. Advance online publication. DOI: 10.3389/fpsyg.2018.02649 PMID: 30627113

Tamatea, L. (2010). Online Buddhist and Christian responses to artificial intelligence. *Zygon, 45*(4), 979–1002.

Tambe, P., Cappelli, P., & Yakubovich, V. (2019). Artificial Intelligence in Human Resources Management: Challenges and a Path Forward. *California Management Review, 61*(4), 15–42. DOI: 10.1177/0008125619867910

Tamizhselvan, V., & Pougajendy, S. (2024). From Data to Insights: Using AI Tool to Improve Employee Involvement and Employee Tenure-Rane Madras. *International Journal For Multidisciplinary Research, 6*(6). Advance online publication. DOI: 10.36948/ijfmr.2024.v06i06.33512

Tan, C. (2020). Digital Confucius? Exploring the implications of artificial intelligence in spiritual education. *Connection Science, 32*(3), 280–291.

Tandon, A., et al. (2017). *AI in recruitment: Limitations to full automation*

Tarafdar, M., Tu, Q., Ragu-Nathan, B. S., & Ragu-Nathan, T. S. (2007). The impact of technostress on role stress and productivity. *Journal of Management Information Systems, 24*(1), 301–328. DOI: 10.2753/MIS0742-1222240109

Tasheva, Z., & Karpovich, V. (2024). Transformation of recruitment process through implementation of AI solutions. *Journal of Management and Economics, 4*(02), 12–17.

Tilmes, N. (2022). Disability, fairness, and algorithmic bias in AI recruitment. *Ethics and Information Technology, 24*(2), 21.

Timbadia, D. H., Shah, P. J., Sudhanvan, S., & Agrawal, S. (2020, February). Robotic process automation through advance process analysis model. In *2020 International Conference on Inventive Computation Technologies (ICICT)* (pp. 953-959). IEEE.

Tong, S., Jia, N., Luo, X., & Fang, Z. (2021a). The Janus face of artificial intelligence feedback: Deployment versus disclosure effects on employee performance. *Strategic Management Journal, 42*(9), 1600–1631. DOI: 10.1002/smj.3322

Trapeznikov, V., & Zinovieva, E. (2024). Neural Networks and Generative AI in Higher Education: International Experience and Russian Practice. *Russian International Affairs Council.* https://russiancouncil.ru/analytics-and-comments/analytics/neyroseti-generativnyy-ii-v-vysshem-obrazovanii-mezhdunarodnyy-opyt-i-rossiyskaya-praktika/

Tsindeliani, I. A., Proshunin, M. M., Sadovskaya, T. D., Popkova, Z. G., Davydova, M. A., & Babayan, O. A. (2022). Digital transformation of the banking system in the context of sustainable development. *Journal of Money Laundering Control*, *25*(1), 165–180.

Turcu, C. E., & Turcu, C. O. (2021). Digital transformation of human resource processes in small and medium sized enterprises using robotic process automation. *International Journal of Advanced Computer Science and Applications*, *12*(12).

Twenge, J. M. (2017). iGen: Why Today's Super-Connected Kids Are Growing Up Less Rebellious, More Tolerant, Less Happy--and Completely Unprepared for Adulthood. Atria Books.

Tyugashev, E. (2025). Clip thinking – a modern form of zero-dimensional thinking. *BULLETIN of Samara State Technical University. Series. Philosophy (London, England)*, *7*(1), 91–102. https://journals.eco-vector.com/2658-7750/article/view/692897/208432

University, H. S. E. (2024). Survey on the Use of Artificial Intelligence by University Students. *Ict.moscow*. https://ict.moscow/projects/ai/research/opros-o-primenenii-iskusstvennogo-intellekta-uchashchimisia-vuzov/.

Upadhyay, A. K., & Khandelwal, K. (2018). Applying artificial intelligence: Implications for recruitment. *Strategic HR Review*, *17*(5), 255–258.

Uppal, A., & Awasthi, Y. (2024). Machine learningbased approaches for enhancing human resource management using automated employee performance prediction systems. *The International Journal of Organizational Analysis*. Advance online publication. DOI: 10.1108/ijoa-07-2024-4643

Ushinsky, K. D. (1990). *Pedagogical works: In 6 volumes* (Vol. 1). Pedagogika.

Vaghani, D. (2024). *Enhancing Employee Engagement and Retention through AI-Powered Human Resource Software Solutions*. DOI: 10.24940/theijst/2024/v12/i5/st2405-003

Vaghani, D. (2024). *Enhancing Employee Engagement and Retention through AI-Powered Human Resource Software Solutions*. The International Journal of Science & Technoledge., DOI: 10.24940/theijst/2024/v12/i5/ST2405-003

Valčo, M. (2023). ETHICAL IMPLICATIONS OF ARTIFICIAL INTELLIGENCE IN HUMAN RESOURCE MANAGEMENT FOR SUSTAINABLE DEVELOPMENT. *The International Conference on Human Resources for Sustainable Development*, 147–160. DOI: 10.51316/icpt.hust.2023.34

Van Der Aalst, W. M. P., Bichler, M., & Heinzl, A. (2018). Robotic Process Automation. *Business & Information Systems Engineering*, *60*(4), 269–272. DOI: 10.1007/s12599-018-0542-4

Van Wynsberghe, A., & Robbins, S. (2019). Critiquing the reasons for making artificial moral agents. *Science and Engineering Ethics*, *25*(3), 719–735. PMID: 29460081

Vanduhe, V., Cemal Nat, M., & Al-Delawi, H. (2020). Continuance Intentions to Use Gamification for Training in Higher Education: Integrating the Technology Acceptance Model (TAM), Social Motivation, and Task Technology Fit (TTF). *IEEE Access : Practical Innovations, Open Solutions*, *20*, 1. DOI: 10.1109/ACCESS.2020.2966179

VC, K. (2024a). The Role of Artificial Intelligence (AI) and Machine Learning (ML) in HR Decision Making Processes. Shanlax International Journal of Management, 11(S1-Mar), 98–107. DOI: 10.34293/management.v11iS1-Mar.8064

Vendramin, N., Nardelli, G., & Ipsen, C. (2021). Task-Technology Fit Theory: An Approach For Mitigating Technostress. In *A Handbook of Theories on Designing Alignment Between People and the Office Environment* (pp. 39–53). Routledge/Taylor & Francis Group. https://doi.org/DOI: 10.1201/9781003128830-4

Vetrova, E. (2024). AI in Education: Statistics, Implementation, Advantages, Problems. *VirtRe*. https://virtre.ru/articles/artificial-intelligence/ii-v-obrazovanii-statistika-vnedrenie-preimushhestva-problemy

Vhora, M. A., Bhandwalkar, V., & Rege, P. M. (2024). AI-driven HR analytics: Enhancing decision-making in workforce planning. *The Scientific Temper*, *15*(04), 3299–3308. DOI: 10.58414/SCIENTIFICTEMPER.2024.15.4.39

Vicci, D. H. (2024). Emotional Intelligence in Artificial Intelligence: A Review and Evaluation Study. SSRN *Electronic Journal*. https://doi.org/DOI: 10.2139/ssrn.4818285

Vijai, C., & Mariyappan, M. (2023). Robotic process automation (RPA) in human resource functions. *Advances in Management*, *2023*(16), 3.

Vishwanath, S. V. (2023). The Future of Work: Implications of Artificial Intelligence on Hr Practices. Tuijin Jishu/Journal of Propulsion Technology, 44(3), 1711–1724. DOI: 10.52783/tjjpt.v44.i3.562

Vivek, R. (2023). Enhancing diversity and reducing bias in recruitment through AI: a review of strategies and challenges. Информатика. Экономика. Управление/Informatics. Economics. Management, 2(4), 0101-0118.

Völker, J., & Mannheim, C. (2021). Tuned in on senders' self-revelation: Emojis and emotional intelligence influence interpretation of WhatsApp messages. *Computers in Human Behavior Reports*, *3*, 100062. https://doi.org/https://doi.org/10.1016/j.chbr.2021.100062

Vologzshanin, G. (2025). What Can the Chinese Neural Network DeepSeek Do on Android and How is it Better than ChatGPT – AndroidInsider.ru. *Androidinsider.ru*. https://androidinsider.ru/obzory-prilozhenij/chto-umeet-kitajskaya-nejroset-deepseek-na-android-i-chem-ona-luchshe-chatgpt.html

Vorobjev, D. (2023). 'They'll Find a Loophole': Analyst on Banning a Chatbot for Writing Diplomas. *National News Service – NSN*. https://nsn.fm/nauka-i-tehnologii/naidut-lazeiku-analitik-ne-verit-v-zapret-chat-bota-po-napisaniu-diplomov

Vrontis, D., Christofi, M., Pereira, V., Tarba, S., Makrides, A., & Trichina, E. (2023). Artificial intelligence, robotics, advanced technologies and human resource management: a systematic review. *Artificial intelligence and international HRM*, 172-201.

Wadley, G., Krause, A., Liang, J., Wang, Z., & Leong, T. W. (2020). Use of music streaming platforms for emotion regulation by international students. *Proceedings of the 31st Australian Conference on Human-Computer-Interaction*, 337–341. https://doi.org/DOI: 10.1145/3369457.3369490

Wadley, G., Smith, W., Koval, P., & Gross, J. J. (2020). Digital Emotion Regulation. *Current Directions in Psychological Science*, *29*(4), 412–418. DOI: 10.1177/0963721420920592

Wahyuning, S., & Sudibyo, S. K. (2024). Leveraging Machine Learning for Talent Acquisition: Predicting High-Performance Candidates in Human Resource Management. *Journal of Management and Informatics*, *3*(1), 87–104. DOI: 10.51903/jmi.v3i1.44

Walter, Y. (2024). The digital transformation in the psychology of workplace spirituality. *Digital Transformation and Society*, *3*(1), 23–49.

Wamba-Taguimdje, S.-L., Fosso Wamba, S., Kala Kamdjoug, J. R., & Tchatchouang Wanko, C. E. (2020). Influence of artificial intelligence (AI) on firm performance: The business value of AI-based transformation projects. *Business Process Management Journal*, *26*(7), 1893–1924. DOI: 10.1108/BPMJ-10-2019-0411

Wang, A. (2024). Advancing Organizational Effectiveness Through Strategic Workforce Planning and Technology Integration. Advances in Economics. *Management and Political Sciences*, *121*(1), 107–112. DOI: 10.54254/2754-1169/121/20242362

Warrier, U., Shankar, A., & Belal, H. M. (2024). Examining the role of emotional intelligence as a moderator for virtual communication and decision making effectiveness during the COVID-19 crisis: Revisiting task technology fit theory. *Annals of Operations Research*, *335*(3), 1519–1535. DOI: 10.1007/s10479-021-04216-8 PMID: 34539017

White, J. (2024). People Want to Know: Which are the Top Seven Branches of Artificial Intelligence? *Tech Rays*. https://techrays.net/top-seven-branches-of-artificial-intelligence/

Willcocks, L., Lacity, M., & Craig, A. (2017). Robotic process automation: Strategic transformation lever for global business services? *Journal of Information Technology Teaching Cases*, *7*(1), 17–28.

Wirth, N. (2018). Hello marketing, what can artificial intelligence help you with? *International Journal of Market Research*, *60*(5), 435–438.

Wixom, B. H., & Todd, P. A. (2005). A theoretical integration of user satisfaction and technology acceptance. *Information Systems Research*, *16*(1), 85–102.

Wuisan, D. S. S., Sunardjo, R. A., Aini, Q., Yusuf, N. A., & Rahardja, U. (2023). Integrating Artificial Intelligence in Human Resource Management: A SmartPLS Approach for Entrepreneurial Success. [ATT]. *Aptisi Transactions on Technopreneurship*, *5*(3), 334–345. DOI: 10.34306/att.v5i3.355

Xue, J., & Shen, B. (2020). A Novel Swarm Intelligence Optimization Approach: Sparrow Search Algorithm. *Systems Science & Control Engineering*, *8*(1), 22–34. DOI: 10.1080/21642583.2019.1708830

Yadav, M., Kakkar, M., & Kaushik, P. (2023). Harnessing Artificial Intelligence to Empower HR Processes and Drive Enhanced Efficiency in the Workplace to Boost Productivity. *International Journal on Recent and Innovation Trends in Computing and Communication*, *11*(8s), 381–390. DOI: 10.17762/ijritcc.v11i8s.7218

Yanamala, K. K. R. (2023). Transparency, privacy, and accountability in AI-enhanced HR processes. *Journal of Advanced Computing Systems*, *3*(3), 10–18.

Yano, Y. (2017). *AI without data: Useless in practice* [Technical report; exact source not located].

Yaprak, B. (2024). Generative Artificial Intelligence in Marketing: The Invisible Danger of AI Hallucinations. *Economica Işletme Ve Yonetim Dergisi*, *8*(2), 133–158. DOI: 10.7596/jebm.1588897

Yashu, Y., Sharma, R., Jain, A., & Manwal, M. (2024). *Enhancing Human Resource Management through Deep Learning: A Predictive Analytics Approach to Employee Retention Success.* 1–4. DOI: 10.1109/iciteics61368.2024.10625175

Yassine, T. K., & Achchab, S. (2024). Predictive Hiring and AI: Elevating Recruitment with Optimized Neural Networks and Gradient Descent. *International Journal of Intelligent Information Systems, 13*(6), 117–127. DOI: 10.11648/j.ijiis.20241306.11

Yeke, S. (2023). Digital intelligence as a partner of emotional intelligence in business administration. *Asia Pacific Management Review, 28*(4), 390–400. DOI: 10.1016/j.apmrv.2023.01.001

Yoon, S. W., Han, S. H., & Chae, C. (2024). People analytics and human resource development–Research landscape and future needs based on bibliometrics and scoping review. *Human Resource Development Review, 23*(1), 30–57.

Yorks, L., & Jester, M. Y. (2024). Applying generative AI ethically in HRD practice. *Human Resource Development International, 27*(3), 410–427. DOI: 10.1080/13678868.2024.2337963

Yu, L. (2019). *"Made in China 2025" China's development strategy through technological innovation.* Universidade de Lisboa.

Yuyun, I., & Suherdi, D. (2023). Components and Strategies for Personalized Learning in Higher Education. *Systematic Reviews.* Advance online publication. DOI: 10.2991/978-2-38476-054-1_23

Zaharia-Rădulescu, A. M., Pricop, C. L., Shuleski, D., & Ioan, A. C. (2017). RPA and the future of workforce. In Proceedings of the 11th International Management Conference. The Role of Management in the Economic Paradigm of the XXIst Century (Vol. 11, No. 1, pp. 384-392).

Zang, Y., & Ye, M. (2015). Big data and human resource management: Efficiency and accuracy through analytics. *Journal of Management Analytics, 2*(1), 1–18.

Zhadan, A. (2023). I Defended my Thesis, which I Wrote Using ChatGPT. https://journal.tinkoff.ru/neuro-diploma/

Zhang, E. Y. A. (2024). *Digitalizations Enhancement in HR Practices: The Impact of Incorporating AI in the Process of Recruitment and Selection. Advances in Economics, Management and Political Sciences, 120(1).* None-None., DOI: 10.54254/2754-1169/120/20242377

Zhang, H. (2024). Exploring the Impact of AI on Human Resource Management: A Case Study of Organizational Adaptation and Employee Dynamics. *IEEE Transactions on Engineering Management*, *71*, 14991–15004. DOI: 10.1109/TEM.2024.3457520

Zhang, H. (2024). Exploring the Impact of AI on Human Resource Management: A case study of organizational adaptation and employee dynamics. *IEEE Transactions on Engineering Management*.

Zhu, Z. (2024). What Businesses Can Learn from McKinsey's 2024 Global Survey on AI Adoption. Mitchell E. Daniels, Jr. School of Business. https://business.purdue.edu/daniels-insights/posts/2024/global-survey-on-ai-adoption.php

Zigurs, I., & Khazanchi, D. (2008). From Profiles to Patterns: A New View of Task-Technology Fit. *IS Management*, *25*(1), 8–13. DOI: 10.1080/10580530701777107

Zinchenko, V. P. (2002). Psychological foundations of pedagogy (Psychological and pedagogical foundations of building a system of developing learning by D.B. Elkonin – V. V. Davydov). – M. – 431 p.

Zinnbauer, B. J., Pargament, K. I., & Scott, A. B. (1999). The emerging meanings of religiousness and spirituality: Problems and prospects. *Journal of Personality*, *67*(6), 889–919.

About the Contributors

Krastev Viliyan Krastev, Doctor of Social Sciences (DSc), Candidate of Geographical Sciences (PhD), Associate Professor of the Department of Economy and Tourism Organization at the University of Economics in Varna, Bulgaria. He is a specialist in political geography, geopolitics and geography of tourism. He has 16 years of teaching experience. He is the author of more than 75 publications, including those indexed in WoS and Scopus platforms. He has lectured at many foreign universities, including La Sapienza (Rome, Italy), BSU (Minsk, Belarus), L.N. Gumilyov Eurasian University. Gumilyov (Astana, Kazakhstan), the University of Latvia (Riga, Latvia), the University of Urbino "Carlo Bo" (Urbino, Italy), etc. Member of the editorial boards of a number of scientific journals: "Geography and Tourism" (Kyiv, Ukraine), "Russian Regions: A Look into the Future" (Moscow, Russia), "Scientific Review" (Saransk, Russia), "Pskov Regional Studies Journal" (Pskov, Russia), "Geotema" (Rome, Italy).

Chandni Rani is currently an Assistant Professor at the University School of Business, Chandigarh University, Mohali, (Punjab) India. With over three years of teaching experience, her research interests span Human Resources, HR analytics, Organizational behavior, green HRM, and the application of artificial intelligence and virtual reality in HR and, the healthcare sector. She is a lifetime member of the International Teachers Association. She is an avid researcher and presented papers at various national and international conferences. Dr. Rani has also played a pivotal role in curriculum development and pedagogy design, enhancing the learning experience at Chandigarh University.

Olga Ergunova is currently an Associate Professor at the Higher School of Production Management at Peter the Great St. Petersburg Polytechnic University. With over 22 years of professional experience in management and marketing, including 14 years in academia, her expertise spans strategic management, project management, urban studies, tourism, sustainable development, and digital transformation. She has held various leadership roles, including President of the Ural Union of the Tourism Industry, and serves as an Expert at the Russian Academy of Sciences. Dr. Ergunova is a prolific researcher with 167 publications, including in the RSCI database, as well as indexed articles in Web of Science and Scopus. Her research interests focus on sustainable urban development, tourism, creative industries, and regional branding. She has received numerous awards, including recognitions for best practices in national relations and sustainable tourism. Additionally, she has led international and regional projects, including initiatives within the framework of the "SMART CITY 2030" program. Dr. Ergunova actively contributes to the development of academic and professional programs, organizing forums, master classes, and scientific-practical events to foster innovation and collaboration in the BRICS countries.

Pooja Kansra is presently working as a Professor and Head of Economics at Mittal School of Business, Lovely Professional University, Phagwara, Punjab (India). She has a teaching experience of fifteen years and research experience of eleven years. Her areas of research include health economics, labor economics, gender economics, insurance and informal sector, digitalization. She is an avid researcher and presented papers in various national and international conferences. She is the recipient of several best paper awards from reputed institutions such MAIMS, IBS, NIT Srinagar, Delhi University and Lovely Professional University. She has to her credit various research papers published in Scopus Indexed Journals including Journal of Consumer Behavior (Wiley, ABDC A category), Economic and Political Weekly (EPW), Journal of Health Management (Sage Publications). Global Business Review (Sage Publications), International Journal of Diabetes in Developing Countries (Springer Publications), Health and Population: Perspectives and Issues (MOHFW) etc. She has the convener of three conferences organized in Lovely Professional University.

Tanveer Kajla is an engineering graduate with doctorate in Tourism Analytics, presently working in NALSAR University of Law, Hyderabad, India. He worked as Assistant Professor with Lovely Professional university. Prior to that he also worked as Research Associate under the ICSSR-IMPRESS Major Project at Punjabi University, Patiala (IN). He has published and presented papers in globally acclaimed conferences and Journals. He has been instrumental delivering expert talks on subjects like Business Analytics, Big Data Analytics, Microsoft Excel, R and Hadoop in academic institutions. His area of research includes Social Network Analysis, Sentiment Analysis, Twitter and Facebook analysis, Text Classification.

***

Garima Bansal is a research scholar in Guru Jambheshwar University of Science & Technology, Hisar and pursuing PhD under the supervision of Prof. B.K. Punia. Her research domain focuses on leadership, prosocial service behavior, and mindfulness. She has presented research papers in national and international conferences. She has also bestowed with "Naari Shakti Samaan" Award from "Sadhbhawana Welfare Society", Hisar because of her remarkable contribution in the upliftment of underprivileged children in Hisar district. Her research journey has been centered around the exploration of mindfulness and life awakening experiences. She has also attended various mindfulness workshops and meditation sessions. She is an active volunteer in an NGO Foundation– "Bhikh Nahi Kitaab Do" from last 4 years.

Pradnya Bhatkulkar is a seasoned HR professional with over a decade of expertise in human resources management, specializing in talent management, employee relations, and organizational development. She excels in implementing strategic HR initiatives aligned with business objectives, fostering a positive workplace culture, and enhancing employee engagement. Pradnya's adept navigation of complex personnel issues showcases her comprehensive knowledge of HR policies and regulations, coupled with effective communication skills. Renowned for her commitment to diversity and inclusion, she has played a pivotal role in implementing programs that promote equality within organizations. Pradnya's adaptability to industry trends and forward-thinking approach make her a valuable asset in the ever-evolving field of human resources. With a proven track record of driving HR excellence and a passion for cultivating collaborative teams, Pradnya Bhatkulkar continues to significantly contribute to the success and growth of the organizations she serves.

Geetha Devi is working as Associate Professor and Program Manager in Chemical Engineering at National University of Science and Technology, Oman. Dr. Devi has more than 30 years of experience as Faculty and researcher.

Mahak Garg is currently a doctoral student in Guru Jambheshwar University of Science & Technology, Hisar under the supervision of Prof. B.K. Punia in the field of Human Resource Management. Her research domain focuses on Spirituality, Artificial Intelligence and Employee Behaviour. She has published various papers and book chapters in referred journals and books.

Kerimbayeva Rysty Kaldykhanovna was born on January 30, 1971 in the village of Akzhar, Baizak district, Zhambyl region. In 1988 she graduated from the S. Seifullin Secondary School in the village of Akzhar. In 1988 she entered the Zhambyl Pedagogical Institute with a degree in "Preschool Pedagogy and Psychology", from which she graduated with honors in 1992. She began her career in 1992 as a teacher at the Zhambyl Pedagogical Institute. In 1993-1996, she studied in the postgraduate program of the full-time department of the Kazakh State Women's Pedagogical Institute, specializing in 13.00.06 - “Preschool Pedagogy and Psychology”. In 1999, she defended her PhD thesis in specialty 13.00.01 – “General Pedagogy” and received the academic degree of candidate of pedagogical sciences. In 2008, she received the academic title of associate professor in the specialty “Pedagogy”. Since 2020 I am a corresponding member of the Academy of Pedagogical Sciences of Kazakhstan. Scientific achievements: - “Best University Teacher-2019” MES RK. - Scientific director and author of the grant project on commercialization. DP23692218 - “Revival of national values of the Kazakh people with the help of toys in a modern style” project for the commercialization of the RNTD for 2024-2026. - Author of 310 scientific works, 6 teaching aids under the stamp of the Ministry of Education of the Republic of Kazakhstan, 14 teaching aids, 5 electronic textbooks, 3 monographs, 2 patents, 9 Scopus articles in scientific journals, 20 KOKONVO articles, 48 author's certificates, Hirsch Index-h-2. From 1992 to the present I am an associate professor at the Department of Social Psychology at Taraz University named after M.Kh.Dulati. Kerimbayeva Rysty

Natalia Khazieva is an associate professor in the Department of Management at the National Research University Higher School of Economics (HSE University), St. Petersburg, Russia. She has experience in business as an economist and financial analyst. She has completed various professional training programs in the fields of project management, digital transformation, business analytics, communications, and others. Her research interests include the digital transformation of business, knowledge management, strategic management, SPACs and IPOs, and the application of AI in marketing. Natalia received her PhD in management from STU, Bratislava, Slovakia.

Yuliya Kuznetsova graduated from the school N°3 in Aktobe. Education: 1992-1997 yy: Education. Higher education. Graduated from Aktobe University named after K.Zhubanov with a degree in “General Technical Disciplines and Labor” 2000-2004 yy.: 2017-2019 yy.: Postgraduate student at K.Zhubanov Aktobe University, specialty “General Pedagogy”, Cipher: 13.00.01 2017-2019 Master's student at the Regional Socio–Innovative University, specialty 6M042100 – Design. In 2019, she was awarded a Master's degree in Art History. Job Experience: Academic: Employment in this organization 1997 to 2025 works at Aktobe Regional University named after K.Zhubanov 1997-1999 yy. 1999 – 2006 yy 2006-2025 yy The list of subjects taught: she worked as a lecturer at the Department of Nature Science Disciplines and Labor she worked as a senior lecturer at the Department of Nature

Science Disciplines and Labor Senior lecturer at the Department of "Artistic Labor and Design" Materials Science, Modern materials in design, Elements and processes of graphic design, Layout and Construction in graphic design, Clothing decoration Employment: Advanced training Full-time employment - "Current issues of the organization of the educational process in the higher education system in the field of GRAPHIC DESIGN" Kama Institute of Design, Naberezhnye Chelny from January 14-25, 2019, 72 hours, certificate of advanced training 162404281059 Registration number 047. - Course: "Management in education ""empire of knowledge" 72 h. 9.11.-21.11.2020 . Certificate No. 00955. - "University 4.0. Digital transformation " International online internship on the educational online platform SKLAD Republican Institute Higher School of the Republic of Belarus 07-23.04.2021 G. 72 hours. - Modern concepts in design. Digital educational resources. International seminar "Creative thinking: methods of developing students 'creativity", held From February 13 to 24, 2023 by Professor Rakesh Bani of Kuruksheta university /India. / 72 hours/. Aktobe-2023. (online) Awards and prizes: Nominal cup for the best organization of the Vernissage (Nursultan, EST. 2021); Medal for achievements in the field of design (NurSultan, 2021); Over the years, she has published more than 20 publications.

Evgenii Makarenko, PhD in Economics, Associate Professor, has over 20 years of professional experience, including more than 10 years in academic and teaching activities. He graduated with honors from the Institute of Management and Economics in Saint Petersburg with a degree in Finance and Credit, and completed the Presidential Management Training Program at the Graduate School of Management of Saint Petersburg State University. He has also undertaken advanced training in project management, digital communications, neural network technologies, and behavioral finance. Currently, he holds the position of Associate Professor at the Graduate School of Industrial Management of Peter the Great St. Petersburg Polytechnic University, and also serves as Associate Professor at the Department of Business Informatics and Management of Saint Petersburg State University of Aerospace Instrumentation. He is the Director of the Competence Center "Innotech." He is the author of more than 200 scientific publications on risk management, insurance, public administration, digital transformation, and the application of neural networks. His monograph "Risk Management in the System of Contractual Relations: Theoretical and Practical Aspects" was included in the list of publications "Economic Book of the Year – 2024" by the VEO of Russia. He is an independent anti-corruption expert certified by the Ministry of Justice of the Russian Federation.

Tawheed Nabi is currently Assistant Professor at Mittal School of Business ACBSP USA, Accredited, Lovely Professional University, Punjab (India). Dr. Nabi received his PhD degree from DOS in Economics, Karnatak University, Dharwad and has been UGC-UPE research fellow. His expertise entails areas like International Trade, Agriculture Economics and Business Models. He has published his research ideas in journals, edited volumes, conference proceedings in the areas of International Economics, Agricultural Economics and Business Models. He has presented several papers in International and National level seminars and participated in various workshops and FDP's.

B. K. Punia is well renowned in the field of human resource management and organizational behavior. He has numerous research papers to his credit in diverse areas and has been chairing expert sessions in various national and international conferences. Apart from being a respectable researcher, he is a great administrator too. He held the prestigious post of Vice chancellorship of famous Maharshi Dayanand University, Rohtak, Haryana. Prior to MDU, he also worked as Dean, Haryana School of Business and also as founding director, Academic Staff College, Guru Jambheshwar University of Science and Technology.

Vandana Punia, Co-director of ICSSR Research project is the Dean & Head Faculty of Education, Guru Jambheshwar University of Science &Technology, Hisar, Haryana. She is having 20 yrs of experience in teaching & research. She worked as a Content writer, Content presenter and Content reviewer in ARPIT 2018, ARPIT 2019. She has also developed an OER and MOOC course on " Happiness: Education of 21st Century from lenses of Happiness" under the aegis of OE4BW, an UNESCO initiative. She has completed two UGC sponsored Major Research Projects and two MHRD Digital Initiatives SWAYAM ARPIT 2018 & 2019. She has authored two books published by reputed National Publisher. Edited two books published by reputed National Publishers. Published more than eighty research papers in various National and International Journals, Developed and published Five Research Tools and one Training Module. She had been awarded Bharat Shiksha Ratan Award (2012), University Gold Medal in M.A. Journalism and Mass Communication, CDLU, Sirsa (2012), Innovative Res. Developers & Publishers– Teaching and Research Excellence Award (2017) & Dr. Radhakrishnan Award for Teaching, Learning and Innovation. Her interests are in Faculty Development and Empowerment Psychology of Teaching and Learning, Technology Integration & Educational Technology. Devoted to upholding professional standards of conduct and ethical conduct. Proficient in accommodating the varied learning methods of students. Constantly on the lookout for the most recent advancements in the field of education.

Dmitry Vyacheslavovich Samorukov, PhD in Engineering, has over 15 years of professional experience, including more than 5 years in academic and teaching activities. He graduated from the National Open Institute of Saint Petersburg with a degree in Industrial Management (2014), from ITMO University (Saint Petersburg National Research University of Information Technologies, Mechanics and Optics) with a degree in Refrigeration, Cryogenic Engineering and Life Support Systems (2016), and from Peter the Great St. Petersburg Polytechnic University with a degree in Commodity Science (2017). He also completed the Presidential Program for Training Engineering and Technical Personnel (2016), along with various professional retraining and advanced training programs in quality management, human resources, pedagogy, technosphere safety, digital communications, and neural network technologies. He undertook an internship at the Akademie für Internationale Wirtschaft in Berlin under the program Business-Prozess beim Qualitätsmanagement der Organisation. He is currently an Associate Professor at the Department of Design and Technology of Leather Products named after Prof. A.S. Schwartz at Saint Petersburg State University of Industrial Technologies and Design. He heads the Competence Center "Light Industry Product Technology." He is the author of 50 scientific publications, including 8 certificates of intellectual property registration and 4 articles indexed in Scopus. His research interests include organizational management, quality management, pedagogical practices, digitalization, and the application of neural networks. He is a certified independent expert in the field of quality management.

Vyacheslav Ivanovich Samorukov, PhD in Pedagogy, Associate Professor, has over 45 years of professional experience, including more than 25 years in academic and teaching activities. He graduated from the Faculty of Psychology at Saint Petersburg State University with a degree in Psychology. Certified psychological trainer (Training Institute, 1997). He has completed various professional retraining and advanced training programs in the fields of quality management, human resources management, pedagogical activity, technosphere safety, digital communications, and neural network technologies. He also completed an internship at the Akademie für Internationale Wirtschaft in Berlin under the program Business-Prozess beim Qualitätsmanagement der Organisation. Currently, he is an Associate Professor at the Department of Professional Certification and Information Implementation of the Academy of Management and Agribusiness of Saint Petersburg State Agrarian University, and Head of the Competence Center "School for Educators." He is the author of more than 150 scientific publications, including 7 monographs, 15 certificates of intellectual property registration, and 11 articles indexed in Scopus. His research interests include organizational management, pedagogical practices, public administration, quality management, agribusiness, digital transformation, and the application of neural networks. He is a certified independent expert in the field of continuing professional education.

Gulnara Kazybekovna graduated from the state farm of Krasnoyar in the Isatai district of the Aktobe region.40 Education: 1981-1986 yy: Higher education, Dzhambul Technological Institute of Light and Food Industry, specialty "Technology of sewing products", qualification - process engineer. 2004 y.: 2008 y.: Candidate of Pedagogical Sciences. Cipher: 13.00.01 - General pedagogy, history of pedagogy and education, ethnopedagogy. Associate Professor in the specialty of pedagogy 56 Job Experience: Academic: Employment in this organization 1993-2004 yy.: Senior lecturer of the "Labor Training" Department 2004-2009 yy.: 2009-2025 yy. Head of the Department, Associate Professor of the "Professional Training" Department Associate Professor of the "Artistic labor and Design" Department Previous jobs in educational organizations: 1980-1981 yy.: 1986-1987 yy.: primary school teacher in Mikhailovskaya secondary school of the Akrabsky district of the Aktobe region. Technologist of the Factory of sewing and repairing clothes in Aktobe 1987-1993 yy.: Teacher of special disciplines of Aktobe Pedagogical College The list of subjects taught: Costume history, Design of fashion design objects I, II, III, IV, Costume design documentation, Integrated product design. Period: Full-time/part-time employment. Full. Over the years, she has published more than 70 publications, including textbooks, monographs, articles in international conferences, Committee for Control in the Field of Education and Science, Scopus, etc., patents, copyright certificates, and many others. She was an opponent of PhD theses and master's Dissertations. She is a member of Republican Educational and Methodological Council on specialties, an expert at the national level. Actively participates in the social activities of the university, regional and national events.

Andrei A. Ternikov is a senior lecturer in the Department of Management at the National Research University Higher School of Economics (HSE University), 194100, St. Petersburg, Russia. His research interests include the analysis of labor market issues and the application and creation of machine learning methods in economics. Ternikov received his PhD in economics from HSE University.

Index

A

B

C

D

E

G

H

I

M

O

P

R

S

T

V

www.ingramcontent.com/pod-product-compliance
Lightning Source LLC
LaVergne TN
LVHW080909300926
849162LV00003B/611